Acting Realism

Acting Realism

Theory and Practice from Garrick to Meisner and Beyond

Stephen Bayly

methuen | drama
LONDON • NEW YORK • OXFORD • NEW DELHI • SYDNEY

METHUEN DRAMA
Bloomsbury Publishing Plc, 50 Bedford Square, London, WC1B 3DP, UK
Bloomsbury Publishing Inc, 1385 Broadway, New York, NY 10018, USA
Bloomsbury Publishing Ireland, 29 Earlsfort Terrace, Dublin 2, D02 AY28, Ireland

BLOOMSBURY, METHUEN DRAMA and the Methuen Drama logo are trademarks of Bloomsbury Publishing Plc

First published in Great Britain 2026

Copyright © Stephen Bayly, 2026

Stephen Bayly has asserted his right under the Copyright, Designs and Patents Act, 1988, to be identified as Author of this work.

Cover design by Alejandro Cañer Labradas
Cover images © Getty

All rights reserved. No part of this publication may be: i) reproduced or transmitted in any form, electronic or mechanical, including photocopying, recording or by means of any information storage or retrieval system without prior permission in writing from the publishers; or ii) used or reproduced in any way for the training, development or operation of artificial intelligence (AI) technologies, including generative AI technologies. The rights holders expressly reserve this publication from the text and data mining exception as per Article 4(3) of the Digital Single Market Directive (EU) 2019/790.

Bloomsbury Publishing Plc does not have any control over, or responsibility for, any third-party websites referred to or in this book. All internet addresses given in this book were correct at the time of going to press. The author and publisher regret any inconvenience caused if addresses have changed or sites have ceased to exist, but can accept no responsibility for any such changes.

A catalogue record for this book is available from the British Library.

Library of Congress Control Number: 2025943254

ISBN: HB: 978-1-3503-2022-2
PB: 978-1-3503-2021-5
ePDF: 978-1-3503-2024-6
eBook: 978-1-3503-2023-9

Typeset by RefineCatch Limited, Bungay, Suffolk
Printed and bound in Great Britain

For product safety related questions contact productsafety@bloomsbury.com.

To find out more about our authors and books visit www.bloomsbury.com and sign up for our newsletters.

The hero of my tale – whom I love with all the power of my soul, whom I have tried to portray in all his beauty, who has been, is, and will be beautiful – is Truth.

Count Leo Tolstoy

Contents

1	Skinning the Cat		1
2	The Realm of Realism		4
3	David Garrick	1717–1779	8
4	Denis Diderot	1713–1784	12
5	From Russia with Love		15
6	Eleonora Duse	1858–1924	23
7	Vladimir Nemirovich-Danchenko	1858–1943	27
8	Adolphe Appia	1862–1928	30
9	Konstantin Stanislavski	1863–1938	32
10	Émile Jaques-Dalcroze	1865–1950	43
11	Frederick Matthias Alexander	1869–1955	45
12	Gordon Craig	1872–1966	48
13	Vsevolod Meyerhold	1874–1940	51
14	Maria Ouspenskaya	1876–1949	56
15	Jacques Copeau	1879–1949	58
16	Rudolf Laban	1879–1958	62
17	Yevgeny Vakhtangov	1883–1922	65
18	Nikolai Demidov	1884–1953	69
19	Charles Dullin	1885–1949	72
20	Richard Boleslavsky (The American Lab Theatre)	1889–1937	75
21	Michael Chekhov	1891–1955	79
22	Erwin Piscator	1893–1966	84
23	Antonin Artaud	1896–1948	89

24	Bertolt Brecht	1898–1956	93
25	Sergei Eisenstein	1898–1948	102
26	Lee Strasberg	1901–1982	106
27	Harold Clurman	1901–1980	111
28	Stella Adler	1901–1992	114
29	Moshe Feldenkrais	1904–1984	119
30	Sanford Meisner	1905–1997	121
31	Viola Spolin	1906–1994	127
32	Robert Lewis	1909–1997	129
33	Elia Kazan	1909–2003	134
34	Joan Littlewood	1914–2002	139
35	Uta Hagen	1919–2004	143
36	Jacques Lecoq	1921–1999	146
37	Sidney Lumet	1924–2011	148
38	Peter Brook	1925–2022	153
39	Julian Beck	1925–1985	157
40	Judith Malina (The Living Theater)	1926–2015	159
41	Augusto Boal	1931–2009	163
42	Susana Bloch (Alba-emoting™)	1931–	166
43	Jerzy Grotowski	1933–1999	169
44	Sydney Pollack	1934–2008	176
45	Charles Marowitz	1934–2014	180
46	Joseph Chaikin (The Open Theatre)	1935–2003	184
47	Eugene Barba	1936–	188
48	Tadashi Suzuki	1939–	192
49	Anne Bogart	1951–	194
50	David Mamet	1947–	198
51	Simon McBurney (Théâtre de Complicité)	1957–	202
52	The Neighborhood Playhouse	1915–1927, 1928–	204
53	The Group Theatre	1931–1941	207

54	The Actors Studio	1947–	211
55	Dramatic Realism in Cinema		213
56	Arrival of the Talkies	1927	215
57	Socialist Realism	1934–1991	217
58	Poetic Realism	1930–1939	220
59	Italian Neo-Realism	1943–1952	223
60	Satyajit Ray	1921–1992	228
61	Kitchen Sink Drama (British Social Realism)	1956–1970	231
62	John Cassavetes	1929–2008	235
63	Ken Loach	1936–	239
64	John Sayles	1950–	246
65	Sean Baker	1971–	249
66	Neo Neo-Realsim		252
67	Magic Realism		260
68	Errors and Omissions		262

1 Skinning the Cat

There's more than one way to skin a cat.[1]

Film directors generally are woefully ignorant of actors' methods. Theatre directors, depending on their education and training, less so. But a knowledge of the actor's formation and processes can provide the key to unlocking the actor's individual talents and skills to maximum effect. Could you, as a director, engage in a conversation with your actor about **Uta Hagen's** *endowment principles*, or **Michael Chekhov's** *psychological gesture*? Could you, as an actor, respond when asked to use **Lee Strasberg's** *sensory memory* or **Charles Marowitz's** *Ur-text*? What about prescribing *Alexander Technique* as a remedy for your actor's voice problems? An actor trained in **Jerzy Grotowski's** *physical theatre* will bring very different resources to their work compared to one trained exclusively in **Sanford Meisner's** techniques. Did you know that some actors' methods in current practice are over a century old? **Rudolf Laban**, whose techniques are taught in acting and dance schools today, was a contemporary of **Konstantin Stanislavski** in the nineteenth century. **Frederick Alexander** (Alexander Technique) predates him.

Even if only used as a conversational gambit, a knowledge of a range of techniques is useful to the director – familiarization of your actor's process will make them relax and trust you. Lamentably not all actors will have mastered *one* 'simple technique perfectly' as proposed by **David Mamet** (see the chapter 'Simple Technique Perfectly' in the companion book, **Working with Actors**).[2] Drama schools tend to offer up a buffet of different tantalizing methodologies, frequently without time to explore any one of them in depth. I asked one of my students – a graduate of a reputable London theatre school – if she had previously studied Meisner technique. 'Oh, yes. We had a couple of days of **Meisner** in our second year.' This notion is anathema to a **Meisner** practitioner, who will have spent a minimum of two years developing the requisite skills.

You will clearly understand, if you have read the companion book, **Working with Actors**, that I'm convinced that **Sanford Meisner's** techniques provide the most useful base for actors and directors. And as the title implies, it is a central point of reference for this book. But to limit oneself to **Meisner** (or any technique) could be self-defeating. There may be no time during rehearsal to do a 'Practical Aesthetics' breakdown to analyse the character's objectives, and work out actors' substitutions, but perhaps a quick fix with a **Michael Chekhov** *psychological gesture* might clear up a blockage, or a bit of **Uta Hagen's** 'endowing', or, *in extremis*, some of **Susana Bloch's** *Alba-emoting*™. There's more than one way to skin a cat. Do you not recognize some of the names of the innovators mentioned above? Carry on reading and you shall. My writing this book grew out of frustration with my own ignorance when actors spoke to me about using Boal's *games for non-actor*s or *Alba-emoting*™. I personally can't bear to be ill-informed in front of someone I'm meant to be guiding.

'We have actors but no *art of acting* [emphasis mine].' So said G. E. Lessing (1729–81), a German playwright and philosopher considered to be the first dramaturg, lamenting the state of acting in his time.[3] As it happens, a few of Lessing's contemporaries (such as **David Garrick** and **Denis Diderot**) were actually grappling with the problem and, as we shall discover in the pages which follow, laying the foundations for a body of theory on acting which eventually elevated the lowly endeavour called 'acting' to an art form. This book attempts to document developments in the art of acting, especially in the realistic vein, and, concomitantly, the art of dramatic representation (the two are inextricably bound). The latter, before the arrival of cinema, meant theatre in its different forms. It stands to reason that a film director wanting to learn about acting techniques needs to understand how the art has developed, and, of course, that was in the theatre.

The writing of this book was an education for its author. I was already familiar with a few of the masters I researched, but the discovery of how one practitioner's thinking affected another – the interconnections of drama theory across international borders – was a revelation. A fascinating cross-fertilization occurred during the first thirty years of the twentieth century – an explosion in Western theatre forms whose legacy we are living today: a commingling of the ideas of **Stanislavski**, **Meyerhold** and **Vakhtangov** in Russia; **Brecht** and **Piscator** in Germany; **Copeau** and **Artaud** in France; and in Switzerland, **Appia** and **Jacques-Dalcroze**.

In addition to the web of influences which revealed themselves, my research unearthed fascinating life stories of these giants of theatre and cinema, e.g. **Meyerhold's** assassination, **Brecht's** philandering, **Michael Chekhov's** nervous breakdown, **Ouspenskaya's** self-immolation, **Eisenstein's** closeted homosexuality. I have presented the chapters chronologically according to the birthdates of the practitioners to give a sense of how their ideas have been transmitted within their life span and handed down over time. I offer a brief biography of each – generally contextualizing their ideas in terms of the culture and politics of their time. I have tried to point out who influenced whom, and who was influenced by whom. References to the gurus and chapters in the book have been **bolded** to help you to cross-reference these influences. You can read the book either as a history of acting/performance theory and praxis, or as a quick encyclopaedic reference guide to a specific guru or technique – which may then lead you on to explore another one. For the newcomer to the field, it is a *primer* of the ideas of some of the great teachers, practitioners and theorists of dramatic art of the nineteenth and twentieth centuries.

As per the book's title, I have focused on acting realism, but it is impossible to trace the lineage of theatrical and cinematic Realism and ignore other forms of expression in theatre art and cinema which have grown up alongside it, been informed by the style, and sometimes reacted against it. It is commonly said that all forms of twentieth-century acting stem back to **Stanislavski**. It's undeniable. He was the first Westerner to attempt to codify the elements of acting and to devise systematic training for the actor. (Eastern modes of theatre, such as Japanese Noh drama or Indian Kathakali, were based on rigorous training programmes). **Stanislavski's** quest was for 'truth' in performance. Even the great promulgator of physical theatre, **Jerzy Grotowski** (1933–99) subscribed to **Stanislavski's** proposition that 'truth' resided in the psyche of the actor – as evidenced in the actor's emotions – but proposed another route into the psyche – the *universal collective unconscious*. Others, such as **Meyerhold**, **Grotowski** and **LeCoq**, shared the quest, but sought to find truth through direct theatrical means of expression reaching to the deepest part of man's nature – unlocking the *anima*, the soul, the unconscious. There are inclusions in the book of other practitioners and theorists for whom 'truth' did not lie in the actor's psychology, such as **Gordon Craig** who treated the actor as a puppet (*Übermarionette*), Appia, who wanted to liberate the actor spatially, and **Brecht**, for whom 'transformation' on the part of the actor was strictly forbidden. They are included because they influenced the theatrical form of Realist artists like **Harold Clurman**, who was greatly stimulated by **Brecht's** ideas, and in the interest of creating a dialectic. Given that my goal is to 'arm' the well-informed director I also deemed it important to include chapters on practitioners such as **Frederick Alexander** and **Émile Jaques-Dalcroze** and others who were not proponents of Realism, but whose techniques are still being taught to in acting schools today.

Nothing comes from nothing, and **Stanislavski** had his references and inspirations for his Realism, such as the literary work of Pushkin, the performances of Italian actress **Eleanora Duse**, the naturalism of The Meiningen Players group, and the realistic acting of the great Russian actor Mikhail Shchepkin . . . as you shall see.

The first textbook on acting theory was written in 1657, written by Valentin Conrart (1603–75), one of the leading lights of the French Academy. Its title was *Treatise on the action of the orator, with respect to elocution and gesture*.[4] Our journey back in time reaches not quite that far, beginning in the early 1700s with the articulation of acting theories based on the performance techniques of the English actor, **David Garrick** (1717–79), and a critique of those techniques by his contemporary, the French philosopher and encyclopaedist, **Denis Diderot** (1713–84).

Art, in common with science, is a process of evolution and influence. Innovators build their ideas on what has already been discovered. We filter the useful from the irrelevant in our experience and make it our own. Our understanding of precedents is the bedrock of our own creativity. For this reason, I have organized this book chronologically in order of birth dates, to be best able to perceive a network of influences over time. British director **Peter Brook** said, 'I think that one exists to receive and give influences. And nothing is worse than to try to deny that. I'm influenced and influencing.'[5]

Notes

1. Expression coined in 1854 by Seba Smith in *Way Down East, Portraitures of Yankee Life*.
2. 'I think the essential tools in any worthwhile endeavour are incredibly simple. And very difficult to master. The task of any artist is not to learn many, many techniques but to learn the most simple technique perfectly.' David Mamet, *On Directing Film* (London: Faber & Faber, 1992), 106.
3. Toby Cole (ed.), *Acting: A Handbook of the Stanislavski Method*. Introduction by Lee Strasberg (New York: Lear, 1947), 11.
4. Valentin Conrart, *Traité de l'action de l'Orateur ou de la Prononciation et du Geste* (Paris: Chez Augustin Corbé, 1657).
5. Margaret Croyden, *Conversations with Peter Brook, 1970–2000* (New York: Theatre Communications Group, 2009), 390.

2 The Realm of Realism

Ceci n'est pas une pipe.

Richard Armstrong begins his book *Understanding Realism* by evoking the famous canvas by Belgian Surrealist René Magritte (1898–1967) depicting a smoking pipe, beneath which is the inscription, 'This is not a pipe.'[1] The painted image of the pipe is almost photorealist, but Magritte's ironic caption reminds us that what we call *realism* is, in fact, a subjective *representation* of a reality.

According to French film and theorist critic André Bazin (1918–1958), Realism springs from a primeval need in man to *represent* things, which is a way of lifting objects out of time and space and making them eternal. It is both a religious and a psychological need. He cites the mummification of Egyptian kings as an example, in which the deceased obtains immortality via mummification, and sculpted models representing the deceased are spread around their tomb in case something should happen to the *actual* mummy.[2] Bazin maintains 'Photography and the cinema . . . are discoveries that satisfy, once and for all and in its very essence, our obsession with realism.'[3]

Realism, in its narrowest definition, was a late-nineteenth-century movement in art, literature and the dramatic arts, lying between Romanticism and Modernism. The term was popularized in the 1840s by the French novelist Champfleury (1821–89) to embrace art and literature, but with specific reference to the work of the Gustave Courbet (1819–77) a painter whose canvases exemplified the style.[4] Realism in its broader sense survived Modernism – a loose collection of trends – and remains today the dominant form of art, literature, drama, and film. Modernism didn't so much kill-off Realism, as to put a different spin on it. As the French writer/filmmaker Alain Robbe-Grillet (1922–2008) pointed out, 'All writers believe they are realists. None ever calls himself abstract, illusionistic, chimerical, fantastic, falsidical . . . Realism [is] a flag under which the enormous majority – if not all – of today's novelists enlist.'[5] Modernism and Post-modernism can be seen simply as new approaches to representing reality.[6] What all emerging forms or subgenres of Realism have in common is that they have created new ways of seeing.[7]

Literary Realism can be said to have started in the earlier part of the nineteenth century in Russia, notably with elements of the novels and plays of Alexander Pushkin (1799–1837). In France there were parallel developments, primarily with Stendhal (1783–1842), who wrote the first psychological novel (*The Red and the Black*, 1830), and Honoré de Balzac (1799–1850), whose works offered an unfiltered view of society, with multi-faceted and – like Stendhal's – morally ambiguous characters. *La Comédie Humaine* (1829–1848) is considered his *magnum opus*. Nikolai Gogol (1809–52), a Russian writer of Ukrainian origins, was greatly influenced by Pushkin. His short stories, novels and plays were written in a realistic vein, increasingly with political undertones (e.g. *Dead Souls*, 1836, *The Government Inspector*, 1842). Gogol greatly influenced the great novelists to follow such as Fyodor Dostoevsky (1821–81) and Leo Tolstoy (1828–1910) during the latter half of the nineteenth century, which saw the full flowering of literary Realism and emergence of the style in the dramatic arts, notably in the Moscow Arts Theatre (MAT).

Key literary works of nineteenth-century Realism

Author	Dates	Key Work	Theme
Ivan Turgenev Russian	(1818–83)	Fathers and Sons (1862)	Explores generational clashes between fathers and their sons in nineteenth-century Russia.
Fyodor Dostoevksky Russian	(1821–81)	Crime and Punishment (1886)	A destitute, desperate former student wanders through the slums of St Petersburg and commits a random murder without remorse or regret.
Count Leo Tolstoy, Russian	(1828–1910)	Anna Karenina (1878)	An extramarital affair scandalizes St Petersburg, and the lovers flee to Italy.
Honoré de Balzac, French	(1799–1850)	Père Goriot (1835)	Three lives are intertwined: the elderly doting Goriot, a mysterious criminal-in-hiding and a naïve law student.
Gustave Flaubert, French	(1821–80)	Madame Bovary (1857)	The obscure life of a discontented provincial doctor's wife.
George Eliot, English	(1819–90)	Adam Bede (1859)	Carpenter in love with an unmarried woman who bears a child by another man.
George Gissing, English	(1857–1903)	New Grub Street (1891)	Battle between integrity and the dictates of the marketplace for soul of an impoverished writer.
Stephen Crane, American	(1871–1900)	Red Badge of Courage (1895)	The psychology of fear in an American Civil War setting.

'Naturalism' is a variation of realism, more generally associated with stories of the working class and poverty, with political overtones. Naturalism is modelled on what is observable in nature and is intrinsically linked with the environment. It is based on scientific and historical accuracy. In the century which followed, American writers such as Clifford Odets (1906–53) would be inspired by it, but in the late nineteenth century Russia its principal practitioner was Maxim Gorky (1868–1936). Gorky's seminal play, *The Lower Depths* (1902) described the suffering of the working class in graphic terms. That the name Gorky is a pseudonym meaning bitter tells us something about the tone of his work.

In France, in 1873, Émile Zola (1849–1902) adapted his naturalistic novel, *Thérèse Raquin*, to the stage. Zola was attempting to explore *temperaments* as opposed to 'fixed' characters, and his playwriting gives great freedom to the actor to explore the nuances. Philosophically, Zola was inspired by Charles Darwin (1809–82) with his scientific explorations of the effect of environment on behaviour, as well as by the inventor of sociology, Auguste Comte (1798–1857) who promoted the 'science of behaviour' and a Positivist philosophy.[8]

Notable among other playwrights who wrote in a naturalistic vein were the Swede, August Strindberg (1849–1912), the Irishman, John Millington Synge (1871–1909), and the German, Gerhart Hauptmann (1862–1946).

As a movement, Naturalism was not so much a distillation of Realism but represented an aesthetic doctrine that was more pointed politically. The earlier Realist writers, such as Flaubert, maintained an attitude of neutrality towards their material, whereas the Naturalist writers such as Maxim Gorky and Émile Zola imposed a very specific view of humanity on their work – scientific and anthropological, informed by the methods and discoveries of nineteenth-century science.[9] Zola's introduction to the second edition of *Thérèse Raquin* is positively Darwinian:

> Thérèse and Laurent are human beasts, nothing more . . . I had only one aim, which was: given a powerful man and an unsatisfied woman, to seek within them the animal, and even to see in them only the animal.[10]

Key literary works of Naturalism

Author	Dates	Key Work	Theme
Émile Zola, French	(1840–1902)	*Thérèse Raquin* (1867) novel, (1873) play	A woman and her lover murder the husband with whom circumstances had forced her to wed.
Maxim Gorky Russian	(1868–1936)	*The Lower Depths* (1902) play	A group of impoverished Russians share a basement shelter.
Arthur Morrison, English	(1863–1945)	*A Child of the Jago* (1890)	A devastating portrait of quarrelling families in an East End slum.
Theodore Dreiser, American	(1871–1945)	*Sister Carrie* (1900)	A small-town girl comes to the big city and is used and abused.

As a theatrical form Realism and Naturalism found their full expression in the Moscow Arts Theatre at the turn of the nineteenth century in the work of **Konstantin Stanislavski** (1863–1938) and **Vladimir Nemirovich-Danchenko** (1858–1943), changing forever the course of theatrical representation and dramatic art (fully explored in a later chapter, **From Russia with Love**).

The arrival of cinema, in the late 1880s, and sound cinema in 1927, assured Realism's predominance as a dramatic art form (see the chapters **Dramatic Realism in Cinema** and **Arrival of the Talkies**). Over time, cinema spawned its own variations of Realism – **Italian Neo-Realism**, **Socialist Realism**, **Social Realism**, **Kitchen Sink Drama** and **Neo Neo-Realism**, **Poetic Realism**, **Magic Realism** – each a subgenre of its own.

Realism as a style of acting was first investigated and taught by Konstantin Stanislavski in his work with the Moscow Arts Theatre at the very end of the nineteenth century. However, its antecedents hark back as far as the early eighteenth century, when the acting methods of a certain English actor stirred up a debate about acting technique that continues to this day. That groundbreaker was named **David Garrick**.

Further reading

Richard Armstrong, *Understanding Realism* (London: British Film Institute, 2005).
André Bazin, *What is Cinema?*, trans. and ed., Hugh Gray (Berkeley: University of California Press, 1967).
Matthew Beaumont, ed., *Adventures in Realism* (Oxford: Blackwell Publishing, 2007).
Alain Robbe-Grillet, 'From Realism to Reality', in *For a New Novel: Essays on Fiction*, trans. Richard Howard (New York: Grove Press Inc., 1965), 157–68.

Notes

1. Armstrong, 1.
2. Bazin 9–10.
3. Ibid., 21.
4. The term *'realisme'* first appeared in 1826 in the *Mercure français du XIXeme siècle* to describe a doctrine based on truth and an accurate depiction of life.
5. Robbe-Grillet, 157.
6. Robbe-Grillet, 165. Robbe-Grillet contends that even Kafka's 'absurdist' writing – to the extent that it is not metaphysical but is grounded in an immediate, direct and detailed materialist reality – should be considered a form of Realism.
7. Ibid.
8. Positivism: a system recognizing only that which can be scientifically or mathematically verified.
9. Sally Ledger, 'Naturalism: "Dirt and horror pure and simple,"' in Beaumont, *Adventures in Realism*, 69.
10. Ibid., 71.

3 David Garrick
1717–1779

Shakespeare and Garrick like twin stars shall shine / and Earth irradiate with a beam divine.[1]

Some 157 years before the Moscow Arts Theatre presented its game-changing version of Anton Chekhov's *The Seagull* – which many claim is the birth of theatrical realism – on an October night in 1741 in the East End of London, a twenty-four-year-old English actor took to the boards to play Shakespeare's *Richard III*, delivering up the crookback king in an acting style hitherto unseen. David Garrick dared to play King Richard as a real person, with real emotions and a psychological makeup.

Garrick's performance became the talk-of-the-town – the buzz in the coffee houses frequented by the likes of Samuel Johnson and James Boswell.[2] Soon carriages were creating nightly traffic jams in front of Goodman's Fields Theatre. Garrick's style of 'naturalistic' acting was pronounced by the 'tattlers' as nothing short of a revolution. Richard Cumberland (1731–1811), a contemporary playwright, described its effect.

> It seemed as if a whole century had been stept over in the transition of a single scene. Old things were done away with and a new order at once brought forward, bright and luminous, and clearly destined to dispel the barbarisms and bigotry of a tasteless age . . . superstitiously devoted to the illusions of imposing declamation.[3]

The contrast between Garrick's acting and the prevailing style was described by an astonished contemporary critic: 'When three or four men are on the stage with him, he is attentive to whatever is spoke, and never drops his character when he has finish'd a Speech, by either looking contemptuously at an inferior performer, unnecessary spitting, or suffering his eyes to wander thro' the whole of Circle of Spectators.'[4] It was common practice at the time, for the actor, having delivered their line, to disconnect with the other actors, to powder their nose, or look into the audience to wink at their girlfriend, until their next line was due.

Garrick's first biographer, Thomas Davies, a contemporary, said this of his acting:

> Mr. Garrick shone forth like a theatrical Newton; he threw new light on elocution and action; he banished ranting, bombast, and grimace; and restored nature, ease, simplicity, and genuine humour.[5]

The actor gained instant notoriety, and triumph after triumph followed in short order: *The Orphan* (1741), *Venice Preserv'd* (1742) and *King Lear* (1742), at Goodman's Fields; *Hamlet* (1742) in Dublin and *The Alchemist* (1743), *Macbeth* and *The Provok'd Wife* in 1744, at Theatre Royal, Drury Lane. By 1747, after only six years on the stage, Garrick's reputation and influence were so substantial that he was invited to manage London's most important theatre – the Theatre Royal at Drury Lane, in Covent Garden, still in existence today.

Garrick's acting was eulogized by contemporaries such as the poet Alexander Pope (1688–1744), as well as the politico and soon-to-be prime minister, William Pitt (1708–78).[6] William Hogarth (1697–1764) captured him on canvas in the role of King Richard, and Sir Joshua Reynolds (1723–92) immortalized him in several portraits.[7] London had at that moment overtaken Paris as the largest city in the world, and its literature, theatre and music (notably George Frederick Handel's operas and oratorios) made it the pre-eminent cultural capital of the globe.[8] Garrick's fame spread to the Continent, and was heightened when he undertook his Grand Tour from 1763 to 1765. He visited Italy, Germany, and Russia, and ended up in Paris. There he struck up a friendship with the essayist and *philosophe*, **Denis Diderot** (1718–84), whose ideas on acting he influenced greatly. During this European peregrination he was endlessly invited to the *soirées* of the rich and famous, where he famously performed 'turns' – scenes, alternating between comedy and tragedy – demonstrating his ability to move seamlessly from one emotional zone to another.

Garrick's acting style was not his only contribution to the dramatic arts. During his twenty-seven years as manager of the Theatre Royal, Drury Lane, he is said to have made significant innovations and reforms to stagecraft in the areas of scenery, lighting, costumes and production procedures. He instituted the unheard-of practice of *casting* for roles, and penalized actors who forgot their lines. One of his first changes was to kick the spectators off the front of the stage, and the jeerers out of the auditorium, making the audience watch the play, rather than each other. Garrick himself played ninety-six roles at Drury Lane. He wrote forty-nine plays, and his adaptations of other works formed an impressive body of dramatic literature of the period. Not the least of these were his adaptations of Shakespeare's plays, about which a brief digression is necessary.

Before the early eighteenth century, Shakespeare's plays had been quite freely adapted – sometimes massacred. Endings were changed (e.g. King Lear survived), new characters were introduced (e.g. Miranda in *The Tempest* was given a sister), entertainments injected (the witches in *Macbeth* sang and danced). At the time no one thought that Shakespeare's original words were sacrosanct or that he should be treated much differently from his peers.[9] However, the 1700s, vastly aided by Garrick, saw the emergence of Shakespeare scholarship, with well-considered editions being published by the likes of Alexander Pope and Samuel Johnson, offering footnotes explaining obscure terms and historical references – much like the style of the Arden edition widely used today. A new respect for the texts emerged, along with a general resistance to adaptation. Bucking the trend, Garrick, to popularize the Bard, adapted freely and with much imagination – but always with complete respect for the poet's words, as laid down in the original Folio editions. Within those parameters, as an actor, he was unique in serving up his characters with real emotions. Allegedly, 'James Boswell wept openly at the poignant frailty of Garrick's Lear, an experience so pleasurable that he returned for more.'[10] Garrick actively promoted the concept of 'Bardolatry', organizing, among other things, the first Shakespeare Festival in Stratford-upon-Avon. (Being England, the first attempt was typically rained-off.) No one – at that time, or since – has done more than David Garrick to popularize the concept of Shakespeare as a British national treasure.

If we saw Garrick performing on the stage today, we would most probably be disappointed and find him to be over the top. Although he was revered at the time for his 'naturalistic' style, subsequently different concepts of 'acting naturally' have evolved. From what I have read of contemporary reactions, in Garrick's day 'naturalism' meant simply representing the changing emotions felt by the character in the flow of the play.

According to his great admirer, **Denis Diderot**, the emotions which David Garrick demonstrated in performance were 'represented' – manufactured technically in gestures, vocal tone, etc., irrespective of what the actor was actually feeling. Garrick claimed otherwise. His secret was that he didn't *try* to evoke specific emotions at a given moment; instead, he entered into the circumstances, into situations. He proposed, effectively, that true 'genius' in acting is 'living in the moment' – thus anticipating Stanislavski's dictum by 150 years. To draw a contrast, Garrick said this about France's leading actress of the time:

> Mademoiselle Clarion is so conscious and certain of what she can do that she never (I believe) had the feelings of the instant come upon her. But I pronounce that the greatest strokes of genius have become unknown to the actor himself, 'til circumstances and the warmth of the scene has sprung the mine, as it were, as much to his own surprise, at that of the audience.[11]

Sadly, Garrick's 'revolution' failed to have a long-term effect on acting methods. The top contemporary actors, Theophilus Cibber (1703–58) and James Quin (1693–1766), carried on as usual, in the same declamatory style, as did other actors at the time.[12] Quin declared cynically, 'Garrick is a new religion' but that he 'would come to church again.' Garrick turned out the following epigram, in reply:

> Pope Quin who damns all churches but his own,
>   Complains that heresy infects the town;
>   That [Garrick] has misled the age,
>   And taints the sound religion of the stage:
> Schism, he cries, has turn'd the nation's brain
>   But eyes will open, and to church again!
>
> When doctrines meet with gen'ral approbation,
>   It is not heresy, but reformation.[13]

Thanks to Garrick, 'truthful emotion' came to be acknowledged as a desirable quality in acting. Unfortunately, the re-emerging Romanticism of the later part of the eighteenth century required an acting style that was overly sentimental and indicated. The Victorian theatre that followed ushered in the era of melodrama and the return of exaggerated acting styles, which were to largely prevail until the re-emergence of psychology in acting, brought on by Anton Chekhov and Konstantin Stanislavski in far-off Russia at the end of the next century.

Further reading

Jean Benedetti, *David Garrick and the Birth of Modern Theatre* (London: Methuen, 2001).

Notes

1. Inscription by Samuel Jackson Pratt on David Garrick's tombstone in Poet's Corner, Westminster Abbey.
2. Samuel Johnson (1709–84) and James Boswell (1740–95) were writers, biographers and diarists, chroniclers of the epoque. Johnson was a personal friend of Garrick.
3. Richard Cumberland, *Memoirs of Richard Cumberland, Written by Himself,* Vol.1 (London: Lackingham, Allen & Co., 1807), 81–2.
4. A writer for *The Champion*, cited by William Angus, 'An Appraisal of David Garrick: Based Mainly Upon Contemporary Sources', *Quarterly Journal of Speech*, XXV (February 1939): 31.
5. T. Davis, *Memoirs of the Life of David Garrick, Esq.* Vol. 1 (London: Longman, Rees, Hurst, and Deme, 1780), 44.
6. Alexander Pope was a poet, essayist and translator. *The Rape of the Lock* was his most famous work. William Pitt was prime minister between 1766 and 1768, a populist, a great orator and promoter of the idea of a British Empire.
7. William Hogarth was an English painter and pictorial satirist, who chronicled the venality and superficiality of society. Sir Joshua Reynolds was a portrait painter of world renown.
8. George Frideric Handel (1685–1759) was a German born composer of Baroque music famous for his Italian-style operas, *concerti grossi*, oratorios and organ music. He was resident in London from 1712 and naturalized in 1727.

9. Richard Schoch, 'How one actor forever changed the way we see Shakespeare', British Council Voices, https://www.britishcouncil.org/voices-magazine/how-one-actor-forever-changed-way-we-see-shakespeare, 19 April 2016.
10. Ibid.
11. Benedetti, 199 (quoting a letter Garrick wrote to a Danish friend, Helfrich Peter Sturz).
12. Davis, ibid. Quin famously said: 'That if this young fellow be right, then we have been all wrong.'
13. Ibid., 45–6.

4 Denis Diderot
1713–1784

Feeling cripples the intelligence at the very juncture when man needs all his self-possession.[1]

Amazing as it may seem, more than 125 years before **Konstantin Stanislavski** was actively making the case in Russia for actors to bring their personal emotions to the stage, Denis Diderot, one of the bright stars of the French Enlightenment, was questioning the value of doing so, and arguing instead for 'faking it', thus provoking a debate which is alive amongst actors and drama theorists to this day.

Diderot was a philosopher, pamphleteer, pornographer, sometimes prisoner. As an outspoken voice of the Enlightenment, he prized rationality and passion, and voiced his radical scepticism at personal peril.[2] As the originator, editor and main contributor to the original *Encyclopédie*, he incensed the Catholic Church and the French State by promoting his rationalist philosophy and his rejection of orthodox Christianity. (The Pope ordered all copies of the *Encyclopédie* to be handed over to local priests for burning.)[3]

Diderot's undoing, however, was his sceptical and atheistic pamphlet entitled *Lettre sur les aveugles à l'usage de ceux qui voient* ('Letter on the Blind') – a polemic against Christian superstition, as uttered by a man in his dying hours. Upon publication, Diderot was arrested and incarcerated in the Vincennes prison in 1749 – without trial. The 'blasphemous' pamphlet had followed closely on the heels of his philosophical and pornographic novel, *Indiscrete Jewels* (1748), which employed the device of talking vaginas (predating the play *The Vagina Monologues* by a mere 248 years[4]). In Vincennes, he was at least able to enjoy frequent visits from his friend and supporter, Jean-Jacques Rousseau (1712–78), doyen of the Enlightenment. Diderot was also much admired by Voltaire (1694–1778), although they only met once, shortly before Voltaire died.

With his 'encyclopaedic' bent, Diderot wrote on many subjects, including acting. Between 1771 and 1778 he penned *Paradoxe sur le Comédien* (published posthumously in 1880 in France, and in English in 1883) in which he examined the nature of emotion in performance. He maintained that the best performances are given by actors who remain personally detached from their own feelings, but who possess techniques for representing emotions which enable them to replicate the same emotions with consistency, night after night.

He condemned the '. . . unequal acting of players who play from the heart. From them you must expect no unity. Their playing is alternatively strong and feeble, fiery and cold, dull and sublime. Tomorrow they will miss the point they have excelled in today . . .'.[5] By contrast, the absence of 'sensibility' (emotion) makes for a sublime actor whose 'tears come from his brain.'[6]

Diderot argued that for the actor to succeed in convincing the audience of the veracity of their emotions, they needed technique. He insisted that 'the actor who performs from reflection and the study of human nature, from constant imitation of some ideal model, from imagination, from memory, will be one and the same in all of his presentations, always equally perfect'.[7]

He was clearly inspired by what he saw of the work of English actor, **David Garrick**. However, his impressions were based solely on impromptu performances of a mixed bag of scenes which he witnessed Garrick performing at various Paris salons, at the time of Garrick's visits with his wife in 1763, and again in 1764–5.[8] The fact that Diderot may have only witnessed scene renderings, may account for his wonderment over Garrick's versatility and his ability to instantly swop from tragic to comic instantaneously. 'Garrick will put his head between two folding doors, and in the course of five or six seconds his expression will change successively from wild delight to temperate surprise, from surprise to blank astonishment, from that to sorrow . . . .'.[9] Diderot assumed, therefore, that Garrick had mastered certain mechanical acting techniques, and was not relying on any 'real' emotion: 'Can his soul have experienced all these feelings, and played this kind of a scale in concert with his face? I don't believe it; nor do you.'[10] Had he seen Garrick in complete performances of entire plays, where the ebb and flow of emotion is pinned to the narrative, he may have reached different conclusions.

Diderot has been criticized for being a failed dramatist (he wrote two not very successful plays), and for lacking any first-hand experience in acting or directing. According to some, he was not even a regular theatregoer. Nonetheless, he triggered a debate in drama theory which has continued down through the years, manifesting itself in opposing camps of 'emotionalists' and 'anti-emotionalists' – arguments as to whether the artist should experience the feelings which they present in performance, and as to the relationship of physiology to emotion. The history of what is known as the 'Great Debate' is laid out in Jean Benedetti's very readable biography of David Garrick in the chapter of that name.[11]

Among the later 'anti-emotionalists', was the internationally known nineteenth-century French actor, Benoît-Constant Coquelin (1841–1909) – a strong advocate of Diderot's point of view. Coquelin was the occasional acting partner of Sarah Bernhardt – the quintessential 'representational' style actor (see notes on Bernhardt in **Working with Actors** and below in the chapter on **Eleonora Duse**). He said,

> I hold this paradox to be literal truth; and I am convinced that one can only be a great actor on condition of complete self-mastery and ability to express feelings which are not experienced, which may never be experienced, which from the very nature of things never can be experienced. And this is the reason that our trade is an art.[12]

Stanislavski was obviously in the 'emotionalist' camp; however, he acknowledged that Diderot's proposal wasn't 'all bad' – that it had been misunderstood and indeed allowed for 'affective feelings'.[13] **Lee Strasberg**, an arch-emotionalist, took a similar position.[14] Also in the emotionalist camp was **Jacques Copeau** (1879–1949) whose take on Diderot was, 'For the actor, the whole art is the gift of himself. In order to give himself, he must first possess himself. . . . Not only does technique not exclude sensitivity: it authenticates and liberates it.'[15]

In modern times, the Chilean psychologist, **Susana Bloch** (b.1931) is an advocate. Her *Alba-emoting*™ technique is predicated on the actor using physical *devices* to 'manufacture' emotion for performance. (See the chapter on **Bloch** and the chapter 'Psychophysiological Mechanisms' in **Working with Actors**.)

Further reading

Jean Benedetti, *David Garrick: The Birth of Modern Theatre* (London: Methuen, 2001).
Andrew S. Curran, *Diderot and the Art of Thinking Freely* (New York: The Other Press, 2020).
Denis Diderot, *The Paradox of Acting*, trans. Walter Herries Pollock (London: Chatto & Windus, 1883).

Notes

1. Diderot, *Paradox*, quoted by Henry Irving in his Preface, x.
2. Adam Gopnik, 'How the Man of Reason got Radicalised' *(The New Yorker)*, issue 1, 4 March 2019, https://www.newyorker.com/magazine/2019/03/04/how-the-man-of-reason-got-radicalized#:~:text=His%20experience%20in%20Russia%20radicalized,not%20have%20a%20decade%20earlier
3. Ibid., 6.
4. *Vagina Monologues* was created by actor/writer Eve Ensler (b. 1953) and first performed in 1996 and deemed by many critics to be one of the most important pieces of political theatre ever written in America.
5. Diderot, 8.
6. Ibid., 1.
7. Diderot as quoted in James Gray, 'Diderot, Garrick, and the Art of Acting', *The Age of Johnson* (Lewisburg, PA: Bucknell University Press, 2007), Vol. 18, 250.
8. F. M. Wilkshire, 'Cher et illustre Roscius: David Garrick's Influence on the Dramatic Theories of Diderot', *L'homme et la nature* (Man and Nature), (1987) Vol. 6, 21–34. https://doi.org/10.7202/1011867ar, 21–2.
9. Diderot, 38.
10. Ibid.
11. Benedetti, 182–200.
12. Benoît-Constant Coquelin, *Art and the Actor*, trans. Abby Langdon Alger (New York: Dramatic Museum of Columbia University, 1915), 56.
13. Jessica Marie Beck, 'Directing Emotion: A Practice-led Investigation into the Challenge of Emotion in Western Performance', PhD thesis, University of Exeter (2011), 62.
14. Ibid., 63.
15. Jacques Copeau, 'An actor's thoughts on Diderot's "Paradox"', 1929, in *Copeau: Texts on Theatre*, trans. and ed. John Rudlin and Norman H. Paul, (London: Routledge, 1990), 77.

5 From Russia with Love

The truth of passion, the verisimilitude of feeling, placed in the given circumstances, that is what our reason demands of a writer, or a dramatic poet.[1]

Alexander Pushkin

Our story starts in Moscow on 29 December 1898. It is the opening night of the Moscow Art Theatre's production of Anton Chekhov's *The Seagull*, starring the playwright's soon-to-be-wife, Olga Knipper as Arkadina, and featuring **Vsevolod Meyerhold** as Konstantin and, playing the role of Trigorin, **Konstantin Stanislavski**, the play's director. Foster Hirsch describes this historic moment in his book, *A Method to Their Madness*.

> As the curtain rose on the first act . . . a group of actors was seated on a long bench, placed at the front of the stage, with their backs turned to the audience. A gasp swept through the opening night crowd in audible response to this violation of theatrical rules – actors turned away from the house, engaged in conversation as the curtain went up – what could the director have been thinking of?[2]

Whether an accidental or inspired gesture on the part of **Stanislavski**, it was, in effect, the first gunshot in a revolution in theatre, which would ricochet down the years, from country to country, from director to director, and find its full expression in the work of **Sanford Meisner**, among others.

But nothing comes from nothing, and we must travel a bit further back in history to understand how *'realism'* arrived onstage on that fateful night in 1898 in the Moscow Arts Theatre, and became, thereafter, the dominant acting technique. It's a rich and colourful chronicle sweeping over tzars and revolutions. All I can offer within the limits of this book is the briefest outline.

Realism Russian style

After the 1848 Revolution in France, Realism emerged in Europe as a recognized art form in the plastic arts, as a rejection of the Romanticism which preceded it – the movement, as mentioned earlier, was led by the French painter Gustave Courbet (1819–77). In Russia, as elsewhere, during the latter part of the nineteenth century, increasing industrialism saw the burgeoning of urban populations, which created new mass audiences in search of entertainment. When the monopoly held by the Imperial theatres was abolished in 1882, along with the strict censorship they imposed, new commercial popular theatres sprung up in Moscow and St Petersburg, with the unfortunate result was that the existing taste in the theatre was degraded even further.[3] The menu on offer consisted of vaudeville, broad comedies (especially French farce) and melodrama. Occasionally more elevated fare, such as Shakespeare or the Greek tragedies, was presented, but the performances were *formulaic*, and the lines were *declaimed* – completely artificial and stilted.

There was one notable exception. The Ukrainian/Russian actor, Mikhail Shchepkin (1788–1863) rose to fame – much as **David Garrick** had a hundred years previously – by portraying real characters with feelings on the stage. Shchepkin detested the prevailing fakery and mannerisms of the acting of his day – above all, the distorted manner of speech. He observed that whenever an actor played a lover, 'the words "love," "passion," and "betrayal" were screamed with as much strength as the actor possessed; but facial expressions were not used.'[4] Almost every word spoken was accompanied by a gesture – the *final gesture* being when the actor was finished a speech and was ready to exit. The convention required that the actor raised their right hand to signal that they were leaving the stage.[5] According to his own memoirs, Shchepkin's acting style developed by accident. Once, when bored during a rehearsal, he lazily delivered all his lines in his normal tone of voice. It was a revelation. It caused him to *believe in* what he was saying, and he felt 'alive' on the stage as he never had before. Shchepkin deserves a chapter of his own. He had an extraordinary life. He was born a serf, and it was only when he was thirty years old, and already a successful provincial actor, that his owners permitted a benefit performance to raise the money buy his freedom. Eventually he became a regular actor at the Maly ('Little') Theatre in Moscow, and even founded his own school of acting. He had a profound influence on **Stanislavski**.

It could be said that in the latter part of the eighteenth century a realistic theatre was inevitable – given the precedents in literature, the scientific breakthroughs of the day (Charles Darwin published *On the Origin of Species* in 1859), an emerging interest in psychology (Freud set up his practice in Vienna in 1886), and the social currents stirred up by industrialization. The work of two great dramatists defined the style. The first, in Norway, was Henrik Ibsen (1828–1906) – usually credited as the 'Father of Realism' – and secondly, in Russia, Anton Chekhov (1860–1904).

Ibsen wrote about ordinary people, frequently bourgeois, in their natural environment – people who suddenly find themselves in existential crisis. He brought an ethical gravity and psychological depth to theatre, and a reality on the stage hitherto unseen. His characters expressed themselves in everyday language, with individual vocabularies. He was a social critic – portraying the injustice and falsity of middle-class social conventions, and the corrosive effect of the secrets that often underlie a respectable middle-class façade. In his plays people frequently say one thing and mean another, which demanded a radically different approach to 'acting'. For actors, it meant that, in addition to dealing with the words their character spoke aloud, they were required to develop the *subtext* to those lines – i.e. what the character might be thinking. Ibsen's playwriting career spanned from 1867 (*Peer Gynt*) to 1890 (*Hedda Gabler*).

The title of 'Father of Realism' equally belongs to the Russian, Anton Chekhov. Chekhov was a qualified doctor, a role which may have offered him insights into the fears and desires of ordinary people. He wrote about tragic events occurring in a *minor* key, as a part of the everyday texture of life. His dialogues show 'life as it is'. His characters give *self-interested answers* to other characters' questions. For everything that is said, there is that much more implied. *Subtext* becomes more important that the spoken *text*. His dialogues are like the tip of an iceberg, with the dangerous mass hidden beneath the water. His plays contain numerous characters, many on the stage at once. This allowed scope for actors to work closely together as an *ensemble*, to discover the dynamic of their character's relationships with other characters, and to plumb the depths of possible emotions. His notable plays spanned from 1887 (*Ivanov* – only performed posthumously) to 1901 (*The Cherry Orchard*). He died of tuberculosis at the age of forty-four.

The famous long lunch

On 16 June 1897 the young director, **Konstantin Stanislavski** – thirty-four years old at the time – was summoned to a fancy Moscow restaurant at 10 am to meet the Director of the Philharmonic Institute

School, **Vladimir Nemirovich-Danchenko**, a playwright, teacher and literary critic. During the legendary 'lunch' which followed (it didn't end until 3 am the next morning) the two men agreed to form what was to be called the Popular Moscow Arts Theatre. They divided up their responsibilities in the endeavour: **Nemirovich-Danchenko** was to have final say in literary matters, business affairs, and was to attend to the daily running of the theatre; **Stanislavski** was to have the last word in artistic and production concerns. According to Foster Hirsch, 'It was a naive separation of powers destined to provoke civil war.'[6] Despite a public show of unity, irreconcilable differences in approach developed over time which, contrary to public appearances, rendered a poisonous atmosphere behind the scenes. 'For Nemirovich, the theatre was a branch of literature; it was its "handmaiden". For Stanislavski the theatre was an art in itself, with the actor at its heart.'[7]

Eighteen months later, while still in the honeymoon of that relationship, Anton Chekhov's *The Seagull* opened to a rapturous response, and the Popular Moscow Arts Theatre was on the map. It should be noted that the author had mounted his play in St Petersburg in 1896, with a more 'comic' tone, but it had received a tepid response, nearly causing him to give up playwriting as a vocation. **Stanislavski**, perhaps understanding the nature of Chekhov's writing better than the author himself, introduced the missing ingredient – *subtext*.

In the chapter on **Stanislavski**, I will provide more details of the actor/director's life and trace the evolution his 'system'. Initially, his early concept of directing, while demanding a certain style of naturalism and truthful acting, was far from what he later promoted. It focused primarily on the necessity for *control* by the director. In the early days of the Moscow Arts Theatre (MAT), he was notoriously autocratic and micro-managed rigidly pre-conceived performances from his actors. He set out a 'score' for each production 'setting down every move, every gesture, exact facial expressions in almost cinematic detail'.[8]

From its inception, until about the time of its first tour of Europe, the Moscow Arts Theatre (they dropped 'Popular' from the name for bureaucratic and financial reasons) mounted numerous plays, with reasonable financial success, and built a reputation for drama in the realistic and naturalist vein – plays by Chekhov, Gorky, Ibsen, Tolstoy, Hauptman and **Nemirovich-Danchenko**, with a few Shakespeares thrown in for good measure. Most were directed by **Stanislavski**, and he acted in many. As an actor in this early period, he was erratic, still finding his feet, and puzzling out what it was that had made the likes of Shchepkin, and Italian actors Eleonora Duse (1858–1924) and Sandro Salvini (1890–1955), all of whom he had seen live on stage in Moscow, so *consistently real* in performance, while he, himself, felt so fake.

The work of the MAT and **Stanislavski** as it developed during the period 1989 to 1905 was, indeed, revolutionary – one of *realistic style*, *ensemble acting* and the use of *subtext*. Posturing and declaiming were replaced with *psychology* and *truthful emotion*. The focus of the actors on the stage was inwards to the actions of themselves and other actors, and not outwards towards the audience. An imaginary 'fourth wall' was constructed along the proscenium.

The uprisings in the streets of Moscow in 1905 meant the MAT needed to close its shutters – it was located very near to the Kremlin. This, of course, meant no income. It was decided to take the troupe on tour in Europe – a financially risky strategy, but one that paid dividends. The first stop was Berlin. At first the Russian actors were met with suspicion and arrogance, but once the run started, the Germans – astonished at the quality of production and acting – heaped praise upon the group. The season was a sell-out – helped in no little measure by the attendance of Emperor Wilhelm to a presentation of Tolstoy's *Tsar Fyodor*. The MAT was now on the map internationally. (The news reached as far as New York, as we shall later learn.)

During the tour, **Stanislavski** was depressed, feeling himself unable to obtain 'truth' as an actor. Immediately afterwards, he retreated to Finland for a vacation and time for reflection. There he sketched out ideas for arming the actor with practical methods to represent their personal truth on stage. He was looking for a 'system' upon which actors could rely to tap into the wellspring of their creative energies. When he returned to the MAT, he began using production rehearsal time to experiment with his new ideas. Some of his actors were not happy to engage in his strange new processes and protested. However, he discovered an ally in Leopold Sulerjitsky, a would-be actor serving as odd-jobs man in the MAT. 'Suler', as he was nicknamed, was an astute observer of actors, and shared **Stanislavski's** conviction that a methodology needed to be devised to aid the actors in their endeavours. For years, Suler became **Stanislavski's** right-hand man, eventually participating in the foundation of the First Studio, in 1912 – which was established specifically as a laboratory for the development of the 'system'. The early ideas devised in the First Studio were those which came to be passed on to the Americans as a result of a fortuitous conjunction of two paths which crossed in New York in 1923 – that of **Richard Boleslavsky** (1889–1937) and the first visit of the Moscow Arts Theatre ensemble.

'The system' becomes 'The Method'

Boleslavsky was a member of **Stanislavski's** and Suler's First Studio at its inception. When the MAT visit to the USA was announced he happened to be in New York, about to return to Russia. He stayed on to receive his compatriots, act with them in the ensemble, and – as he had acquired a modicum of English – to become their spokesperson. The Russian language productions of the MAT took Broadway by storm and left the Americans hungry to know the secret of their realistic and detailed acting – the likes of which Americans had never seen. The group had promised the authorities to return to Russia, but a few, including **Maria Ouspenskaya** – another First Studio member – defected. She joined **Boleslavsky** as a teacher in the newly formed **American Lab Theatre** (ALT), where they taught for ten years – essentially promulgating the principles taught by Suler and **Stanislavski** in the First Studio, upon which the ALT was modelled. Some of the key ideas of the 'system' as it existed in 1923 are outlined here:

Key elements of Stanislavskian dramatic realism (at the time of the First Studio)
ACTION
Drama is action, and action is only meaningful if motivated.
BELIEVABLE TRUTH
The actor's main job is to be believed – not to 'become' the character, but to take their own personality (psychological makeup) onto the stage, and make the audience believe in the character by believing the truthful emotions of the actor.
ENSEMBLE PLAYING
When actors have relationships off-stage, then acting on stage can be more 'potent', more engaged and more natural. Every role, large or small, must 'engage'.
EMOTIONAL MEMORY
Also called 'affective memory', possibly evoked through the senses ('sensory memory'): the application of emotions one has experienced from the past, to the circumstances given to the character by the author.

WHAT IF?
The actor asks: 'What would I do if I were in similar circumstances to my character?'

OBJECTIVE and SUPEROBJECTIVE
What the character wants to achieve within the scene, and, more largely, within the story. Objectives are the motivation driving the action. All actions must serve the SuperObjective or 'spine'.

The 'system' also involved a rigorous training programme for actors, starting with *relaxation* and *concentration*, practiced in the First Studio, and this was essentially what **Boleslavsky** delivered to New York in the **American Lab Theatre**. It only remained for a group of interested Americans to take what was taught further and adapt it to an American style, making adjustments for American culture. *Subtext*, for example, had a different value to the Americans, who were used to speaking their mind, whereas the Russians lived in conditions where much of one's ideas and feelings could not be stated outright in conversation, therefore the notion of *subtext* was commonly understood there. Psychology, on the other hand, was anathema to Soviet thinking (especially in the doctrinaire Stalinist era) but the Americans were crazy for it, which impacted significantly on the American interpretation of **Stanislavski**, as you will see.

Via their stage presentations, lectures given by **Boleslavsky**, and the teaching of the **American Lab Theatre**, the Russians inspired four young idealists – **Harold Clurman**, Cheryl Crawford (1902–86), **Lee Strasberg** and **Sanford Meisner** – who, in turn, were galvanized in 1931 to recruit twenty-eight actors, writers and directors, to form the **Group Theatre**. This was to become a permanent ensemble dedicated to realistically dramatizing the struggles of the times – mounting original American plays which would mirror – even change – people's lives. Playwright Clifford Odets (*Waiting for Lefty*, 1935) was a member, as was actor/director **Elia Kazan**, director **Robert Lewis** and actors **Stella Adler**, John Garfield, Franchot Tone and Francis Farmer. **Adler**, like **Clurman** had taken classes with **Boleslavsky** and **Ouspenskaya** at the ALT, and **Strasberg** and John Garfield had both been enrolled in the full-time acting course there.

The story of the **Group Theatre** is set out in its own chapter. The body of theory that arose out of their work around **Stanislavski's** ideas was to define what was later called the 'American' style of acting – **Lee Strasberg's** The Method. **Strasberg** was a young *wunderkind* who dominated the **Group Theatre** in its earlier years, serving as principal director and teacher. **Strasberg** became focused on, and obsessed with, the *affective memory* aspects of **Stanislavski's** teaching (which demands that if a part calls for fear, the actor must remember fear from their own experience and bring this honest emotion to the stage). Similarly, he promoted *sensory memory,* using imaginary objects relating to your emotional past to induce a remembered emotional state.

Strasberg, who was something of a self-promoter, named his version of **Stanislavski's** 'system', 'The Method'. **Stanislavski** had insisted 'system' be written in lower case, or set in quotes, or named his 'so-called system', to acknowledge that it was not immutable, but was continually evolving. **Strasberg's** ideas, however, did not evolve, but were largely stuck with the techniques **Stanislavski** had developed until 1923 – as promulgated by **Boleslavsky** and the Lab Theatre. **Strasberg** embellished his teaching with some ideas of **Yevgeny Vakhtangov** and **Vsevolod Meyerhold**, and arrogantly claimed that his 'Method' was an improvement upon **Stanislavski's** ideas.[9]

Change was in the wind. **Stella Adler** and **Harold Clurman**, following a visit to Moscow along with **Strasberg**, to witness the workings of the MAT and get to know Russian theatre first-hand, went on to Paris without **Strasberg**, where they met with **Stanislavski**, who was convalescing from illness. The master gave **Stella** several weeks of one-on-one tuition, during which she learned that he had greatly revised his ideas, most especially about affective memory. Upon her return to New York in August 1934, **Stella** joined one of **The Group's** famous summer retreats in the countryside, and excitedly expounded upon these revelations – most importantly **Stanislavski's** discovery that *imaginary circumstances* could be more effective than affective memory, and that emphasis should be placed on *action* over *psychology*.

To a few of **The Group** members, notably **Sanford Meisner** and **Robert Lewis**, **Stella's** revelations were music to the ears. They felt (as **Stanislavski** had, ten years earlier) that *affective memory* was limiting. Meisner, more than anyone, was excited by a new, more useful direction for finding the actor's truth – *imaginary circumstances* offered exciting possibilities. **Adler**, under sufferance from **Strasberg**, gave two lectures to the **Group** on **Stanislavski's** new ideas. **Strasberg**, with his psychological approach, felt undermined and resentful. Moreover, there was a backlash mounting from the actors against his autocratic direction in productions. He was finally ousted by the members in April 1937. **The Group** carried on under **Harold Clurman's** leadership until 1940, staging numerous plays, but no hits. After a long string of flops, it folded in 1941.

The troika

The impact of the **Group Theatre** was pervasive and continues to be felt today. It changed the face of American theatre, produced the leading acting teachers of the day – **Stella Adler**, **Lee Strasberg**, **Sanford Meisner** – and created from its Russian antecedents a style of film acting evermore to be known as the 'American School'.

With respect to 'American Realism' the twin dramatic arts of theatre and cinema had come late to the party. There was already a movement in full flower in American literature by the 1920s with novelists such as Stephen Crane (1871–1900), Upton Sinclair (1878–1968), Theodore Dreiser (1871–1945) and John Dos Passos (1896–1970). Similarly, in fine art a movement was afoot. In 1910, a loose fraternity of artists known as the Ashcan (or Ash Can) School rebelled against American Impressionism and began documenting everyday urban life in a *naturalistic* vein. Artists such as George Bellows (1882–1925), Robert Henri (1865–1929) and John French Sloan (1871–1951) painted the low life of New York and Philadelphia with an unromantic verisimilitude. In the theatre world there had been much discussion for the need of a 'new Realism', but no one was capable of delivering it until the Russians arrived.

In the 1930s the realism of **Stanislavski's** theatre found its true home in Hollywood. The establishment of the **Group Theatre** and the emergence in New York of a more realistic style of acting coincided with the development of sound in the cinema – both forms demanding a more credible, nuanced, spoken performance (see **Arrival of the Talkies**). In the ten years following the advent of the 'soundtrack' **Group Theatre** actors such as John Garfield and Franchot Tone and directors such as **Elia Kazan** and Harold Hecht (1907–1985) were swept up in Hollywood's rush to find actors who could play credibly in close-up, and directors who could deliver the more multi-dimensional and psychologically layered characters required for the slick Hollywood films of the 1930s and 1940s. It was a propitious moment for **Lee Strasberg**, who went west to Hollywood to work as an acting coach and teacher. He had great success in Los Angeles, before being lured back to New York by **Elia Kazan** in 1950 to become head of teaching at the **Actors Studio**, where he was able to give full rein to his 'Method', imparting it to the likes of Robert De Niro and Rod Steiger. Extremely self-promoting, he made the **Actors Studio** his own, and built a loyal following of high-profile actors.

Stella Adler had her own mentees, including Marlon Brando (1924–2004) and James Dean (1931–55). **Adler's** method started with an analysis of *character*, then worked backwards to find 'emotional truth' from resources within the actor, emphasizing *imagination* over *affective memory*. The actor was exhorted to first find the character from the 'big ideas' of the script and then inhabit it. **Sanford Meisner**, for his part, took a different approach, where the character develops organically out of an essential emotional truth inherent in the actor, which is stimulated by action.

Sanford Meisner started teaching at The Neighborhood Playhouse (School of Theatre) in 1935, while still an active member of **The Group**. He remained there, as Head of Drama, until moving to Hollywood in 1958 to become Director of the New Talent Division of 20th Century Fox.

Of the 'troika' of great American acting teachers (and the satellite teachers which they spawned) one can make the case that **Sanford Meisner** was the true inheritor of **Konstantin Stanislavski's** 'system'. **Stella Adler** reported upon her return from Paris that following the demise of the First Studio the master had developed new concepts. These were, principally: 'The Method of Physical Actions', and later 'Active Analysis' (elaborated in the chapter on **Stanislavski**). Both approaches involved a shift away from emotional introspection and psychology, and an emphasis on spontaneous action based on *what comes at you* from the other actor. As I have demonstrated elsewhere, this principle, coupled with the use of imaginary circumstances, is the very essence of **Meisner's** teaching: 'Don't do anything until something happens to make you do it . . . What you do doesn't depend on you; it depends on the other fellow.'[10]

Meisner's famous *repetition* exercises can be seen as an adaptation of **Stanislavski**/Suler's *concentration* exercises – especially in the first levels (The Listening, and Perceptive repetitions), in which one places one's focus on something other than oneself. Two-way repetition is a concrete form of what **Stanislavski** called 'Communion'.

In his later years and after his death Stanislavski's 'system' of realistic acting was appropriated as a tool for **Socialist Realism**. Consequently, 'The system' in an edited form, became the dominant body of acting theory in the Soviet bloc, as well as China and Communist Asia. Meanwhile, in the USA 'The Method' became universally known as the 'American School' of acting. Given the global predominance of American cinema, 'The Method' caught on in all English-speaking countries, as well as much of Europe and Latin America.

Sanford Meisner's lower profile meant that he was not broadly known. In 1990, a former student of his, director **Sydney Pollack**, produced a documentary entitled 'The American Theatre's Best Kept Secret', which revealed **Meisner's** methods to a larger audience and featured some of the brilliant screen actors who had studied with him. Since then, his fame has spread, and it can be said that **Meisner Technique** has become the most highly valued acting methodology in the USA, with its reputation spreading internationally. **Meisner** died in 1997, but there is a new generation of teachers, me included, dedicated to disseminating his ideas globally.

A chronology of theatrical realism

Stendhal 1783–1842
Shchepkin 1788–1863
Pushkin 1799–1837
Balzac 1799–1850
Gogol 1809–52
Ibsen 1828–1906
Invention of photography 1826, in France
Chekhov (Anton) 1860–1904
Zola 1840–1902
Strindberg 1849–1912
Charles Darwin, On the Origin of Species *1859*
Stanislavski 1863–1938

Gorky 1868–1936
Sigmund Freud 1896, coins term 'psychoanalysis'
Chekhov (Michael) 1891–1955
Moscow Arts Theatre 1897
Strasberg 1901–82
Adler 1901–92
Meisner 1905–97
American Lab Theatre 1925 (Boleslavsky and Ouspenskaya)
The Jazz Singer (the first 'talkie') 1927
Group Theatre 1931
Adler and Clurman visit Stanislavski 1934
Meisner to Neighborhood Playhouse 1935
Strasberg to Actors Studio 1947

Notes

1. This epigraph was oft quoted by Stanislavski and was written at the top of the handwritten chart explaining his 'system', which he gave to Stella Adler in Paris. A copy of this fascinating chart can be found in Robert Lewis, Method or Madness? (New York: Samuel French Inc, 1958).
2. Foster Hirsch, *A Method to Their Madness: The History of the Actors Studio* (New York: Da Capo Press, 1984), 24.
3. Laurence Senelick, *Historical Dictionary of Russian Theatre* (Lanham, Maryland: Scarecrow Press, 2007), xxiv.
4. Jean Benedetti, *Stanislavski: An Introduction* (New York: Routledge, 1982), 7, quoting from 'Memoirs of a Serf Actor', *Zhizn í Tvorchestvo,* Vol. 1 (Moscow, 1984,104).
5. Benedetti, 8–9.
6. Hirsch, 24.
7. Konstantin Stanislavski, *My Life in Art*, trans. Jean Benedetti (New York: Routledge, 2008), xxvii.
8. Jean Benedetti, *Stanislavski: A Biography* (London: Methuen Drama, 1990), 75.
9. Mel Gordon, *Stanislavski in America* (Abingdon: Routledge, 2010), 61.
10. Sanford Meisner and Denis Longwell, *Sanford Meisner on Acting* (New York: Vintage Books/Random House, 1987), 34.

6 Eleonora Duse
1858–1924

All that I have to offer as an artist is the revelation of my soul.[1]

Throughout her career during the first half of the twentieth century the Italian actor Eleonora Duse brought to the stage a natural quality which enthralled audiences worldwide and fascinated teachers of realistic acting such as **Stanislavski** and **Sanford Meisner**, who longed to unearth her secrets for creating an emotionally truthful performance. In the debate on *indicating* vs. *organic* acting (set out in the chapter 'Indicating' in **Working with Actors**) Duse is compared to her contemporary, Sarah Bernhardt (1844–1923) as having a 'presentational' style of acting, versus Bernhardt's 'representational' style – which is to say Duse 'presented' her own inner emotional life to create the illusion of a character.[2] As noted in the chapter on **Denis Diderot**, the contrasting approaches have been hotly debated, with Sarah Bernhardt's frequent acting partner, Benoît-Constant Coquelin, coming down on the side of a technical, non-emotional approach to representing the character.[3]

The comparison of the two styles was vividly put in relief in 1895 when the two leading ladies went head-to-head in London, both playing the role of Magda in Hermann Sudermann's play *Heimat* – Sarah Bernhardt at Daly's Theatre and Eleonora Duse at Drury Lane. This clash of the Titans was a key event in the long-standing rivalry between two of the world's greatest actors of the time, and solidified Bernhardt's contempt for the younger thespian (by fourteen years). The Irish playwright and critic George Bernard Shaw (1856–1950) availed himself of both performances. He offered his critique in a subsequent review, pointing out the stark differences in technique and coming down fully on the side of Duse, saying she had 'annihilated' Bernhardt.[4] He pointed out that externally they could not have been more different. Bernhardt arrived on stage fully and impeccably made-up, lavishly costumed and perfectly manicured – 'beautiful with the beauty of her school [but] entirely inhuman and incredible.'[5] Shaw noted that this applied veneer was excused by the audience because everyone understood it was artifice and accepted it as part of the form. Duse, on the other hand, entered the stage wearing no perceptible make-up. Shaw wrote 'You are welcome to take your opera glass and count whatever lines time and care have so far traced on her.'[6] Duse, herself, reflected 'I did not use paint. I made myself up morally.'[7]

In terms of acting style, Shaw observed that Bernhardt does not 'enter into' a character, but she 'substitutes herself for it' with a package of well-studied gestures and effects. 'All this is precisely what does not happen in the case of Duse, whose every part is a separate creation.'[8] He praises the delicateness of her feelings in contrast to the conscious 'Mona Lisa smile' of Bernhardt – effective in the sense that 'it not only appeals to your susceptibilities, but positively jogs them.' In contrast, 'Duse with a tremor of the lips which you feel rather than see . . . touches you straight on the very heart.'[9]

The most frequently referenced remarks in Shaw's review – cited by **Meisner** and the others of the **Group Theatre** school (**Adler**, **Lewis**, **Strasberg**, **Hagen**) – concerned Eleonora Duse's blush. It occurred at a moment in the play when the protagonist, Magda, is confronted with her lover, who had abandoned her years before not knowing she was pregnant with his child. As Shaw tells it, when Duse looked at him 'a terrible thing happened to her. She began to blush; and in another moment she was conscious of it, and the blush was slowly spreading and deepening until, after a few vain efforts to avert her face . . . she gave up and hid the blush in her hands.'[10] One cannot manufacture a blush. 'It seemed to me a perfectly genuine effect of the dramatic imagination.'[11]

Duse was born in Lombardy of Armenian descent (her birth name was Dusian). Her father and grandfather were actors, frequently itinerant, and she travelled with them, acting on stage from the age of four, and living under austere and unhealthy conditions, which surely contributed to a weakness in her lungs. Her mother died of tuberculosis when Duse was fourteen, and her father, who had been her inspiration and mentor, died when she was eighteen. When her uncle died a year later, she was left totally alone in life.

Despite her poverty, she doggedly determined to follow a career as an actor. A lucky break when she was understudy to an actress who fell ill gave her an invitation to a Naples-based company as the company ingénue playing opposite a famous leading lady, Giacinta Pezzana (1841–1919). Their version of the Zola's naturalistic play *Thérèse Raquin* was a *succès d'estime* and Duse's reputation was set. At a very young age she had a baby by another actor who abandoned her. The boy subsequently died. She joined the Cesare Rossi company in Turin, eventually marrying a fellow actor in the group. In 1882, a daughter was born, who she named Enrichetta. She left the child with an honest couple in a nearby suburb and returned to the stage.

Duse was known to have had many lovers in her life, of both sexes and mostly of an artistic bent, including a count who was a painter. She was not especially promiscuous, but relationships never lasted. One of the longest and most intense was with the poet, novelist, playwright, and aristocrat Gabriele D'Annunzio (1863–1938). It was a passionate, artistically symbiotic relationship. He wrote several plays with wonderful roles for her, and her interpretations helped bring his work to public attention. It lasted for five years falling apart explosively when D'Annunzio dared to offer the lead in his play *La Citta Morta* to Sarah Bernhardt.

The shadow of the Divine Sarah seemed to envelop Duse. It was a relationship marked by rivalry and admiration – at least on the part of Duse. She had been on the verge of dropping out of acting altogether in the Naples company, when Sarah Bernhardt was contracted to perform at her theatre.[12] Duse watched every performance awestruck by both the charisma and highly developed skills of la grande Sarah, and the hold she had on her audience. Duse determined to emulate her success. There is an inherent irony that the very person whose acting techniques were later in direct opposition to her own (Bernhardt was known as *la cabotine de genie* in her native France),[13] and who treated her with distain, was the very person who stimulated her desire to master the techniques of acting and to embrace the theatre with all her heart and soul.

Inspired, she set out in 1884 on what was to become an upward rising trajectory. She took on more challenging roles, including some that Bernhardt had made famous. She honed her technique, formed her own company, played at the best theatres in Italy, and later elsewhere in Europe. In 1889 she toured Latin America, and in 1893, the USA. She played Russia (including the Maly Theatre in Moscow where **Stanislavski** would have seen her), Berlin, London, and in 1897 she dared to play on Sarah's home ground, Paris, at Bernhardt's own theatre, La Renaissance. Her performances captivated audiences around the globe.

In 1909, at the age of fifty-one and the height of her career, she suddenly announced she was giving up the theatre. She retired to Asolo, a hill town near Venice. The reasons are a mystery. She certainly had health problems – recurrent respiratory ailments had plagued her since childhood. Eva Le Gallienne posits that she was simply – in today's terms – 'finding her mojo', spending her days reading books of philosophy, religion, mysticism.[14] Perhaps Duse was contemplating a return to the stage, but then the War broke out such possibilities diminished. In 1921 she acted again, first in Rome, where she was rapturously received. Then Milan, London, Germany, Austria, and in 1923–4, the USA (sold-out appearances in New York, Philadelphia, Washington, Boston, New Orleans, Los Angeles and Havana). Her last booking was in 1924 in Pittsburgh (which she called *la plus hideuse ville du monde*).[15] In an unfortunate incident on an icy evening, Duse insisted on walking to the theatre, even though it was raining. By accident she tried to enter the wrong side of theatre and consequently was locked out in the freezing rain for half an hour. She shivered that afternoon in her dressing room, unable to get warm before what was to become her last performance. She died days later in her room at the Hotel Shenley of pneumonia resulting from influenza. She was sixty-five.[16]

Despite all the interest in Duse's technique, she professed to having none, and derided all attempts to make a science of her art. One thing she understood, in common with **Stanislavski**, is that there is a natural harmony in the movements of human beings – *as long as they are unaware of being watched*. Her naturalness came from training herself to lose self-consciousness in the scene – precisely the skill that **Sanford Meisner** tried to inculcate in his students years later. According to Eva Le Gallienne, her biographer and friend, on stage Duse 'seemed oblivious of being watched.'[17] She fully understood **Stanislavski's** concept of being 'private in public', and that concentration was the key to losing self-awareness. A Danish critic, Hermann Bang, said that her powers of concentration were 'unequalled'. 'It is not only the very essence of her art; it is also – and this is what makes her so unique – the only means she uses; it takes the place of all the usual means, which she discards.'[18]

Not from training but through experience on the stage Duse understood concepts which **Stanislavski** promoted in his 'system', and which subsequent teachers like **Meisner** emphasized – the importance of *listening* and the *reality of doing*. Eva Le Gallienne saw those skills as the essence of Duse's technique:

> She did not need physical motion, not even facial expression, to convey her thoughts; she conveyed them because she *really thought them* . . . She did not pretend to listen – she *really* listened . . . Sometimes her thoughts and feeling swept over [her face and body] with a logic and an immediacy that convinced one she had never thought or felt these things before.[19]

The naturalness of her performance led some to believe that it was improvised. According to Le Gallienne, who observed Duse playing the same scenes a number of times, that was far from the truth. The 'architecture' of her performance was always carefully planned, her relationship to other characters determined in advance; however, 100 per cent concentration enabled her to *live* the role, so inevitably variations to *her reactions surfaced in the moment*.[20] Duse also mastered the use of silence – *deep* silence – using it boldly in ways most actors wouldn't dare to try, understanding that silence embraces an action – that of thinking on behalf of the character.

Eleonora Duse loathed publicity, and never gave interviews – in stark contrast to her rival, Bernhardt. She was fiercely self-critical, in the sense that she was humble in respect to her characters, and asked herself if she was serving them well. 'Whenever she gave a superlatively great performance she never felt that *she* had given it, but rather that it "had been given her" to give.'[21]

Further reading

Eva Le Gallienne, *The Mystic in the Theatre: Eleonora Duse* (London: The Bodley Head, 1966).
Helen Sheehy, *Eleonora Duse: A Biography* (New York: Alfred A. Knopf, 2003).

Notes

1. Widely quoted, e.g. https://www.quotemaster.org/q335b9a5dbf2da2d04a76280eef6b3bcd
2. The two approaches are elaborated upon by Uta Hagen in her book *Respect for Acting* (Hoboken: John Wiley & Sons, 1973), 12.
3. Benoît-Constant Coquelin, *Art and the Actor*, trans. Abby Langdon Alger (New York: Dramatic Museum of Columbia University, 1915).
4. George Bernard Shaw, 'Duse and Bernhardt', 15 June 1895, *Dramatic Opinions and Essays, Volume One* (New York: Brentano's, 1906), 139.
5. Ibid., 136.
6. Ibid.
7. Widely quoted, e.g. https://inspiration.rightattitudes.com/authors/eleonora-duse/
8. Shaw, 'Duse and Bernhardt', 136.
9. Ibid., 137.
10. Ibid., 141.
11. Ibid.
12. Le Gallienne, 33–4.
13. Ibid., 36. Translated: 'a genius of ham acting'.
14. Ibid., 175–7. She was particularly taken with the writings of the French archbishop François Fénelon (1651–1715), who counselled us to stop dwelling on the past and to continually move forward.
15. Sheehy, 320.
16. The circumstances of Duse's final performance and death are fully recounted in Sheehy, 320–2.
17. Le Gallienne, 123.
18. Ibid., 126.
19. Ibid., 129.
20. Ibid., 136.
21. Ibid., 24.

7 Vladimir Nemirovich-Danchenko
1858–1943

I don't create at the Art Theatre, all I have really done is create an institution where others create.[1]

Nemirovich-Danchenko's fascination with the theatre started at the age of nine, when a summer theatre was being built opposite his house in Tiflis, Georgia. He spied on the actors from the scaffolding, then imitated them in his own games of 'rehearsal'. By the age of thirteen he had written a five-act play, among other literary works. His graduation paper from the Tiflis Gymnasium was on Pushkin and Gogol, indicating an early interest in Realism.[2]

At Moscow University he studied physics and mathematics but spent his spare time writing theatre criticism – which was published. Upon leaving university he devoted himself to writing fiction and plays with remarkable success. His plays were produced in Moscow and St Petersburg, were much admired, and won several national prizes. He met Anton Chekhov (1860–1904) in 1888. They clicked and became close friends. It was Nemirovich-Danchenko who encouraged Chekhov to write *The Seagull*. When his own play, *The Worth of Life* (1896), was awarded the coveted Griboyedov Prize over *The Seagull*, Nemirovich-Danchenko objected to the judges – but to no avail.

In 1891 he took up a role teaching acting in the Moscow Philharmonic Society, a school which he admitted had a 'bad reputation'.[3] At first, he was less than happy there, especially with the quality of students, but eventually his teachings were commended, and his course and its productions gained a high reputation. Among his students were Olga Knipper (1868–1959), who later married Chekhov, and two actors, eventually turned directors, **Vsevolod Meyerhold** (1874–1940) and **Yevgeny Vakhtangov** (1883–1922), whom he would later invite to join Moscow Arts Theatre (see their respective chapters). While teaching at the Philharmonic School, Nemirovich-Danchenko published, in addition to several plays, two works of fiction (*The Governor's Inspection* (1896) and *Dreams* (1898), plus a book on acting, translated as *Drama behind the Scenes* (1896).

The famous 'long lunch' with **Stanislavski** occurred in June 1897 (see **From Russia with Love**), and the Moscow Art Theatre (MAT) was born. Nemirovich-Danchenko, as a man-of-letters, was to be in charge of the selection of works to be presented, and business matters. **Stanislavski** would attend to the acting and the staging of productions. It was Nemirovich-Danchenko who persuaded his new partner to mount *The Seagull* after it had bombed in St Petersburg – some say to make amends for his winning the prestigious Griboyedov Prize over his friend Chekhov. The astonishing success of the play's history-making opening night is recounted in detail in Nemirovich's autobiography.[4]

The first signs of antagonism in what was meant to be a symbiotic relationship appeared only a year into the new enterprise. A wealthy investor whom **Stanislavski** had invited to join the board of the MAT – Savva Morozov (1862–1905) – had become a very assertive principal shareholder. Nemirovich-Danchenko feared both a loss of control, and a surrendering to commercial values, and challenged **Stanislavski**.[5] 'Did I start this business with you for some capitalist to come along and try to turn me into – how shall if put it? – a kind of secretary'?[6] This was the first in a string of feuds, resentments, artistic differences and clashing egos between the two men, which bubbled under the surface during the duration of their association, but was carefully covered up to the outside world, for fear of some outside attack on the MAT institution itself, most especially during the Soviet era. Another example was the influence on **Stanislavski** of Leopold Sulerjitsky (1872–1916) and his inclusion in the First Studio project, which deeply rankled Nemirovich-Danchenko.[7] Over the years there were numerous failed directorial collaborations between the two. For example, during rehearsals of *Ghosts* in the 1904–5 season the two co-directors couldn't bear to be in the room with each other.[8] There were also conflicting strategies for the development of the MAT. **Stanislavski** wanted to branch out regionally, whereas Nemirovich-Danchenko wanted more investment in the theatre's productions.[9] Nemirovich resisted **Stanislavski's** insistence on making 'the system' the house style for all MAT productions, especially taking against the *études* – improvisations tangential to the original text – which he saw as irrelevant. This last issue came to a head in a production of *Drama of Life*, in 1905.[10] Nemirovich considered **Stanislavski's** rehearsal methods, where memorizing lines came later in the process, to profane the sanctity of the text. Things came to a head when Stanislavski discovered that Nemirovich-Danchenko had been in discussion with the Maly Theatre regarding a possible merger of the two houses. In February 1906 he tendered his resignation – but following a conciliatory letter from Nemirovich-Danchenko, he quickly rescinded it.[11]

Towards his former pupil **Vsevolod Meyerhold**, Nemirovich-Danchenko developed a great antipathy. **Meyerhold's** attraction to Symbolism – then later Constructivism – did not fit the MAT's brand of realism, and Nemirovich was pleased to let him go and create his own theatre in St Petersburg in 1902[12] – but *not* pleased to see him return, under **Stanislavski's** wing, to form the Experimental Theatre in 1905.

While **Stanislavski** had been enamoured of opera since his youth, Nemirovich-Danchenko was keen on musical theatre, and as an adjunct to the Moscow Art Theatre he founded the allied Moscow Art Musical Studio in 1919. In 1926, the school's name was changed to the V.I. Nemirovich-Danchenko Musical Theatre (and still later to the Stanislavski-Nemirovich-Danchenko Musical Theatre). That year it mounted a season in New York to great acclaim.[13]

With respect to drama theory and actor training, Nemirovich left little to posterity. His early writing on the subject, mentioned above, was based on his teaching methods in the Philharmonic Institute, which focused on the character's psychology and the individual particularities of the actors (innovatory in the 1890s) – it was quickly eclipsed by **Stanislavski's** work.[14] Later, he struggled to adopt **Stanislavski's** ever-developing methods to his own directing work, but he never really grasped them fully and, as mentioned above, thought that they demeaned the text, towards which he was ever-reverential. His conservative attitude to the script, his respect for the classics, and his belief in Realism made him 'acceptable' to the new Soviet cultural police in the 1930s, and he was able to steer the MAT through the hazardous waters of Stalinism. He declared that the three 'truths' of the theatrical act consisted of the *social* (the staging must integrate ideological imperatives), *living* (the characters respect a psychological truth) and *theatrical* (the staging must render the author's style expressively). Together these verities meet **Socialist Realism's** criteria, and Nemirovich was thought of as the model Soviet director.[15]

Apart from the visionary act of establishing the MAT, Nemirovich-Danchenko was not considered a great *innovator*. Instead, he was highly respected as an *enabler*. There is some truth in his self-deprecation in this chapter's epigraph, but at the same time he directed innumerable plays in his time at the MAT, with considerable flair. History has left Nemirovich-Danchenko in the shadow of **Stanislavski**, largely due to the popularization of the latter's teaching in the USA. But the legacy of the Moscow Arts Theatre was a shared one. Lest we forget, it was Nemirovich-Danchenko, *the enabler*, who proposed and acquired the plays of Chekhov, Gorky and Tolstoy, and shaped the MAT as the bastion of the new Realism. These principles, and the teachings of **Stanislavski** which enabled them, were enshrined in a final act by Nemirovich-Danchenko in the formation of the Moscow Art Theatre School,[16] which opened in the year of his death, 1943, and to this day bears his name.

Further reading

Marie-Christine Autant-Mathieu, '"I am not a theorist, I am an inspirer": How Nemirovich-Danchenko interpreted the Stanislavski system', *Stanislavski Studies*, 5, issue 1 (2017).

Vladimir Nemirovich-Danchenko, *My Life in the Russian Theatre*, trans. John Cournos (London: Geoffrey Bles, 1968). Contains a 'Chronology' compiled by Elizabeth Hapgood, 359–65.

Jean Benedetti, *Stanislavski: A Biography* (London: Methuen, 1988).

Notes

1. Benedetti, 170.
2. Elizabeth Hapgood, 'Chronology', in Nemirovich-Danchenko, 359.
3. Nemirovich-Danchenko, 43.
4. Ibid., 184–93.
5. Benedetti, 120.
6. Ibid., 100, quoted from his letters.
7. Ibid., 166–7.
8. Ibid., 147.
9. Ibid., 237.
10. Ibid., 166.
11. Ibid., 169.
12. Ibid., 119.
13. Hapgood, in Nemirovich-Danchenko, 393.
14. Autant-Mathieu, 124.
15. So-named by Pavel Markov in the 1943 Yearbook of the Moscow Art Theatre; cited in Autant-Mathieu, 126.
16. Co-founded with **Nikolai Demidov**, who became its director.

8 Adolphe Appia
1862–1928

I directed all my efforts in order to liberate the actor . . . deep in my heart and before making any designs, I knew the production means the performer.[1]

Appia was Swiss. He trained as an architect. He made virtually no contribution to the craft of acting. Despite the declaration cited above, he had limited regard for actors other than as ciphers. And while he staged a few productions later in his career, he is principally noteworthy for his scenic designs and his contribution to drama theory, in common with his contemporary, **Gordon Craig** (1872–1966) – who similarly produced relatively little on stage. He was a proponent of Symbolism – a particular cultural/artistic strand in theatre which emerged in the late nineteenth century, running parallel with, and in opposition to, the new Realism proposed by **Stanislavski**. This artistic movement originated in France and was the precursor of Expressionism, which emerged in Germany at the beginning of the next century. Appia was a leading proponent of Symbolism in the theatre, rejecting both the Romanticism of the past and the new Naturalism which had taken its place.[2]

His interest in stagecraft grew out of his early interest in opera, especially the works of Richard Wagner (1813–83), which he had followed enthusiastically since his youth. His Symbolist designs were a radical break from the traditional painted flats, *trompe l'oeil*, and realistic detail of those early productions he witnessed, which functioned only on two planes – the *horizontal* floor, and the *perpendicular* flats and curtains. By using simple suggestive forms, like massive boulders, staircases, ramps and drapes, the stage became a three-dimensional landscape, allowing for a unity of staging involving actors in fluid motion, lighting, and music. His desire to 'liberate' the actor, in the epigraph above, meant freeing them spatially to move in rhythm and in unity with the director's concept.

Wagner's notion that dramatic art should 'return to its distant sources . . . nourished again on myth, dream, and archetype'[3] was a rallying cry for the Symbolists. Appia's most notable designs were for Wagnerian operas, a few of which he actually *staged* in later years. 'Staged' is a better word than 'directed', because Appia's over-riding principle was that theatre has its basis in the artistic unity of the director and designer. Actors were malleable commodities who were there to serve the director's symbolic vision of the work and were frequently asked simply to *pose*.

In 1906, Appia met and became friends with fellow-Swiss **Émile Jaques-Dalcroze** (1865–1960**)**, the inventor of Eurythmics (who also influenced **Stanislavski** and his Russian cohort). Subsequently Appia came to believe that the *rhythm* inherent in a text is the key to *mise-en-scène*, and to every movement and gesture the actor makes in performance. Basing his ideas on the principles of Jaques-Dalcroze he proposed in his 1899 book, *Music and the Art of the Theatre,* the 'Word-Tone Drama' – a symbiosis of dance, symphonic music, speech and pantomime, all under the despotic unifying control of the director.[4]

Appia began designing for the stage at the time of the advent of electrical lighting, and one could claim that he was the first lighting designer. He proposed that light had a far greater potential than simply the utilitarian illumination of the actors and the flat stage-sets of the time. He proposed 'active light', which did not mean moving the lamps, but a *dynamic* use of light. He maintained that light was a *key element* in the unified dramatic effect of the work.

He was in correspondence with, and shared ideas with **Gordon Craig**, and he inspired **Jacques Copeau** (1879–1949) and **Antonin Artaud** (1896–1948), among others. Copeau became a close friend and called himself a 'disciple' of Appia. He designed his theatre in Paris, the Vieux-Colombier, around Appia's ideas. Later, he carried those principles with him to New York, where a generation of young designers became profoundly influenced by Appia's theories and designs.

Although acknowledging that performance was central, Appia stressed the supremacy of the author and the rhythm of the text over the actor. 'It is the will of the poet-musician that evokes life for the actor and acts as interpreter between him and the inanimate setting.'[5]

Further reading

Richard C. Beacham, *Adolphe Appia, Artist and Visionary of the Modern Theatre* (Reading: Harwood Academic, 1994).

Appia's complete works can be found in French, edited by Marie-Louise Bablet-Hahn: 'Œuvres Complètes', Volume 4, 1921–8, *l'Age d'Homme* (Lausanne: Société Suisse du Théâtre, 1991).

Notes

1. Beacham, 22.
2. Symbolism aimed to eliminate all traces of naturalistic acting, and all romance and melodrama. The actor became a depersonalized symbol pointing to a meaning beyond what was visible on the stage.
3. Beacham, 2.
4. Adolphe Appia, *Music and the Art of the Theatre*, 1898, English ed. 1918, trans. Robert D. Corrigan and Mary Douglas Dirk (Coral Gables: University of Miami Press, 1962).
5. Beacham, 53.

9 Konstantin Stanislavski 1863–1938

What does it signify to write down what is past and done? The system lives in me but it has no shape or form. The system is created in the very act of writing it down. That is why I have to keep changing what I have already written.[1]

Formative years

Konstantin Stanislavski was enamoured of the theatre from childhood and made his first amateur public appearance as an actor at the age of fourteen. Even from his first performance on stage, the young Konstantin felt his acting to be hit-and-miss, and puzzled over what made some moments successful and others dreadful.[2] He fleetingly attended an acting school at the age of twenty-two but having joined his father in the family textile business, found it impossible to keep up, and the teaching he received was not satisfying to him. For some years Stanislavski had to content himself with amateur dramatics – but what amateur dramatics they were! His father, a wealthy textile manufacturer, supported his endeavours as an actor to the extent of building a theatre at their home, where for years – through his teens and twenties, accompanied by his sisters and numerous cousins and visiting professionals, he was able to develop work on a semi-professional level, even to the extent of hosting the Imperial Little Theatre (The Maly) for a production of *The Lucky Man* by **Vladimir Nemirovich-Danchenko**, the most talented and popular playwright in Russia at the time – later to become his partner.

Stanislavski loved being on stage. However, from his teen years on, he worried about his own inadequacies as an actor, and through the duration of his entire acting career of sixty years, he religiously recorded in notebooks his self-evaluation of his successes and failures – critical for his later analysis of acting technique.[3]

The line of Russian Realism (set out in the chapter **From Russia with Love**) started with Alexander Pushkin (1799–1837), who planted the seeds within the Romanticism of the earlier half of the century for more realistic depictions of life. He was greatly admired by Stanislavski, who never tired of quoting him: 'The truth of passion, the verisimilitude of feeling, placed in the given circumstances, that is what our reason demands of a writer, or a dramatic poet.'

Stanislavski had two notable Russian antecedents in theatre, both dead before he was born – the actor Mikhail Shchepkin (1788–1863) (see **From Russia with Love)** and the actor/playwright Nikolai Gogol (1809–1852). While Shchepkin presented a more natural style of acting, Gogol (*The Government Inspector*, 1836), brought psychology to the stage, insisting that the actor's motivating force was much more important than appearances. Politically, according to Gogol, the role of theatre was to inform and teach the audience, and the actor's job was to serve that goal through the transmission of real emotion. Gogol loved the irony of the fact that he had once failed an audition for the Imperial Theatre because his performance was considered too 'real'.[4]

While working his 'day job' for his father, Stanislavski skipped out to visit the Maly Theatre, where Shchepkin had regularly played when alive. He watched the Italians **Eleonora Duse** (1858–1924) and Tommaso Salvini (1829–1915).[5] La Duse already had a global reputation for performances gave free rein to her inner compulsions, across a range of emotions, and used her body as a vehicle for expression. Stanislavski took careful notes.[6] As for Salvini, Stanislavski was intrigued by the range and intensity of his emotions, which seemed to change dramatically in accordance with the given circumstances of the text, adding layers to the personality of each character he portrayed. Stanislavski devotes an entire chapter in *My Life in Art* to Salvini's work in *Othello*, emphasizing (for the benefit of student readers) his professionalism in *preparing* for a performance.[7] The reality and truthfulness of the performances of these actors made an indelible impression on the young Konstantin, and set benchmarks to which he referred during his long career.

In 1874 the Meiningen Ensemble from Germany started touring Europe. The troupe was formed by an aristocrat-intellectual, the Duke of Saxe-Meiningen – who directed and designed most of the plays. The productions amazed their audiences with their use of detailed and historically accurate sets and costumes, huge crowd scenes, and actors naturalistically inhabiting the reality of the epoque in which the play was set, right down to reproducing period gestures and manner of speech. Young Stanislavski saw every one of their Moscow performances and was deeply impressed. The Meiningen work greatly informed his later approach as a director – both his search for verisimilitude, and his love for supernumeraries on the stage. The latter he was able to indulge to some extent in the semi-amateur productions he directed – largely operettas – for his Alexeiev Dramatic Circle (which later became the Moscow Musical-Dramatic Amateur Circle), drafting in not only his first, but second and third cousins, to fill its ranks onstage. It seems Stanislavski also took notes on the duke's directing style – autocratic and micromanaging – which he applied in his early days of directing.

In his early twenties Stanislavski was offered a semi-honorary job – vacated by a cousin – as Director of the Russian Musical Society and Conservatory. At a very young age he was able to have contact with musicians and artists at the highest level and it gave him a cultural street cred in Moscow circles. Between this administrative job at the Musical Society and his Alexeiev productions, he became 'noticed'.

During this period, he was briefly struck with the romantic notion of becoming an opera performer, and he enrolled in private tuition with a famous tenor, Fyodor Komisarjevsky (1832-1905). However, while gearing up for his semi-professional debut, performing alongside professional singers, he realized just how mediocre was his vocal talent, and he gave it all up. He said, 'I realised my dream was broken and there was nothing else left to me than to occupy myself with the drama. But I knew the latter was the hardest and most exacting of all forms of scenic art.'[8] Through his operatic explorations with Komisarjevsky, especially from work they did on 'mimodrama', Stanislavski developed an interest in rhythm – not the surface beat of the music, but a more fundamental personal 'inner rhythm', which he later developed – after exposure to **Appia** and **Jacques-Delcroze** – as 'tempo-rhythm', which became part of his 'system' of acting.[9]

Vladimir Nemirovich-Danchenko was a successful playwright and critic who had found his way on the Repertoire Committee of the Imperial Theatre, and membership of the Russian Society of Authors. In 1897, around the time that he invited Stanislavski to the famous 'long lunch' (see **From Russian with Love**), various schemes Nemirovich-Danchenko had proposed for the creation of a new 'popular' theatre had been rejected by the Imperial Theatre administration. He was experiencing a general frustration with bureaucracy.[10] Given that he did not know Stanislavski personally, but that the lavishness of the latter's semi-amateur productions was legendary in Moscow, the smell of some private financial backing may have motivated Vladimir to approach the well-healed young actor/director.

The famous performance of Anton Chekhov's *The Seagull* in December 1898 was not the first Moscow Arts Theatre (MAT) production. They had mounted Tolstoy's *Tsar Feodor* earlier in the year, to good reviews, but it was *The Seagull* that launched the MAT's reputation. While it captivated the audience, the production was clumsy and, in many ways, amateurish. Stanislavski, frustrated in his inability to explain to his actors how to achieve some sort of truthful reality in their performance, badgered and bullied them, and became increasingly autocratic – something he retrospectively regretted. He knew what he wanted – he had worked everything out in detail – not only the *mise-en-scène* and blocking, but the characterization of each role, right down to parsing the text. But he did not know how to get what he sought from the actors. This feeling of inadequacy spurred him on in his quest to find a systematic approach to achieving the kind of performance that Chekhov's plays demanded. The impact of that first *Seagull* production lay in its realistic detail, the organic unity of its elements, and, of course, the revolutionary use of *subtext*.

Over the next thirty-nine years, until illness at the age of seventy-four prevented him from continuing with his final production, Verdi's *Rigoletto*, Stanislavski, as both actor and director, never ceased in his quest for the illusive nature of the actor's truth, which he attempted to codify in some form, for the elucidation of all actors and directors.

The system, AKA 'the system'

The task of organizing and simplifying Stanislavski's teachings for the reader is daunting. For one thing, as per the epigraph at the beginning of this chapter, his ideas never ceased evolving. Moreover, he never managed to put them on paper in a manner which was succinct and consistent. It was only in his later years that he attempted to commit his ideas to the page – with mixed success. His first volume, *My Life in Art* (1926), published when he was sixty, consisted of rambling memories dictated to a ghost writer. This is the most readable of his works, full of auto-biographical detail.

In 1930 he embarked on the task of putting 'the system' on paper. But he was not a writer by nature, and what he produced over the following years was a series of works that were dense, rambling, verbose and sometimes seemingly contradictory. He constantly amended his writings as his ideas changed – a posthumous editorial nightmare. The resulting works, heavily edited in numerous versions, and contradictory translations, with different nomenclatures, remain a difficult read.

The first versions of the works available in English were:

1 *An Actor Prepares*: which covers his work between 1906–14, when his emphasis was on the 'inner process' – what his biographer Jean Benedetti calls 'the psycho-technique'. This material basically covers the first year of actor's training. He called it the 'Internal Theatrical State'.

2 *Building a Character*: based on work he did between 1914 and 1920, where the emphasis is on physical and vocal techniques (the 'External Theatrical State'). This material would correspond to the second year of his actor's training programme. Stanislavski died before he completed this work, which was conceived as part two of a larger book, *An Actor's Work on Himself*, incorporating *An Actor Prepares*. It was completed by editors. (See Further Reading below.)

3 *Creating a Role* (the Russian title was *An Actor's Work on Himself in a Role*): covers the work he did between 1916 and 1937. Stanislavski never actually started this book. It is really 'material for a book' – a compilation of articles and draft material, edited after his death.[11]

On the assumption that the reader hasn't the time or inclination to work their way through this maze, I have attempted to encapsulate Stanislavski's theories, as I understand them, over their thirty-nine years of evolution – each development building on top of the preceding one.

Stanislavski's teachings

EVOLVING NOTIONS 1898–1905 The practical experience of directing and acting at the MAT	• Believable truth. • Realistic action, in a realistic environment. • Actors focused on the action of other actors – the existence of the 'fourth wall'. • Ensemble playing. • Psychological depth and inner truth. • The subtext.
DEVELOPMENT OF A SYSTEM 1906–23 The First Studio, with Sulerjitsky	• Emotional Memory and Sensory Memory, derived from Théodule Ribot's writings on affective memory. • Introduction of prana yoga concepts – rhythmic breathing, creative circle, etc. • Exercises on relaxation and concentration. • Analysis of the character's tasks, in terms of Objectives and the SuperObjective. • Finding the 'magic if' to the author's Given Circumstances. • The script as a series of units (bits, or beats), and objectives (tasks) which must cohere, via the through-line. • Actors need to read broadly on human experience and study culture.
SHIFTS IN EMPHASIS 1933–8 Opera Studio and Opera Drama Studio 'Method of Physical Action' and 'Active Analysis'	• Affective memory is limited. • Life on stage emanates from the imagination. • Physical action is a way of reaching the emotions within the actor's creative centre. • The logic and coherence of physical actions sequentially directed to a task (What do I want? What do I do to get it?) results in a logical and coherent (i.e. believable) psychological life. • 'Active Analysis' of smaller units or events, and use of improvisations (*études*) to explore action. • Actor's dependence on the actions of other actors to stimulate an emotional reaction. • Recognizing the tempo-rhythm of the work. • Greater emphasis on dramatic conflict.

Evolving notions

In his years of formation, Stanislavski derived inspiration from numerous sources, cited above. He had learned from great actors such as Shchepkin, Duse and Salvini that the 'truth' existed within the actor. With the formation of the Moscow Arts Theatre troupe, he was able to begin to explore methods for achieving this 'believable truth'. He recognized that the actor's job on the stage was not to *'become' the character*, but to be *believed*, by taking their own personality onto the stage. The audience would believe in the character by believing the truthful emotions of the actor.

From the Meiningen Ensemble he had learned that what the actors did on stage had to be convincingly real. The way they spoke, the way they dressed, their manner of moving – all had to bespeak of a time and place and cultural milieu. In short, the external elements required verisimilitude. He was also inspired by the Meiningen notion of 'ensemble', where an actor could play the lead role in one performance and be the spear-carrier in another. The ensemble principle became enshrined by Stanislavski and Nemirovich-Danchenko in the Moscow Arts Theatre, and subsequent studios which they created.

In his early MAT days, he had a director-centric approach to the work, largely inspired by the Meiningen directors. A play required an organic unity of its elements – design, acting, movement, music, etc. and, above all else, it was the director's job to achieve this unity. Unfortunately, by his later self-admission, to achieve unity he also imitated the tyrannical methods of the Meiningen directors, especially one Ludwig Chronegk (1837–91) – at the expense of getting the best from his actors.

On the stage, he focused his actors on each other, and made them play off one another, and not to the audience. Effectively, he constructed the invisible 'fourth wall'. He required his actors to plumb for psychological depth and inner truth, and in working with Chekhov plays, discovered a route to that truth via the conscious understanding of the subtext, which he called the 'Inner Monologue'. He started his rehearsal process with intensive group readings of the script, in which the text and subtext were thoroughly analysed. (He rejected the group reading concept in later years.)

All the while, in these early years of the MAT, Stanislavski, the actor, was seeking – even agonizing – to get hold of the illusive magic within himself and other actors which made for a truthful performance.

Development of 'a system'

Following the European tour of the MAT, Stanislavski set up the First Studio (1906). In this endeavour he was aided and abetted by Leopold Sulerjitsky (1872–1916), dubbed 'Suler' by the writer Maxim Gorky (1886–1938) (see **From Russia with Love**). The aim was to experiment with acting methods and pull together Stanislavski's ideas into a workable 'system' around a 'psychophysical' construct.

He started from the point of view that *acting* is *action*. He said, 'On the stage, you must always be enacting something; action, motion, is the basis of the art followed by the actor.'[12] But all action needs to be motivated. What about the psychology behind the action? There were two key influences in Stanislavski's thinking. One derived from a book, *Problèmes de Psychologie Affective* (1910), by a French psychologist, Théodule-Armand Ribot (1839–1916), in which the author identified that humans possess an 'affective memory' – i.e. emotions experienced in the past, embedded in the brain, which can be unlocked through sensory memory. Experimentation with this idea led to Stanislavski creating his key concept of 'Emotional Memory', where emotions from the actor's past could be applied to the circumstances in which their character found themselves in the moment.

The second influence most probably came from Suler, via his psychologist friend **Nikolai Demidov** – yoga for actors. This was a totally novel idea at the time, but it made sense. In practical terms, yoga techniques can aid the actor in relaxation, concentration and communication. But more than that, Stanislavski became convinced that the discovery of one's *prana* (life force), reached through rhythmic breathing, is the key to unlocking the actor's creativity ('Inner Creative State'). Physical action could be used as the conscious means to reach the 'subconscious' or 'soul' of the actor. From 1916 on, he frequently used a slogan: 'to the subconscious via the conscious'.[13] This concept later crystalized as 'The Method of Physical Actions'.[14]

As a route to the actor's subconscious (unconscious), Stanislavski proposed a relationship between what he called the 'Given Circumstances' of the author and the 'inner life' of the actor. This device was termed the 'magic if', in which the actor imagined how they would react if they found themselves living in the given circumstances of the character in the script. (For example: a scene in which the character's husband tells them after ten years of an apparently happy marriage that he had never loved them. The actor asks: 'What would I do if that happened to me? How would I feel?') Taking it a step further, identifying the emotions one might feel in those imaginary circumstances provides a springboard for the actor's exploration of an appropriate Emotional Memory. (For example: remembering when someone you love rejected you, and the conditions – physical/sensorial – in which the event occurred.)

Physical action needs to be motivated. It is not random. Hence Stanislavski's concept of the 'Task', which has also been translated as the 'Objective'[15] – a problem, or obstacle, embedded in the given circumstances that the character needs to overcome. What does the character want to get or achieve in the scene? And from each other character? The pursuit of successive tasks – one after another – forms a 'through-line' of action. What does the character want to obtain within their overall situation or specific circumstances throughout the work? It's this *desire* which drives the narrative. This overall objective he called the 'Supertask', also called the 'Super-Problem' or 'SuperObjective'. (The numerous translations are maddening!) The pursuit of one task after another forms a 'through-line' of action. The SuperObjective can be thought of from two angles: on one level for the protagonist, in terms of their over-riding objective within the given circumstances of the script, but also in terms of the author's or director's objective in writing (or presenting) the work. The moral of the story lies within the SuperObjective. Director **Harold Clurman** (1901–80), along with other Stanislavski-influenced directors, used this analysis as the basis of the director's quest to find the 'spine' of the work.

Stanislavski considered each play, and each scene, to be made up of divisible 'units', each consisting of a chain of actions, each action with an objective, whether a simple banal one, like opening a door, or one with more weight, like coming to get a confession of guilt from someone. He maintained that nothing the actor does can be extraneous, and that all the actions must all add up to something meaningful.

> That inner line of effort which guides the actors from the beginning to the end of the play we call the 'continuity' or the 'through-going-action'. This through-line galvanizes all the small units and objectives of the play and directs them toward the SuperObjective. From then on, they all serve the common purpose.[16]

In terms of the actor's development of their 'instrument', the exercises in relaxation and concentration in Stanislavski's training programme, provided *baseline conditions* for effective acting.

> Properly relaxed and concentrated, the actor has a chance of slipping into a creative state, where he can begin to reach the usually obscured depths of his subconscious, there to discover a stream of pure, flowing, usable emotions, memories, and images.[17]

Once relaxed, the actor is free to put their attention on something other than themself. Stanislavski suggests focusing on a 'circle of attention' – e.g. an object or another actor – forget the circumstances of the theatre and lose oneself in the circumstances of the play. With full concentration in the 'circle of attention' the actor is able to achieve 'solitude in public.'[18] It's a technique one would have observed in the performance of **Eleonora Duse**.

The 'system' also demanded that the actor read broadly and be versed in 'culture' manifested in other art forms – great literature, poetry, music, ballet, the fine arts. This was also considered part of an actor's growth and a key to understanding human nature.

While developing his 'system' in the First Studio, Stanislavski was also looking over his shoulder at his protégée, **Vsevolod Meyerhold** (1874–1940), who had left the MAT, rejecting its naturalism, and taking up the emerging fad for Symbolism. This primarily literary movement originated in France and Belgium in late nineteenth century. *Les Fleurs du Mal, a volume of poetry by Charles* Baudelaire (1821–67) kick-started a rich literary tradition including writers Stéphane Mallarmé (1842–98), Paul Verlaine (1844–96) and Arthur Rimbaud (1854–91). It was picked up in Russia in the St Petersburg salons, by artists such as the poet Alexander Blok (1880–1921) and composer Alexander Scriabin (1872–1915). Symbolism sought to express an individual's emotional experience through suggestive symbolized language. It explored the unconscious (and frequently darker) side of human nature, and this is what attracted Stanislavski.[19] In 1906, Meyerhold produced an acclaimed Symbolist production of Blok's *The Puppet Show*. Not to be outdone, Stanislavski mounted a much-appreciated Symbolist production of *The Blue Bird* by the Belgian Maurice Maeterlinck (1862–1949). Still in a Symbolist vein, in 1911 he collaborated with **Gordon Craig** – an English actor-theoretician, Constructivist and Avant-gardist – in a production of *Hamlet* which was curiously conceived as a 'monodrama' – a concept developed by Russian Symbolist critic and playwright Nikolai Evreinoff (1879–1953).[20] A 'monodrama' is a dramatic representation of what passes in an individual's mind. Everything one witnesses on stage is portrayed from the perspective and mental state of the protagonist.

Once Stalin succeeded Lenin, **Socialist Realism** became the only permitted art form. Symbolism – which was individualistic, mystical, and deified the act of creation – was banned. His continued adherence to the form was to become the death of Meyerhold – literally – but Stanislavski had, by then, abandoned the style.

Shifts in emphasis

When **Stella Adler** returned to the USA from her Paris visit with Stanislavski in 1934, she announced to the **Group Theatre** that the master had rejected the concept of *Emotional Memory*, supplanting it with another device – *Imaginary Circumstances*. In this case the actor didn't try to imagine themself living through the 'given circumstances' (the 'magic if') but, instead, using their imagination, found parallel personal circumstances, feasible and credible in the reality of their own lives which might engender emotions suitable for the character's situation. It was called the 'as-if' – the actor's *'substitution'*, to use Adler's term. **Sanford Meisner** saw Imaginary Circumstances as a panacea. The actor, in their substitution, could go anywhere, to any height or depth.

Adler also reported a conceptual shift in the process of the actor accessing their 'inner truth', whereby the actor uses physical *action* as a way of provoking their instinctive emotional makeup – the *unconscious*. It was what Stanislavski later was to describe as the 'Method of Physical Actions'. By committing a unique physical act, the actor connects with the psychological and emotional element of the action, by reflex. Every action has an objective, and within every physical action, via the objective, a psychological element comes into play. Conversely, every inner (emotional) experience has an external physical expression. The new Stanislavskian dictate was that the text should be approached in terms of objectives and actions, and not in terms of emotions and psychology.

Reconciliation of the concept of living 'the moment' on the stage, with the intellectual analysis of objectives and action, according to Stanislavski, involves 'adaptation'. He pointed out that in life we constantly adjust ourselves, emotionally, in reaction to the way that others behave towards us, and so it should be on the stage. 'Each change of circumstance, setting, place of action, time – brings a corresponding adjustment.'[21] 'Objectives' (the 'Why') and 'action' (the 'What') could be worked out in the analysis of the text, but the 'adaptation' (the 'How') had to happen in performance, in reaction to another actor, or physical obstacle. Therefore, adaptation means making an adjustment in-the-moment. For that to occur, the actor needed to be in a state of 'communion'. In communing, he said: 'we send out rays and receive them, we use our eyes, facial expression, voice and intonation, our hands, fingers, our whole bodies, and in every case we make whatever corresponding adjustments are necessary'.[22]

The seedbed of these ideas was a new studio, created in 1918. It was called the Opera Studio and was a coproduction with the Bolshoi Theatre. When originally proposed, Stanislavski jumped at the suggestion, partly as a chance to explore whether the 'system' could stand up to, or perhaps be further illuminated by, the constrictions of the opera format. But also, as a space to explore his notions of the actor's 'tempo-rhythm', the seeds of which had been germinating since his youthful flirtation with opera under the tutelage of Fyodor Komisarjevsky. He observed that an opera score sets out the basic speeds and generates an impulse for each 'unit' of action. He began to apply the rhythmic principle to dramatic theatre and exhorted his actors to find the speed and rhythm within themselves that the actions dictated. Just as music had various movements (legato, staccato, andante or allegro) in a continuous line, so should stage action and speech. Discovering the tempo-rhythm enabled the flow of emotions within the actor. It is best explained in his own words to the young opera-singers-cum-actors:

> From the instant the music begins you are completely in its power. Your nerves, blood, heartbeat must all be in accord with the rhythm proposed by the music. . . . The simplest thing is to beat the measures, the stresses. That is the easiest to accomplish, yet this affects only the extremities, the periphery of your body. It is not this rhythm which will determine the essentials of the composition played or your life as part of it. I am speaking here of the inner rhythm which makes you act differently, breathe differently. It is the thing that carries away your emotions, arouses them, giving them both keenness and power.[23]

Apart from 'tempo-rhythm', the programme of teaching for the Opera Studio basically corresponds to that set out in *An Actor Prepares*. Pavel Ivanovich Rumyantsev (1890–1962) has written an eye-witness account of his experience as a student in the Opera Studio, in which one can clearly hear the voice of Stanislavski's fictitious 'master', Tortsov, and his flock of keen students in *An Actor Prepares*, as they are put through exercises in 'Concentration', 'Faith and a Sense of Truth', etc.[24]

On 15 November 1935, Stanislavski opened the doors to his final studio, the 'Opera-Dramatic Studio'. It was not to be a performance studio, but strictly a training ground. It involved a course of study of four years, the first two consisting of technique and method – essentially the ideas contained in *An Actor Prepares*, but including what came to be known as the 'Method of Physical Action', followed by two years of work as outlined in his book *Creating a Role*, in which he used *Hamlet* and *Romeo and Juliet* for working on character development. The most significant development of the Opera-Dramatic Studio was the concept of 'Active Analysis' – his very last invention. Due to censorship and its consequent banning by the State, this idea did not surface in Russian actor training establishments until the 1960s.

Active Analysis

'Active Analysis' turned the prevailing MAT method of rehearsal on its head, ending the tradition of interminable 'table work' – reading and analysing the play prior to the actors 'getting on their feet'. In this process, the script is broken down into scenes (events), and each one is worked on individually. Postponing memorizing of the lines, the actors explore the interactive dynamics of a story by means of '*études*', improvisations of the actions and objectives contained in the scene – but in the actors' own words. After an '*étude*', the actors go back to the table to analyse the dynamic of what occurred in the improvisation; then perhaps set up another '*étude*', or perhaps rehearse the scene (or event) with the written text, before moving on to the next one. Noted Russian director Georgi Tovstonogov (1915–89), who perfected this method in his own work, labelled this first step in rehearsal '*physical reconnaissance*'.[25] Gradually, as the actors test the actions and conflicts that tell the story, they come to need their lines. Gradually, the scenes are tacked together, and the through-line becomes more evident. In that way 'Active Analysis' steps away from the text to learn it. It is active because from the first rehearsal to the very last performance the actors are on their feet, actively engaging with each other, and with the text. The technique is action-based and is an advance on the concept of the 'Method of Physical Actions' in that one's choice of physical actions depends wholly upon one's stage partner. It is not contradictory to the other elements of 'the system' but could be said to embody them.

The '*études*' can also be used to examine the backstory or the pre-circumstances of a scene. **Elia Kazan** used to do this regularly.[26] **Sanford Meisner** used '*études*' in working up scenes, and with his insistence that his actors 'don't do anything until the other fellow makes you do it', was using 'Active Analysis', even if he didn't label it as such. Similarly, **David Mamet's** 'Practical Aesthetics' incorporates these principles, without acknowledging them. My own rehearsal techniques incorporate 'Active Analysis'. Directors may wish to explore it further for their own use, to which end I have listed a special bibliography below. Maria Knebel (1898–1985) is the only author on the list who worked with Stanislavski during this period – and 'has it from the horse's mouth'. This notion of action generated in reaction was one of the late, and most important shifts in Stanislavski's thinking – focusing more intently on the underlying patterns of dramatic conflict. Sanford Meisner, in his rejection of **Lee Strasberg's** 'Method', gravitated towards this methodology, meaning that Meisner was the American teacher most closely aligned to Stanislavski's ultimate practices.

Bowing out

A final biographical note. In 1937, at the time that his health was seriously deteriorating, Stanislavski re-engaged with his old friend and pupil, **Vsevolod Meyerhold**, whom he regarded somewhat as a son – albeit a prodigal one, given their divergent, almost antithetical approaches to theatre.[27] Both men shared a fascination with opera, and Meyerhold, having become a much more sober director in his maturity, had taken an interest in Stanislavski's opera studios. Jean Benedetti suspects that they were, in fact, secretly working towards a synthesis of Meyerhold's 'Biomechanics' and the 'Method of Physical Action'.[28] Stanislavski was mounting a production of Verdi's *Rigoletto* at the time, and bit-by-bit Meyerhold became involved, much to the bewilderment of cast and crew, who knew of the schism in the past. In the event, Stanislavski died some months later, and Meyerhold took over the production and mounted it. It was the last thing either of them were to direct.

Previously, Stanislavski had been in direct communication with Stalin regarding the MAT, and the opening of the Opera-Dramatic Studio. Stalin saw the MAT as an asset – a vehicle for the pursuit of his concept of **Socialist Realism** – and neither **Nemirovich-Danchenko** nor Stanislavski disabused him of that idea. Nonetheless, Stalin was keeping an eagle eye on his internationally high-profile representative of Russian theatre. Using the principle of 'isolate and preserve' he *personally* appointed Stanislavski's doctors, who carefully controlled his meetings and his routine, and attended his death, 7 August 1938.

Stanislavski escaped getting into trouble with the Soviets over his flirtation with Symbolism. He had long since moved on from that idea, in the sense that he no longer considered the acting process to be 'individualistic'. One's attention was no longer on oneself, but on the other actor, whose actions would enable one to unconsciously access one's inner self, in reaction. In other words, the *social dynamic* between individuals (in terms of their objectives towards each other) was paramount. The emphasis was now safely removed from individual 'psychology' and conformed to the politics of the collective. Stanislavski's 'system' – in its materialistic form – became the doctrinaire methodology of acting for the new Socialist Realism.

Further reading

Jean Benedetti, *Stanislavski: An Introduction* (New York: Routledge, 1982).
Jean Benedetti, *Stanislavski: A Biography* (London: Methuen, 1988).
Konstantin Stanislavski, *My Life in Art*, trans. Jean Benedetti (New York: Routledge, 2008). (Recommended over the original 1924 publication, trans. J. J. Robbins.)
Konstantin Stanislavski, *An Actor's Work* (New York: Routledge, 2016). This is Jean Benedetti's compilation of *An Actor Prepares*, and *Building a Character*, which is clearer and easier to read than earlier translations of those books.

Active analysis further reading

Maria Knebel, *Active Analysis* (Abingdon: Routledge, 2021).
Georgii Tovstonogov, *The Profession of Stage Director*, trans. Bryan Bean (Moscow: Progressive Publishers, 1972).
James Thomas, *A Director's Guide to Stanislavsky's Active Analysis* (London: Bloomsbury, 2016).
Sharon Marie Carnicke, 'Improvisations and études: an experiment in Active Analysis', *Stanislavski Studies*, 7, no. 1, 2019.

Notes

1. Quoted in Jean Benedetti, *Stanislavski and the Actor* (New York: Routledge, 1998), xxii.
2. Benedetti, *Biography*, 14.
3. Benedetti, *Introduction*, 3.
4. Ibid., 13.
5. The Maly was referred to as the House of Shchepkin, in memoriam, as noted in Benedetti, *Biography*, 16.
6. **Sanford Meisner** was fond of relating that George Bernard Shaw had reported once seeing **Eleonora Duse** blush in performance – evidence of *acting truth*, as a blush can't be faked. Sanford Meisner and Dennis Longwell, *Sanford Meisner on Acting* (New York: Vintage Books/Random House, 1987), 191.
7. Konstantin Stanislavski, *My Life in Art*, trans J. J. Robbins (London: Geoffrey Bles, 1945), 265–76.
8. Ibid., 133.
9. Ibid., 134.
10. Cassandra Brooks, 'Cultural Exchange: The Role of Stanislavsky and the Moscow Arts Theater's 1923 and 1924 American Tours', MA diss., University of North Texas (August 2014), 24.
11. These volumes were translated by the American, Elizabeth Hapgood, in direct contact with Stanislavski during the last years of his life. The subsequent mix of US, British and Russian publications, and which material was used in each, is highly confusing; Jean Benedetti sets out clearly the convoluted evolution of the publications in an appendix to *An Introduction*, 103–8.
12. Constantin Stanislavski, *An Actor Prepares* (London: Geoffrey Bles, 1937), 36.
13. Sergei Tcherkasski, 'The System Becomes the Method: Stanislavski-Boleslavsky-Strasberg', abstract of PhD diss., St Petersburg Theatre Arts Academy (November 2013), 98.
14. Sharon Marie Carnicke, *Stanislavsky in Focus: An Acting Master for the Twenty-first Century*, 2nd ed. (Abingdon: Routledge, 2009), 187, 189.
15. The original translator of Stanislavski's 'trilogy', Elizabeth Hapgood, uses the term 'objective'. Later Jean Benedetti retranslated his works in a tighter, more literal fashion, and insisted on 'task'. I prefer 'objective' because it suggests an internal motivation as opposed to something assigned, or external, which one takes on board.

16. Stanislavski, *Prepares*, 273.
17. As explained by Foster Hirsch, *A Method in Their Madness* (Boston: DaCapo Press, 1984), 38.
18. Stanislavski, *Prepares*, 87.b
19. Paul Schmidt, ed. and trans., *Plays of Anton Chekhov* (New York: Harper, 1997). Schmidt points out that the late works of Chekhov can be thought of as Symbolist, in that they deal with individual psychological undercurrents.
20. Nikolai Evreinov's key critical work is *The Theatre in Life,* trans. A. I. Nazaroff (London: George G. Harrap, 1927), containing wide-ranging essays on aspects of theatre, railing against major themes such as 'Realism', and minor ones such as the 'intermission' as a practice, as well as children who squirm in their seats. More about this provocative character can be found in Sharon Marie Carnicke, *The Theatrical Instinct, Nikolai Evreinov and the Russian Theatre of the Early Twentieth Century* (New York: Peter Lang, 1989), 71–80.
21. Stanislavski, *Prepares,* 226.
22. Ibid.
23. Pavel Ivanovich Rumyantsev, and Konstantin Stanislavsky, *Stanislavsky on Opera* (New York: Routledge, 1975), 12.
24. Ibid., 1–45. Drawing on the copious notes he took as a student, Rumyantsev sets out the Opera Studio teaching programme, stylistically in the manner of *An Actor Prepares*, with student-master dialogues.
25. Tovstonogov, 239.
26. Michel Ciment, *Kazan on Kazan* (London: Secker and Warburg, 1973), 41.
27. Regarding his two other 'surrogate' sons, **Yevgeny Vakhtangov** (1833–1922) had died, and **Michael Chekhov** (1891–1955) had gone to the USA.
28. Benedetti, *Biography*, 344.

10 Émile Jaques-Dalcroze
1865–1950

> Musical training is a more potent instrument than any other, because rhythm and harmony find their way into the inward places of the soul, on which they mightily fasten, imparting grace . . .[1]
>
> **Plato**

Born in Vienna, Jaques-Dalcroze moved with his family to Geneva in 1875, at the age of ten. Musically inclined, he enrolled in the Conservatoire de Musique when twelve years old. In his youth, he had the good fortune to study with Gabriel Fauré (1845–1924) and Léo Delibes (1836–91), and much later, in Vienna, with Anton Bruckner (1824–96). From 1892 he became Professor of Harmony at the Geneva Conservatory. During 1886 he had the additional good fortune to be assigned an assistant conductorship in Algeria. Exposure to Arab music exploded his Western concept of rhythm and opened his eyes to the connection of music to dance.

In 1910, he established his own school in Hellerau, near Dresden, from where he began to promulgate his theories, in a system which he named 'Eurhythmics'. His work quickly gained renown in the world of dance and music, and his school was frequented by numerous leading practitioners of contemporary dance, such as Marie Rambert (1888–1982) and **Rudolf Laban** (1879–1958). He was frequently visited by fellow Swiss, **Adolphe Appia**, who was heavily influenced by Jaques-Dalcroze in the development of his 'Word-Tone Drama' concept.

Dalcroze's pedagogy resulted from his deep dissatisfaction with the music instruction he witnessed in the conservatories – theory and notation were taught as abstractions, disassociated from the sound, movements and the feelings they represented. He believed that the first *instrument* that the musician needed to train was *the body*.[2]

> There are two physical agents by means of which we appreciate music. These two agents are the ear, as regards sound, and the whole nervous system, as regards rhythm. Tone is evidently secondary, since it has not its origins and model in ourselves, whereas movement is instinctive in man, and therefore primary. I begin the study of music by careful and experimental teaching of movement.[3]

Having carefully observed the physical effect of the act of playing music on a musician's body – for example, the tensions in the crescendo and relaxation in the final coda – Dalcroze's developed his system of 'Eurhythmics', comprising numerous dance-like exercises relating one's body to music, *especially to rhythm*. Some of the earlier exercises are catalogued in his book, *Eurhythmics Art and Education*, and are widely used in music education today.

In 1911, Dalcroze and his students visited St Petersburg and Moscow and presented their work at the Moscow Arts Theatre. The visit was timely, corresponding as it did with the period in which Russian theatre sets were shrinking in scale, due to both budgetary restrictions and the emerging taste for abstraction (Symbolism and Constructivism), thus making the actors' movements and their placement on stage more critical (as had been promoted by Appia). These changes caused **Stanislavski** to re-evaluate his actor training, deciding that an actor's proficiency in modulating speech and voice was not enough: '. . . we not only needed good speech in the right tempo and the right rhythm but . . . we also needed to be able to move in rhythm. This discovery spurred me on to a whole new series of investigations.'[4] Key to his new approach was Dalcroze's Eurhythmics, which he found highly useful – although too *mechanical*. He adapted Eurhythmics to his own concept of 'Tempo-Rhythm', to include an inner justification for, and an awareness of each movement. The exercises were taught in the Opera Studio by Stanislavski's brother, Vladimir.[5] Conversely, Dalcroze assimilated aspects of Stanislavskian training, subsequently reflected in Dalcrozian music education, including ensemble work, intention and emotion, and the evolution of psychophysical performance.[6]

Nowadays, basic forms of Eurhythmics are taught quite widely in music classes for children all over the world, especially in Steiner schools, and is taught in greater depth and detail in the early stages of training in music and dance conservatories, as well as some drama schools.

Further reading

Émile Jaques-Dalcroze, *The Eurhythmics of Jaques-Dalcroze*, The Gutenberg Edition, [EBook No. 21653], 2007 (Boston: Small Maynard and Company, 1915).

Notes

1. Plato, *The Republic, Volume Four*, eds Hare & Russell, trans. Benjamin Jowett, Book III (398–403), 165–71 (London: Sphere Books, 1970).
2. 'Émile Jaques-Dalcroze', https://en.wikipedia.org/wiki/Émile_Jaques-Dalcroze.
3. Émile Jaques-Dalcroze, *Eurhythmics Art and Education* (London: Chatto & Windus, 1930), 8.
4. *Stanislavski Collected Works, Volume 1* (Moscow, 381–2), quoted by Jean Benedetti, Introduction, 67.
5. Ibid., 68.
6. Andrew Davidson, 'Konstantin Stanislavski and Émile Jaques-Dalcroze: historical and pedagogical connections between actor training and music education', *Stanislavski Studies* (2001), DOI: 10.1080/20567790.2021.1945811

11 Frederick Matthias Alexander
1869–1955

The stupidity of letting children go wrong is that once they go wrong, their right is wrong; therefore, the more they try to be right, the more they go wrong.[1]

The techniques proposed by F. M. Alexander over a hundred years ago, while not acting techniques *per se*, are taught in drama schools globally to this day as base physical skills for actors for the enhancement of voice and movement.

Alexander, a Tasmanian by birth, started his acting career in Melbourne, Australia, around 1891, in the amateur theatre. He was starting to gain a reputation as a 'reciter' of Shakespeare in the Victorian declamatory style when his voice began to let him down. He first became aware of a problem when fellow actors reported to him that they could hear him gasping for air during performances. He also began to experience hoarseness, and eventually lost his voice completely during a show. Doctors recommended 'resting his voice' for a few days, and when that didn't work, for a few weeks. This only had the effect of allowing him to *begin* a performance in full voice before the problems surfaced once again mid-show. He deduced that something was occurring *during* performance. He began to study himself speaking in mirrors and observed that when he began to recite a speech, he tensed his neck muscles and put his head back somewhat, which in turn caused him to have short breaths. Further observation showed that the position of his neck was also causing his shoulders to narrow, and his posture generally to collapse. He concluded that he didn't have a voice problem, he *was* the voice problem.

These discoveries led to empirical research, in which Alexander was able to identify the *natural* body posture in which there exists the least amount of tension and the maximum free function of organs, especially for breathing. He understood that many of us misuse our bodies constantly, and develop a 'manner of doing' which runs counter to natural 'use', thereby creating many health and well-being issues, such as chronic back pain.[2] The procedure he proposed for correcting this, relies on us un-learning bad habits (he calls it *'inhibiting'* them), and *learning* the 'manner of doing' things which least stress the body – the *right* and *wrong* referred to in the epigraph about children above. Alexander identified that the head leads the entire body posture, so if one gets the head right, the body follows suit. He named this conscious positioning of the head 'primary control'.[3]

Fundamental to his technique was the idea that 'it is impossible to separate 'mental' and 'physical' processes in any form of human activity.'[4] He identified that stress and corporal misuse are a two-way street – one can cause the other. The end goal is 'psychophysical integrity', which comes with awareness. One needs to 'inhibit' one's bad habits in posture, and consciously choose good habits. For example, to achieve 'primary control' of the head-body relationship, one can imagine a piece of string attached to the top on one's head, pulling one gently upwards. He developed exercises in standing, sitting and semi-supine positions, to enable us to understand how best to move, and to recognize when 'psychophysical integrity' is achieved. These exercises are facilitated by trained teachers, who physically guide the student into the required positions, hands-on, on an individual basis. (One-on-one training is deemed important in that our organisms, and our points of equilibrium, are unique.) Alexander observed that modern man/woman – even 120 years ago – was always in a hurry to accomplish something. This state of being he called 'end gaining'. He observed the effect on posture, namely that people in a state of 'end gaining' tend to lean forward while in motion, and their skeleton goes completely out-of-line. The reader may have observed this in certain busy people one knows. This is just one example of corporal misuse. It is correctable with some tutoring, leading to a different mind-set.

For performers these methods can be extremely helpful. For actors and singers, assuming the Alexander Technique (AT) posture opens the airways, and additionally allows the diaphragm to function properly, greatly enhancing voice projection. In movement, dance and musical performance achieving 'psychophysical integrity' allows free movement, avoiding the damage one might be doing to one's body. For the layperson, relief from certain types of corporal pain can be attained in practicing AT. To offer one example, the recommended AT *semi-supine position* on the floor, if practiced with all points of the body in proper relationship to each other, can melt away muscle spasm in the lower back (I can attest to its efficacy). The position is sometimes called 'active rest' – actively correcting bad habits while resting.

In Melbourne, Alexander gradually gave up acting and concentrated on teaching his newly discovered methods, which gained popularity in turn-of-the-century Australia. His methods developed, his fame spread, and he moved to London, where in 1904 he set up practice, and attempted to insinuate himself into the medical community. Soon after his arrival, a prominent ENT specialist sent him a famous actress as a client, and that in turn led to more actors employing his services – the likes of actors Henry Irving (1838–1905) and Herbert Beerbohm Tree (1852–1917).[5] His fame spread.

At the outset of First World War, Alexander was invited by a Montessori educationalist to go to New York to set up a practice. It was extremely successful, and his fame spread even further. In 1931, he returned to London and set up a teacher training course, alongside his practice, which ran until the outset of the War (at which time he returned to New York for two years while England dealt with Hitler). During the inter-war years in Britain, Alexander had many high-profile clients, including actress Viola Tree (1884–1938), novelist Aldous Huxley (1894–1963) and playwright George Bernard Shaw (1856–1950). **Moshé Feldenkrais** was another of his London 'patients'.

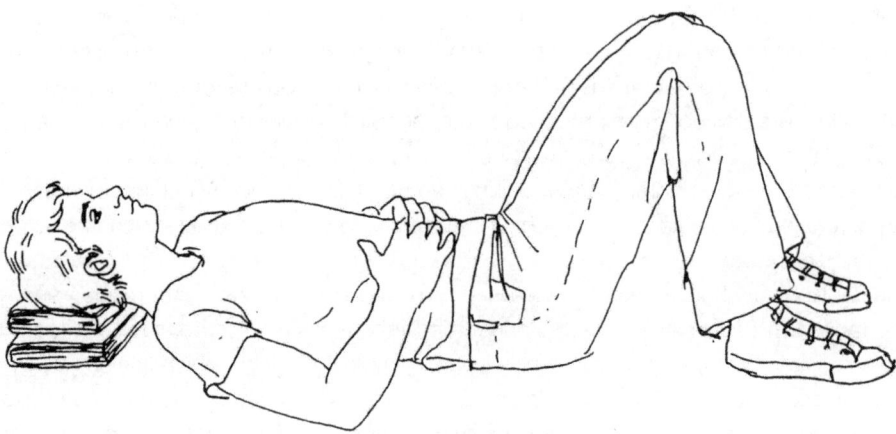

Figure 11.1 Alexander semi-supine position. Drawing: Jose Angel Nazabal.

Proponents of AT, and Alexander himself, have at times made claims that its practice can provide relief for asthma, headaches, osteoarthritis, insomnia and stress. There has been no medical evidence in all these years to support these claims. However, the British National Health Service do recommend AT for long-term back pain, long-term neck pain, and to relieve certain symptoms of Parkinson's disease. The Technique has shown some success in alleviating stuttering, but it has not proven to be a panacea.

Between 1910 and 1912 Alexander penned three volumes, *Man's Supreme Inheritance, Addenda* and *Conscious Control* – later, in 1918, they were consolidated into one book under the first volume's title. In 1932 he wrote *The Use of Self*. In these writings Alexander rather pretentiously couches his practical observations, according to a former student, in a 'cosmic and evolutionary philosophy', which are not 'half so persuasive as the technique itself.'[6] Further stating, 'Mr Alexander's empiric idea and practice are too valuable to be wrapped up in a philosophy that is not just as vigorously integrated and intelligently guided as the muscular system which he skilfully directs towards perfect functioning.'[7]

For anyone interested in pursuing Alexander Technique, I would recommend one of the contemporary books describing it, such as those listed below, in lieu of Alexander's own writings.

Further reading

F. Matthias Alexander, *The Use of the Self* (London: Chaterson Ltd, 1932).
F. Matthias Alexander, *The Resurrection of the Body: The Writings of F. Matthias Alexander,* ed. Edward Maisel (New York: University Books, 1969).
F. Matthias Alexander, *Man's Supreme Inheritance*, 7th ed. (London: Mouritz (1918), 2011).
Michael Bloch, *F. M. The Life of Frederick Matthias Alexander* (New York: Little, Brown, 2004).
Richard Craze, *Alexander Technique* (London: Hodder and Stoughton, Ltd. 1996).
Kelly McEvenue, *The Alexander Technique for Actors* (London: Bloomsbury Methuen, 2016).

Notes

1. Alexander, *Resurrection*, 10.
2. Alexander, *Use of the Self*, 2. Note: 'use' is defined in a wider sense by Alexander as applying to the working of the organism in general'.
3. Craze, 10.
4. Alexander, *Use of the Self*, 1.
5. Bloch, 67–9.
6. Ibid., 116–17, citing from an essay by a former student Randolph Bourne entitled 'Making Over the Body', Appendix A in the 1996 Mouritz edition of *Man's Supreme Inheritance*.
7. Ibid.

12 Gordon Craig
1872–1966

Realism is a vulgar means of expression bestowed upon the blind.[1]

Craig was an English actor, illegitimate son of the popular actor Dame Ellen Terry (1847–1928) and the architect Edward Godwin (1833–86). He was virtually brought up backstage, and as a young man he acted for a while in the theatre company of his godfather, Sir Henry Irving (1838–1905), actor and impresario.[2] He gave up acting to study wood carving – from whence he moved into stage design. His initial endeavours – designs for Purcell's and Handel's operas, and Ibsen's *The Vikings at Helgeland* – were well received. However, disappointed by the lack of significant success in Britain, he emigrated to Germany in 1904.

There he wrote his seminal work, published in English in 1911, *On the Art of the Theatre*, sometimes described as 'the theatre's door to Modernity'.[3] The Symbolist manifesto was a diatribe against the new Realism (see epigraph above), and a paean to puppetry. In it he presented the concept of the actor as *Übermarionette*. 'The actor must go, and in his place comes the inanimate figure.'[4] He maintained that emotion conspires against art.[5] 'Acting [in the naturalistic vein] is not an art. It is therefore incorrect to speak of the actor as an artist. For accident is the enemy of the artist. Art is the exact antithesis of pandemonium.'[6]

He argues that the only use an actor has for the study of *nature* is to find *symbolism* for the expression of their thoughts. 'Art arrives by design . . . The whole nature of man tends towards freedom; he therefor carries the proof in his own person that, as material for the Theatre, he is useless.'[7]

Craig proposed that audiences go to the theatre to *see*, rather than to *hear*. The design elements of a play transcend reality and function as symbols, thereby communicating a deeper meaning, rather than simply reflecting the real world, as in Realism. Craig found a kindred soul in his contemporary, **Adolphe Appia** (1862–1928). These two men from quite different backgrounds became friends and correspondents, and shared the common view that Realism was a wholly inadequate expression of theatrical art.

It was Craig who originated the idea of doing away with traditional footlights. The stage was, for the first time, lit from above; colour and variations in light became part of the stage designer's palate. The actors also became an integral part of the design – just one element in a work of movement, line, sound, light, and colour – all orchestrated by the director/designer. Professionally, Craig was considered by many to be extremely difficult to work with, always refusing to direct or design any project over which he did not have complete artistic control. Gradually he was marginalized and was unable to produce practical work in the last forty years of his life.

Craig lived in straightened circumstances during most of his life, leaving little inheritance to his numerous progenies. He was married and had five children in the four years he spent with his wife. He then lived for many years with a violinist, who bore him two children. He also had a daughter with an actress, another with the dancer (Isadora Duncan, 1877–1927), a son with a poet, and yet another daughter with his secretary. I count that as eleven. (His daughter with Duncan, Deirde Beatrice Craig, died in a car which accidentally plunged into the River Seine in Paris in 1913, profoundly affecting the dancer.)

In 1908, Isadora Duncan introduced him to **Stanislavski**. The latter at that point was getting over his failed experiment with **Meyerhold**. He proposed a collaboration with Craig which led to the vaunted MAT production of *Hamlet*, which opened in December 1911. It was the product of an uneasy alliance embracing two diametrically opposed views of theatre (Symbolism and Realism) which miraculously led to a groundbreaking, game-changing work. It was the first production in which Craig used sliding screens – for which he became famous – as the principal staging device. Craig constructed the play as a continual, uninterrupted piece, with *Hamlet* watching all the action from the wings. He wanted the screens to be moved in sight of the audience by specially costumed stagehands, but Stanislavski vetoed the idea, and, instead, curtains were drawn between scenes. Nonetheless, it was a *succès d'estime*, and the production established Craig's reputation globally as a theatre designer. Subsequently, he moved to Florence, where he formed a school of theatrical design (the Arena Goldoni).

Craig left a body of published work. In *On the Art of the Theatre* he waxed lyrical about puppets, positing their potential for a new art form.[8] He wrote a cycle of puppet plays, the *Drama for Fools*, as well as producing a theatre magazine entitled *The Marionette* (1918). 'There is only one actor – nay one man who has the soul of the dramatic poet, and who has ever served as the true and loyal interpreter of the poet,' he proclaimed, and 'this is the marionette.'[9] In his 1910 article 'A Note on Masks', Craig expounded the virtue of using masks as a mechanism for capturing the audience's attention, imagination, and soul. In 1913, he published *Towards a New Theatre* – essentially a catalogue of his designs, vividly demonstrating the dramatic power of light.[10] *The Theatre Advancing*, published in 1919, is a rant against the pretension and lack of substance of his contemporary theatre, and a proposal for creating both more durable (weightier) and more perishable (experimental) forms of theatre.[11] It is easy to understand how Craig inspired **Meyerhold**, **Copeau**, **Lecoq**, **Brecht** and **Brook**, and many other directors, including, curiously, **Lee Strasberg**.[12]

Further reading

Gordon Craig, *On the Art of the Theatre* (London: Heinemann Ltd, 1911).
J. Michael Walton, ed., *Craig on Theatre* (London: Methuen Drama, 1983, 1991, 1999).

Notes

1. Craig, 287.
2. Craig wrote a well-received biography of his godfather: *Sir Henry Irving* (London: J. M. Dent, 1930).
3. Lorenzo Mango, 'The Manuscripts of The Art of the Theatre', *Acting Archives Review Supplement*, 7 April 2011: 2.
4. Craig, 81.
5. Ibid., 57. 'It sways his voice to join in the conspiracy against his mind . . . Therefore the mind of the actor, we see, is less powerful than his emotion, for emotion is able to win over the mind to assist in the destruction of that which the mind would produce: and as the mind becomes the slave of the emotion it follows that accident upon accident must be continually occurring.'
6. Ibid., 55.
7. Ibid., 56.
8. Walton, 25. In an essay, 'Gentlemen, The Marionette!' (1912) he writes, 'The marionette, through his two virtues

of obedience and silence, leaves to his sons a vast inheritance . . . the promise of a new art.'
9. Ibid., 24.
10. Gordon Craig, *Towards a New Theatre* (London: J. M. Dent and Sons, 1913).
11. Gordon Craig, *The Theatre Advancing* (Boston: Little, Brown & Co., 1919).
12. Lee Strasberg, *A Dream of Passion: The Developments of the Method* (Boston: Little, Brown & Co., 1987), 27–9. Strasberg, an arch emotionalist, says that Craig's writings were the intellectual stimulus for him to engage in theatre, and claims that Craig's *Übermarionette* concept is widely misinterpreted, being not a proposal to replace the actor, but an encouragement to the actor to achieve the precision and skill of the marionette.

13 Vsevolod Meyerhold
1874–1940

A theatre built on psychological foundations is as certain to collapse as a house built on sand. On the other hand, a theatre which relies on physical elements is. . . assured of clarity.[1]

Deeply impressed by the prodigious talent of the twenty-four-year-old Vsevolod Meyerhold, his teacher at the Moscow Philharmonic acting school **Vladimir Nemirovich-Danchenko** invited him in 1898 to join the Moscow Arts Theatre as one of the original *ensemble*. As a member of the MAT, Vsevolod acted for, studied under and worshipped **Stanislavski**. His first important role was that of the angry young playwright, Konstantin, in the ground-breaking production of Chekhov's *The Seagull*. Meyerhold played opposite Stanislavski, who played Trigorin, a worldly writer of considerable experience. The casting was prescient. Chekhov's frustrated young Konstantin declares: 'What we need are new artistic forms, and if we don't get new forms, it would be better if we had nothing at all . . . I don't want to show life as it is, or the way it should be, but the way it is in dreams', presaging Meyerhold's future Symbolist credo and the looming artistic conflicts he would have with his 'master'. The character Trigorin, given to strolling about jotting down observations of human behaviour, was, like Stanislavski, treading the path of Realism. The would-be actress Nina eventually spurns the love-sick idealist Konstantin, and takes up with the 'safer bet', Trigorin – a disastrous choice, as it turns out. Meyerhold's biographer, Paul Schmidt points out the final irony: like poor Nina, the October Revolution spurned Konstantin/Meyerhold and chose instead Trigorin/Stanislavski. Stalin and his commissars rejected – we should say *obliterated* – Symbolism (and with tragic consequences for Meyerhold) and embraced the MAT's brand of Realism – adapting it to the doctrine of **Socialist Realism**, discussed later in its own chapter.[2]

In the three years following *The Seagull*, Meyerhold became increasingly disillusioned with Stanislavski's naturalism (along with the internal organization of the MAT). He left under a cloud in 1902 and drew together a group of other disaffected young MAT actors. They established a new theatre in Ukraine, which came to be called the Fellowship of the New Drama. It was there that Meyerhold cut his teeth on directing, and his first work was totally in the realistic vein of Stanislavski. He later justified himself: 'There is no danger in imitation for the young artist; it is an almost inevitable stage.'[3] While in Ukraine he discovered the work of the 'Symbolists' and was especially taken by the Belgian poet and playwright, Maurice Maeterlinck (1862–1949). He began to try out new ideas.

In 1905 Stanislavski, entering a period of intense self-doubt, and having heard about some of the cutting-edge work taking place in the Fellowship, invited Meyerhold back to the MAT to be the head of a new theatre studio, which was to be dedicated to 'experimentation'. In his own work Stanislavski was seeking something fresh, more modern in spirit. Symbolism filled the bill. As he put it, 'The time for the unreal on the stage had arrived. It was necessary to picture not life itself as it takes place in reality, but as we vaguely feel it in our dreams, our visions, our moments of spiritual uplift.'[4]

However, after a year of trial and error, and a failed attempt by Meyerhold to mount a production of Maeterlinck's *The Death of Tintagiles*, the 'experiment' was brought to a halt. Stanislavski didn't negate the concept, but contended that Meyerhold's actors lacked the proper training and experience to deliver what the director intended.

After the demise of the Experimental Theatrical Studio, Meyerhold was patronized by noted actress and theatre manager, Vera Komissarzhevskaya (1864–1910), who some called the 'Russian Duse'.[5] She set him up in the theatre she owned and managed in St Petersburg. There he was further able to develop his avant-garde ideas. The collaboration with Komisarzhevskaya was short-lived, lasting only one year. Meyerhold's new-found Symbolist approach left no space on the stage for the actress's prodigious emotional style and theatricality, so she dismissed him. Moreover, he was allegedly becoming notoriously arrogant and tyrannical towards his actors, which did not win him any favours.

Biographer Paul Schmidt justifies Meyerhold's 'tricky' personality as typical of many directors – he was paternalistic and authoritarian. 'Like all lonely people he was difficult, and like lonely people of intelligence he surrounded himself with crowds, worked always in full view, in public. Yet those who surrounded him were followers, subordinates.'[6] The film director **Sergei Eisenstein**, a student of Meyerhold's who idolized him, said of him: 'He was living proof that genius and maliciousness can both abide within one human being.'[7] Director and erstwhile assistant to Meyerhold, Leonid Varpakhovsky (1908–76) commented: 'Meyerhold's friendship turned eventually, and quite regularly, into its diametrical opposite, and the rejected friend had to suffer in succession his indifference, coldness, suspicion, dislike, hostility, and hatred.'[8]

There is an interesting comparison to be made between Meyerhold and his mentor in terms of directorial style. In the early days of the MAT, Stanislavski, taking a leaf from the book of the authoritarian directors of the Meiningen Players, saw it as his duty to impose his *directorial vision* on every miniscule aspect of the production, including a dictatorial approach to his actors' performance. Later, dissatisfaction with his own acting and that of his group, led him increasingly to appreciate – and make room for – the 'inner creative impulses' of the actor, and to work collaboratively to access them. Conversely, Meyerhold, along with other of the Symbolists and Constructivists, became increasingly concerned with matters of form over content and exerted ever more control over his actors. 'His aim was to convey not the feelings of individual characters but purified 'extracts' of emotion. The actors were trained to speak in a form of *recitative* limited to three notes and to move in a slow, hieratic style. Often it seemed as though Meyerhold was trying to turn his actors into puppets . . .'[9] His actors were increasingly regarded as *Übermarionettes* – he was exposed to **Gordon Craig's** theories while in Berlin in 1907, and afterwards incorporated them into both his productions and his teaching.[10]

As he geared up for his 1909 production of *Tristan and Isolde* at the Marinsky Opera, Meyerhold read up on Wagner, and in doing so discovered Wagner's designer, **Adolphe Appia**. Consequently, his notions about rhythmical movement, and his visualization of the actor and stage space in three-dimensional terms, assumed a new coherence.

In the fallow years between revolutionary outbreaks, he became fascinated by the *commedia dell'arte*, with its masks, its freedom of improvisation, its lack of psychological nuance, and its fascination with the grotesque. Mirroring his contemporary in France, **Jacques Copeau**, he proposed that the 'cabotin' (strolling player) was the 'instrument needed to energize the Russian theatre'.[11] He studied Noh drama and other oriental theatre, with its formal externalized techniques. He established his own school, where he experimented with *commedia*, the circus and oriental theatre, and laid the foundations for the programme of 'Biomechanics', which he began to promote after the 1917 Revolution.

Around 1920–1 Meyerhold began to teach 'Biomechanics', which is both an acting technique and a production style. It took its inspiration from **Jaques-Dalcroze's** Eurhythmics in relating movement to rhythm.[12] It is framed by two widely different external influences: the *objective psychology* of Ivan Pavlov (1849–1936), famous for exploring 'conditioned behaviour' in dogs, and the *assembly-line efficiency* postulated by American industrialist Frederick Winslow Taylor (1856–1915). Pavlovian ideas were central to Meyerhold's approach – that our behaviour is essentially a chain of *reflex responses* to conditions of the external world. Essentially, we don't *act,* but we *react*. 'Taylorism' involved a time-and-motion approach, ensuring that the actor did not waste one calorie of their energy.[13] Based on Taylor's analysis of *working cycles*, Meyerhold's constructed his concept of stage movement in terms of *acting cycles*: *intention*, *realization* and *reaction*. Movement had three sequential parts, each with its own rhythm: (1) preparation for an action (then pause), (2) the action itself (then pause) and (3) its corresponding reaction. Like a dancer, the actor's every movement or gesture made on stage is calculated, controlled and never spontaneous.[14]

Rhythms could be enforced with devices such as the 'pose-pause', where action is frozen momentarily for emphasis (Charlie Chaplin employed this). *Gesture* was an elemental device, enabling the actor to clarify an intention, qualify it, or contradict it. Meyerhold's 'Gesture' was marked by three traits: 'First, it was never casual or spontaneous, but always deliberate and significant; it partook of the nature of a rhythmic contribution to the performance . . . and finally that it was a movement which reverberated through the whole body.'[15] Just as in Japanese theatre hands were agents of expressiveness, other elements of the body were used as a form of 'plastic movement'.[16] Biomechanical exercises were self-descriptive, including 'Shooting from the Bow', 'Throwing the Stone', 'Stab with the Dagger' and 'Leap on the Chest'. The classic forms are still deployed today by practitioners of Biomechanics.

Characterization in Meyerhold's theatre was a vehicle for revealing social relationships rather than a search for personal meaning – a dialectical materialist view of stage life and real life, positing that '*dramatis personae* are not real people, and to suppose they are is to misunderstand the very basis of art'.[17] In this way Meyerhold presages **Bertolt Brecht**. The character is an '*action-function*'.

Biomechanics was perfectly suited to Meyerhold's newly found interest in Constructivism – the revolutionary Russian architecture and art movement sparked off by Vladimir Tatlin (1885–1953) and Alexander Rodchenko (1891–1956) featuring geometric abstraction, industrial materials and functionality. Two noteworthy Meyerhold productions marrying Biomechanics with Constructivist staging were *The Magnanimous Cuckold* (1922) and *The Government Inspector* (1926). Both stripped the stage of any remnant of Realism. Both were hugely successful.

Throughout his directing career, Meyerhold developed new concepts for the relationship of the play to the audience, which would later be embraced and elaborated upon by the likes of **Piscator**, Brecht, **Brook** and **Grotowski**. He attempted to engage the audience in a visible manner – for example, keeping the lights in the auditorium lit during performances. He broke out of the proscenium, constructing ramps leading from the stage into the audience. None of this would surprise us when we enter a theatre today, but in the early 1900s these ideas were unheard of.

In 1932 both Stanislavski and Nemirovich-Danchenko came out in sharp criticism of 'formalistic innovators' (pointing a finger at Meyerhold). They defended Realism as the only sound tradition.[18]

> As the outward side of our productions retreated more and more to the background, so in the other theatres of Moscow and Petrograd more and more interest was displayed in the outer appearances in contra-distinction to the inner contents of the play.[19]

While the theatre under Lenin had been allowed to experiment with new forms in the name of creating art of the proletariat, when Stalin came to power in 1934 **Socialist Realism** became the only permitted art form in both theatre and film, and Meyerhold's ideas were denounced. The MAT's version of Realism, with a few 'tweaks', adapted itself neatly to the Stalinist formula, and, as indicated in the chapter on Stanislavski, the MAT and its principals were able to carry on with only a modicum of State surveillance. In contrast, early in 1938, Meyerhold's theatre was closed, and he was branded 'an enemy of the State'.

Stanislavski came to his rescue, taking him on as assistant director at the Opera Theatre, in a famous reconciliation between the master and his errant student. In August 1938 Stanislavski died, and Meyerhold completed the master's production of *Rigoletto*.

Unfortunately, not long after, the outspoken Meyerhold disgraced himself during a government-sponsored colloquium of theatre directors – convened to bring everyone onboard the Party-line on Socialist Realism. He was sent to an Arctic concentration camp, subsequently charged with being a German spy, tortured, given a secret trial and executed in a prison basement in Moscow (February 1940). In parallel, his wife was brutally disfigured and murdered. Meyerhold's name and his image were literally eradicated from Russian theatre history until after the death of Stalin.

Meyerhold's legacy lived on directly in the work of **Brecht**, **Artaud**, **Brook**, **Grotowski**, **Piscator**, **LeCoq**, **Chaikin**, **Malina** and **Michael Chekhov**. Sergei Eisenstein was a student of Meyerhold. More generally, his innovations in theatre technique and staging were embraced by the wider community, even the Realists and 'Method'-ists, such as **Harold Clurman**, **Lee Strasberg** and the **Group Theatre**. The obsolescence of the proscenium arch is just one example of this legacy.

Meyerhold was posthumously rehabilitated in Russia, and his teachings taken up again there in the early 1970s, principally in the Theatre of Satire. Now Biomechanics are alive and well and living in various niches in the USA, of which the Institute in Theatrical Biomechanics at Tufts University is pre-eminent.[20]

The most authoritative source on Meyerhold is *Meyerhold on Theatre* – his own writings, edited and elucidated by Edward Braun. Its fourth edition was published by Bloomsbury Methuen Drama in 2016, with an introduction by Jonathan Pitches. The perfect complement for further study would be Pitches' biography, *Vsevolod Meyerhold*, which, among other things, sets out in simple clear terms the basic skillset of Biomechanics, as well as the exercises to achieve them. Similarly, the forms are clearly illustrated in Law and Gordon's *Meyerhold, Eisenstein, and Biomechanics*. There are numerous audio-visual representations of Biomechanics on You Tube.[21]

Further reading

Edward Braun and Jonathan Pitches, *Meyerhold on Theatre*, 4th ed. (London: Bloomsbury, 2016).
Alma Law and Mel Gordon, *Meyerhold, Eisenstein, and Biomechanics* (Jefferson, NC: McFarland & Co., 1996).
Robert Leach, *Vsevolod Meyerhold* (Cambridge: Cambridge University Press, 1989).
Jonathan Pitches, *Vsevolod Meyerhold* (London: Routledge, 2003).

Notes

1. Braun and Pitches, 245.
2. Paul Schmidt, ed., *Meyerhold at Work*, trans. P. Schmidt, I. Levin and V. McGee (New York: Applause Books, 1996), xi.
3. Braun and Pitches, 22.
4. Konstantin Stanislavski, *My Life in Art* (New York: Little Brown & Co., 1924), 434.
5. Braun and Pitches, 24.
6. Schmidt, xviii.
7. Ibid., 5.
8. Ibid., 181.

9. James Roose-Evans, *Experimental Theatre from Stanislavsky to Peter Brook*, (London/Melbourne: Routledge & Kegan Paul, 1984), 22.
10. Braun and Pitches, 136.
11. Robert Leach, *Directors in Perspective* (Cambridge: Cambridge University Press,1986).
12. 'Whether we use a saw poorly, whether we handle a knife and fork clumsily, whether we walk awkwardly on the stage, we can all learn from Dalcroze. Every master-blacksmith, foundry worker, actor must have a sense of rhythm.' Sergei Eisenstein, 'The Actor of the Future and Biomechanics' in Law and Gordon, 142–3.
13. Braun and Pitches, 244.
14. Roose-Evans, 28. For a lucid explanation of the technique, including YouTube references, see: https://thedramateacher.com/meyerholds-biomechanics-for-theatre/
15. Leach, 59–60.
16. Meyerhold's term, Leach, 61.
17. Leach, 74.
18. Roose-Evans, 21.
19. Ibid., 20.
20. Jane Baldwin, 'Meyerhold's Theatrical Biomechanics: An Acting Technique for Today, *Theatre Topics*, Vol. 5, No. 2, September 1995: 181–5.
21. One of many YouTube references to Biomechanics: https://www.youtube.com/watch?v=dUUgaQqgBS0

14 Maria Ouspenskaya
1876–1949

No book could be valid. Now is all.[1]

Film buffs best remember Maria Ouspenskaya as the gypsy woman who teaches the werewolf rhyme to Lon Chaney Jr (1906–73) in *The Wolf Man* (1941), a role which she subsequently reprised in *Frankenstein Meets the Wolf Man* (1943), and which has been lampooned in other films such as Mel Brooks' *Dracula: Dead and Loving It*. Maria was famously parodied as Marjory the Trash Heap in the puppet series *Fraggle Rock*. It is forgotten that this 'tiny very wrinkled actress with a commanding presence'[2] and heavy Russian accent was once a leading lady on the Moscow Arts Theatre stage, highly respected on Broadway, and had won a Best Supporting Actor Oscar nomination for in her very first Hollywood film, *Dodsworth* (1936), and again, three years later, playing a wise old grandmother in *Love Affair* (1939). It is also largely forgotten that she was very much responsible for the formation of **Stella Adler**, **Lee Strasberg** and **Sanford Meisner** – all of whom studied with her, and in some ways replicated her manners and teaching methods. Because she refused to write a textbook, or have one written about her teaching, as did the 'troika', her pedagogy has not survived to be digested in books. As she said: 'Now is all.' Instead, her legacy has been handed down, via the three great **Stanislavskian** teachers above, and now is alive in the classrooms of the successive generations of teachers who have followed, including myself.

Ouspenskaya was a character actor, and quite a 'character' in her own right, given to dressing dramatically in black and toting a long cigarette holder. Conducting her classes at the **American Lab Theatre** she was described as 'awesome'. 'Sitting in her chair, her feet on a footstool, her head covered by a shawl, she would smoke a small black cigar, and with a piercing look command her students to begin an exercise.'[3] **Stanislavski** called her one of the best teachers of 'the system'. And Strasberg respected her greatly as both an actress and teacher, '. . . better in both capacities, probably, than any of the other Russian actors of the time who emigrated to this country'.[4]

With a background in singing from the Warsaw Conservatory and some initial acting training at Adasheff's School in Moscow, Ouspenskaya studied the emerging 'system' for three years with Stanislavski's assistant Leopold Sulerjitsky (Suler), before officially being invited to joining the MAT in 1909. She then became a member of the First Studio at its inception in 1912. She was one of the MAT's most esteemed actors and very famous in her native Russia. She travelled to New York with the troupe in 1923 and toured with them until **Richard Boleslavsky** persuaded her to stay on and join him to teach in the American Lab Theatre. Her significant contribution to acting pedagogy is set out in the chapter on **Boleslavsky and the American Lab Theatre**. You can pick up her story there.

After the Lab closed Maria set up the Maria Ouspenskaya School of Dramatic Art in Manhattan – a thriving enterprise. She also began to pick up some stage roles in New York, but eventually decided to follow **Boleslavsky's** trail and try her luck in Hollywood. During her later years became a respected film character actor, making seventeen films and garnering the two Best Supporting Oscar nominations mentioned above. In later years she became deeply immersed in astrology and would consult an astrologist daily before showing up on the set. Her insistence that her work revolved around the stars – the *astrological* ones – and an imperious attitude meant she was not well-liked amongst cast and crew.

After the graduation of her students in 1939, she moved the New York studio to Hollywood and continued teaching Stanislavski's methods. She once said she could not live without acting nor could she live without teaching.

In 1949, at the age of seventy-three, she died, having accidentally set fire to her bed and burning down her house. Her life-long addictions to smoking and alcohol got her in the end – albeit in an unexpected manner. According to Mel Gordon, her reported net worth when she died was $352.32.[5]

Further reading

Mel Gordon, *Stanislavsky in America* (New York: Routledge, 2010).

Notes

1. Gordon, 26.
2. So described by critic James Robert Parish in his book *Hollywood Character Actors* (New York: Arlington House, 1978).
3. David Garfield, *A Player's Place: The Story of the Actors Studio* (New York: Macmillan, 1980), 11–12.
4. Ibid., 12.
5. Gordon, 33.

15 Jacques Copeau
1879–1949

The stage is the instrument of the creative dramatic artist. It is the place for drama, not scenery and machines. It belongs to the actors, not to stagehands and painters. It must always be ready for the actor to use, for action.[1]

In France, at the turn of the twentieth century, there were three types of theatre:

- The theatre of the *Boulevard* – highly commercial popular plays performed by *'marquee'* actors).
- The *classical repertory* of the *Comédie-Française* – heavily biased towards Molière.
- The *naturalistic movement* of the independent theatres – spearheaded by André Antoine (1858–1943).

André Antoine, a director/impresario, was the leading proponent of Realism and naturalism on the French stage, having taken his inspiration largely from Émile Zola (1840–1902). In 1887 he founded a workshop studio, the Théâtre-Libre, a place for trying out new writing with disregard to box office. The project lasted seven years primarily presenting short plays, and when it closed for financial reasons, it was reconstituted in the form of the Théâtre Antoine, which lasted another ten years. In his directing, Antoine emphasized 'connected' acting, psychology and social settings, predating **Stanislavski's** experiments in Russia. He frequently built the sets and asked the actors to inhabit them before starting rehearsals, as a way of grounding the characters. Sometimes he decided late in the rehearsal process which of the four walls to remove to present to the audience. Ultimately frustrated at the business of theatre, he turned to silent film direction, primarily doing literary adaptations such as *La Terre* (Earth) based on Zola's 1887 novel. In that film and others, he presaged **Italian Neo-Realism** and **Neo Neo-Realism** by mixing non-actors with professionals in every-day settings. Antoine ended his career just as Jacques Copeau had begun his . . . as a theatre (and film) critic.

Having failed to graduate from the Sorbonne in philosophy in 1902, Jacques Copeau took up theatre criticism in order to put bread on the table. He was an avid theatregoer, and, at that time, an ardent admirer of Antoine. (Later, as a critic, he rejected that director's fixation on naturalism, and his over-emphasis on the literary text.) Copeau had tried his hand at writing a few plays while at university, but his break-through as a 'professional' didn't come until the 1911 of his adaptation of Dostoevsky's *The Brothers Karamazov*, directed by Jacques Rouché (1862–1957), and featuring actors **Charles Dullin** (1885–1949) and Louis Jouvet (1887–1951), with whom Copeau was to maintain close relationships. Given the massively favourable notices, Copeau was able to revive *Karamazov* three times, which, in turn, led to a certain amount of fame in the theatre worlds of Paris, London and Europe.

What Copeau did take from Antoine – who in later years became an admirer and friend, despite their different views of theatre – was the concept of 'ensemble' acting. Like **Stanislavski**, Antoine had learned this through the example of the Meiningen Players. Copeau quickly realized the value of creating a well-trained ensemble of actors, who, working together over time, could play effectively off each other. This principle became fundamental to his work.

By 1912, Copeau, now with a bit of practical experience under his belt, as both actor and director, crystallized his ideas, largely in reaction to the prevailing state of the French theatre. He felt that the exaggerated naturalism of Antoine had become an obstacle to an understanding of the text and to the fullest development of character. Moreover, he was determined to sweep away the tawdry, cheap commercialism of the Boulevard, as well as the 'ham' acting ('*cabotinage*') that characterized it. With respect to the Comédie-Française approach to Molière, he sought a new style of presenting the classic work stripped of its puffed-up ornamentation. His determination to mount an alternative to the current theatre scene, emboldened by his modicum of experience in staging *Karamazov*, plus his innate passion, moved him to establish a theatre of his own.

In 1913, Copeau founded what was to become one of the world's most renowned theatres – the Vieux-Colombier. He assembled a troupe of enthusiastic, trusting actors, and took them off to his country house to work as an *ensemble* to prepare a season of plays. These were duly presented in the theatre in October of that year. A mix of the classic (primarily Molière) and modern, the season culminated with a legendary production of *Twelfth Night*, which was a *succès d'estime*. Paris was enthusiastic. Unfortunately, this auspicious start was cut short by the outbreak of the First World War. Copeau's actors were conscripted, and the theatre closed. Copeau, luckily, was seconded to Paris, where he was at least able to keep up with his correspondence.

In 1915, he took up an invitation to visit **Gordon Craig**, with whom he had been corresponding, at Craig's school, Arena Goldoni, in Florence. He stayed several weeks. Craig's views on staging, lighting, the role of the director and designer provided solutions to many of Copeau's unanswered questions. The principal aspect on which their opinions diverged was the role of the actor. Copeau believed that the actor was the *centre* of the theatrical experience, and not a peripheral adjunct to the director's vision – unlike Craig's *Übermarionette*. Craig apparently said to Copeau, 'You believe in the actor. I do not.'[2] The additional benefit of the visit was to learn how to set up and run a school, which stood Copeau in good stead later, when he established his own École du Vieux-Colombier.[3]

In the summer of 1916, Copeau was asked to go to Geneva as a 'cultural ambassador'. He profited from this 'gig' by frequently visiting the school of **Jaques-Dalcroze** (1865–1950), composer and music teacher, who had developed a system of movement using *rhythm* as the 'universal and essential component of all expression'.[4] Copeau was captivated by the manner in which, through improvisation and experimentation using 'Eurhythmics' – as Dalcroze's exercises were called – students could learn to bring the body into a unified theatrical expression. He incorporated the Eurhythmics into his own curriculum, but later rejected it on the basis that it made the actor too self-conscious of their movement.[5]

While in Switzerland, he also met with **Adolphe Appia**, at his castle on Lake Leman – a meeting considered 'to have been a decisive factor in the evolution of Copeau's theatrical thought.'[6] While he was dazzled by Appia's ideas for staging, he shared with him the idea of the primacy of the actor in the theatrical experience. Thereafter he called Appia his 'master'. Copeau didn't imitate Appia or Craig; instead, he provided a conduit through which their idealistic visions could take shape.[7]

With respect to the actor's technique, Copeau did not incline towards **Diderot's** view in *Paradox* that real feeling gets in the way of the actor's performance, or that technique precludes feeling, stating 'The absurdity of the "paradox" is to oppose professional technique to liberty of feeling and deny that they exist simultaneously in an artist.'[8]

In 1916 Jacques Copeau was sent to New York, again as a 'cultural ambassador' for France (the original plan was to send his entire ensemble, but by then, most were fighting the War). There he delivered a series of lectures expounding his theories on an ideal theatre, including a lecture at the **American Lab Theatre** (see chapter on **Boleslavsky**). These lectures captured the imagination of the US theatre world, and were attended, among others, by **Harold Clurman**, who later said that Copeau was his *first* formal instructor in theatre.[9] Clurman claimed that Copeau was the inspiration for his and **Strasberg's** formation of the **Group Theatre** ensemble.[10] One particular enthusiast, a philanthropist named Otto Kahn (1867–1934), proposed setting up a season of Vieux-Colombier plays within the framework of the moribund Théâtre Français de New York. With Kahn's money, and the help of his usual collaborator, Louis Jouvet, Copeau remodelled the Garrick Theatre, the Théâtre Français' home space, in line with his new concepts of staging – stripped back, minimal, and inspirational.

With the renovations completed, and the War drawing to its conclusion, Copeau brought his troupe to the USA and mounted a diverse season of twenty-one French-language plays. They were deemed a great success. One critic said, 'The Vieux-Colombier . . . has set for us a new and practicable standard by which American dramatic art may be tested.'[11]

Returning triumphantly to Paris, the company enjoyed great success in their old theatre, peaking in 1922–3, when the entire season sold out. Nonetheless, the economics of the small theatre finally determined Copeau to close it, rather than give in to a more commercial approach, and it was liquidated in the summer of 1924. He bequeathed his actors and repertoire to Jouvet and moved lock, stock and barrel to Burgundy, where he established a small workshop, called Les Copiaus, specializing in the study of *commedia dell'arte*. He lived and worked in the wine-producing village of Pernand-Vergelesses until his death in 1949.

During his career, Copeau wrote numerous articles and pamphlets, but he never set down his ideas in a handbook. His pedagogy was based on *movement* training to foster spontaneity, playfulness and creativity in the actor – and, additionally, to generate the chemistry of *ensemble* – notions which he passed on to his student, **Jacques Lecoq**.[12] The main thrust of Copeau's training, was for the actor to discover the *child's instinct for play*, a concept later fully developed by Lecoq, and explored in depth in the USA by **Viola Spolin**.

For Copeau, in the dramatic arts the writer reigns supreme, and the director's role, above all else, is to illuminate the text for actors and audience alike.

In his later years, Copeau promoted the study and modernization of mime. Étienne Decroux (1898–1991), a French actor who specialized in corporeal mime, and Marcel Marceau (1923–2007) the noted mime artist, both trained with him, as did actor and mime artist, Jean-Louis Barrault (1910–94).

Copeau was not oblivious to the work of **Stanislavski**. They had corresponded regularly since 1916, and had much in common, even if Copeau rejected the exaggerated realism that had emerged in France, in imitation of the MAT. He insisted that slavish Realism could be an obstacle to a substantive understanding of the text and to inspired character development. They finally met when the Vieux-Colombier hosted the Moscow Arts Theatre in Paris in December 1922, presenting productions of *The Cherry Orchard* and other plays.[13] Copeau and his actors were deeply impressed, and from that time adopted three basic Stanislavskian principles: 'the importance of sincerity and truth; that action must be linked to a psychological state; that movement should originate from need'.[14] Both men had talked of jointly founding an international centre of theatre art, but it never came to fruition.

In late 1925, Copeau returned to New York to direct the legendary American thespian couple Alfred Lunt (1892–1977) and Lynne Fontaine (1887–1983), in an English version of *The Brothers Karamazov*. Harold Clurman was his assistant director.[15] The Theatre Guild production opened in January 1927. During his time in the States, Copeau gave another series of enthusiastically attended lectures, spreading his influence even further. He had no 'system' to proselytize. What he offered was an inciteful critique of current theatre, along with notes on a different way of working. His influence was great but subtle. His biographer Mark Evans opines: 'In all respects his legacy has become so pervasive that it is in danger of becoming invisible.'[16]

Further reading

Jean Benedetti, *The Art of the Actor* (Abingdon: Routledge, 2007), Chapter 10.
Jacques Copeau, *Registres I, Appels*, ed. Marie-Hélène Dasté and Suzanne Maistre, (Paris: Gallimard, 1974).
Mark Evans, *Jacques Copeau* (London: Routledge Performance Practitioners, 2007).
J. Rudin and N. Paul, *Copeau Texts on Theatre* (Abingdon: Routledge,1990).

Notes

1. Copeau, 214.
2. Rudin and Paul, 22.
3. Albert M. Katz, 'The Genesis of the Vieux-Colombier: The Aesthetic Background of Jacques Copeau', *Educational Theatre Journal*, Vol. 19, No. 4 (December 1967): 439.
4. Evans, 17.
5. Ibid., 63.
6. Katz, 441.
7. Evans, 19.
8. Benedetti, 161, quoting an article by Copeau entitled 'To the Actors'.
9. Boleslavsky was the second. Harold Clurman, *On Directing* (New York: Fireside Books, 1997), 28.
10. Evans, 155.
11. Mabel Hayes Barrows Mussey, 'The Stimulus of the Vieux-Colombier', *The Nation* (March 1919): 482.
12. Simon Murray, *The Life of Jacques Lecoq* (London: Routledge, reprinted 2017), 29.
13. According to Stanislavski's principal biographer, Jean Benedetti, Copeau, while having corresponded at length with Stanislavski, never actually met him – as he was in New York at the time of the MAT visit to Paris (Benedetti, 159). However, according to Copeau's biographer, Mark Evans, the Frenchman was waiting at the Gare du Nord in November 1922 to meet and welcome the man he called 'master to us all' (Evans, 29).
14. Mira Felner, *Apostles of Silence: The Modern French Mimes* (London: Associated University Presses, 1985), 39.
15. Clurman first met Copeau was while studying in Paris in the 1920s. Clurman, *The Fervent Years* (New York: Harcourt, Brace, Jovanovich, 1975), 5.
16. Evans, 151.

16 Rudolf Laban
1879–1958

When mime, and with it the significance of movement, is entirely forgotten or neglected, the theatre is dead.[1]

He was Hungarian born – as Rudolf *von* Laban – into a once-noble French family. He studied architecture at the École des Beaux-Arts in Paris, where he developed a fascination for the relationship of *movement* to the *spatial environment*. In 1909, that interest took him to Munich to study Expressionist dance (*Ausdruckstanz*) with leading choreographer Heidi Dzinkowska (1884–1922). There his architectural inclinations transmuted into those of a dancer/choreographer, leading him to begin the painstaking development of his extraordinary *movement notation* system, explained below. It was eventually completed in 1926 and unveiled in a polished form in 1928 as *Kinetography Laban*. It later came to be known in the USA and UK as *Labanotation*.

Notation for scoring music had been around since the mid-seventeenth century, but Laban saw the utility of being able to describe dance movement on paper in a similar manner to musical notes. Since 1928, Labanotation has become a universal method for committing choreography to record, thus enabling ballets, for example, to be replicated years after they were conceived. The notation uses a *stave* – as in music – the centre line of which corresponds to the *spine*, with each peripheral line representing the extremities of the body. For the curious, one can find a visual explanation of the system on Christian Griesbeck's webpage, 'Introduction to Laban Notation'.[2]

From Munich, Laban went on to Switzerland, where he established a 'movement commune' in Ascona (1911–14). There he was able to explore the *mystical* potential of music.[3] Despite possessing an extremely rational methodical mind, Laban had a penchant for the occult. His exposure as a younger man to Sufi Dervish culture, with its whirling dances and trance-like states, had created a belief in the *magical* potential of movement.[4] This, coupled with his affinity to the Rosicrucians, gave a spiritual dimension to his work. He claimed: 'Sensitizing the body to be receptive to inner and outer forces of energy . . . could lead to psychic experiences.'[5]

Following the Ascona experience, he established a school of dance and movement in Zürich. He developed the concept of the *'movement choir'*, where large numbers of people move in unison, but in a manner which includes personal expression. Between 1919 and 1929 he branched out, establishing twenty-five Laban schools and movement choirs and dance troupes, in Austria, Germany (which became his base), Paris, Zagreb and Latvia.

Inspired by new forms emerging in the fine arts, especially in the work of Klimt, Kokoschka and Kandinsky, and the music of Arnold Schoenberg – he determined to find an equivalent in the dance. He was inspired by the Swiss composer, **Jaques-Dalcroze**, and the American dancer Isadora Duncan (1877–1927). He proposed abandoning the traditional steps, relying instead on the *music* to *structure the dance*, freeing the body to find its own rhythms and create its own steps, revelling in the medium of space. Thus, Laban gave birth to 'Der Freier Tanz' (Free Dance), and, in that sense, he can be called the Father of Modern Dance.[6]

In 1927 he moved to Berlin, opening the Choreographisches Institut, from where he initiated several Dance Congresses. In 1930, Laban was made director of the Prussian State Theatres, until 1934, when he was promoted to director of the Deutsche Tanzbühne – an 'official' appointment under the aegis of Josef Goebbels, Propaganda Minister – a position in which he sometimes felt restrained in having to compromise his principles.[7] In 1936 he fell out of favour over the production of a large movement choir to celebrate the opening of the Olympic Games, which Goebbels found too 'individualistic' – he banned the work.[8]

Feeling that his days in Nazi Germany were numbered, Laban used permission to travel to Paris as a stepping stone to England. By 1937 he was making ends meet by teaching in residence at Dartington Hall in Devon, a progressive arts centre in a medieval estate. Upon arrival he had just missed meeting another Dartington Hall émigré teacher, **Michael Chekhov**, who had, only weeks before, re-emigrated to the USA. The campus was still buzzing from Chekhov's influence, and Laban was able to learn much, albeit second-hand, concerning Chekov's idea of *Psychological Gesture* as the door to an 'inner quality'.[9]

During the War he was employed by the British Government, who asked him to use his techniques of Labanotation of movement to do time-and-motion studies in factories for the War production effort. Just as **Meyerhold** had used Frederick Winslow Taylor's time-and-motion studies for the efficient movement of his actor.[10] Laban based much of his theories on 'Fordism' – motion analysis pioneered by Henry Ford in the USA to analyse assembly-line workers movements in the manufacturing processes.[11]

In 1946, in partnership with Lisa Ullmann, Laban opened the Art of Movement Studio in Manchester. He and the school moved to Addlestone in Surrey in 1953. He died five years later. In 1975, the school moved to south London where it exists today as the Trinity Laban Conservatoire of Music and Dance. Having little regard for the materialistic aspects of life, Laban was always poor, never owning a home or possessions. He left nothing but his papers when he died, in addition to nine children somewhere in Europe, progeny of two marriages which had fizzled out by 1919.[12] His publishing legacy consists of ninety-seven books and articles, including *Modern Educational Dance* (1948),[13] a basic handbook for teaching dance which is still in use in many British schools.

Laban's contribution to dance is indisputable. In terms of acting, he emphasized mime as a core skill – it is the pure expression of movement: 'Mime, built on movement occurrences, both in its content and form, is the basic theatrical art.' The performer's 'truth' lies in mime. 'Too many words and too much music are both apt to overshadow the truth of this effort display as it becomes apparent through the performer's bodily actions.'[14]

Laban followed his earlier analytical work on Labanotation for dance, with the study of 'kinesiology' (i.e. body movement), for which he developed a theoretical framework which he named 'Laban Movement Analysis' (LMA). The two basic elements of LMA are 'Eukinetics', the study of *effort*, and 'Choreutics', the study of *spatial harmony*. For these theoretical constructs he applied numerous practical exercises for actors, incorporating what he saw as the *four basic elements of movement*: Time, Weight, Space, and Flow. 'Effort' – a key concept – was defined as 'the inner impulses from which movement originates'; the manifestation of in-the-moment impulses engendered by feelings or emotions.[15] This part of his analysis relates to the questions posed by **Stanislavski** and Meyerhold as to *what generates action*. These four elements were expanded in the theoretical constructs of later practitioners such as Mary Overlie and **Anne Bogart**.

While Laban's influence on modern dance is incalculable – in theatre, it's noteworthy, but not seminal – much more appropriate to physical, than realistic theatre. Most British drama schools today teach a module on Laban. **Joan Littlewood** used Laban movements in interpreting Brecht. **Peter Brook** was a fan. In France, **Jacques Copeau's** exercises were influenced by Laban, and he, in turn, influenced **LeCoq**. Laban was a friend and correspondent of psychiatrist Carl Jung (1875–1961), as well as physiotherapist Joseph Pilates (1983–1967).

The best way to understand LMA is to practice some of the exercises. For that, I recommend Barbara Adrian's book, *Actor Training the Laban Way: An Integrated Approach to Voice, Speech, and Movement*, which lays out the principles clearly, and maps out a series of exercises from basic to advanced level.

The LMA is analytical, theory-based, and demands self-consciousness on the part of the actor, so cannot be considered a useful frontline acting tool for a Meisner- or Method-trained actor. Its value is in honing the actor's 'instrument', as per **Stanislavski's** notion of the 'actor's work on himself'. It can be used as a functional skillset to support the actor's expressive impulses, alongside, or *in lieu* of, Pilates, **Feldenkrais** and **Alexander Technique**.

Further reading

Barbara Adrian, *Actor Training the Laban Way: An Integrated Approach to Voice, Speech, and Movement* (New York: Allworth Press, 2008).
Rudolf Laban, *The Mastery of Movement* (London: Macdonald & Evans, 1960).
Rudolf Laban and F. C. Lawrence, *Effort: Economy of Human Movement* (Plymouth: Macdonald and Evans Ltd, 1974).

Notes

1. Laban, *Mastery*, 98.
2. Labanotation illustrated by Christian Griesbeck, 1996: https://studylib.net/doc/5868566/introduction-to-labanotation
3. Adrian, 29.
4. Ibid.
5. Ibid., 26.
6. Trinity Laban Conservatoire of Music and Dance, London, website: https://www.trinitylaban.ac.uk/about-us/our-history/rudolf-laban, 4.
7. In 1933 Laban allegedly exclusively selected Aryan candidates for his dance school. Source: Lillian Karina and Marion Kant, *Hitler's Dancers: German Modern Dance and the Third Reich*, trans. J. Steinberg (New York and Oxford: Berghahn Books, 2003).
8. Adrian, 32.
9. Vladimir Mirodan, 'The Way of Transformation (The Laban Malgrem System of Dramatic Character Analysis)', PhD diss., University of London (1997), 31.
10. For a full discussion of Meyerhold's use of 'Taylorism' see Eduard Braun and Jonathan Pitches, *Meyerhold on Theatre*, 4th ed. (London: Bloomsbury, 2016), 70.
11. Adrian, 32.
12. Trinity Laban website, 3.
13. Rudolf Laban, *Modern Educational Dance* (London: Macdonald and Evans, 1948).
14. Rudolf Laban, *The Mastery of Movement* (London: Macdonald & Evans, 1960), 10.
15. Ibid., 18.

17 Yevgeny Vakhtangov
1883–1922

One must surrender entirely to the power of one's artistic nature. It will do all the necessary things. Don't impose any solution upon yourself in advance. The quality to develop in an actor is courage.[1]

In the constellation of Russian star directors created by the 'Stanislavski effect' in the early twentieth century, the 'supernova', Yevgeny Vakhtangov, burned brightly, then burned out, suddenly, at the young age of thirty-nine. He was a friend of and fellow traveller with **Michael Chekhov**, **Vsevolod Meyerhold** and **Richard Boleslavsky.** He was a favourite student of **Stanislavski**, Sulerjitksy and **Nemirovich-Danchenko**. He was a central force in the development of the First and Third Studios of the Moscow Arts Theatre, and the Jewish Habima Theatre. He was a teacher of 'the system', and a transformer of Stanislavski's ideas in ways that would, in turn, inform and transform the master's own investigations. Several of the paradoxes and dilemmas of the art of drama posed by Stanislavski were resolved by Vakhtangov in the final two years of his short creative life.[2]

Yevgeny Vakhtangov's recruitment to the Moscow Arts Theatre by Sulerjitsky and Nemirovich-Danchenko in March 1911 was endorsed by Stanislavski, who quickly pegged him as a better teacher/director, than actor.[3] He possessed well-practiced stenographic skills and took copious notes of his early sessions with Stanislavski, who quickly took him on as an assistant teacher. Stanislavski affectionately used him as a model for Kostya – the keen young actor-in-training who was the narrator of his book, *An Actor Prepares*. When the First Studio was formed in 1913, Vakhtangov was appointed 'leader', sharing the teaching responsibilities with Sulerjitsky. In that capacity it's said that he was able to articulate the 'master's' ideas more clearly than the man himself, and subsequently, to modify them and incorporate them into his own production methodology.

Vakhtangov's first production for the First Studio was a German play, *Das Friedensfest* ('The Peace Festival'). When Stanislavski and Nemirovich-Danchenko attended the dress rehearsal they found it overly didactic and political – at variance with MAT principles – and *too naturalistic*.[4] They grudgingly permitted the play to open, but it caused an artistic rift in the master-pupil relationship which never quite healed, and which galvanized Vakhtangov to plough his own furrow artistically.[5] He set up his own school which in 1920 became the Third Studio of the MAT.

Central to Vakhtangov's approach was the idea of 'Creative Individuality'. Each actor is unique and deserves a different 'approach' from the director. This creativity is sourced from *within* – it relates to the actor's individual psyche, and it is what they brings to the performance. According to Vakhtangov an actor should never force or predetermine emotions.

> Everyone feels differently. If feelings do not come to an actor – he should not imitate them. Without feelings – what is there to act? Whatever combination of feelings creates itself – an actor should allow it.[6]

He shared this emphasis on the actor's innate creativity with fellow Stanislavski 'acolyte', **Nikolai Demidov**.

Stylistically, Vakhtangov's mature directorial work represent a reconciliation of Stanislavski's Realism and Meyerhold's experimental ideas. By the early 1920s there was an emerging general trend towards 'non-naturalistic' acting, which led Vakhtangov to experiment with the concept of 'The Grotesque' – which he first applied to a 1921 First Studio production of August Strindberg's *Erik XIV*. Michael Chekhov allegedly gave an engrossing performance as the Swedish king, in which he had managed to capture a deep 'inner truth' while wearing exaggerated non-realistic makeup, characteristic of the style.[7] Stanislavski was intrigued by the work. He interviewed Vakhtangov about The Grotesque and deduced that the style demanded a 'vivid, external, audacious justification of enormous inner context, which is so all-embracing as to verge on exaggeration . . . going to the brink of over-acting.' Vakhtangov maintained that The Grotesque was something that only a highly talented actor could achieve, because it involves an enormous creative energy springing from the unconscious.[8]

At this time, Stanislavski became involved in a company of Jewish actors resident in Moscow, who had petitioned the MAT for support. With them he re-established the Habima Theatre Company, and – feeling overstretched by his own obligations – appointed Vakhtangov to run it. Stalin signed its charter. The 'master' lectured the young actors – when available – but young Yevgeny whipped them into shape along Stanislavskian lines. In 1921 he staged with the troupe what was to become another twentieth century landmark production, *The Dybbuk* – in a style he called Fantastic Realism. The play concerned a young woman who on the day of her marriage is possessed by an ugly spirit called a dybbuk. The production ran continually until 1926, when the company set off on a world tour. At home in Stalinist Russia things were getting 'tricky' – the work had been branded 'counter-revolutionary'. The tour ended up in Palestine, where the entire troupe settled. The Habima Company eventually evolved into what is now the Tel-Aviv Habima – the National Theatre of Israel. Vakhtangov's 'grotesque' treatment of *The Dybbuk* predated – and probably influenced – the 'Theatre of Cruelty' of **Antonin Artaud** (1896–1948). It caused one critic to say: 'In *The Dybbuk* Vakhtangov demonstrated how cruel his talent was, how dear the beauty of ugliness was to his soul'.[9]

The second, and last example of Fantastic Realism was the Third Studio production of Count Carlo Gozzi's (1720–1806) fairy-tale, *Princess Turandot* (1922), based in *commedia dell'arte*, using improvisational techniques, and expressionist design (towels were used as beards, and a tennis racket as a sceptre). The mechanics of theatre were on full display – the actors changed costumes and applied makeup on stage. This production became a theatrical landmark, regularly reprised down through the years since 1922. Vakhtangov's approach was to bring the actor's *point of view* towards their character into the foreground, foreshadowing **Brecht's** principle of 'alienation'.[10]

Despite his *penchant* for non-naturalistic stylization, the essence of Vakhtangov's approach lies in the Stanislavskian belief in the actor's faith on the stage – the moment of truth.

> Psychological, inner truth – is the great truth. Truth is what I believe at this particular moment . . . When the falseness of theatrical events becomes truth for an actor – this is stage truth.[11]

This 'truth' he called '*inner justification*', and, unlike Stanislavski, he said it didn't have to come from the given circumstances of the play, but the actor could invent his own secret reality to justify their actions. This is what **Sanford Meisner** later proposed with the actor's '*as if*'. Vakhtangov shared Stanislavski's idea that the script must be approached in 'bits' (which we now call 'beats'), and that only when one part was mastered should one move on to the next.[12] Like his mentor he believed in *action*.

> Only things active are worthy of the stage . . . Without action nothing onstage is received [by the audience] . . . When a human being lives passively, he cannot convey his feelings.[13]

In terms of his legacy, Vakhtangov influenced both the *realists* and those looking *beyond* realism, including **Brecht**, **Artaud**, **Peter Brook**, and, of course, **Jerzy Grotowski**, who trained in Moscow under Vakhtangov's protégée, Yuri Zavadsky (1894–1977).

Vakhtangov's pedagogy arrived in the USA via the **Group Theatre**. During one of their summer retreats, a visiting MAT actor left a copy of an essay by Vakhtangov, entitled 'Preparing the Role' – in Russian, of course. Fortuitously, the camp cook spoke the language and obligingly translated the article, then read it to the assembled actors after dinner one night. They were enthralled with Vakhtangov's lucid articulation of Stanislavski's early principles – none more so than **Lee Strasberg**, who was drawn to the Vakhtangov's notions of 'inner justification' and 'creative individuality', reinforcing his own emphasis on individual psychology. Apart from his biography, *My Life in Art,* 1924, Stanislavski had not yet published a textbook setting out his 'system'. In Vakhtangov's 'Preparing the Role' Lee Strasberg had found his Bible!

Sadly, there were no further English-language publications of Vakhtangov's writings before Malaev-Babel's translations and biography (2011–13). The chef's translation of Vakhtangov's essay appeared in *Acting: A Handbook of the Stanislavski Method* in 1947, containing treatises from Stanislavski and his acolytes, but based solely on early work at the First Studio.[14]

On his trip to Moscow in 1934, Strasberg saw the reprised version of Vakhtangov's *Turandot* and was impressed that, even with its theatricality, the roots of the 'system' were in evidence.[15] He said:

> If you examine the work of the Stanislavski System as made use of by Stanislavski, you see one result. If you examine it in the work of one of his great pupils, Vakhtangov – who influenced our thinking and activity – you will see a completely different result. Vakhtangov's work was skilfully done, his use of the Method even more brilliant and more imaginative than Stanislavski's . . . [16]

Yevgeny Vakhtangov died of cancer at the age of thirty-nine. He was convinced that the new theatrical forms he was exploring were in the service of the Revolution, yet had he lived it's likely that by expounding his doctrine of 'creative individuality' he would have quickly fallen out of favour with the authorities and been marginalized along with Meyerhold.

To anxious students trying to 'find' their character I am fond of quoting Vakhtangov . . . 'We don't need characters, characterizations. Everything you have makes up your characterization; you have individuality – this is your character.'[17]

Further reading

Andrei Malaev-Babel, ed. and trans., *The Vakhtangov Sourcebook* (Abingdon: Routledge, 2011).
Andrei Malaev-Babel, *Yevgeny Vakhtangov: A Critical Portrait* (Abingdon: Routledge, 2013).

Notes

1. Malaev-Babel, *Sourcebook,* 99.
2. Laurence Senelick, *Historical Dictionary of Russian Theatre* (Lanham, MD: The Scarecrow Press, 2007), 419.
3. Jean Benedetti, *Stanislavski: A Biography* (London: Methuen, 1988), 207.
4. Malaev-Babel, *Critical Portrait,* 73. The leading actress reported: 'He accused us of naturalism – we probably truly became too zealous in our striving for the truth of life in its most heavy and ugly expressions.'
5. Benedetti, 233.
6. Malaev-Babel, *Sourcebook*, 10–11.
7. Benedetti, 257.

8. Ibid., citing a note from Stanislavski in 'The Last Conversation with Yevgeni Vakhtangov'.
9. Malaev-Babel, *Sourcebook*, 5.
10. Malaev-Babel, *Critical Portrait*, 2.
11. Malaev-Babel, *Sourcebook*, 92.
12. Ibid., 95.
13. Ibid., 95–6.
14. Toby Cole, *Acting: A Handbook of the Stanislavski Method* (New York: Lear, 1947), 116–24.
15. Paul Gray, ed., 'Stanislavski and America: A Critical Chronology', *The Tulane Drama Review*, Winter, 1964, Vol. 9, No. 2: 35.
16. Cited in Wikipedia article on Vakhtangov: https://en.wikipedia.org/wiki/Yevgeny_Vakhtangov, edited 31 January 2021.
17. Malaev-Babel, *Sourcebook,* 21.

18 Nikolai Demidov
1884–1953

After Stanislavsky and Nemirovich-Danchenko, Nikolai Demidov, is the largest figure in Russian, Soviet theater. And, perhaps, no less large than Stanislavsky and Nemirovich.[1]

Oleg Okulevich

This extravagant tribute from a respected Russian film and theatre actor caught my attention. The name of Demidov had popped up several times during my research on Russian theatre, and he appeared to be highly regarded by all sources. Investigations revealed that, like the epithet applied to Sanford Meisner, 'Hollywood's Best Kept Secret', Nikolai Demidov is sometimes called 'Russian Theatre's Best Kept Secret'.[2] In common, both men took the best of **Stanislavski's** pedagogy, and incorporated it into an effective methodology for creating *truthful* performances.

While still a young man undertaking his studies in psychiatry and homeopathy (with a side-line in yoga) at the University of Moscow Medical School, he was introduced to **Konstantin Stanislavski** by his good friend, Leopold Sulerjitsky (see **From Russia with Love**). They hit it off, and Demidov formed a personal friendship with the 'master', who enlisted the young man to tutor one of his sons. He effectively became a family friend. Demidov had done some acting in his youth, and during his years of medical study he was increasingly drawn into Sulerjitsky's world, attending classes at the First Studio. He completed his medical degree and dutifully entered practice as a psychologist, but remained drawn to his personal interest in theatre. In 1919, encouraged by Sulerjitsky and Stanislavski, he abandoned practice and joined them in the Opera Studio. He showed great aptitude for the 'system', even to the extent that Stanislavski consulted him as an editor for *An Actor Prepares*. It was most likely Demidov who persuaded Stanislavski to incorporate elements of yoga into his methods. Demidov grew to be a master teacher of Stanislavski's 'system' during the height of its development. He was founding Director of the Fourth Studio (1921–5). Once, near the time of his death, Stanislavski proclaimed that Demidov was the *only student* who understood 'the system'. When the MAT troupe left for its tour of the USA in 1922, Demidov became Director of the Moscow Art Theatre School.

Up until the breakout of the Second World War, he continued being an influential teacher working in several Russian acting institutions. As he did so his ideas crystallized – beginning to diverge from, and even contradict elements of 'the system', challenging the 'governmentalized' version of Stanislavski promoted by the Stalinist ideologues. In common with Stanislavski, Demidov focused on the theatre of 'experiencing', looking for *truth* in-the-moment on stage. But he concluded that Stanislavski's approach was too analytical and fragmented.

> By rationally dividing into elements the indivisible creative process, we murdered the main thing: spontaneity and the involuntary nature of life onstage, i.e. we murdered the creative process itself.[3]

Demidov wrote five incisive volumes on actor training, which he dubbed *The System for Practical Pedagogy of Acting*, containing revisions of Stanislavski's methods, and based on the deepest respect for the master's efforts to create the *science* of the actor's art. Both for political reasons and professional territorialism, his writings did not appear in print in Russia until after the beginning of this century. He had dared to bring the 'subconscious' back into the discussion – a dirty word in Stalinist Russia. In 2016 the five volumes were edited, abridged and published in English, in a single book, *Becoming an Actor-Creator* (details below).

The second of these volumes, *Actor Types*, proposes four generic types of actor, each with self-descriptive names:the Imitator, the Emotional (or emotionally wilful), the Rationalist (or rationally wilful) and the Affective (meaning 'passionate'). He proposed that the actor should understand to which type they belong *by nature* and pursue training in that specific vein.

For Demidov, the *Affective* actor is the most desirable type, because they are much closer *to the subconscious*. In Russian, affective emotion means *heightened* or *passionate* emotion. Demidov's 'Affective Technique' was subsequently adopted by **Vakhtangov**. In lieu of Stanislavski's idea that the actor should live truthfully via the *given circumstances*, Demidov and Vakhtangov proposed that the actor should live through a heightened perception, passionately – 'the creative state' – overriding, as it were, the reality of the stage.

> An actor creates a new artistic reality on top of the actual reality of the stage . . . included in it, but it is so insignificant in comparison with the new artistic reality that it literally dissolves in it.[4]

This idea is not antithetical to **Sanford Meisner's** teaching, in that when the actor lives off the emotions engendered by their 'as-if', it allows a 'heightened perception' of what's going on in the scene which surmounts the given circumstances.

Demidov suggests that acting in-the-moment involves a sort of 'cognitive automatism', which is to say that *action* is *not* the starting point – *perception* is.

> A different law of stage behaviour has now developed and formulated itself; action does not constitute the primary cause of our emotional state: rather our perception should be considered the primary cause, both of our action and of our emotional state.[5]

This required the use of a uniquely different type of *étude*. Stanislavski's improvisations sprung from an analysis of the characters' objectives. Demidov and Vakhtangov proposed improvising from a stripped-down version of the text which allowed one to act, based on one's gut feelings in the scene – working through *perceptions*.

Demidov urged his students to have the courage to freely go with their impulses – which emanated from the subconscious – without knowing where they might lead, and to have the patience to wait for an impulse when there was none. He described the character's 'essence' as the 'embryo'. The embryo is something discovered in the first reading of the script – something intuitive, lying within the subconscious of actor, which relates to the character, appearing 'as soon as they understand a role, feel it, and begin to burn with desire to act it.'[6] As the role develops, the embryo remains in the centre of it. A gradual, 'organic' rehearsal process is required for the embryo to develop into a full-blown role.'[7]

After the death of Stanislavski, Stalin's 'thought police' denounced and hounded Demidov. His case for the role of the subconscious in acting resulted in a ban from teaching. His name was removed from the history of the Moscow Arts Theatre and all Russian theatre studies. He retired to the provinces to escape persecution, only returning to Moscow for health reasons, spending his last three years in ill health trying to complete his writings. He died in 1953.

Demidov Technique, using *études*, is once again being taught in Russia. In the USA specialist Andrei Malaev-Babel currently teaches Demidov Technique at the Florida State University Asolo Conservatory, and in London it is now taught at the Demidov Studio.

Further reading

Nikolai Demidov, *Nikolai Demidov: Becoming an Actor-Creator*, eds and trans. Andrei Malaev-Babel and Margarita Laskina (New York: Routledge, 2016).

Andrei Malaev-Babel, 'Nikolai Demidov – Russian Theatre's Best Kept Secret', *Stanislavski Studies*, 3:1 (2015): 69–81.

Notes

1. https://en.wikipedia.org/wiki/Nikolai Vasilievich_Demidov, last revised 4 October 2022. Oleg Okulevich (1921–2006) was a well-known theatre and screen actor who was a student of Demidov and was married to Demidov's biographer, Margarita Laskina.
2. Demidov, 30.7 / 2499.
3. Ibid., 45.7 / 2944.
4. Malaev-Babel, *Best Kept Secret*, 70.
5. Ibid. (The debate over which comes first, cognition or emotion, is covered in **Working with Actors**, **'What's Love Got to Do with It?'**)
6. Demidov, 570.0 / 2944.
7. Andrei Malaev-Babel, ed. and trans., *The Vakhtangov Sourcebook* (Abingdon: Routledge, 2011), 23.

19 Charles Dullin
1885–1949

Charles Dullin . . . his playing sometimes brought to mind an image of a pneumatic drill penetrating the toughest of walls.[1]

Antonin Artaud

To say that Charles Dullin had an 'exceptional' childhood is an understatement. He was born the youngest child of eighteen children (only thirteen survived), of a father aged sixty-four and a mother of forty. His father, Jacques Dullin, a judge, who by all accounts had an admirably kind disposition, had regularly impregnated his forbearing wife since marrying her at the age of sixteen. Charles was not the most robust of infants and suffered fragile health during most of his life.[2]

They lived in a crumbling old medieval castle named Châtelard, which, according to Charles's sister, Pauline, was 'enchanted'. It was thought locally that the house was peopled with ghosts of the dead. There appeared to be an actual *living* one as well – an 'unbalanced' uncle Joseph, living in seclusion in one of the towers, who beguiled young Charles with the poems of LaFontaine and the plays of Molière, and who the boy discovered many years later, was not an *uncle* at all, but an *aunt*.[3] Possibly the 'magical' atmosphere of his childhood contributed to Dullin's penchant for mystery, fantasy, the metaphysical and the theatrical, which he brought to his acting and his teaching. **Antonin Artaud** said of him, 'Hearing Dullin teach I feel that I'm rediscovering ancient streets and a whole forgotten mystique of production'.[4] Jean-Louis Barrault (1910–94), actor and mime artist, quoted him, 'My vocation for the stage is made up of all these fantasies which people my childhood.'[5]

Charles Dullin was a well-known and much-loved French actor of stage and screen during the 1930s, with an impressive body of work. But he is best remembered as a teacher, counting amongst his students Artaud, Jean-Louis Barrault and Marcel Marceau (1923-2007).

He was a member of **Jacques Copeau's** original Vieux-Colombier troupe, in 1913, at the age of twenty-eight, then again in 1917–18. The gap was due to the Great War, when actor members of Copeau's company, including Dullin, melted away into the ranks of the French Army. Dullin was sent to the frontline, but instead of twiddling his thumbs while waiting for the War to finish, he formed his own company of amateur soldier actors, specializing in improvisations.[6]

At that time Copeau had been sent as a cultural emissary to the USA and was setting up in the Théâtre Français in New York. He was able to reconstitute the Vieux-Colombier in Manhattan, as his actors, including Dullin, obtained dispensations from Army service. Before leaving France for his transatlantic voyage, Dullin, an avid horseman and lover of the silent Wild West films of actor William S. Hart (1864–1946), bought for himself a red bandana and cowboy hat, imagining them to be *de rigeur* apparel in the USA.[7]

When Dullin originally joined the Vieux-Colombier experiment in 1913, he already had a body of professional work behind him, and much practical experience. Since abandoning his studies in a seminary as a youth, he had worked his way up the ladder in theatre, apprenticing with walk-ons, then playing melodrama in small theatres, eventually moving up to larger naturalistic roles with director André Antoine at the Odéon Theatre.

From the outset, Dullin had a conflictive relationship with Copeau, which he described as being more *master-student* than *director-actor*.[8] On one hand, the two men shared a passion for theatre and the belief that it needed renewal. They became great personal friends. Dullin, wrote to Copeau from the frontlines, confessing his undying admiration for his mentor ('I believe in you') and his steadfast loyalty ('You must count on me until death').[9] Nonetheless, from his earliest days in the company, Dullin criticized Copeau for being too literary in his approach. 'Copeau and I don't see eye-to-eye. He is basically less alive than me. He is a literary type and prefers books to reality.'[10] Later in life, he admitted that he greatly admired Copeau for his respect for the text, and the narrative line of the work, and admitted that, at least in that area, he had learned much.[11] Dullin engaged in his own acting with ferocious energy (see Artaud's comment in the epigraph), and he dreamed of creating a theatre which was actor-centric rather than text-centric.

The rupture occurred while in the USA. There was much discontent on the part of the troupe, feeling that they were being pushed beyond their physical limits of endurance (twenty-six productions in one year), and were being exploited financially. When Copeau, mentally and physically exhausted, abandoned his group to go to a country retreat, rebellion fomented. When he returned, he fired a few of the actors. Dullin took their side and tendered his resignation.

Having left the Vieux-Colombier, he began to mix acting jobs and teaching gigs in Paris. Then, in 1921, he established his own 'laboratory theatre', the Théâtre de l'Atelier, in an old barn in Néronville, 84 km (52 miles) south of Paris. In August of that year, he published its manifesto. 'Theatre is like life, multifarious, fluid and mysterious, while its basic elements remain eternally the same.'[12] The initial intake of students was small, and the group lived communally. Dullin was copying Copeau in the attempt to build an *ensemble*, and work without distraction in the countryside. Among the 'communards' was Antonin Artaud, who studied with Dullin for the next eighteen months. In 1922, the Théâtre de l'Atelier established its base in Paris in the Théâtre Montmartre, and there it remained until the onset of the Second World War.

Dullin's methods were eclectic but conformed to one central idea – to strip acting of its artificiality, as practiced on the stages of the 'Boulevard' and replace it with something organic which emanates from the soul of actor. Like Stanislavski, he believed in the 'complete actor': good diction, a fully developed voice, and physical training to expand the actor's means of expression, including dance and pantomime. Dullin's classes lasted ten or twelve hours per day and included demanding physical training such as gymnastics. The actor's work on themself preceded the work on the role. An actor had to 'look and see before describing, hear before answering his partners, and feel before trying to express himself'.[13]

This quest for the actor's truth mirrored what Stanislavski wrote in *An Actor's Work on Himself*. Stanislavski hadn't yet published, but it is probable that Dullin acquired some formal knowledge of these methods via Aleksandr Sokolov (1906–96) and Muni Seroff (1895–1979), former students of the Moscow Arts Theatre, who taught from time-to-time in Dullin's atelier during the 1930s.

Dullin's actor-training programme included improvisation – the effectiveness of which he had discovered with his amateur soldier troupe during the War. It was a relatively new concept at the time. They helped the actor to *interiorize* the moment, instead of *acting* it. Much of this work related to creating *sensations* felt in Nature. An example might be to improvise a walk in the forest, using all five senses to create an imaginary experience. He contended that first of all the actor needed to get in tune with '*la Voix du Monde*' (Voice of the World), by making contact with one's surroundings. This would then enable the actor to reach their own true voice, '*la Voix de Soi-Même*'.[14] Jean-Louis Barrault, who studied with Dullin from about 1931, put it simply: 'He was teaching us authenticity in our sensations; to feel before expressing.'[15]

Another of Dullin's innovations in improvisation was the use of the mask. The mask was substituted, in some measure, for the actor's personality. The forced depersonalization of the actor, and the introduction of the sacred and mystical were Dullin's *counterpoints* to the personal, psychological approaches of realistic acting. Artaud was greatly taken by the use of masks (as discussed in his chapter), and took the idea into performance, whereas Dullin thought their use was only suitable for improvisations.

The theatre of the Orient was another of Dullin's interests. He taught aspects of Japanese and Chinese acting methods in his classes, which inspired Artaud, in turn, in his explorations. But, unlike Artaud, he didn't propose to adapt Oriental theatre lock, stock and barrel, appropriating its language and style, but only to use *certain* of its techniques to help create a more organic and physical actor. It could be said that Artaud, in his largely theoretical work, tended to push Dullin's modest ideas to the extreme.

Further reading

Clément Borgal, *Metteurs en Scène* (Paris: Fernand Lanore, 1963).
František Deák, 'Antonin Artaud and Charles Dullin: Artaud's Apprenticeship in Theatre,' *Educational Theatre Journal*, Vol. 29, No. 3, October 1977.
Thomas John Donahue, *Jacques Copeau's Friends and Disciples* (New York: Peter Lang, 2008).

Notes

1. Antonin Artaud, *Oeuvres Complètes*, Vol. viii (Paris: Gallimard, 1971), 215.
2. Borgal, 99.
3. Ibid., 100.
4. Deák, 315.
5. Ibid., 350.
6. Donahue, 78.
7. Deák, 305.
8. Borgal, 107.
9. Donahue, 79.
10. Borgal, 106. *'Copeau n'est pa tout à fait de mon avis. C'est qu'au fond il est moins vivant que moi. C'est un litéraire qui préfère les livres à la réalité.'*
11. Ibid.
12. J. Rudin and N. Paul, *Copeau Texts on Theatre* (Abingdon: Routledge, 1990), 224.
13. Deák, 347.
14. Ibid.
15. Ibid., 349.

20 Richard Boleslavsky
1889–1937
The American Lab Theatre
1923–1933

An actor cannot be made between lunch and dinner.[1]

Boleslaw Ryszard Srzednicki (aka Richard Boleslavsky) was the *connection* and *conduit* for the enthusiastic American adoption of the Stanislavskian method of acting, which changed the face of dramatic art in the USA and saw what was known as the 'Russian' style of acting transformed into what became the 'American Style' (see **From Russia with Love**).

Scion of an aristocratic family, he moved to Moscow from a part of that country under the control of the Russian Czar. **Stanislavski** had accepted him for the Moscow Arts Theatre in 1906 with the caveat that he lose his Polish accent – which he successfully managed to do. He enrolled in Stanislavski's programme of teaching at the time that the master himself was developing his 'system' and became a leading actor in the MAT troupe. In 1912, along with **Maria Ouspenskaya**, he was one of the founding students in the First Studio, for which, in 1916, he was appointed joint head, alongside **Yevgeny Vakhtangov**. In the midst of the chaos of the continuing Bolshevik revolution swirling around the MAT in the Moscow streets, he directed a very successful *Twelfth Night*, with **Michael Chekhov** excelling as Malvolio. By 1919 his relationship with Stanislavski had deteriorated,[2] and in April 1920 he escaped with his Russian wife, Natasha, and a group of actors, across the border into the newly formed Poland.

In Warsaw Richard put his talents to use directing a couple of spectacles in the Teatr Polski, and to making a documentary for the Ministry of War celebrating the Polish victory at the Vistula River over the Soviet forces. He also landed a role in a German silent film directed by Danish director Carl Theodor Dreyer (1889–1968). He joined a group of ex-MAT actors who formed the Moscow Art Theatre of Prague and directed a noteworthy *Hamlet* which toured Vienna and Berlin. When the Prague MAT disbanded Boleslavsky stayed in Berlin. By the early 1920s Berlin was teeming with ex-patriot White Russians – and Paris, more so. Using émigré talent, Richard mounted the *Revue Russe*, a cabaret show imitating the extremely popular Russian language *La Chauve-Souris*, which had originated at the MAT in Moscow with producer-director Nikita Balieff, and was playing to acclaim in Berlin, and later Paris.

Serendipity was at work – the show was spotted in Paris by Elizabeth (Bessie) Marbury – an irrepressible top New York impresario, Francophile, and one of the first females in the business. Her competitor, the famous producer Morris Gest, had already brought *La Chauve-Souris* to the US, with great success. Hoping for the same, Bessie booked the *Revue Russe*, with its director and compère, to open in New York and Philadelphia. Thus, Richard Boleslavsky was able to make his way to the USA.

The show opened on 5 October 1922 and was a flop. It died after twenty-one performances.[3] Bessie, at that point sixty-six, and winding down her career, got on with publishing her autobiography, *My Crystal Ball*.[4] Boleslavsky, who had had a busy but chaotic time after leaving Russia in 1920, decided to stay on for a while and try his fortune in New York, with one eye on Hollywood. After several months, it looked as if staying in the USA was not going to pan out for him. He was making plans to return with his wife Natasha to Europe, when something arrived out of the blue. Morris Gest, on the back of the success of *La Chauve-Souris*, had invited the Moscow Arts Theatre to tour the USA. Stanislavski, one imagines swallowing some pride, contacted Boleslavsky and asked him to stay on, to facilitate some arrangements, and receive the group.

On 3 January 1923 the MAT arrived in New York. Boleslavsky booked the additional actors and walk-ons, and the season started. No one could have imagined the success it would have. The productions, in Russian, played to full houses wherever they travelled – 380 shows in twelve months. In New York there was a captive audience – a mixture of the intelligentsia and the Russian Yiddish immigrants from the Lower East Side. But in touring, surprisingly, the programme had equal success, as spectators marvelled at the *veracity* and *detail* in the acting the likes of which they had never seen – even if in a language they couldn't understand. Boleslavsky stood-in for several of the actors, even replacing an ailing Stanislavski in a production of *The Lower Depths*.

As the only quasi-English speaker in the group, Boleslavsky was asked by Morris Gest to give a series of lectures at the Princess Theatre on the artistic theories of the MAT. These were attended by the likes of **Harold Clurman**, **Stella Adler**, **Lee Strasberg** and Cheryl Crawford – all wildly enthusiastic – the future instigators of the **Group Theatre**. Even before the MAT had returned to Russia, *Theatre Magazine* in April 1923, published an article Boleslavsky had written: 'Stanislavsky – The Man and His Methods'.[5] This cemented his position as spokesperson and front man for the Russian theatre revolution which was taking the US by storm.

In attendance at Boleslavsky's first lecture was an enthralled Miriam Stockton, a socialite and would-be actor-writer, who described the experience 'like the coming of a new religion which could liberate and awaken American culture'.[6] It was Stockton who convinced Boleslavsky to set up the **American Lab Theatre** in 1923 and pulled together a group of interested professionals to make all the arrangements.

The original grandiose idea was that the American Lab Theatre was to have been a counterpart of the MAT in New York. The plan was to train a company of actors for three full years, before beginning public performances in a rep theatre. However, economic factors dictated an earlier start to performances, the first being mounted in April 1925 – *The Sea Woman's Cloak*. It did not get favourable reviews. The earliest hit from the theatre was in October 1925, with Boleslavsky's energetic and innovatively directed performance of *Twelfth Night*.

From the inception of the Lab Theatre, Boleslavsky's time was divided between the project and other commitments. He persuaded Maria Ouspenskaya, to join him as a teacher once she had finished her stint with the second tour of the MAT, in November 1924.

The Lab offered a full-time drama school programme, reflecting what Boleslavsky and Ouspenskaya had studied in the First Studio under Suler and Stanislavski – with potential membership in its theatre company. Teaching was divided into three sections:

1. The outer means of expression (body and voice).
2. The inner means of expression (connecting the experience and imagination of the actor to the given circumstances of the author).
3. Intellectual and cultural awareness.[7]

Maria largely concerned herself with the day-to-day teaching of the second part – the 'acting' bit – drawing on what she had learned from Suler and Stanislavski. Amongst the students attending various courses were Stella Adler, Harold Clurman and John Garfield (1913–52).

Boleslavsky's reputation was enhanced in 1933 with publication of his book, *Acting, the First Six Lessons*. Using a device similar to that of Stanislavski in *An Actor Prepares* (in which Stanislavski writes about a fictitious self in the guise of acting teacher Tortsov talking with his student, Kostya), Boleslavsky delivers his lessons autobiographically (unfortunately with a patronizing and quite sexist attitude) to a beautiful young eighteen-year-old female, given to moist eyes, who he dubs 'The Creature'. The six lessons are imparted over time so that the student has time to internalize one before moving on to the next (note this chapter's epigraph). They are based on Stanislavski's First Studio programme, and consist of:

>Concentration
>
>Memory of Emotion
>
>Dramatic Action
>
>Characterization
>
>Observation
>
>Rhythm

Boleslavsky sets out three forms of training necessary to become an actor: (1) physical training: fencing, gymnastics, dancing, or other, requiring one-and-a-half hours per day minimum; (2) intellectual training: devouring books, especially on the arts and psychology; (3) training of the soul, which is about self-discovery and understanding one's emotional makeup. The second chapter refers directly to 'affective memory', citing the French psychologist Théodule-Armand Ribot (1839–1916), from whom Stanislavski adapted the concept. The fourth chapter, 'Characterization' concerns the 'externals' – asking oneself how one's character might dress, make themself up, hold their head, or walk down a flight of stairs – all of this framed by the *period* and *place* in which the author has set the piece. In the fifth chapter he wisely enjoins the Creature to observe life in detail '. . . the only thing which can stimulate inspiration in an actor is constant and keen observation every day of his life.'[8]

It is important to note that the Lab was only imparting Stanislavski's ideas up to 1923. The later shifts in the master's thinking were not known to them. This contributed to the fact that one ardent student in the full-time course – **Lee Strasberg** – became fixated with *affective memory*, which became the basis of his own later teachings, which he dubbed 'The Method'.

Ouspenkaya's exercises became quite famous, and some – especially the 'symbol' exercises – were the subject of lampooning. Actors were asked to transform themselves physically and psychologically into objects, such as a cup of tea. By the time I did my first actor training in the 1950s, these exercises had become *de rigueur*. I remember having to 'become' a pebble on the beach, rolling on the floor as the sea washed over me. By all accounts they are still used today in drama schools. Mel Gordon has usefully documented Ouspenskaya's exercises, as well as those of the Group Theatre, Michael Chekhov, and other drama 'masters' in his book: *Stanislavsky in America: An Actor's Workbook*.[9]

Ouspenskaya, diminutive in stature (she weighed 90 lbs.), had a formidable personality. She was a chain smoker and an alcoholic – even in her Moscow MAT days. In her classes during the Prohibition era in New York, she usually had a vessel of some sort on a table next to her – a 'cough medicine bottle' or a pot of 'tea' – containing bathtub gin.[10] But withal, she had an acerbic wit, and was a scathing critic of her students' work. She insisted on being addressed as 'Madame', and that students stand at attention as she entered and exited the studio. Mel Gordon sees her as a role model for some of the American teachers who followed in her footsteps, notably Lee Strasberg, Stella Adler, **Bobby Lewis** and **Sanford Meisner** – all of whom were sharp-edged, and known to not suffer fools gladly.[11] Her legacy to American theatre is far-reaching. In her lifetime she passed on the Stanislavskian principles directly to some 1,500 students.

This doesn't account for the many thousands who were eventually tutored in turn by her former students, including the likes of Strasberg. Boleslavsky may have been the *connection*, but Ouspenskaya provided the *substance*.

In 1929, with the production side of the Lab Theatre not generating sufficient revenues and, facing the growing the disaffection of the board of directors, Boleslavsky with his increasing outside commitments, resigned. A year later, the venture closed – both the school and production wings. Following an earlier aspiration, he found his way to Hollywood, where he directed several films until his sudden death from a heart attack in the middle of filming. He was only days shy of forty-eight years of age.

Further reading

Richard Boleslavsky, *Acting: The First Six Lessons* (New York: Theatre Arts, (1933), 1987).
J. W. Roberts, *Richard Boleslavsky: His Life and Work in the Theatre* (Ann Arbor: UMI Research Press, 1981).

Notes

1. Edith J. R. Issacs, Foreword to Boleslavsky, *Acting*, 22.
2. This may have had to do with Boleslavsky's pro-Tzarist politics. Stanislavski professed to be apolitical, and Nemirovich-Danchenko was trying to steer the ship of the MAT through neutral political waters, difficult at the time. In any event, Stanislavski was angry with him for emigrating and taking with him some of the MAT actors.
3. *Playbill* online, https://playbill.com/production/revue-russe-booth-theatre-vault-0000001873
4. Elizabeth Marbury, *My Crystal Ball, Reminiscences* (New York: Boni & Liveright, 1924).
5. Richard Boleslavsky, 'Stanislavsky – The Man and His Methods: A Glimpse of the Head of the Moscow Arts Theatre and the Secret of His Success,' *Theatre*, Vol. 38 (April 1923).
6. Roberts, 108.
7. The course is quite fully described in Ronald A. Willis' article 'The American Lab Theatre' in the *Tulane Drama Review* (Autumn, 1964): 112–16.
8. Boleslavsky, 99.
9. Mel Gordon, *Stanislavsky in America* (New York: Routledge, 2010).
10. Ibid., 24.
11. Ibid., 25.

21 Michael Chekhov
1891–1955

Find an imaginary body for your character. First you define the character, then, imagine the body the character might have, then . . . you clothe yourself, as it were, with this body; you put it on like a garment. After a while you will begin to think of yourself as another person.[1]

It is said that **Stanislavski** changed his ideas about emotional memory after a classroom episode with student-actor Michael (Mikhail) Chekhov, nephew of the writer, later to become another great acting teacher. Chekhov was asked to enact a dramatic situation using 'affective memory'. He acted out very realistically a moving scene depicting the character's father's death. Stanislavski, deeply moved, assumed from the truthfulness of the performance that Chekhov had lost his own father and offered his condolences. Chekhov explained that he had cheated – the old man was alive and in sound health, and that he had *imagined* his death (a real person – imaginary circumstances). Angered by his non-compliance with the exercise, Stanislavski banned the young actor from attending class for a fortnight for his non-compliance, but a lightbulb had illuminated. He began to explore *imaginary circumstances* as a tool.[2]

Chekhov, given his relationship of being related to the writer whose play had kickstarted the success of the Moscow Arts Theatre (MAT), was hand-selected by Stanislavski in the company's early days and given preferential treatment (including private tuition) which other members of the troupe resented. But he rose above their gripes and grumbles and proved himself to be an actor of exceptional depth and quality. First for the MAT under Stanislavski, and later for the First Studio under Vakhtangov, Chekhov astonished audiences with his multi-layered characterizations – creating human beings who embodied contradictions, revealing surprising facets of a character arising from what he, the actor, confronted in the moment. In agreement with Stanislavski's later thinking, he rejected *emotional memory* in favour of *imagination* – but for Chekhov a different type of imagination was required. He proposed that the actor starts by intuiting an understanding of the character, then uses imagination emanating from their subconscious – 'cleansed of all personal [conscious] associations'.[3]

Chekhov was heavily influenced by **Yevgeny Vakhtangov**. One biographer, Charles Marowitz, has pointed out that he inherited many of that director's ideas: 'the almost total immersion in improvisation, the quest for deeply rooted living matter beneath the psychological subtext, the belief that only subconscious energy can truly ignite the actors' imagination, the conviction that *artifice* can contain a greater dollop of truth than can ever be produced by strict *verisimilitude*'.[4] Chekhov succeeded Vakhtangov as Director of the First Studio, which was subsequently renamed the Second Moscow Arts Theatre. From that position, he publicly claimed that Stanislavski's realism was bankrupt and urged moving away from the mere *'photographic'* representation of life, seeking *'truth'* in more inspiring ways. He declared that 'life on the stage differentiates itself from the everyday common place, and needs to be bold, expressive, and theatrical'.⁵ A rift developed between the 'master' and his star pupil over those pronouncements, which never fully healed.

During the Russian Revolution, Chekhov's first wife, silent film star Olga Tschechowa (1897–1980) divorced him to take up with her lover. He was devastated. Emerging, via hypnotism, from a long bout of alcoholism and depression – these were life-long tendencies – Chekhov discovered the esoteric quasi-mystical ideas of the Austrian philosopher, Rudolf Steiner (1861–1925). Steiner promoted the concept of *anthroposophy*, defined as 'a pathway to developing a conscious awareness of one's humanity'.⁶ Chekhov began to incorporate this idea of the subconscious and its relationship to a collective unconscious in his work as Artistic Director of the Second MAT. Steiner proposed: 'Whenever art is formed from a truly artistic conviction it bears witness to the connection of the human being with the supersensible world'.⁷ Chekhov began to explore how the actor can access the unconscious creative 'higher' self through indirect non-analytical means. These ideas were labelled as 'mysticism' by the authorities. He was told to drop them and to immediately desist from his 'Steiner-style' approach to *Hamlet*, which was playing to rapt Moscow audiences at the time. He refused. A warrant was issued for his arrest. He and his second wife, Xenia, left the country before it was served, and they never returned. All references to his association with the MAT were eradicated from their records, and for the next fifty-odd years his autobiography and teachings were banned in the Soviet Union.⁸

Before leaving Chekhov's MAT era, I must mention the influence of Leopold Sulerjitsky (who possibly merits a chapter of his own). A free-spirited chap who had been a fisherman, sailor, farmhand, revolutionary, sometimes indigent, and a friend to Count Leo Tolstoy (1828–1910), Sulerjitsky spent a year in Canada, at the behest of Tolstoy, acting as a sort of major-domo for a cult which had emigrated from the Caucasus in search of religious freedom. Named the Doukhobors, they rejected all church and civil authority, obeying only their 'inner light'.

Returning to Russia, Sulerjitsky ended up as an odd job man at the MAT. His interest and aptitude soon made him an indispensable asset to the theatre, and he became assistant to, and later collaborator with Stanislavski and Vakhtangov (see **From Russia with Love**). It is to Sulerjitsky, encouraged by **Nikolai Demidov**, to whom we can directly attribute both Stanislavski's and Chekhov's interest in the practice of yoga. The concept of 'the inner light' which he had learned from the Doukhobors, fed directly into the more transcendental ideas of Stanislavski, and was a good fit with Chekhov's version of Steiner's *anthroposophy*.⁹

In Germany – Chekhov's first country of refuge – he had some success as an actor, albeit in lighter fare, but was unable to establish a company as he had wished. Additionally, there was the looming threat of Nazism. He was tempted to resettle in Lithuania when he was offered the prospect of having his own ensemble – a plan which foundered when the Fascist majority solidified their control there. Conveniently, he was invited to the USA to form a touring company called the Moscow Art Players and to be its principal actor. Following a short season in America, with only limited success, Chekhov was enticed by wealthy progressive philanthropists Dorothy Elmhirst (1887–1968) and her husband Leonard (1893–1974) to move to England and found a school and company at their Dartington Hall arts complex in Devon. It was a very rewarding time for Chekhov. His student company was talented and attentive to his teachings (Russian actor Yul Brynner joined at one point), and their work was highly praised. In 1938, **Bobby Lewis**, in London directing a play, dropped in on him. Lewis told him that he and other members of the **Group Theatre** (including **Adler** and **Meisner**) had been deeply impressed with what they had witnessed in New York, and that he would always be welcome there. As war clouds darkened over England, he found it expedient to resettle in the USA, setting up his own school in Connecticut. Again, Brynner was a student. The Second World War drew many of his actors away, and Chekhov and Xenia moved to Los Angeles where he had been offered a contract by the Selznick Studio. Once there he set up shop in his modest house in Benedict Canyon and started giving classes. His reputation had preceded him, and an A-list of actors signed up.

As a teacher Chekhov was authoritative, charismatic, with a Stanislavskian-Vakhtangov 'pedigree' unequal to any other, and his ideas were received hungrily by American actors of the 1940s and 1950s. One noteworthy student was Marilyn Monroe. Chekhov was, in fact, Marilyn Monroe's first mentor and father-figure, before her entanglement with Lee Strasberg.

ACTORS WHO STUDIED WITH CHEKHOV
Ingrid Bergman
Yul Brynner
Gary Cooper
Clint Eastwood
Anthony Hopkins
Marilyn Monroe
Patricia Neal
Jack Nicholson
Jack Palance
Gregory Peck
Anthony Quinn

Chekhov's pedagogical starting point was that the *actor is an artist*, and thus endowed with the ability to see and experience things which are obscure to the average person. As such they should be able to tap into their subconscious mind and a universal experience of humanity, which would go beyond a limited conscious experience. Using a 'psycho-physical approach', he proposed a series of exercises to connect *movement* to *psychology*, starting with finding one's 'centre' – an imaginary nucleus in one's chest which is a source of inner activity and power, from which one can 'send' energy to all parts of the body. This energy could be expressed in four different types of movement: *moulding, floating, flying, radiating* – all emanating from the centre and used, in a sense, to *dominate* or master one's environment.

He proposed that movement could also be used by the actor to embody four essential qualities for use in the creative process: *Ease, Form, Beauty* and *Entirety*. 'Ease' uses floating and flying movements, to relax both body and spirit. 'Form' uses moulding movement to dictate *how* you play a character. Training for 'Beauty' begins with the observation of beauty in other humans, later *internalizing* those feelings in one's 'centre' before *externalizing* them, using all four forms of movement. 'Entirety' is a mental exercise to train the actor to have a consistent and comprehensive overview of their character's nature – what Stanislavski called the 'Unbroken Line'.

Development of the actor's *imagination* was one of the tenets of Stanislavski's training, and Chekhov placed it centre-stage in his concept of 'Creative Imagination'. In his book *To the Actor,* he cites Rudolph Steiner's view on creation, 'Creation is inspired not by that which is, but by that which may be; not by the actual, but the possible.'[10]

Chekhov stressed the importance of *atmosphere* as a collective reciprocal experience between the actors and the audience. He proposed exercises to make the actor sensitive to atmospheres in their daily life, and to carry that skill to the stage, the idea being that the atmosphere will help one 'feel' the content and the very essence of the scene.

The process Chekhov proposed for developing a character starts first with envisioning the character, as something not connected to the actor, and then imagining how the character might behave in certain circumstances, given its psychological makeup. This approach relates more to Stanislavski's 'what-if?' than it does to Meisner's 'as-if', in which the actor determines the character's *objective* and imagines parallel and *personal* circumstances in which the actor could achieve a similar objective (see 'Taking it Personally' in *Working with Actors*).

One of the fundamental and most-discussed principles of Chekhov's teaching was the 'Psychological Gesture' (or 'PG' as he named it) in which the actor determines the character's overall or SuperObjective and then represents it in the form of an over-exaggerated physical gesture, created initially externally, but then incorporated internally. These are based on archetypal human gestures: open, close, push, pull, lift, embrace, penetrate, ring, tear, smash and throw. With a quality or emotion added to emanating from the character's objective, the archetypal gestures become Psychological Gestures. He contended that the PG represented the 'soul' of the actor, and the *physical memory* of the gesture would then inform the actor's performance on an unconscious level. This *inner event,* as it is being experienced by the actor, is witnessed by the audience in its outward expression, which they can only read within the framework of its context in the drama. In Chekhov's book, *To the Actor,* he offers illustrations of the PGs – bodies frozen in an all-embracing gesture, like sculptures caught mid-action – which represent the physical manifestation of the drive behind different types of characters.

In **Working with Actors**, in the chapter **'Psychophysical Mechanisms'** I illustrate that a physical gesture (perhaps we should call it a 'pg', in lower case?) can be used to generate a specific emotion (e.g. the clenched fist, the furrowed brow, etc.), but Chekhov's idea is more comprehensive. He proposes that the PG is not a superficial stimulus for a specific emotion, but an internalized physical symbol of the character's *desires* which emanates from the actor's *subconscious depths*. It is part of the actor's 'creative individuality' (as per Vakhtangov), or unique essence, which sets them apart from any other artist – 'the dominant idea, which like a leitmotif, pervades all his creations'.[11] It is the route via which the actor can rise above mere naturalism.

In practical terms, Chekhov proposed that, following an initial reading of the entire script, the actor finds a PG to represent the character's *inner being*. They should do this on an intuitive basis, using their 'creative imagination and artistic vision'. I do not find this approach useful. It is introspective, happens *in isolation*, and preconceives the essential nature of the character before the actor has had a chance to work through their relationship to other characters – perhaps blocking rich possibilities which could evolve from those relationships. It could, additionally, be wildly 'off' the director's vision of the character. And, while the method purports to be anti-intellectual, it is based on an analysis of the text, thus cannot be totally instinctive but is inherently logical.

Chekhov had a long career as a movie actor, mostly in 'character' roles. He started out in silent film in Russia in 1913 and continued through his years in Europe and the USA. His best-known film role is in Hitchcock's 1945 film *Spellbound* in which he played psychiatrist Dr Brulov opposite former student Gregory Peck – a perfectly executed Stanislavskian realistic performance for which he received an Oscar nomination. For all his esoteric teaching, when it came down to the nitty-gritty, Chekhov realized that basic techniques for realism were what was required in cinema. According to the actress Mala Powers, his acolyte and estate executrix, 'He deplored the fact that naturalism/realism had become the main criteria for opinions about good theatre and good performances, when, in truth, naturalism is only one style. He understood, however, that in order to work in their chosen profession, actors must master the style.'[12]

Further reading

Michael Chekhov, *To the Actor: On the Technique of Acting*, Forward by Simon Callow and historical overview by Mala Powers, 2nd ed. (London: Routledge, 2002).

Charles Marowitz, *The Other Chekhov: A Biography of Michael Chekhov, the Legendary Actor, Director and Theorist* (New York: Applause Theatre and Cinema Books, 2004).

Notes

1. Chekhov, 78–9.
2. Marowitz, 39.
3. Ibid., 58.
4. Ibid., 61.
5. John Gillett, *Acting Stanislavski* (London: Bloomsbury, 2014), xxviii.
6. https://sydneyrudolfsteinercollege.com/articles/anthroposophy/
7. H. Biesantz and A. Klingborg, *The Goetheranum: Rudolf Steiner's Architectural Impulse* (London: Rudolph Steiner Press, 1979), 49.
8. Mala Powers, Intro., Chekhov, xxxv.
9. Marowitz, 41–4.
10. Chekhov, 5.
11. Ibid., 61.
12. Mala Powers, Intro., Chekhov, xlii.

22 Erwin Piscator
1893–1966

We do not conceive of the theatre as a mirror of the times, but as a way of changing the times.[1]

In the history of theatre Piscator is often overlooked, overshadowed by the higher profile of **Bertolt** Brecht – his mentee and some-time collaborator. Yet Piscator had a more perceptible and indelible effect than Brecht on theatre arts and acting styles, especially in the USA – injecting theatricality into Realism and inspiring experimentation.

Erwin Friedrich Maximilian Piscator was a German writer, director and producer, who inspired and later collaborated with Brecht in proposing 'Epic Theatre'. This was a politically-based theatre that emphasized the socio-political content of drama, over its emotional manipulation of the audience, or the production's formal beauty.

In line with his rejection of Realism, Piscator was an innovator in theatrical design, eschewing scenic realism for *Constructivism*. His concept of 'Total Theatre' involved abolishing the 'fourth wall'. He was the first to use still and cinema projections as part of the set, and frequently set the action on elaborate scaffold stages on different levels. A good portion of his legacy to the theatre lies in his technological invention. He endeavoured to employ 'all the technological means available to make the stage a dynamic organism'.[2] The moving floor surface – a belt upon which an actor walks – was just one of his trademark inventions. Lighting from below was another.

'Total Theatre' was a term originally used by the architect Walter Gropius (1883–1969) – who once collaborated with Piscator – to describe a totally flexible space. Piscator adapted it to embrace what *occurred* in the space – theatre in its many incarnations – to 'represent the drama of life as a whole' – a full-on theatrical experience, achieved by the 'total mechanization of the stage', using lights, projections of film or still photos, movements of all sorts, sounds, sets and costumes – all orchestrated by the director.[3]

Piscator's theatre was unabashedly political, as a vehicle for *changing* society, not simply reflecting the status quo. In October 1920 he opened the short-lived Proletariat Theatre in Berlin, aspiring to a popular political theatre. Unfortunately, the Berlin workers did not fully support it with their patronage, in addition to which the police refused it a license for political reasons. It was forced to close in April 1921.[4]

In 1924, Piscator had the good fortune to be made artistic director of the Volksbühne (People's Theatre), where he was able to mount plays in line with his politics. Internal conflicts in the Volksbühne made him again desirous of establishing his own theatre, and in 1927 he moved to the Piscator-Bühne, where he enjoyed his first collaborations with Bertolt Brecht. In 1928, aided by Brecht and others, he directed *The Good Soldier Svejk*, based on the Czech novel by Jaroslav Hašek. The play, with sets by artist Georg Grosz (1893–1959), became a theatrical landmark, and Piscator's direction of that play is now seen as the prototype example of Epic Theatre – a concept picked up and developed further by Brecht.

In 1929, Piscator wrote his autobiography, *The Political Theatre*, reflecting on his work in the emerging Weimar Republic 'agit-prop' theatre, in which plays were brought to the people to illuminate social unrest and political struggle. He classified these as 'Documentary Drama' and 'Topical Theatre', dealing with the realities of the street: breadlines, housing problems, etc.

Piscator was a Communist, committed to the ideas of the Russian Revolution. In 1931, he was invited to Russia to direct a movie, which ended up, for bureaucratic reasons, being a drawn-out affair, during which time Adolf Hitler came to power, and systematically began crushing left-wing theatre in Germany. Piscator decided to remain in the USSR. **Gordon Craig** visited him in Moscow, and personally delivered a message from Joseph Goebbels. Hitler's Minister of Propaganda wanted Piscator to come back to the German theatre and offered him a post. The reply was: 'Tell Goebbels I'll be back – when he's gone.'[5]

There are marked similarities in Piscator's approach to that of **Meyerhold.** They only met once, in 1930, but it is likely that Piscator was exposed to Meyerhold's work during his sojourn in Moscow. Referring to Piscator's staging, one of Meyerhold's biographers said: 'I can state with a clear conscience that I have seen no scenic device [used by Piscator] that Meyerhold had not used earlier . . .'[6] Piscator also used elements of Meyerhold's 'Biomechanics' in training his actors. He promoted rigorous gymnastic training, so the actors might gain more exact physical control, and to be able to move freely in the more open spaces of his 'Total Theatre' stages.

Meanwhile, in 1936, across the Atlantic in New York, **Harold Clurman** and the **Group Theatre** mounted a version of Theodore Dreiser's *An American Tragedy*, which Piscator had co-written, entitled *The Case of Clyde Griffith*. It was directed by **Lee Strasberg**. Piscator never saw the version, which only ran for nineteen performances. In 1936 he emigrated to the Soviet Union. Although he was certainly not Jewish – he was descended from Johannes Piscator, the famous Lutheran theologian who translated the Bible in 1600 – he had been designated a Jew by the SS.[7] In 1937 he moved on to Paris, where he married dancer Maria Ley. He had thought of returning to Russia but was warned that purges had started in the theatre. Instead, Erwin and his new wife emigrated to the US in 1939.

He wrote to Brecht shortly after his arrival in New York – in a state of *deep culture shock*. As a Communist finding himself in the epicentre of Capitalism, and as a German at the time of the outbreak of the Second World War, he felt severely ill at ease. Moreover, in the world of theatre he was confronted by a predominance of **Stanislavski** and psychology, and a commercially controlled market – all deeply dismaying. He soon got over his ill ease. It was only a few months later that he urged his friend, Bertolt Brecht, to join him in the US for a brief stay, which the latter did.

His equivocal relationship with Brecht entails a long and involved story, impossible to relate here in full.[8] For Piscator it was *'love-hate'*. He admired Brecht's intellect, their politics were aligned, and Brecht had formidable dramaturgical skills which Piscator found lacking in himself. Brecht on the other hand, respected Piscator's political commitment, found his ideas on staging to be inspired, and freely put them to use in his own work, rarely acknowledging their source.[9] Brecht did irreparable damage to the relationship in the 1940s when Piscator discovered that he was preparing his own version of *Svejk*, turning his back on a collaboration which Piscator – originator of their project – had proposed.[10]

Brecht, on the day following what must have been an unnerving interrogation (as a friendly witness) by the House Un-American Activities Committee, fled the States to the 'safe haven' of East Berlin, where his position as a pre-eminent artist was assured. He later tried to tempt Piscator to join him in East Germany, with the prospect of some collaboration. Piscator found the prospect quite limiting, artistically and socially. However, in 1951 – when his application for US citizenship was finally refused – he opted to return to his old family home in Dillenburg in West Germany. According to biographer, John Willett, he called this period the 'Cold Shoulder' – a long lean period, unloved and unappreciated in West Germany and only obtaining scraps of directorial work.¹¹ His 'comeback' arrived in 1960, when he was invited to direct *Death of a Salesman* in the West Berlin Freie Volksbühne ('Free' in contrast to its East German counterpart, of which he had once been director). It was a great success, and in 1962 he accepted that theatre's artistic directorship, symbolically coming full circle. It was at that point that he was offered, and mounted Rolf Hochhuth's *The Deputy*, the scandalous play about Pope Pius XII's complicity with Nazi slaughter, which rocked the foundations of the Vatican, and became a hit worldwide. Piscator was well and truly back on the map. In 1966, in the full flower of his 'second life', he died unexpectedly at the age of seventy-two due to complications of a gall bladder operation.

In 1939 Piscator had settled in New York relatively quickly, and he was fortunate to have been asked, soon after his arrival, to establish and run the Dramatic Workshop, a newly formed department of drama at the New School. The first students entered in January 1940. Under his contract with the New School, he was also able to establish a Studio Theatre, where he did his most significant directorial work in the USA.

Piscator took a hands-off approach to teaching actors, but hired in various teachers, including Herbert Berghof (1909–90), **Stella Adler** and Lee Strasberg – all of whom later founded their own schools. It is said that there was a rivalry between Piscator and Adler, representing the dichotomy between Stanislavskian Realism and Meyerhold's theatrical expression. Adler was looking for 'sympathetic students of human behavior, while Piscator saw actors as the servants of the director'.¹² 'There was Stella downstairs in the basement, screaming "Don't act! Stop acting!" . . . While Piscator upstairs on the main stage, shouting, "Be big! Bigger!"'¹³ The Dramatic Workshop can be said to be the precursor to the **Actors Studio**.¹⁴ Actors such as Marlon Brando, Tony Curtis, Sylvia Miles, Ben Gazzara, Walter Matthau, Rod Steiger, Elaine Stritch, Harry Belafonte, Eli Wallach, and playwright Tennessee Williams – all passed through – not necessarily for the complete course. Brando was groomed by Stella Adler in her classes there, but later was thrown out by Piscator for impudence (as was Walter Matthau). And, of course, there was **Judith Malina** – who went on to be a founder of the highly political Living Theatre, the American incarnation of Epic Theatre.

Piscator's pedagogical idea in the Dramatic Workshop was not to teach actors one method, but to offer an eclectic menu, all of which, ideally, was to be put to the service of a new – Epic (Brechtian) – mode of theatre. Actor Sylvia Miles (1924–2019) said that the only 'method' she learned directly from him was 'result direction'. Basically, he told you – even showed you – what to do, and you did it. She said it was a useful technique only in the sense that it trained the actor to find within themselves a *justification* for the action.¹⁵ As a teacher, what he imparted to them was less about technique and more to do with his deep moral sense and socialist values. Without most knowing that he was a Communist, his students nonetheless took on his idea that theatre was a political act, even if they didn't subscribe to some of his techniques.¹⁶

'Epic Theatre' required the creation of a new 'Objective Acting', in which the object of the actor's focus is members of the audience, as opposed to the other actors on the stage – meaning that the 'objective' actor was *inspired by*, *transformed by* and *responsible to* the spectator. This was in direct contrast to the Stanislavskian idea of the actor working from within themself based on their personal understanding of the character, and then focusing their attention on what was going on within the supposed four walls of the stage. 'It is not true that your [the actor's] centre of attention lies in the middle of the stage. When you play before a public, the public must be the centre of your attention.'¹⁷ As Judith Malina points out, 'Objective Acting is not performance technique, it's an aesthetic political position.'¹⁸ Maria Piscator, wife and collaborator, explained: Objective Acting 'is to learn to see the world not through the sense only, as in Stanislavski, but to move away from the individual, as in Brecht. In objective acting we do not judge . . . We're interested in conveying ideas more than emotion'.¹⁹

Piscator did not agree with Brecht regarding alienation (or *'estrangement'* as it is sometimes translated), considering it to be a *romantic* concept 'formulated on the basis of oriental classical theatre' – basically Noh drama.[20]

He considered theatre to be a *'director's art'*. The process of developing a play was 'top-down' with the director as the spokesperson for the playwright, imparting their superior understanding of the play. He was aware of **Gordon Craig's** Über-marionette concept, and according to some, he put it into practice.[21] As Sylvia Miles pointed out, with Piscator there was very little room for 'psychology'.[22]

As successful as he was in those New York years 1939–51, he always considered it to be only an interregnum from his full-on directing career – he called it 'an interim achievement'.[23] Piscator's profound influence on Brecht has been noted. While it is possible to trace his *direct* influence on numerous directors – **Grotowski**, Mnouchkine and **Boal** to name a few – the most direct legacy of Piscator's ideas was in the Living Theatre.

Further reading

C. D. Innes, *Erwin Piscator's Political Theater: The Development of Modern German Drama* (Cambridge: Cambridge University Press, 1972).
Judith Malina, *The Piscator Notebook* (New York: Routledge, 2012).
Irwin Piscator, *The Political Theater* (London/New York: Eyre Methuen, 1980).
John Willett, *The Theatre of Erwin Piscator* (London: Methuen, 1978).

Notes

1. Piscator, 246.
2. Malina, 159.
3. Innes, 150–1.
4. Malina, 152.
5. Leo Kerz, 'Brecht and Piscator', *Educational Theatre Journal*, Vol. 20, No. 3 (October 1968): 368.
6. Juri Jegalin, quoted in Innes, 186.
7. Malina, 3.
8. This relationship is well documented. Herbert Knust gives a detailed account in his article, 'Piscator and Brecht: Affinity and Alienation', in *Essays on Brecht*, eds Siegfried Mews and Herbert Kunst (Chapel Hill, NC: University of North Carolina Press, 1974).
9. Ibid., 64, Knust uncovered a 1955 note in Piscator's papers saying: 'Nowhere does Brecht mention me, and yet: in everything he does there is part of me.'
10. Ibid., 51–2.
11. Willett, 175.
12. Malina, 23.
13. Ibid., 24.
14. 'There wouldn't have been an Actors Studio without Piscator's Workshop.' Actor Jack Garfein, as quoted in Foster Hirsch, *A Method to Their Madness* (New York: DaCapo, 1984),118.
15. Malina, 21–2.
16. Malina, 22. Sylvia Miles confessed: 'I never knew he was a Communist – or was he a socialist?'
17. Erwin Piscator, 'Objective Acting', in *Actors on Acting*, eds Toby Cole and Helen Krich Chinoy (New York: Crown Publishers, 1949). 287.

18. Malina, 150.
19. Hirsch, 119.
20. Ibid., 152. Piscator was very suspicious of the Brecht's love of Noh drama, thinking it to be formalistic. Brecht, on the other hand, thought Piscator's interest in Kabuki Theatre was *bourgeois*.
21. Innes, 189. Referring to remarks made by Bauhaus director, Oskar Schlemmer (1888–1943).
22. Malina, 22.
23. Ibid., 11

23 Antonin Artaud
1896–1948

Psychology, which works relentlessly to reduce the unknown to the known, to the quotidian and the ordinary, is the cause of the theatre's abasement and its fearful loss of energy, which seems to me to have reached its lowest point. And I think both the theatre and we ourselves have had enough of psychology.[1]

Artaud was not an accomplished practitioner, neither as actor nor director. He was an 'ideas man'. His provocative and anarchistic thinking inspired generations of theatre-makers aspiring to a revolution against the prevalent dominant forms of Realism. Susan Sontag (1933–2004) perhaps overstated the case in saying, 'the course of all recent theatre in Western Europe and the Americas can be said to divide into two periods – before Artaud and after Artaud'.[2] (This generalization fails to acknowledge that the unbroken dominance of Realism in the twentieth century took little or no notice of Artaud's proposals.) Sontag was a supporter of **Judith Malina** and the **Living Theatre**. Malina's principal line of influence ran from **Craig** and **Meyerhold**, through **Piscator,** only later referencing Artaud.[3] However, once Malina and her partner **Julian Beck** discovered Artaud, his theories of theatre were tested and embedded in a practical sense in the work of their Living Theatre (see Malina's chapter).

Milling and Ley in *Modern Theories of Performance* suggest we consider Artaud in two time-frames – the first being the period between the Wars, in which he was alive and 'productive', and the second, post-1960, well after his death, when his influence came fully into play, most visibly in the political theatre of Judith Malina and her imitators.[4] In similar terms, David Shafer points to the existence of *two* Artauds: 'the one who lived and the one of our ideas', likening him to 'a palimpsest upon which we inscribe what we want to find in him'.[5] Artaud's *cri de guerre* has especially resonated with those dramatic artists such as **Peter Brook** and **Charles Marowitz**, jaundiced by contemporary practice and looking for some higher meaning.[6] As Milling and Ley point out, 'The construction of Artaud may be a necessity, at least for some, as much of an act of continuing defiance and self-determination, as a set of propositions for a particular practice.'[7]

The boy Antonin was sickly with meningitis. Then, as a teenager, he was traumatized by a random violent knife attack. He was in and out of sanatoriums and mental hospitals during his entire his life, spending most of his last nine years institutionalized (which included receiving electroshock treatments, so in vogue at the time). His taste in reading was on the dark side – Rimbaud, Baudelaire and Poe. His fine art references were Grunewald and Hieronymus Bosch. He was addicted to heroin and other opiates. All of this points to a psychological makeup well suited to producing an angry proclamation such as *'The Theatre of Cruelty'*. Published in *La Nouvelle Revue Française* in 1932, the manifesto was based on an existential philosophy which runs something like this:

Existence is evil. That is the base state of the universe. Goodness is an act of will, requiring an effort. Hence, to live well, or live a good life requires an act of will – of great effort – necessary to counteract the evil inherent in existence. It is cruel to have to continually make the effort to live without evil.[8]

His proposal is not, as you might imagine, an incitement to sadism and horror, but, in the face of a stagnant bourgeois theatre, it is a call for 'rigour, implacable intention, and reason, irreversible and absolute determination', as **Harold Clurman** described it.[9] Artaud wished to create a new theatrical language of 'totem and gesture', devoid of dialogue, which would appeal to all the senses. His Theatre of Cruelty would look and sound something like this:

> Every spectacle will contain a physical and objective element, perceptible to all. Cries, groans, apparitions, surprises, theatricalities of all kinds, magic beauty of costumes taken from certain ritual models; resplendent lighting, incantational beauty of voices, the charms of harmony, rare notes of music, colours of objects, physical rhythm of movements whose crescendo and decrescendo will accord exactly with the pulsation of movements familiar to everyone, concrete appearances of new and surprising objects, masks, effigies yards high, sudden changes of light, the physical action of light which arouses sensations of heat and cold, etc.[10]

Artaud's first training in theatre was as an actor, just after the First World War at Théâtre de L'Oeuvre in Paris, known for its Symbolist approach – but he was let go. In the words of his teacher: 'his make-up, his behavior, were of a painter lost in midst of actors'.[11] His real theatre 'apprenticeship' was with **Charles Dullin** in the Théâtre de Atelier, which he joined in 1921. He related easily to **Dullin's** distain for naturalism. **Dullin** found him to be a dedicated student and commented on the effect of Artaud's *poetic imagination* on his acting. Artaud especially took to **Dullin's** improvisation and mask work.[12]

As a youth he had been captivated by the Symbolist/Decadent poets, Rimbaud (1854–91) and Verlaine (1844–96), which led him to try his hand at writing poetry – unsuccessfully. He devoured the doctrines of Surrealism, as set out by the likes of André Breton (1896–1966) and in 1924 he became involved with the Surrealist movement. In 1926 he founded, with fellow traveller playwright Roger Vitrac (1899–1952), the Théâtre Alfred Jarry, named after the author of the seminal satirical Symbolist play *Ubu Roi*. It was a short-lived venture – mounting only four productions over two years – but it at least provided some concrete practical experience of production upon which to later build his Theatre of Cruelty vision. Ultimately, Artaud rejected Surrealism as being simply a mechanism for shocking bourgeois sensibilities without an elevating inspirational element – and for its dogmatic attachment to Marxism. He was publicly 'excommunicated' from the Surrealist movement. For Artaud, *theatre* had a higher value. He was 'unique in providing the modern theatre with a sense of itself as something sacred'.[13]

Surrealist theatre tended towards the 'exotic'. As a result of attending the Balinese dance festival at the Paris Colonial Expo of 1931, Artaud developed an admiration for Eastern forms of theatre. He was attracted by its codified, highly ritualized and precise physicality – especially as exemplified in Balinese dance. 'The Balinese, who have a vocabulary of gesture and mime for every circumstance of life, reinstate the superior worth of theatrical conventions.'[14] The narrative was expressed in dance and gestures, and *not* verbally.

In 1933 he published 'Theatre and the Plague' – the second most widely discussed of Artaud's themes – in which he sees the process of theatre as analogous to the plague.

> If the essential theater is like the plague, it is not because it is contagious, but because like the plague it is the revelation, the bringing forth, the exteriorization of a depth of latent cruelty by means of which all the perverse possibilities of the mind, whether of an individual or a people, are localized.[15]

In 1935 he produced, acted in and directed the only play he wrote – an adaptation of Percy Bysshe Shelley's *The Cenci*. It was an opportunity to put into practice theories contained in his manifestos. The production was reviled by the critics, who emphasized Artaud's histrionic and melodramatic style of acting. Soon afterwards, disillusioned with the theatre world of Paris, he travelled to Mexico, where he lived in the mountains for a period with the Tarahumaran people, experimenting with peyote. (The account of this sojourn was published in English in 1976 under the title of *The Peyote Dance*.)[16]

Perhaps peyote was still synaptically affecting his brain when, in the following year, he went to Ireland on an obscure mission carrying what he believed to be actual the staff of St Patrick. After numerous misunderstandings (he spoke neither Gaelic or English), confrontations and arrests, he was unceremoniously deported. Aboard ship he created such a fracas that he had to be constrained in a straitjacket. Upon his arrival back in France on 12 February 1937, he was committed to an asylum in Rodez in the south of France, and remained institutionalized for most of the remainder of his life.[17]

Artaud wrote numerous essays, manifestos and critiques, some of which are collected in his seminal work, *The Theatre and Its Double*,[18] including the manifesto with which we most closely associate him – the Theatre of Cruelty. In the chapter 'No More Masterpieces', he attacks the prevailing realist aesthetic based on psychology, by implication laying the blame at **Stanislavski's** door. He exhorts us to replace the written word with spectacle, movement, lighting, music, shouts, cries and other sound effects. These elements are used to *disturb* the audience and to take them to a place that transcends the intellect.

> In the anguished, catastrophic period we live in, we feel an urgent need for a theatre which [current] events do not exceed, whose resonance is deep within us, dominating the instability of the times . . . Everything that acts is a cruelty. It is upon this idea of extreme action, pushed beyond all limits, that theater must be rebuilt.[19]

I've mentioned Artaud's brief career in stage acting, but I should also note that he had some experience in movies – essentially small roles in several silent films, including *Napoléon* (1927, dir. Abel Gance), in which he played Marat – a role he suited well – and *The Passion of Joan of Arc* (1928, dir. Carl Dreyer). He had twelve further parts in the talkies between 1929 and 1935. Silent film may have been more suited to his acting style. Artaud had very striking features and was cast in small character roles and bit-parts such as 'the thief', 'a delirious soldier', 'a knife-seller' (the last being in Fritz Lang's 1934 film, *Liliom*). Of those of his performances I've seen there was little attempt at realism.

Artaud's view of actors was close to **Gordon Craig's** and the notion of *Über-marionettes*. He somewhat begrudgingly acknowledged the necessity of actors, but saw them as subservient, valued much on the same level as the scenery and lighting.

> The actor is both an instrument of first importance, since it is upon the effectiveness of his work that the success of the spectacle depends, and a kind of passive and neutral element, since he is rigorously denied all personal initiative.[20]

In the 'second', arguably more important epoque of the Artaud 'story' as conceived by Milling and Ley – the posthumous one – his ideas came to inspire the whole of the *Avant Garde* movement – what Clurman calls the 'New Theatre' – of the 1960s and 1970s covering the *gamut* of experimental theatre from Grotowski, to 'happenings', to Total Theatre, to the Living Theatre. His ideas are clearly detectable in the writing of the 'Theatre of the Absurd', for example, in the works of Albee, Beckett, Ionesco and Genet. His influence was heavily felt in the work of two theatre giants, English director **Peter Brook** and French director **Jacques LeCoq**. Another of Dullin's protégées, French actor/director Jean-Louis Barrault (1910–94) counted Artaud as one of the primary forces that shaped him, as does the French *avant-gardist*, Ariane Mnouchkine (1939–

), a former student of LeCoq and director of earlier versions of *Cirque du Soleil,* who borrows much from Artaud's playbook.

Susan Sontag was clearly a fan. She has edited and introduced Artaud's formidable output: verse, prose poems, essays on film, film scenarios, a historical novel, plays and essays on the theatre, art, and literature – published by University of California Press in 1988.

Further reading

Antonin Artaud, *The Theatre and its Double*, trans. Mary Caroline Richards (New York: Grove Press, 1958). Original publication Paris: Gallimard, 1938.

Antonin Artaud, *Selected Writings*, ed. and Intro. Susan Sontag (Berkeley: University of California Press, 1988).

David A Shafer, *Antonin Artaud* (London: Reakton Books, 2016).

Notes

1. Artaud, *The Theatre,* 77.
2. Quoted in Natasha Tripney, 'Antonin Artaud and the Theatre of Cruelty', Discovering Literature: 20th Century, British Library online, published 7 September 2017, https://www.bl.uk/20th-century-literature/articles/antonin-artaud-and-the-theatre-of-cruelty
3. It was her partner, Julian Beck, who obsessed with Artaud and introduced his ideas to Malina, which justified many of their ideas and fed their anarchistic tendencies. See chapter on Beck.
4. J. Milling and G. Ley, *Modern Theories of Performance* (London: Palgrave Macmillan, 2000), 87.
5. Shafer, 9.
6. The concept of the 'sacred' clearly influenced Peter Brook and forms the centrepiece of the chapter 'The Holy Theatre' in his book, *The Empty Space* (New York: Touchstone/Scribner, 1968).
7. Milling and Ley, 87–8.
8. Based on the analysis of Mark Russell in *Twentieth-Century Theatre: Antonin Artaud, Annotated Bibliography* (Dundee: Learning and Teaching Scotland, 2001), 1.
9. Harold Clurman, 'The New Theatre, Now', *The Collected Works of Harold Clurman*, eds. Marjorie Loggia and Glenn Young (New York: Applause, 1994), 770.
10. Artaud, *The Theatre,* 93.
11. František Deák, 'Antonin Artaud and Charles Dullin: Artaud's Apprenticeship in Theatre', *Educational Theatre Journal*, Vol. 29, No. 3 (October 1977): 345.
12. Ibid., 346.
13. Milling and Ley.
14. Artaud, *The Theatre,* 98.
15. Ibid., 94.
16. Antonin Artaud, *The Peyote Dance* (New York: Farrar, Strauss & Giroux, 1976).
17. Artaud's madness and institutionalization under the care of Dr Gaston Ferdière is the subject of Charles Marowitz's play *Artaud in Rodez* (London: Marion Boyars, 1977).
18. Original publication *Théâtre et son Double,* Paris, Gallimard, 1938.
19. Artaud, *The Theatre,* 86.
20. Ibid., 98.

24 Bertolt Brecht
1898–1956

Why should an actor give the audience an emotional experience when he could give them an opportunity to learn?[1]

In considering Bertolt Brecht's relationship to acting we must take into account that he was first and foremost a *playwright*. His plays demanded a unique *style*, and to get his ideas across properly, he found it necessary to direct his own work. He had no formal training as a director, nor was there a tradition of actor-training in existence in Germany at that time.[2] Acting was not Brecht's principal concern: 'Stanislavski when directing is first of all an actor. When I direct I am first of all a playwright.'[3] In the service of his plays he provided his actors with a *framework for performance* which described their relationship both to (1) their character and, uniquely, (2) their audience, but offered little specific technique. It was rather an 'approach' to acting. The methods he suggested were designed to *breakdown* a realistic performance, rather than build one.

Brecht's style derives from his Marxist political perspective grounded in Hegelian dialecticism – one that eschews individual psychology and the projection of one's personality in favour of the individual's *role in society*. Like that of his mentor **Erwin Piscator**, his was a didactic theatre in which he wanted the spectator to *learn*, and not to *feel*. Hence, he had little time for 'early' **Stanislavski** – centred on psychology – and even less for 'The Method' as he witnessed it being practiced in the USA. I will discuss Brecht's techniques later, but first I offer a brief biography of this fascinating self-styled giant of the theatre.

Brecht's life story divides neatly into four periods:

1 Bavaria – his birth in 1898 until his move to Berlin in 1924.
2 Berlin during the Weimar Republic (1925–33).
3 Exile from Nazi Germany and the Second World War (1933–45).
4 Return to East Germany during the Cold War (1945–56).

Bavaria

Although he sometimes affected peasant roots when questioned about his background, Brecht came from a middle-class family. His father was the managing director of a papermill.[4] His mother was a devout Protestant and served up the Bible as the young Bertold's indoctrination to 'epic literature'. They lived in Augsburg. When the First World War broke out, Brecht, to avoid military service, enrolled as a medical student in Munich. Once matriculated, he switched to the study of dramatic literature. In Munich he frequented the cabaret theatre, where he was dazzled by the performances of the actor/playwright Frank Wedekind (1864–1918). Cabaret became an abiding interest, heavily influencing his work. He wrote his first play, *Baal* (1920), at the age of twenty-two, followed by *Drums in the Night* in 1922. In addition to playwriting, he earned pocket-money as drama critic for an Augsburg newspaper. He became a young father in 1920, when his first son, Frank, was born to his then girlfriend, Paula Banholzer. A performance of *Drums in the Night* was favourably reviewed in Berlin, and Brecht began to build upon connections there, eventually setting up a production company with Austrian playwright Arnolt Bronnen (1895–1959). At that point he fancifully changed his name from Bertold to *Bertolt* to sound more like that of his associate, Arnolt. During the Munich period he had a prodigious output of ten plays, published or performed, yet he still found time to exercise his legendary libido.

In 1922 he married Viennese opera singer Marianne Zoff, who gave birth to his second child – a daughter, Hanne Hiob. The relationship was not to last long due – one imagines due to Brecht's serial infidelities. Among other paramours were his writing collaborator, Elisabeth Hauptmann (1897–1973), and his leading actress, Helene Weigel (1900–71), who, in 1924, bore him another son, Stefan. Brecht and Weigel later married and had a daughter, Barbara, in 1930. Weigel remained married to him until his death in 1959, tolerating his string of lovers, of both sexes, who were sometimes his close collaborators, as was the case with Margarete Steffin (1908–41), actress, translator and poet – a working class woman who helped Brecht write the proletarian dialogues and situations for *The Mother* (1932) and other plays; and the actress/photographer Ruth Berlau (1906–74), who met him during his exile in Denmark. Berlau followed him to New York, where she gave premature birth to his fifth (known) child, who died in infancy. Auguring the Hippies' credo of forty years hence, Brecht rejected the bourgeois notions of monogamous love as an extension of the capitalist concept of property ownership – conveniently justifying the 'fluidity' of his relationships.[5]

Brecht cut his teeth on directing in Munich and Leipzig. His single attempt to direct a play in Berlin ended badly – he was scathing about the actors in his cast. Several walked out, and he was replaced as director.[6] His most notable success was in 1923 at the Munich Kammerspiele – his own adaptation of Christopher Marlowe's play, *The Life of Edward II of England* (c. 1592). During this time in Munich, he was introduced to Marxist texts by Helene Weigel – an active supporter of the Russian Revolution.

Berlin

A job as dramaturg for the renowned director/impresario Max Reinhardt (1873–1943) took Brecht to Berlin in 1924 – at a moment when that city was in its heyday as a pre-eminent global centre of culture. It was the era of Marlene Dietrich (190–92), Bauhaus architecture, the painter George Grosz (1893–1959), crowded kinos, flapper fashions, cabarets (political and decadent), short-haired women wearing trousers and smoking cigarettes, drag balls, sexual libertinism – all moving to the tune of imported American jazz. He collaborated with Reinhardt on a variety of plays including Shaw's *St Joan* and Pirandello's *Six Characters in Search of an Author*. His pleas to Reinhardt to allow him to direct Shakespeare fell on deaf ears, but he was able to mount his own play, *Jungle: Decline of a Family*, which turned out *not* to be a success. He was let go after a year.

Encouraged by Elizabeth Hartmann, by then his regular lover and collaborator, he ramped up his studies of Marxism, with a profound effect on his concept of theatre: 'When I read Marx's Capital, I understood my plays.'[7] An artistic exhibition in Mannheim entitled 'New Objectivity' – a post-Expressionist movement including artists like George Grosz (1893–1959) – inspired Brecht to form a post-Expressionist collective of his own, consisting of writers and actors. It became the vehicle for his first major work in Berlin, *Man is Man* (1926).

In 1927 he joined a group of dramaturgs working with Erwin Piscator's company, enthusiastically embracing the concepts of *'epic theatre'* and *'theatre mechanics'*. In the same year, he began a fruitful collaboration with the composer Kurt Weill (1900–50), initially on a small production entitled *The Little Mahagonny*. Weill continued his collaboration with Brecht on *The Threepenny Opera* (1928), *Happy End* (1929) and *Rise and Fall of the City of Mahagonny* (1930/31), as well as various lieder and cantatas with texts by Brecht. In 1930, Weill, a Socialist, broke with Brecht over the latter's more radical politics, saying he had no interest '[in setting] the Communist Manifesto to music'.[8]

Mounting *The Threepenny Opera*, based on Englishman John Gay's eighteenth-century *The Beggar's Opera*, was originally the idea of Elisabeth Hauptmann, who had already translated it and had begun to adapt it when Brecht presented it (as his own work) to the impresario Ernst Josef Aufricht (1898–1971). Aufricht agreed to finance it, after which Brecht and Hauptmann collaborated on the final script, hand-in-glove with Kurt Weill.[9] *The Threepenny Opera* was a huge success, with over 400 performances in two years in Berlin, playing internationally thereafter. The music to which Weill set Brecht's texts vividly captures the atmosphere of Berlin in the 1920s – jazz mixed with German dance music – giving us classics such as *Mack the Knife* and *Pirate Jenny*, alongside equally evocative music from their next collaboration, *Happy End* (1929) – songs such as *Surabaya Johnny* and *The Bilboa Song*. (A 'listenography' is presented below to give you a flavour.)

In this same period, Brecht's writers collective – now consisting of Hauptmann, Emil Hesse-Burri (1902–66), and later Steffin and Berlau among others – began creating a series of *Lehrstücke* (1926–33), literally translated 'teaching plays' – which Brecht called 'learning-plays' or 'didactic cantatas'.[10] 'With the learning-play . . . the theatre becomes a place for philosophers, and for such philosophers as not only wish to explain the world but to change it.'[11] These plays were designed to appeal to workers, and involved music and gestures capable of being performed by 'proletarians' as well as professionals. Some were plays for schools. Some, small operas. Much of the music of the *Lehrstücke* was composed by three German giants of contemporary music: Kurt Weill, Paul Hindemith (1895–1963) and Hanns Eisler (1898–1962). These works challenged the audience to think or to enter into a dialogue.[12] Questionnaires were frequently handed out at the end of the performance, and the plays rewritten in accordance with the feedback. Years later in Brazil, **Augusto Boal**, a Brecht devotee, extended the idea with his *'spect-actor'* concept, in which members of the audience actively intervene in the drama. Early examples of *Lehrstücke* include *The Mother* (1932) and *Lindberghflug* (Flight Across the Ocean,1928–9).

Exile

On 28 February 1933 – one day after the Reichstag fire – Brecht, with Helene Weigel at his side, fled Germany, following in the footsteps of numerous Jewish and left-wing associates. They spent several peripatetic years, first – in rapid succession – in Prague, Zurich and Paris, then a much longer stay in Denmark (punctuated with trips to Moscow, Paris and the USA). When the Germans moved into Norway and Denmark in 1939, the Brecht menagerie moved to Sweden, then Finland, until finally receiving visas to travel to the States in May 1941. Brecht felt he was 'changing countries more often than shoes'.[13]

Brecht's American sojourn – as vividly set out in James K. Lyon's biography *Brecht in America* – is characterized by disenchantment, thwarted ambition, culture clashes and alienation – largely as a product of his overinflated ego and political arrogance towards the Americans. He had already succeeded in garnering a negative reputation in his earlier 1935 visit to New York when he was invited to supervise the left-wing Theatre Union's production of *The Mother*. He attended rehearsals with Hanns Eisler, argued repeatedly with the director, and got the lead actress fired. Eventually both he and Eisler were banned from rehearsals.[14]

He had several staunch supporters and collaborators in the US, amongst them the director Joseph Losey (1909–84), who was mounting a series of 'Living Newspaper' productions much admired by Brecht.[15] Losey co-directed *Galileo* on Broadway with Brecht in 1947, but was later blacklisted by the House Un-American Activities Committee (HUAC), and moved to Britain where he had a successful career in movies. Brecht naturally gravitated to Hollywood where there existed a veritable diaspora of German artistic talent – all fully employed![16] In Los Angeles, Brecht co-wrote the screenplay for *Hangmen Also Die!* (1943), directed by another German émigré Fritz Lang (1890–1976). It was Brecht's *only* script for a Hollywood film. The story concerned Reinhard Heydrich, the notorious 'Hangman of Prague', who was Himmler's right-hand man in the SS, and a chief architect of the Holocaust. The film won Hollywood kudos for *three* German refugees from Hitler, which included an Academy Award nomination for Hanns Eisler's score.

Brecht's most notable success in the US was the play and film, *Galileo* in collaboration with the eminent actor Charles Laughton (1899–1962). There are, in fact, three versions of this play: Danish, American and (later) German. The original Danish version was written with Margarete Steffin (1938/9) during Brecht's exile in Denmark and was eventually performed in Zurich in 1943. The American version (1944–7) was an extraordinary collaboration with Charles Laughton. The English actor was a perfect fit for Brecht. Both men shared an ability to think theatrically and concretely. Laughton understood the power of language, and quickly grasped Brecht's concept of the 'gestus'.[17]

> [Laughton] spoke no German whatsoever and we had to decide the gest of the dialogue by my acting it all in bad English or even in German and then his acting back in proper English in a variety of ways until I could say: that's it. The result he would write down . . . Some sentences, indeed many, he carried around for days, changing them continually. This system of performance-and-repetition had one immense advantage in that psychological discussion was almost entirely avoided.[18]

Thus, the resulting English-language text was borne out of theatrical gesture on a piecemeal basis rather than by the objective-based psychological pathway proposed by the Stanislavskians. **Harold Clurman** was an admirer of Brecht, calling him 'one of the world's outstanding directors'.[19] Clurman offered to mount *Galileo* on Broadway. In Brecht's eyes, the esteemed Clurman – due to his association with the Group Theatre – was tarred with the brush of 'The Method'. Brecht, months earlier, had watched disapprovingly as **Lee Strasberg** rehearsed one of the *Lehrstücke*, *The Measures Taken*, with the Group Theatre.[20] Regarding his overtures to direct *Galileo*, he told Clurman: 'I'd rather a circus director do it. You are a Stanislavski man and cannot possibly understand how to approach my play. . . . You will try to get "atmosphere"; I don't want atmosphere. You will establish a "mood"; I don't want a mood.'[21] This was a gross misreading of Clurman, who, at this point had become greatly receptive to 'formalist' influences such as those proposed by **Meyerhold** and was probably the American who best understood Brecht's approach. Clearly, Brecht would have had much greater success in the USA if he been less arrogant and had hitched his wagon to Clurman's star.[22]

Brecht's playwriting output over his exile years was prolific. In the earlier years much of it was in reaction to the National Socialist and Fascist movements in Germany from which he had fled, for example: *The Life of Galileo* (1938 and 1945), *Mother Courage and Her Children* (1939), *The Good Person of Szechwan* (1938–41), *The Resistible Rise of Arturo Ui* (1941), *The Caucasian Chalk Circle* (1944), *Fear and Misery of the Third Reich* (1938). Despite the distracting culture clashes and ego clashes he experienced in the USA, and the time wasted in a cul-de-sac in pursuit of a film career in Hollywood, he also managed to write *The Visions of Simone Machard* (1942), *Schweik in the Second World War* (1943) and an adaptation of Webster's *The Duchess of Malfi* (1946).

Return

In 1947 Brecht fell victim to the McCarthy witch-hunt. Along with ten other writers and directors (The Hollywood Ten) he was blacklisted by the studios, then subpoenaed by the HUAC. In solidarity with the Ten, he first refused to appear. Then, seeing his plans to return to Europe in jeopardy, he relented. The others were cited for contempt, and Brecht, not unlike **Elia Kazan** during his second inquisition, was considered to have betrayed his fellow artists. The day after his appearance, 31 October 1947, he flew to Switzerland. He spent a year in Zurich, where he mounted a 'non-Aristotelian' version of Sophocles *Antigone*, before moving to East Berlin.

There, in 1949 he was warmly welcomed by the Communist government, and established with Helene Weigel the Berliner Ensemble, eventually to be permanently based in the glorious Baroque-style *Theater am Schiffbauerdamm*, where the first performance of *The Threepenny Opera* had taken place in 1928. The company is still resident there today, regularly mounting Brecht's work.

Epic Theatre

Piscator had heavily influenced Brecht, who took from him the concept of 'epic theatre' and expanded it, introducing the dimension of *dialectics*, derived from his studies of Marx and Hegel, which holds that society cannot be thought of as *static*, but as in a continual *process of change*, arising out of *contradictions*. The resolution of one contradiction leads to another, as the drama of daily life plays out. History is dynamic. Thus, Brecht's concept of theatre is based on the idea that society can and needs to be changed, and that theatre and film should be an agent for change.

As conceived by Brecht, 'Epic Theatre' rejects the Aristotelian form of drama, especially the notion of 'catharsis', defined as *release*, or the *purging of emotion* via the drama. This is diametrically opposed to the 'Realism' developed by the Moscow Arts Theatre, and Stanislavski in particular. Brecht held that when the audience relates emotionally to the characters their sensibilities are numbed, leading to a state of 'hypnoses' in which the spectator loses their critical faculties and fails to see the contradictions – and consequently, the *need for change*. In Epic Theatre, the actors are 'playing in such a way that the audience was hindered from simply identifying itself with the characters in the play'.[23] In other words, the spectator should not be allowed to 'empathize'.

To create the dialectic, Epic Theatre employed – in both writing and acting – the technique of *'Verfremdung'* ('alienation' – shorthanded as the 'V-Effekt' or 'A-effect' in English). V-Effekt does not mean alienating the audience to the drama itself. It is simply a device to give the spectator a sense of *reorientation* or detachment. In writing this can be affected when there is a change of perception of the relationships of the characters. Brecht gives this example:

> To see one's mother as a man's wife one needs a V-Effekt; this is provided . . . when one acquires a stepfather. If one sees one's form-master hounded by the bailiffs a V-Effekt occurs; one is jerked out of a relationship in which the form-master seems big into one where he seems small.[24]

The technique which produces a V-Effekt is the exact opposite of that which aims at 'empathy'.

Acting Brecht

V-Effekt demands a different approach to acting – even a new kind of actor. One who prioritizes *thought* over *belief*. It requires a sort of schizophrenic state, in which the actor is one moment 'in' the character and the next standing outside of it questioning it. Brecht had a Eureka moment in Moscow in 1935 when he saw the Chinese actor Mei Lan-fang in performance: 'without makeup, costume or lighting . . . an actor who seemed to stand aside from his part and "make it quite clear he knows he is being observed".'[25] Brecht established his new rules for acting based on what he learned about Chinese theatre, in which, 'It was for the author and [director] to present the world in an unfamiliar light. It was the actor's responsibility not to take the edge off that unfamiliarity by losing himself in the play.'[26]

'Transformation' – integrating oneself with the character – was not allowed: 'He is not Lear, Harpagon, Schweik; he shows them.'[27] All of this, of course, goes totally against the grain for an actor trained in any variation of Stanislavski. Brecht demanded that the actor 'expresses his awareness of being watched',[28] which is to acknowledge the presence of the audience. Brecht tore down the 'fourth wall' that Stanislavski had carefully built. In addition to a new relationship to the audience, the actor had a new relationship with themself: 'A further means is that the artist observes himself.'[29] Thus, in a schizophrenic manner, the actor is required to represent the character and ask themself at the same time *how* they are representing the character.

This split is difficult to achieve and goes against an actor's instinct. In rehearsal, Brecht used techniques such as asking the actor to speak about their character in the third person or to speak out the stage directions. Brecht allowed for some 'empathy', but only in the sense of demonstrating how a character might act or react. 'He uses these means just as any normal person with no particular acting talents would use them if he wanted to portray someone else, i.e. show how he behaves. Which is something we do normally in life.'[30]

Having written diatribes against the Stanislavskian use of psychology he grudgingly admitted its utility in creating the illusion of a living character, and he allowed its use in a very specific way in rehearsal. He proposed three stages of rehearsal. The first stage involves reading, thinking, contextual analysis – a lot of it – especially looking for the *contradictions* in the character. In the second phase one looks for the 'truth' of the character in the subjective (psychological) sense. 'And then there is a third phase in which you try to see the character from the outside, from the standpoint of society.'[31] Psychology was only allowed in the second phase of rehearsal, *never* in performance.

Another essential Brechtian concept which applies to acting is the 'gestus'. As Brecht used the term loosely, it's been difficult for his biographers to agree on a precise definition.[32] In general terms, it is a determination of the social position and history of the character, an expression of the contradictions of the character. For the actor, it is finding the manner of gesture and expression that a given 'type' of person (defined by socio-economic status, occupation, age, etc.) would convey in a given social 'situation' (e.g. confronting one's boss about a pay rise). The actor's job was to find an appropriate gesture and take possession of it. He said, 'To make gestures quotable is the actor's most important achievement.'[33]

Brecht did not prioritize putting his ideas on paper, nor creating a manifesto on 'Epic Theatre'. His writing impulse was mostly directed towards his plays and his poetry – he left us over 2,500 poems.[34] Although he was a 'compulsive articulator'[35] his theories found expression in his plays, the journals he kept, and in conversations and correspondence with friends. Three published exceptions were (1) *Messingkauf* ('Buying Brass') consisting of a witty dialogue between two actors, a dramaturg and a philosopher about a new way of making theatre, written, then revised from 1939 to 1955; (2) a series of *Modelbooks* written from 1930 to 1948, and (3) *A Short Organum for the Theatre*, originally published in 1948 and republished in 1953.[36]

Brecht's critique of Stanislavski was mediated by two sources geographically poles and years apart. He was familiar with the 'Realism' of the MAT from his visits to Moscow, but his negative view of Stanislavski's techniques was largely informed by his exposure to the Strasberg's 'Method' as practiced in the USA (which, as we have pointed out elsewhere, misrepresented Stanislavski's teaching). Years later, having returned to Communist East Germany, Brecht became acquainted with the prevailing Stalinist version of Stanislavski – '**Socialist Realism**', equally repugnant to him. Meanwhile, via a mutual friend – Russian constructivist writer Sergei Tretiakov (1892–1937) – he gained exposure to the ideas of **Vsevolod Meyerhold**, whose formalist and Constructivist style mirrored his own in many respects. Brecht was also impressed by what he knew of **Yevgeny Vakhtangov's** work, seeing it as a bridge between Meyerhold, the wayward student and the master: 'Meyerhold is strained, Stanislavsky slack: the latter an imitation of life, the former an abstraction.'[37] For Brecht (and others) Vakhtangov represented a synthesis. While there are similarities in approaches, Meyerhold's and Vakhtangov's evolved directly from theatrical realism, which forms their base reference, whereas Brecht's point of departure is a political-didactic construct which did not emerge from pre-existing drama theory, but where writing and ideas had pride of place.

Limited as Brecht's contribution to acting technique may be his ideas on the nature of theatre have had a profound effect. Elements of Epic Theatre have been taken up by directors such as **Jerzy Grotowski**, **Peter Brook**, Augusto Boal, **Judith Malina** and numerous others who followed narrowly in his footsteps. But more broadly – and with a largely unrecognized debt to Piscator – Brecht had the effect of opening up the staid realistic staging which had become entrenched in the USA and elsewhere. If nothing else, he drove the nail in the coffin of the 'fourth wall' convention.

In cinema, as well, his ideas had some coinage – at least temporarily – and dove-tailed neatly with the dialectical '*semiotics*' applied to cinema in the 1960s and 1970s. The *V-Effekt* can be found in films by directors such as Jean-Luc Godard (b.1930), e.g. *Pierrot Le Fou* (1965); Nagisa Oshima (1932–2013) e.g. *Death by Hanging* (1968); and Rainer Werner Fassbinder (1945–82) in films such as *Katzelmacher* (1969). While such works were enthusiastically embraced by cineastes, they failed to capture the attention of a wider public, and by the 1980s Realism had become deeply entrenched as the dominant form of mainstream cinema.

Brecht/Weill listenography

Listed below are five Kurt Weill songs performed by one of Brecht's star performers, Lotte Lenya (1898–81), who was also Weill's wife. With her gravelly, languid drugged-sounding voice, and detached manner of performance, Lenya was the perfect fit for Brecht's V-Effekt style and Weill's music.

1 'Mack the Knife', *The Threepenny Opera* (1928), in German. https://www.youtube.com/watch?v=aPG9GcykPIY
2 'Surabaya Johnny', *Happy End* (1929), in German. https://www.youtube.com/watch?v=aSLTvKC-P3Y
3 'Pirate Jenny', *The Threepenny Opera* (1928), in German, from 1937 film. https://www.youtube.com/watch?v=Ec0clERjQ5A
4 'Moon of Alabama', *Little Mahagonny* (1927), sung originally in English. https://www.youtube.com/watch?v=x-5ata4jDyk
5 'Bilboa Song', *Happy End* (1929), in German. https://www.youtube.com/watch?v=uC2tnJm6GZw

Further reading

Walter Benjamin, *Understanding Brecht*, trans. A. Bostock (London: Verso, 1998).
Bertolt Brecht, *Brecht on Theatre: The Development of an Aesthetic*, ed. and trans. John Willett (London: Methuen; USA, New York: Hill and Wang, 1964).

Bertolt Brecht, *Brecht on Performance: Messingkauf and Modelbooks*, eds. T. Kuhn, S. Giles and M. Silberman (London: Bloomsbury Academic, 2014).

James K. Lyon, *Bertolt Brecht in America* (Princeton, NJ: Princeton University Press, 1980).

Peter Thomson, 'Brecht on Actor Training: On Whose Behalf do we Act?', in *Actor Training*, ed. A. Hodge, 2nd ed. (Abingdon: Routledge, 2010), 98–112.

P. Thomson and G. Sacks, eds, *The Cambridge Companion to Brecht* (Cambridge: Cambridge University Press, 1994).

John Willett, *The Theatre of Bertolt Brecht*, 3rd ed. revised (London: Eyre Methuen, 1977).

Notes

1. Jean Benedetti, *The Art of the Actor* (Abingdon: Routledge, 2007), 189.
2. Thomson, 100.
3. Brecht, 'Notes on Stanislavski', *Tulane Drama Review*, (1964) Vol. 9 (2): 165.
4. https://en.wikipedia.org/wiki/Bertolt_Brecht, edited 1 December 2021.
5. Lyon, 23.
6. Thomson, 101.
7. Brecht, *On Theatre*, 23.
8. Acc. to Weill's wife, Lotte Lenya (1898–1981) https://en.wikipedia.org/wiki/Kurt_Weill), edited 3 November 2021.
9. https://en.wikipedia.org/wiki/The_Threepenny_Opera, edited 1 December 2021.
10. Brecht, *On Theatre,* 90.
11. Ibid., 80.
12. The semantics around the term *'Lehrstücke'* have created a debate as to whether they are meant to comprise a recipe for political action or the teaching of *dialectics* as a way of thinking. See Roswitha Mueller, 'Learning for a New Society: The Lehrstück', *The Cambridge Companion to Brecht* (Cambridge: Cambridge University Press, 1994), 85.
13. Lyon, 21.
14. Ibid., 7–8.
15. Ibid., 17.
16. Ibid., 46, quotes H. R. Hays, a friend of Brecht: 'By one count in 1944 there were fifty-nine refugee German screenwriters in Hollywood, thirty-three directors, twenty-three producers, ten actors, and nineteen composers working for the film industry.'
17. Benedetti, 203. 'Gestus' can be defined as a gesture or movement which defines a character's role in society as opposed to a psychological state.
18. Brecht, *On Theatre*, 165.
19. Lyon, 94.
20. Benedetti,198.
21. Lyon, 93.
22. Lyon, 92.
23. Brecht, *On Theatre*, 91.
24. Ibid., 177.
25. Willett, 178.
26. Ibid., 179.
27. Ibid., 136.
28. Ibid., 92.

29. Ibid.
30. Ibid., 136.
31. Brecht, 'Notes', 159.
32. Thomson, 109.
33. Benjamin, 11.
34. Edward Mackinnon, 'Living in dark times: the poetry of Bertolt Brecht,' *Culture Matters*, 6 July 2020, https://www.culturematters.org.uk/index.php/arts/poetry/item/3433-living-in-dark-times-the-poetry-of-bertolt-brecht.
35. Thomson, 102.
36. Brecht, *On Performance*. *The Short Organum for the Theatre* can be found at https://archive.org/details/139brechtashortorganumforthetheatre/page/2/mode/2up
37. Brecht, *On Theatre*, 238.

25 Sergei Eisenstein
1898–1948

The Moscow Arts Theatre is my deadly enemy. It is the exact antithesis of all I am trying to do. They bring their emotions together to give a continued illusion of realism. I take photographs of reality and then cut them up so as to produce emotions.[1]

It is little known amongst film students that the seeds of the cinematic concepts of one of the greatest pioneers of film as a plastic art – no less than the 'Father of Montage' – emanate from the theatre, and that he developed a unique training system for actors which was practiced widely in Russia, rivalling the Biometrics system of his mentor, **Vslevod Meyerhold**. For those reasons, and more, Sergei Eisenstein merits a short chapter of his own.

Sergei Mikhailovich was a theatre enthusiast from boyhood. Although raised in a classic *haute bourgeois* environment, he was also a fervent believer in the Bolshevik Revolution – *political* from a young age. He trained as an architect/engineer, but enthusiastically joined the Red Army before he could take up practice, thus alienating his father – a White Army sympathizer. In 1920 he was seconded by the army to Minsk in Belarus where, oddly, he encountered Japanese Kabuki, opening his eyes to possibilities beyond the realistic theatre that was dominating the Russian stage at the time. This enthusiasm led him to embark on Japanese language studies, hoping in time to travel to Japan to study. Returning to Moscow, he was deflected from this goal by being offered 'the job [he] was dreaming of' – scenic design director of the First Workers' Theatre of the Moscow Proletkult.[2] At the Proletkult he became a proponent of agit-prop theatre and rejected what he called the 'traditionalist' theatre of **Stanislavski**. He was able to enrol in the Proletkult studios to take classes in **Jaques-Dalcroze's** 'Eurhythmics', and he revelled in the effect the physical exercises had on his sense of well-being.[3]

When Meyerhold was appointed director of the State Higher Theatre Workshops in 1921, Eisenstein auditioned and was given a place in the company, becoming Meyerhold's protégée for a spell. Eisenstein excelled in Biomechanics and was later enlisted by Meyerhold to teach the method.[4] Additionally, he put his architectural and engineering talents to good use designing sets and stages for Meyerhold. He may possibly have seen and been impressed by **Gordon Craig's** Moscow *Hamlet* collaboration with Stanislavski. He certainly read with relish Craig's essays on the *Übermarionette*.[5]

Eisenstein was promoted in 1922 to head the theatre department at Proletkult, and during the summer developed his own actor-training programme, incorporating Biomechanics, 'eccentric movement', sports, acrobatics, boxing, fencing, diction and speech.[6] This eclectic programme centred on his concept of 'Expressive Movement' described as:

> [Movement] that was executed with animal- or machine-like efficiency but was bound up with human psychology – a dialectic of instinctive and rationalized reaction. If a Proletkult performer was requested

to commit a strangulation on the stage, his behavior and action would more closely resemble the rhythm and pacing of a mindful cobra attacking a rabbit than the stagy indications of a proscenium actor.[7]

He used 'Expressive Movement' in performance, where certain common gestures like unclenching a fist, or the chattering of teeth, were enlarged. By manipulating the choreography, the spectator's eyes were directed towards these individual expressive moments, which could be said to herald Eisenstein's theatrical version of a closeup. Commenting on the acting methods employed in his first professional production, *Enough Stupidity for Every Wise Man* (1923), by the Realist playwright Alexander Ostrovsky (1823–1886)[8] he said, '. . . we must look at the dual principle of its composition which ran through the entire production. Its stylistic premise derived from a very simple starting point: the proposition that every action by an actor should expand in intensity to pass beyond the bounds of that activity itself.' He gives the example that if an actor needed to register astonishment, it wasn't enough to be startled with a small gesture, one had to do a backwards somersault.[9]

Given the Symbolist and Constructivist bent of his mentor, Meyerhold, it's easy to see why Eisenstein's developing cinematic interests inclined to *'formalism'* and *'theatrical effects'*. He never approached theatre from the point of view of the actor, eschewing the actor's personal journey and any notion of psychological realism.[10] This is clearly reflected in the way he used actors in his films. In place of following a single actor's psychological journey, he proposed that a multiplicity of faces in its variety can make a point more effectively. He called this 'cut' acting.

> . . . the method of 'cut' acting makes possible the construction of entirely new methods. Replacing one changing face with a whole scale of facial types of varying moods affords a far more acutely expressive result than does the changing surface, too receptive and devoid of organic resistance, of any single professional actor's face.[11]

To devise and then cast his characters, Eisenstein espoused 'typage' – consciously using actors based on their looks and behaviours, largely as stereotypes. Bourgeois characters are always obese, drinking, eating and smoking, whereas the worker characters are slim and athletic. To this purpose, he frequently cast non-professionals. 'I do not pick my actors from the profession . . . [non-professionals] do not act roles. They simply are their natural selves. I get them to repeat before the camera just what they have done in reality.'[12] 'Typage' was not a lazy shortcut for Eisenstein. According to Seton he carried out extensive observational research to discover the characteristics, both physically and psychologically of any given 'type' – a street-cleaner, for example – before inserting them in the film.[13] He wanted his 'types' to be instantly recognizable and deliver an emotional impact on the spectator, so while he was searching for something 'real' in the each image, he wasn't creating Realism. He said, 'I get away from realism by going to reality.'[14]

Like **Adolphe Appia** and Gordon Craig, Eisenstein believed in the engagement of the spectator as a participant, consciously manipulating all the elements of his works for maximum emotional impact on the spectator, to achieve a *specific political goal*. 'The spectator himself constitutes the basic material of the theatre; the objective of every utilitarian theatre . . . is to guide the spectator in the desired direction (frame of mind).'[15]

Laying out a theoretical approach to his production of *Enough Stupidity for Every Wiseman* he coined the term: *'montage of attractions'*.

> An attraction is any aggressive aspect to the theatre; that is, any element of the theatre that subjects the spectator to a sensual or psychological impact, experimentally regulated and mathematically calculated to produce in him certain emotional shocks which, when placed in their proper sequence within the totality of the production, become the only means that enable the spectator to perceive the ideological side of what is being demonstrated – the ultimate ideological conclusion.[16]

Later, he applied the 'montage of attractions' concept to filmmaking, in movies such as *Strike* (1924), *Battleship Potemkin* (1925), *October* (1927) and *Old and New* (1929) developing his revolutionary 'montage' technique using the aggressive juxtaposition of isolated images arranged in a way to *engage the audience intellectually and emotionally* by creating shock and surprise. The quintessential example is the unforgettable sequence of shocking images in the famous Odessa Steps scene in *Battleship Potemkin*. Actors (in most cases non-actors) were asked to produce exaggerated representations of emotional states and simple actions. It was the assembly (montage) of actions and gestures which forms the *emotional line* of the narrative, strongly underscoring the political point. If you haven't seen the movie, this classic scene is readily available to view on the internet.

Once **Socialist Realism** had become the obligatory artistic style, Eisenstein, like his fellow avant-garde filmmakers, struggled to conform. The film *Bezhin Meadow* (1937)[17] was meant to be a Soviet propaganda movie about a farm boy's efforts to stop his father doing damage to the collective – standard Socialist Realism fare – but in the hands of Eisenstein the film was becoming poetic and formalistic. The production was stopped by the powers that be, and Eisenstein was made to recant publicly, confessing that his work was 'patently groundless politically, and anti-artistic in consequence.'[18] The filmed material was destroyed.

There has been much speculation about whether Eisenstein was homosexual, an assumption roundly rejected by the Russian authorities. 'Gay-spotters' point to the undue weighting to the dormitory scenes and other shots of half-clad sailors showing off their torsos in *Battleship Potemkin* as evidence of his predilection for men. A public scandal over his importing homoerotic drawings from Mexico added fuel to the fire. It was commonly held at the time in Moscow's arty circles that he was of that disposition. Certainly, he had a deep and intense relationship with the director Grigori Aleksandrov (1903–83) spanning ten years and ending abruptly when Aleksandrov married at just the time, perhaps coincidentally, when homosexuality became a criminal offence. Eisenstein also married at about the same time, but both men claimed that there was never a sexual relationship. An alleged dalliance with a Mexican male tour guide called Cañedo while scouting for his film *Que Viva Mexico* (never completed) was exploited in Peter Greenaway's 2015 film *Eisenstein in Guanajuato*.[19] Greenaway's movie was banned in Russia, and his proposal never gained much ground due to the generally poor notices and a limited distribution of the film.

Further reading

Sergei Eisenstein, *Film Form, Essays in Film Theory*, ed. and trans. Jay Leyda (New York: Harcourt Brace and World, 1947).

Alma Law and Mel Gordon, *Meyerhold, Eisenstein, and Biomechanics* (Jefferson, NC: McFarland & Company, Inc., 1996).

Mike O'Mahoney, *Sergei Eisenstein* (London: Reaktion Books Ltd., 2008).

Marie Seton, *Sergei M. Eisenstein* (London, Dennis Dobson, rev.1978).

Notes

1. Seton, 115.
2. Law and Gordon, 76. Proletkult was an experimental art institute that arose out of the Russian Revolution of 1917. The name is a portmanteau of the words 'proletarskaya' and 'kultura'. Its aim was to create a working-class aesthetic in all the arts.
3. Ibid.

4. Ibid., 78.
5. Ronald Bergan, *Sergei Eisenstein: A Life in Conflict* (London: Little, Brown & Co., 1997), 63, 79.
6. Law and Gordon, 83.
7. Ibid., 84.
8. Alexander Ostrovsky was a prolific Russian playwright in the mid 1800s, much admired by Tolstoy and Gogol for his realism. He was a keen sociological observer, a commentator on bourgeois greed and abuse of power, whose works were constantly censored by the Imperial authorities. He can be seen as a precursor to Chekhov.
9. Sergei Eisenstein, *Towards a Theory of Montage*, eds. Michael Glenny and Richard Taylor (London: I. B. Tauris & Co. Ltd., 2010), 230.
10. Sergei Eisenstein, 'A Personal Statement' (essay written in 1926), in *Film Essays and a Lecture by Sergei Eisenstein*, ed. Jay Leyda (Princeton, NJ: Princeton University Press, 1968), 14.
11. Eisenstein, 42.
12. Seton, 81.
13. Ibid., 80–1.
14. Ibid., 115.
15. Quoted in Lars Kleberg, 'Theatre of Attractions', in *Theatre as Action: Soviet Russian Avant-Garde Aesthetics* (New York: New York University Press, 1993), 77.
16. Sergei Eisenstein, 'Montage of Attractions: For "Enough Stupidity in Every Wiseman"' (trans. Daniel Gerould), *The Drama Review*, No. 18 (1974): 78.
17. *Bezhin Meadow* [film], directed by Sergei Eisenstein (Moscow: Mosfilm, 1937). The film was eventually partly restored in numerous versions and has become a popular subject in film history studies.
18. The full recantation reads, 'How could it have happened that more than ten years after the victory of *The Battleship Potemkin*, on the twentieth anniversary of October, I came to grief with *Bezhin Meadow*? What caused the catastrophe that overtook a picture I had spent about two years working on? Where lay the original error in my world view that flawed the work, so that, despite the sincerity of my feelings and my dedication, it turned out to be patently groundless politically, and anti-artistic in consequence? Asking myself that question again, and with much soul-searching, I have begun to see my error and to understand it. My error is rooted in a deeply intellectual, individualist illusion. An illusion which starts off on a small scale but can lead to major and tragic mistakes and consequences. An illusion that Lenin did not approve of and that Stalin has constantly unmasked.' Sergei Eisenstein *Volume III Selected Works: Writings, 1934–47*, ed. Richard Taylor, trans. William Powell (London: BFI Publishing, 1996), 100.
19. *Eisenstein in Guanajuato* [film], dir. Peter Greenaway, Pyramide Distribution, 2015.

26 Lee Strasberg
1901–1982

If we say that cornflakes in their very nature cannot be poetic, we deny in acting what we accept in other arts.[1]

An interested observer of theatre since boyhood, Lee Strasberg had the good fortune in his youth to witness performances of some of the greatest actors of the time when they played New York – **Eleonora Duse**[2] (1858–1924), Giovani Grasso (1888–1963) and Jacob Ben-Ami (1890–1997), among others. He didn't seriously contemplate becoming an actor until 1923, at the age of twenty-two when he attended performances of the visiting Moscow Arts Theatre (MAT) at the 59th Street Theater, directed by **Konstantin Stanislavski**. There he witnessed 'for the first time . . . greatness being shared by talents that were not necessarily on the same level, yet were capable of the same intensity, reality, belief, and truth'.[3]

Born Israel Strassberg, in 1901 in Budanov, in what is now Ukraine, Lee Strasberg emigrated to the United States at the age of seven. His parents settled in the Jewish enclave of New York's Lower East Side. Having been taught in Yiddish and Hebrew, he can't quite remember how and where he started speaking English, but eventually he was fluent enough to be sent to a school for intellectually gifted children. However, he dropped out at the age of seventeen following the death of his brother, which affected him profoundly. He found employment as a shipping clerk and bookkeeper for a wig company.

His first taste of theatre had been as a teenager, playing a small part in a Yiddish-language production being performed by the Progressive Drama Club. Later he was persuaded by a friend to join the Chrystie Street Settlement House's drama club, where he acted in small parts. He was talent-spotted there by Philip Loeb (1891–1955), casting director of the Theatre Guild, but he turned down Loeb's offer of work, saying that he had no interest in becoming a professional actor. But then in 1923, he saw the Moscow Arts Theatre New York productions. **Richard Boleslavsky** and **Maria Ouspenskaya** had established a new school, called the **American Lab Theatre** (ALT) – to be based on the teachings of Stanislavski and the MAT. Strasberg auditioned and was given a place. Meanwhile, Loeb cast him in a Theatre Guild production, *Processional* – his first professional stage role.

Strasberg was a notoriously avid reader. As a very young man his imagination was fired up by reading **Gordon Craig's**, *On the Art of the Theatre*[4] which promoted theatre as 'a uniform and coherent art form worthy of the highest respect and admiration.'[5] Strasberg said: 'I doubt that I ever would have actually embarked in the theatre professionally if not for this eye-opening sense of what theatre was, could be, should be, might be.'[6] It was also in this book that he first got wind of Stanislavski and the MAT.[7]

While attending the ALT he remained involved in Chrystie Street, trying his hand at directing amateur actors. One of his productions was a play written by **Jacques Copeau** about the Frenchman's grandparents. Copeau dropped into see it and, according to Strasberg, at one point wept, moved by the realistic portrayals of his progenitors.[8]

At the American Lab Theatre Strasberg met and became friends with **Harold Clurman**, **Stella Adler** and **Robert Lewis**, later to become collaborators in the **Group Theatre**. In 1926 he married Nora Krecaun. Sadly, she died childless three years later. While studying at the ALT, and after, Strasberg maintained his connection with Loeb and the Theatre Guild, working as a stage manager, and acting in several plays.

The Group Theatre was formed in 1931 by Clurman, Cheryl Crawford and Strasberg, conforming to their vision of a new, innovative, progressive theatre company following the ensemble principles of the MAT, with the lofty goal of producing a wholly new *American* theatre. Harold Clurman became shepherd-of-the-flock – a father figure for The Group – while Strasberg was principal director and ideologue. As he consolidated his power in The Group during their first idyllic summer workshop in the Connecticut countryside, Strasberg's personality, according to Clurman, changed: 'There came into his humble demeanour something tight and autocratic, driving and fierce. He would alternate between a childish self-indulgence in people's good opinion of him and an almost sadistic fury when he was balked.'[9]

Towards the end of his reign over The Group, Strasberg married one of his students, the actress Paula Miller, in 1934. Their honeymoon was a subsidized trip to Russia, along with Clurman and Stella Adler – by now Clurman's wife – to survey contemporary theatre. In Moscow, Strasberg was generally disappointed with the prevailing 'sovietized' performances of the MAT but was greatly taken with the work of the Yevgeny Vokhtangov's theatre, which hooked him on that director's version of Stanislavski.

With Paula Strasberg he had two children: Susan, an actress, and John, an acting teacher, with whom he appears to have lacked emotional connection. In her autobiography, Susan talks about how cold and unaffectionate he was, paying much more attention to his books and music than to her.[10] John said about him, 'he was incapable of expressing his own feelings . . . except in his work. He got lost in the need for people to express themselves, because it was his need; he never resolved his own problem.'[11]

His intellectual rigidity, emotional aloofness in personal relations, explosive temper during artistic disputes and his autocrat's hatred of having his authority questioned, meant that Strasberg was often at the centre of The Group's internecine squabbles. His refutation of what Stella Adler enthusiastically reported to The Group members following her encounter in with Stanislavski in Paris alienated many of them. Perhaps the last straw for some was his arrogant statement, 'Stanislavski doesn't know. I know.'[12] In 1937, in response to a letter originated by The Group's Communist cell, and signed by most of the members, he resigned.

During the next ten years he drifted, a bit rudderless, trying his hand at different things. He directed a few plays on Broadway and elsewhere, with not much success. He became a naturalized United States citizen on 16 January 1939. He taught at **Piscator's** Dramatic Workshop and gave classes at the American Theatre Wing, as well as at Yale University. He spent most of his time between 1941 and 1948 in Hollywood, directing screen tests. He returned to New York City to direct on Broadway, again with only a modicum of success.[13] At **Elia Kazan's** bidding he took up teaching at the **Actors Studio** in 1948 and became its Director in 1951. It was there he found his niche. The chapter on the Actors Studio describes his work and the parade of high-profile actors who passed through under his aegis.

The legendary Svengali-style relationship of Marilyn Monroe and Lee Strasberg was symbiotic in nature – she was under his spell, and he, under hers. She had entered the movies from being a call-girl, poorly educated, never having seen a play in a theatre in her life. Following the making of *Gentlemen Prefer Blondes* (1953) her Hollywood housemate, Shelley Winters (1920–2006), who had trained under Strasberg, suggested that *serious actor training* would help her break out of the 'dumb blonde' mould. Strasberg was the guru she needed, and he welcomed her with open arms. A self-publicist and inveterate 'star f--ker' he offended many Studio members by the special manner in which he treated Monroe, and other "famous" actors working out in the Studio'.[14] There are conflicting reports as to how active Monroe actually was in the Studio. By some accounts she was more of an observer than a participant. However, Lee gave her private lessons, possibly more in the vein of psychotherapy than acting lessons. Cindy Adams, in her book *The Imperfect Genius of the Actors Studio* states, 'She was a little scared kid . . . It's shaky and scary at the top. Marilyn Monroe was a person with human relationship problems, worries, fears, inadequacies, insecurities.'[15] Monroe became integrated into the Strasberg family. She regularly hung out in their apartment. Paula became her private acting coach and minder, employed to be with her during filming, working with her on her roles and attempting to moderate her drug dependency and addiction to champagne. As a result of this relationship Marilyn Monroe bequeathed 75 per cent of her considerable estate to Strasberg. Even if she had been more of an observer than participant in the Studio, there is clear evidence of 'The Method' in her film performances.

Marlon Brando's name is also associated with Strasberg, but he was incensed when Strasberg claimed to be his mentor, 'I sometimes went to the Actors Studio on Saturday mornings because Elia Kazan was teaching, and there were usually a lot of good-looking girls there, but Strasberg never taught me acting. Stella did – and later Kazan.'[16]

Paula Miller Strasberg died April 1966 of bone marrow cancer. Strasberg married Anna Mizrahi in 1968. By 1970, he had become less involved with the Actors Studio and, together with Anna Mizrahi, he opened the Lee Strasberg Theatre and Film Institute with branches in New York City and in Hollywood where he taught (and his protégés still teach) 'The Method' in an acting-school context.

Strasberg was cast as an actor in several movies. He is probably best known for his supporting role as the gangster Hyman Roth, alongside his former student Al Pacino in *The Godfather Part II* (1974), a role he took at Pacino's suggestion after Elia Kazan had turned it down, and which earned him an Oscar nomination for Best Supporting Actor. He also had roles in *Going in Style* (1979) and *. . . And Justice for All* (1979).

He died suddenly of a heart attack two days after dancing in the Rockettes chorus line at Radio City Music Hall along with Al Pacino and Robert De Niro in a benefit performance for an actors' charity.

'The Method'

The essence of Strasberg's 'The Method' is what Stanislavski proposed in his 'system', namely, *living truthfully, experiencing real human emotions, in the moment*. In terms of the routes to arrive at those emotions, Strasberg adopted an early idea of Stanislavski – namely that the actor should reach *inwardly* to find appropriate emotions deep within their *psyche* for the scene.

The key to unlocking the actors' emotions, for Strasberg, was the senses. 'Actors must understand their own nature and how to respond sensorially before transforming into a character.'[17] He used the word 'sensorially' to convey the necessity of experiencing life, the world, people and objects through the five senses: what you see, smell, hear, touch and taste.

In his training programme, Strasberg had the same starting point as Stanislavski – the base skill of *relaxation* – the emotional and physical state required to enter what he called the 'creative mood'. Only once relaxed can one concentrate. 'Relaxation and concentration [are] the "two sides of the acting coin".'[18] While suspicious of many auxiliary classes in actor training, especially those physically based, which he found inimical to Method skills, he proposed T'ai Chi Ch'uan studies as excellent training for relaxation, concentration, flexibility and expressivity.[19]

Like Stanislavski, Strasberg defined 'acting' as 'doing' – not just the outward physical manifestation, but as 'the inner motivation and activity of the character; it is the reason and necessity for the actor's appearance on the stage. Action should be described by a [transitive] verb, instead of the infinitive "to be".'[20]

He maintained that actors also need to train the senses, starting with 'overall sensations' (which he termed the 'Overalls') – Strasberg proposed exercises intended to provoke responses to imaginary physical conditions, such as the heat of the sun, a cold shower, etc. This taught the actor how to experience their physical self in relationship to external circumstances.[21] The actor then needs to explore their own personal emotional relationship to sensory events and build a sensory 'memory bank' (my term). For example, perhaps the smell of ironing might generate a warm sense of security related to having watched your mother iron. During his time as principal teacher of the Group Theatre, he initiated the 'Emotional Memory' exercise, in which the actors are encouraged to dredge up and re-live a significant once in a lifetime event from their past and allow the feelings the memory generates to erupt in an articulated action. Clurman tells us,

> Strasberg was a fanatic on the subject of true emotion. Everything was secondary to it. He sought it with the patience of an inquisitor, he was outraged by trick substitutes, and when he had succeeded in stimulating it, he husbanded it, fed, and protected it. Here was something new to most of the actors, something basic, something almost holy. It was revelation in the theatre, and Strasberg was its prophet.[22]

Sense Memory and Emotional Memory, collectively called Affective Memory, are proposed as a method for unlocking personal emotions which are appropriate to the life of the character. Method training is intensely personal and *self-involving* and includes exercises such as the 'Private Moment' which Strasberg used to get actors to overcome inhibitions in the presence of the audience – engaging in an activity in front of spectators in the studio which would normally cause one embarrassment to do publicly. It was derived from Stanislavski's concept of being 'private in public', with an emphasis on concentration and focus. As mentioned elsewhere in the book, 'affective memory' is only *one* element of the actor's preparation eventually proposed by Stanislavski. While Boleslavsky was proselytizing for the earlier 'psychological' aspects of 'the system' in New York, Stanislavski was busy updating it in Moscow, refocusing on 'action' and the use of 'imaginary circumstances'.

The process of character development in Strasberg's Method, as described by Harold Clurman, involves first *describing* the character, then finding its 'inner life' in oneself. The goal is to represent in a realistic manner the psychological construct of the character by bringing one's own psychological makeup, or psyche, to the role. 'The Method' involves dredging up memories from one's past to provide a 'substitution' for what the character – in the circumstances of the script – must be feeling. This is explored in improvisations, which require the actors to do 'extemporaneous scenes based on situations emotionally analogous to those in the play, but not actually part of the play's text'.[23]

The popular idea that 'method acting' demands that an actor lives 'in character' offstage, as practiced by actors such as Daniel Day-Lewis is not actually taught as part of 'The Method'. The technique was tried by Stanislavski but abandoned when he found the results 'never fully satisfactory'.[24] Neither was it promoted by Strasberg.

Strasberg was well-versed in the writings of Sigmund Freud and promoted the idea of psychoanalysis as a tool for acting. 'An actor knows that his body and personality is his instrument of expression. The more he knows about himself the more he is able to make use of himself. Therefore, to the extent that being psychoanalyzed helps an actor know more aspects of himself, it helps him to be a better actor.'[25]

Read the chapter on **Sanford Meisner** to compare his significantly different approach, focused on *action* rather than *psychology*. Both Strasberg and Meisner based their ideas on those of Stanislavski – the former essentially on his earlier proposals. Strasberg's 'value added' to Stanislavski was primarily in the intensification of the psychological aspects of his methods, whereas Meisner, with his application of 'active analysis', his repetition exercises, his use of imagination, and his development of the 'as if' enriched Stanislavski's later teaching. In effect, Strasberg appropriated only certain elements of Stanislavski's system (as filtered through Vakhtangov) and offered a more limited approach to the pursuit of the actor's truth.

Further reading

David Garfield, *The Actors Studio, A Player's Place* (London: Collier MacMillan Publishers, (1972) 1984).
Robert H. Hethmon, ed., *Strasberg at The Actors Studio: Tape Recorded Sessions* (New York: Theater Communications Group, 1991).
Foster Hirsch, *A Method to Their Madness: The History of the Actors Studio* (New York: Da Capo Press, 1984).
Lee Strasberg, *A Dream of Passion: The Development of the Method* (Boston: Little, Brown, & Co., 1987).

Notes

1. Strasberg cited in Hethmon, 67.
2. 'Duse on stage was terrifying. There was a sense of revealing the innermost parts of herself.' 'Her inner technique was intense, her outer expressiveness was beautiful beyond description, but it was never beauty on its own.' Strasberg quoted in Hirsch, 146.
3. Strasberg, 40.
4. Gordon Craig, *On the Art of the Theatre* (London: William Heinemann Ltd., 1911).
5. Garfield, 5.
6. Ibid., 6.
7. Ibid., 8
8. Lola Cohen, ed., *The Lee Strasberg Notes* (New York: Routledge, 2010), 114–15.
9. Harold Clurman, *The Fervent Years* (New York and London: Harcourt Brace, 1945), 52.
10. Susan Strasberg, *Bittersweet* (New York: G. P. Putnam's Sons, 1980), 25. 'His material and spiritual needs were for more knowledge, more books, more music, more poetry, as if through these he would be able to understand the core of human behaviour.'
11. Hirsch, 222.
12. Hirsch, 79.
13. These included *Clash by Night* with Tallulah Bankhead, 1949; *The Big Knife* with John Garfield, 1949; *House of Bernardo Alba* at the Habima Theatre in Tel Aviv, 1949; *The Country Girl* w/ Uta Hagen, 1951.
14. Hirsch, 162.
15. Cindy Adams, *Lee Strasberg: The Imperfect Genius of the Actors Studio* (New York: Doubleday, 1980), 259.
16. Marlon Brando and Robert Lindsey, *Songs My Mother Taught Me* (New York: Random House, 1994), 85. Brandon further remarks on Strasberg: 'He was an ambitious, selfish man who exploited people who attended the Actors Studio, and he tried to project himself as an acting oracle and guru. Some people worshipped him, but I never knew why. To me he was a tasteless and untalented person whom I didn't like very much.'
17. Cohen, 3.
18. Ibid., 4.
19. Garfield, 134–5.
20. Strasberg quoted in John Gassner, *Producing the Play* (New York: Dryden Press, 1944), 160.
21. Cohen, 54.
22. Clurman, 44.
23. Ibid., 43, describing the processes used in the Group Theatre summer workshops.
24. Strasberg, 44.
25. Strasberg quoted in a *Saturday Evening Post* article, referenced by Paul Gray, 'Stanislavski and America: A Critical Chronology', *The Tulane Drama Review*, Winter, 1964, Vol. 9, No. 2: 47.

27 Harold Clurman
1901–1980

Directing is often compared to conducting an orchestra . . . there is one important difference. While a conductor knows the exact properties, possibilities and limitations of each instrument, the director is never certain with the actor whether he is to be stroked, scratched, plucked, or thumped![1]

Harold Clurman has been called the most influential figure in the history of the American theatre. His output as a director was prodigious – he directed over forty plays between 1935 and his death in 1980. He authored seven books. From 1953 until 1980 he was drama critic for left-leaning magazine, *The Nation*, and a regular contributor to *The New York Times* and *The New Republic Magazine*. His influence as co-founder and leader of the **Group Theatre** in the 1930s helped change the face of acting and directing on the American scene. He lectured sporadically but never became a teacher of acting like his colleagues **Meisner**, **Adler** and **Strasberg**, and so left no legacy *in the flesh* as they did, i.e. actors who promoted their teachers' methods. Stella Adler laments that he never created 'an heir', but I marvel that she doesn't acknowledge **Uta Hagen** as someone who was formed and inspired by Clurman and went on to inspire countless other actors.[2]

As a committed internationalist, he was positioned in the centre of a swirling constellation of new influences from Europe in the early twentieth century. He possessed the intellect and open-mindedness to absorb and synthesize these progressive ideas about theatre and realistic acting, and channel them via the Group Theatre, and in his work as a director and pre-eminent theatre critic, in a manner that profoundly influenced the way we now work. He was a theatre man through-and-through – never seriously tempted by Hollywood, although his guru-ship of The Group and his guidance as a director helped mould several great movie actors of the 1950s and 1960s.[3]

In common with Strasberg, Clurman had Russian Ukrainian roots, but he was born in the USA – on the Lower East Side of New York. As a boy he was taken to see plays in the Yiddish theatre, and became stagestruck, even if he couldn't speak Yiddish. He attended Columbia University and then the University of Paris. In Paris he shared a flat with the quintessential composer of 'American' music, Aaron Copland (1900–90), who introduced him to Sanford Meisner. He chose to write his thesis on French theatre and was able to meet **Jacques Copeau** and see the Moscow Arts Theatre in action. By the time he returned to New York, he was thoroughly committed to a career in the theatre and managed to obtain work backstage in the Theatre Guild. He attended the lectures of **Boleslavsky** and **Ouspenskaya** and signed up for classes at the **American Lab Theatre**. In 1925, Jacques Copeau brought his production of *Brothers Karamazov* to New York, and Clurman served as his assistant. At Copeau's suggestion Clurman read **Gordon Craig's** book, *On the Art of the Theatre* but professes to have not understood it.

Clurman was the visionary behind the Group Theatre, persuading Strasberg and producer Cheryl Crawford, with whom he had worked at the Theatre Guild, to establish a company based on the *ensemble* models used by Stanislavski and Copeau, to practice the precepts of Stanislavski, and to establish a *new American theatre*. Of the three founders, Clurman was the 'father figure' and intellectual guru, sharing directing chores with Strasberg (and others) and coordinating with Crawford the business and administration. His central role is set out fully in the chapter on the Group Theatre. In his memoire, *The Fervent Years*, he vividly chronicled the rise and fall of The Group and levelled significant criticism at Lee Strasberg.

Besotted by the actress Stella Adler, who he met in the ALT, he persuaded her to join The Group, and eventually married her in 1943. They visited Moscow together, and he was with her when she studied briefly under Stanislavski in Paris. As a director he was grounded in Realism, having embraced Strasberg's 'Method' as his principal *modus operandi*, but as a critic he enlarged his vision of theatre to include other forms. He was exposed to formalistic Symbolistic ideas by **Vsevolod Meyerhold**, who he met in Moscow, as well as the anti-Realism of Jacques Copeau.[4] Clurman was interested in **Piscator's** ideas on political theatre, and produced the German's play, *The Case of Clyde Griffiths* (1936) in New York, directed by Lee Strasberg.[5] He later made a failed bid with **Bertolt Brecht** to direct his play *Galileo* with Charles Laughton in the lead. In journals he expressed his fascination and support for **Judith Malina's** and **Julian Beck's Living Theatre** – the North American embodiment of Piscator's teaching.[6] Clurman was 'broad church' in his theoretical view of theatre but was most comfortable with the basic principles of Realism for his practical work.

As a director Clurman didn't develop a proprietary and distinct body of theory of his own. His actor-centric approach was largely based on Stanislavski, as framed by Strasberg, promoting a form of acting in which the actor discovers the character through their own personality and psychology. While he didn't discount 'affective memory', he also laid stress on the later ideas of Stanislavski, regarding *action* to be the generator of emotion, and imaginary circumstances as an effective device to create an actor's substitution. He realized that each actor was unique, had their own personal process, and had to be dealt with individually (as per the epigraph). Clurman's pedagogical contribution to the field of directing was his invaluable book, *On Directing*. Rich in examples, anecdotes and common-sense advice gleaned from his own long career – the book offers to the director a fundamental Stanislavskian approach to a project, be it for theatre or cinema. According to Clurman, the director's starting point, and principal responsibility, is to determine the 'spine' of the work – its *through-action*. Once defined, one must determine how the spine is *to be executed* – the *style* (tone, atmosphere, central metaphor, emphasis and dimension). This includes the *style of acting*. Clurman uniquely proposed that early on in their analysis the director read all parts separately to understand the spine of each individual character, which is to say their SuperObjective. 'The character's spines had best be stated as *active verbs*. The spine is an active response to a wish: the characters want something and do something to satisfy that wish.'[7] Clurman further proposed that the director draws a map, or 'score' of their production as a useful way of tracking the characters' arcs and conflicts.

In addition to being an 'actor's director', Clurman was a political creature – he was deeply concerned with the social context of theatre, while eschewing didacticism or party affiliation. One of the reasons, according to Clurman, that the Group Theatre fell apart was that it was *politically* bankrupt, despite its members' liberal, even Communist sentiments. 'The truth is that none of them has anything but the most rudimentary, naïve understanding of politics; they were all essentially apolitical no matter what they may have once argued.' He went on to criticize The Group for falling prey to commercialism and the 'star system'.[8]

Clurman was the least parochial of the North American critics and directors – a true internationalist. One of his most prized possessions was his *Legion d'Honneur* medal.

Further reading

Harold Clurman, *On Directing* (New York: Macmillan Publishing Co., Inc, 1972, reprint: Fireside Books NY, 1997).
Harold Clurman, *The Fervent Years* (New York: Harcourt, Brace, Jovanovich, 1975) reprinted 1983.
Marjorie Loggia and Glenn Young, eds., *The Collected Works of Harold Clurman* (New York: Loggia & Young, Applause Book, 1994).

Notes

1. Clurman, *On Directing*, 171.
2. Stella Adler, Intro, *Fervent*, vii.
3. For example, Franchot Tone (1905–68), John Garfield (1913–52), Frances Farmer (1913–70).
4. Clurman, *Fervent*, 325.
5. The play is based on the novel *An American Tragedy in New York*, by Theodore Dreiser (1871–1945).
6. Harold Clurman, 'New Theater Now', *Harper's Magazine*, February 1971.
7. Clurman, *On Directing*, 77–8. The concept of the 'spine' is covered thoroughly in the **Working with Actors** in the chapter 'A Director Prepares'.
8. Clurman, *Fervent*, 306–7.

28 Stella Adler
1901–1992

There's nothing more important than Shakespeare: he's God, darling.[1]

Stella Adler, of whom it has been said of her, 'Acting was not *in* her blood. It *was* her blood,' lived to the age of ninety-one. Eighty-seven of the ninety-one years were devoted to her passion for acting. Her stage debut was at the age of four – in Yiddish. Her parents, Jacob and Sarah Adler were highly renowned actors in the Yiddish theatre, which was thriving at the time. (Between 1900 and 1920 1.5 million European Jewish refugees arrived in the USA, and most settled in the Lower East Side of New York.)[2] At the age of twenty-one, Stella finally made her English language debut – on Broadway, no less, in *The World We Live In* (1922*)*. Her theatrical family travelled widely in the USA and abroad, presenting plays to Yiddish-speaking audiences – including London, where, at the age of eighteen, in 1923, Stella played Naomi in *Elisa Ben Avia*. This production ran for a year, and during that time young Stella was seduced by a dashing young Englishman of Russian noble ancestry named Horace Eliashcheff. They were married two years later when he moved to New York, but it gradually became evident to Horace that Stella's first love was the theatre, and he eventually went his own way, leaving Stella with her only child, Ellen, born in 1927.

Adler was an early arrival to the table of Russian Realism. Although she was in London in 1923 when the Moscow Arts Theatre (MAT) took New York by storm, the reverberations reached her across the Atlantic. Once home, she watched a performance of a play which **Richard Boleslavsky** directed using his **Stanislavskian** approach. She was mesmerized by the truthfulness of the acting. Her attendance at some of Boleslavsky's public lectures further whetted her appetite and she enrolled in his two-year course at the **American Lab Theatre** (ALT) – ignoring the protests of her parents who told her she already knew how to act.[3] Fellow students at the ALT included **Lee Strasberg**, later to become her nemesis, and **Harold Clurman**, later to become her husband.

When the **Group Theatre** was formed in 1931 to train and perform in the 'new Realism', she was asked to join by Harold Clurman, and she did so initially with enthusiasm. However, during her ten-year association and despite (or perhaps because of) Clurman's encouragement, she never quite fit in. He later observed: 'She was both attracted to and repelled by The Group'.[4] She was used to being a 'star' in the Yiddish theatre star-system, and the idea of playing supporting roles in an ensemble troupe did not hold much appeal. Secondly, she had caught Clurman's eye, and they had become involved in an intimate relationship, creating jealousies and suspicions among other members of The Group. The frequent and obvious tensions in their relationship spilled over into their work. Elia Kazan said of her: 'We all resented the lady, believed that she'd scattered Harold's concentration and corrupted his good sense.'[5] However, he admits to liking her later in life.[6]

In 1934, while travelling in Europe, Stella and Harold met Stanislavski, who was convalescing in Paris. Bemused by her accounts of how his teachings were being mis-construed in New York, he agreed to take her on as a private student for five weeks. During that time, she learned that Stanislavski had rejected the use of *affective memory* (it had contributed to mental breakdowns in a few of his students, including **Michael Chekhov**), and had discovered the power of *imaginary circumstances* as an actor's substitution. He had also expanded his earlier emphasis on *action* into what his followers posthumously termed a 'Method of Physical Action', which used improvisational work on actions (*études*) arising from the given circumstances of the script. He also mapped out for her a diagram of the workings of 'the system', later published by **Robert Lewis** in his book, *Method – or Madness?*[7] (An explanation of that chart can be found in the chapter on Robert Lewis, below.)

When she returned from Paris, clutching her diagram and full of excitement with her discoveries, Lee Strasberg grudgingly consented for her to give a few lectures to the membership. In them she explained that Stanislavski currently proposed that when the actors simply acted on the character's objectives, as set out in the given circumstances, their emotions would take care of themselves. And that using *personal imaginary circumstances* was a more effective way to explore appropriate emotions than *affective memory*. These new ideas were received enthusiastically, especially by Robert Lewis and Sanford Meisner, but they were anathema to Strasberg – The Group's principal director and pedagogical leader, who had based his entire approach on *affective memory*. He would brook no further discussion and attempted to close Adler down, saying, 'I don't teach Stanislavski's method, I teach Strasberg's Method!'[8] As a result, Adler, Lewis and Meisner drifted away, the latter going on to develop his own version of Stanislavski's teachings at the **Neighborhood Playhouse**.

Adler did some of her best stage work with The Group, notably her role as Bessie Berger in Clifford Odet's *Awake and Sing*. Even though praised for her role in *Success Story* (1932) – a Group Theatre production on Broadway – she was frustrated having to work with Lee Strasberg. She found his autocratic direction intolerably limiting, and he found her to be too 'emotional'.[9] Elsewhere on Broadway she played several roles, but rarely played the leads. Frustrated, in 1937 she went to Hollywood where she stayed for six years and acted in three unremarkable movies using the name Stella Ardler – one was a lead role (*Love on Toast*, 1937) and two in supporting parts. In 1941, she returned to New York, disheartened and disappointed with the Hollywood system. Her acolyte Marlon Brando believed that her being Jewish was a limiting factor in the roles she was given. 'Like many Jewish actors of her era, she faced a cruel and insidious form of anti-Semitism; producers in New York, and especially Hollywood wouldn't hire actors if they "looked Jewish," no matter how good they were.'[10]

Back in New York she started teaching for **Erwin Piscator** at the New School for Social Research (where Marlon Brando turned up in her class), and in 1949 founded her own school, the Stella Adler Conservatory. Over the decades innumerable highly talented actors have walked through her door.

ACTORS WHO STUDIED WITH STELLA ADLER
Robert De Niro
Marlon Brando
Warren Beatty
Harvey Keitel
Shelley Winters
Susan Sarandon
Roy Scheider

> Elaine Stritch
> Martin Sheen
> Mark Ruffalo
> Benicio Del Toro
> Candice Bergen
> Salma Hayek

She was a spirited and flamboyant teacher – very much in the *grande dame* vein – but could be cutting and was not above humiliating recalcitrant students.

In terms of her methods, she promoted *characterization* and *role interpretation* over psychology. She rejected Lee Strasberg's technique: 'The actor cannot afford to look only to his own life for all his material nor pull strictly from his own experiences to find his acting choices and feelings.'[11] On the day of Strasberg's death she famously proclaimed to her class: 'It will take a hundred years before the harm that man has done to the art of acting can be corrected.'[12] While she had rejoiced in the discovery of Stanislavski's concept of *imaginary circumstances* she never developed it into a system, at least not as Sanford Meisner did with his '*études*' (improvisation regime). In practice she promoted a balanced approach, evidenced in the work of former students such as James Dean and Marlon Brando (both of whom additionally attended the **Actors Studio** under Strasberg, and both of whom frequently reverted to affective memory, giving introverted performances, working off themselves).[13]

The thing that set Adler apart from other former Group teachers was her notion of the supremacy of the author. This distinct approach stemmed from the literary foundations of the Yiddish theatre in which she grew up. The author's job was to create the great characters required for the 'SuperObjective' of the work. She said, 'A playwright is like God. He makes a world, needs man and woman to live in it, and creates them in his own image.'[14] Of course there was no god greater than Shakespeare. It was the actor's job to step up to the 'size' of the character – to imagine the character's world: 'The ideas of the greatest playwrights are almost always larger than the experiences of even the best actors.'[15] Adler rejected the idea that the character emanates from the actor: 'Use your creative imagination to create a past that belongs to your character. I don't want you to be stuck with your own life. It's too little.'[16]

Adler's process involved an initial analysis of the *given circumstances* of the script, teasing out aspects of the character (the actor had to sometimes double-guess the author's intentions for the character). Actors were also required to research the *background* and the *environment* the character inhabits. 'Every time we perform an action, we have to be aware of the world in which the action takes place.'[17] Only at a second stage would the actor *personalize* the objectives and the character's situations. It was a more outside-in approach than the more organic inside-out approach of Meisner.

In common with Sanford Meisner, Robert Lewis and **Uta Hagen**, Adler put the accent on action. 'Everything we do in the theatre is an action,' she said, 'That's what acting means.'[18] 'Acting and doing are the same. When you're acting, you're *doing* something, but you have to learn not to *do* it differently when you *act* it.'[19]

But not any-old action would do. An action needed to be 'justified'. She proposed: 'In an action you need to know *what* you do, *where* you do it, *when* you do it, and *why* you do it. But you don't need to know *how* you do it. The how is spontaneous and unexpected.'[20] Justifications should be simple, non-emotional – to get one from A to B – and the actions, *doable*. She urged her actors to be definite, 'big', and carry through with actions (which may explain why actors such as Marlon Brando and Harvey Keitel always have such weight and physical presence in their scenes). '*Size*' was a concept she inculcated in her actors – physically in terms of strong bodies and voices, in their actions, but also in terms of their interpretation – to bring a bigger meaning to the text. The actor needs a *sense of the epic* – to be 'worthy' of the stage.[21]

A further form of justification used by Adler concerns the *pre-circumstances* to the scene. 'You must prepare for every entrance by creating the circumstances of where you've come from. This need not be elaborate . . . You must . . . justify every entrance. There must be a reason why you have entered the circumstances of the play.'[22]

Adler, like Uta Hagen, emphasized the need to *imbue* actions with *reality*, even when the *actual* act can't be performed in the scene (for reasons of danger or technicalities). As with Hagen's '*endowing*', she said the key to finding the reality was in careful attention to the sensorial or physiological aspect of the action. 'The muscles don't accept lies. The muscles are very precise. They can tell the difference between a full bottle and a half-empty bottle, between a jar whose lid is loose and one whose lid is much too tight.'[23] She additionally stressed that the actor should *imbue* each prop they use, and the set, and all the elements within it with a reality, using one's imagination. 'Realism means the ability to be at home on the stage, and the way you do that is to make every object around you meaningful.'[24]

The Stella Adler Studio of Acting, opened in 1949, with its partner school in Los Angeles. The Studios offer a wide variety of acting courses and workshops on numerous levels, including a practical four-year course, tied to a bachelor's degree at the Tisch School of the Arts of New York University.

Further reading

Stella Adler, *Stella Adler: The Art of Acting*, ed. Howard Kissel (New York: Applause, 2000).
Sheana Ochoa, *Stella!: Mother of Modern Acting* (Milwaukee: Applause, 2014).

Notes

1. Quoted in Foster Hirsch, *A Method to Their Madness* (New York: DaCapo, 1984), 219.
2. Ochoa, 90. As a testament to the Yiddish Theatre's extraordinary popularity, upon his death in 1926 between 50,000–100,000 people followed Jacob Adler's funeral cortege.
3. Ibid., 92.
4. Harold Clurman, *The Fervent Years* (New York: Harcourt Brace Jovanovich, 1975), 84.
5. Elia Kazan, *Elia Kazan: A Life* (New York: Da Capo Press,1997), 193.
6. Ibid., 149.
7. Robert Lewis, *Method – or Madness?* (New York: Samuel French Inc., 1958).
8. Robert Lewis interview with former student Robert Ellermann, cited in Ruthel Honey Darvas doctoral dissertation, 'A Comparative Study of Robert Lewis, Lee Strasberg, Stella Adler and Sandford Meisner in the Context of Current Research About the Stanislavski System', Detroit: Wayne State University, 2010, 15.
9. Ochoa, 139.
10. Marlon Brando and Robert Lindsey, *Songs My Mother Taught Me* (New York: Random House, 1994), 78.
11. Adler, 65.
12. Michel Ciment, *Kazan on Kazan* (London: Secker & Warburg, 1973), 143.
13. Joanne Woodward – Meisner trained – hated working with Brando. 'He wasn't there,' she complained, 'He was somewhere else. There was nothing to reach out to.' She quipped that the only way she'd work with him again would be 'in rear projection'. Aubrey Malone, *Sidney Lumet, The Actor's Director* (Jefferson, NC: McFarland & Co. Inc., 2020), 33.

14. Stella Adler, *On Ibsen Strindberg and Chekhov* (New York: Vintage Books, Random House Inc., 2000), 52.
15. Adler.
16. https://www.imdb.com/name/nm0012245/bio?ref_=nm_ov_bio_sm
17. Adler, 45.
18. Ibid., 53.
19. Ibid., 44.
20. Ibid., 119.
21. Adler expounds on the need for the actor to be 'epic' in YouTube: https://www.youtube.com/watch?v=kf6UM_vXZN8
22. Adler, 140.
23. Ibid., 60.
24. Ibid.

29 Moshe Feldenkrais
1904–1984

The past is history, the future only a guess – the present makes them both what they are. If we do nothing to change our emotional pattern of behaviour, tomorrow will resemble yesterday in most details except the date.[1]

Moshe Feldenkrais contended that the route to changing our emotional patterns of behaviour is via the development of our self-image, and this is achieved through an understanding of our way of moving. 'Our self-image is in general more limited and smaller than our potential,' and achieving 'awareness through movement' can help us to meet our potential.[2] You *are* how you *move*.

Feldenkrais was a sort of twentieth-century Renaissance man who lived in many places, spoke numerous languages, and achieved a variety of accomplishments in life. Born in Ukraine, he emigrated to Palestine at the age of thirteen. He lived in Paris in the 1930s, obtained an engineering degree, followed by a doctorate in physics. He worked in the famous Curie Radium Institute before fleeing to Britain when the Nazis invaded France in 1940. He studied judo and was the first European to obtain a black belt. Having reactivated an old soccer knee injury when slipping on the deck of the submarine during war-time service, he explored self-rehabilitation and somatic awareness techniques,[3] and this became the basis of the methodology which was to be his abiding interest in life.

His legacy is the Feldenkrais Method of Somatic Education, a system of exercises for actors, dancers, athletes and musicians, which is taught and practiced in acting schools internationally. **Peter Brook** invited Feldenkrais to teach at the Théâtre des Bouffes du Nord in Paris, and subsequently used it as the basic movement training for his actors. The 'system' consists of exercises and gentle manipulation of the body, with the goal of improving somatic functioning, better posture, increasing self-awareness through movement, and a sense of well-being.

In the late 1960s, Feldenkrais began to train corps of practitioners to propagate his methods, first in Tel Aviv and later in the USA, starting with 'New Age' communities growing up around San Francisco at that time. He formed the Feldenkrais Guild in 1977, to promote his techniques and to accredit certified teachers.

While Feldenkrais cannot be said to have made a *direct* contribution to acting technique, many actors have trained in his methods, as have dancers and musicians, and Feldenkrais's technique is taught in drama schools alongside **Laban**, **Dalcroze** and other schools of movement training.

Feldenkrais describes four components of action – *movement*, *sensation*, *feeling* and *thought*, present in varying degrees.[4] He contends that *action* always involves '*self-image*', and to change our self-image we need to change the balance within the framework of those four components, with special emphasis on movement. In the words of Feldenkrais teacher Victoria Worsley, 'When you know what you do, you can do what you want.'[5]

The Feldenkrais Method is practiced in two forms, using methods of *experiential learning,* i.e. exercises, which claim to help the artist or individual to make intelligent choices about everyday movement and action.

The first form, 'Awareness Through Movement' (ATM), is taught in group sessions, and the second, Functional Integration (FI), in private sessions. Both are designed as a means of enabling the individual to experience the 'transformative miracle of efficient, integrated, and pleasing movement', to quote the promotional jargon. Moshe Feldenkrais's book, *Awareness Through Movement* (1972, and subsequent editions), spells out the techniques, and contains pictorial references of exercises and movements.

Early in his research, Feldenkrais began to relate his methods both to Modern Dance (*Ausdruckstanz*) and to the established German system of '*Reform-Gymnastics*', which purported to develop an awareness of the student's '*inner rhythms*' and of the requirements of their organism. He was also aware of **Stanislavski's** training in the use of psychophysical mechanisms as a route to discovering one's 'inner rhythms', a concept akin to Feldenkrais own rationale for privileging movement to access an awareness of the *unity* of whole self.[6]

Feldenkrais's starting point is '*self-image*' – one's image of oneself defines our way of moving, and vice versa. Movement is the basis of awareness and conversely awareness is the basis of movement. 'For Feldenkrais an awareness of how we do something can change the quality of what we do, and who we are in the world.'[7]

> Self-image is formed by the unique identification of oneself in gravity and proprioceptive space, but most importantly it is to be understood through the sense in which we feel that our own particular way of doing something – walking, speaking, thinking, or play a musical instrument for example – is sensed as uniquely our own . . .[8]

It follows that the Feldenkrais Method, functioning as it does on the basis of self-image, is by nature introspective, encouraging *self-awareness* in the actor. Hence, it is anathema to Meisner performance, which is all about the *loss* of self-awareness. Stanislavski, with respect to 'inner rhythms', wisely proposed that all actors need to develop their 'instrument'. To that end, the value of exercise and somatic (movement) training such as the Feldenkrais Method lies in an actor's preparatory work on themselves and not what they bring to performance.

Further reading

Moshe Feldenkrais, *The Potent Self: A Study of Spontaneity and Compulsion* (Berkeley, CA: Frog Ltd., 1985).
Moshe Feldenkrais, *Awareness Through Movement: Health Exercises for Personal Growth* (New York: Harper Collins, 1990).
Victoria Worsley, *Feldenkrais for Actors, How to Do Less and Discover More* (London: Nick Hern Books, 2016).

Notes

1. Feldenkrais, *Potent Self*, Preface, xxxv.
2. Feldenkrais, *Awareness,* 15.
3. Somatic: relating to the body (the bits which are not organs) as distinct from the mind.
4. Feldenkrais, *Awareness*, 10.
5. Worsley, 29.
6. Thomas Kampe, 'Dancing the Soma-esctatic: Feldenkrais and the Modernist Body', *The Feldenkrais Method in Creative Practice: Dance, Music, and Theatre*, ed. Robert Sholl (London: Methuen Drama, 2021) DOI: 10.5040/9781350158412.0007, 96.0/816
7. Ibid., 45.4/816.
8. Sholl, Introduction, 43.0-45.4.816.

30 Sanford Meisner
1905–1997

He has been the most principled teacher of acting on this country for decades now, and every time I am reading actors I can pretty well tell which ones have studied with Meisner. It is because they are honest and simple and don't lay on complications that aren't necessary.[1]

Arthur Miller

The death of his five-year-old brother when Sanford Meisner was only three, and the ineptitude of the inference on the part of his parents that *he* was to blame, was the defining event of Meisner's childhood. 'I have had considerable experience in psychoanalysis, so I know quite clearly that the death of my brother . . . was the dominant emotion influence in my life from which I have never recovered.'[2] Knowing this, it is easy to understand why Sanford Meisner readily rejected **Lee Strasberg's** reliance on 'affective memory' as the fundamental tool for actors searching for the emotional truth – to be explored later in this chapter.

Like his contemporary, **Robert Lewis**, Meisner's first course of study in the arts was music. He won a scholarship to train as a concert pianist at what is now the world-famous Julliard School of Music. However, economic necessity meant that he had to work in his father's fur business – it was the time of the Great Depression. His music endeavours were abruptly cut off. But another artistic interest was rekindled. He had wanted to be an actor since his teen years, putting on plays for the family – as one does. One day, after his graduation from high school at the age of nineteen, he heard that the Theatre Guild was hiring youngsters for a play called *They Knew What They Wanted*. He took courage in his hands and went along for an interview. He got the job – as an extra. Once he set foot on the stage, there was no looking back.

He went on to win a scholarship to the Theatre Guild School, and while there, through a mutual friend – the young composer Aaron Copland (1900–90) – he was introduced to a young man of the world, just back from studying at the Sorbonne in Paris – **Harold Clurman**. In turn, Clurman introduced him to the slightly older Lee Strasberg. Meisner was initially deeply impressed by Strasberg, and acted for him in a small production at the Chrystie Street Settlement House.

It was 1924–5 . . . 'heady' times in the New York theatre. **Boleslavsk**y had established the **American Lab Theatre**. **Jacques Copeau** returned to New York to mount his version of *The Brothers Karamazov*. '**Stanislavski**' was the word on everyone's lips. A new dawn from the East was awakening the slumbering American theatre, and Sanford, Harold and Lee wanted to be in the vanguard. Clurman, already a published theatre critic, started giving lectures to invited members of the acting community, and Meisner hungrily devoured the news he imparted about the Moscow Arts Theatre, Stanislavski's ideas on acting and the need for a *new American theatre*.

Meisner enthusiastically supported Clurman and Strasberg, along with a dynamic young Theatre Guild producer, Cheryl Crawford, in establishing a new theatre company based on those ideas. The **Group Theatre** was formed in 1931, and Sanford Meisner was a founding member.

During the ten years of The Group's life, Meisner directed or acted in more than a dozen plays, among others, *Waiting for Lefty*, which he co-directed with its writer, Clifford Odets (1906–63, another Group Theatre member). Later during his time with the Group Theatre, Meisner also started teaching at the **Neighborhood Playhouse**, beginning in 1935, and assuming headship of the acting programme in 1940.

When **Stella Adler** returned from Paris announcing that 'affective memory' was redundant, the limits of 'The Method' became apparent, and Meisner researched other possibilities for achieving the elusive goal of the 'truthful' performance. Under the aegis of the Neighborhood Playhouse, he began to develop a set of techniques based on *action* and *imagination* to supplant the teachings of Strasberg.

LIMITATIONS OF 'THE METHOD' – 'AFFECTIVE MEMORY'
It can be psychologically damaging – especially if the actor relives traumas.
It is not directable. It can mean only one thing to the actor.
It is limited to what the actor has experienced.
Memory dims and distorts – experience *remembered* is not the same as experience *lived,* thus emotional recall is not necessarily *truthful.*
It makes for an introspective actor who only works off themself, and with whom it is often difficult for other actors to engage.

In evidence of the first limitation, consider how many famous 'Method'-style actors have suffered nervous breakdowns while working on a role, starting with one of the earliest practitioners of 'emotional memory', **Michael Chekhov**. Later examples include Marlon Brando (1924–2004), Rod Steiger (1925–2002) and Daniel Day-Lewis (b. 1957). The latter, in reaction to seeing the ghost of his own father while acting in *Hamlet*, fled the stage mid-performance in Richard Eyre's 1998 production, vowing never to return to theatre again. He later said: 'Of course, if you're working on a play like *Hamlet*, you explore everything through your own experience.'[3]

Method actors are also notoriously difficult to direct – they don't want to shift from their individual notions of which emotions and motivations are appropriate for the character, because they derive, in effect, from *their own experience* – which belongs uniquely to them. These actors can become introspective and selfish, working strictly off themselves, and leaving their partner actors in the lurch. There are several clear examples of this on-screen in James Dean's 'Method' performances in *Rebel Without a Cause*,[4] and *East of Eden*,[5] when he leaves his fellow actors high and dry.

What an actor can produce using emotional recall is *only* as wide or deep as their *experience of life*. I encounter this problem frequently in teaching eighteen- to twenty-one-year-olds. In the personal monologues that we do in class it is sometimes difficult for the students to come up with any *profound* emotional experience from their past, such as a death, abuse, heartbreak or a devastating hurt. Moreover, memory dims and distorts, is elusive, or is partly blocked due to being traumatic or painful, and a certain *dishonesty* and *self-deception* can creep into the recall process.

In place of emotional memory Meisner proposed using *imagination*, which he claimed was more *potent* and more *workable*. 'Sandy', as he is affectionately called by his students, felt that he had discovered a healthier, broader, more versatile way of achieving realistic and truthful performances.

When the Group Theatre collapsed in 1941, Meisner put his full attention to his role as Head of Drama at the Neighborhood Playhouse, while fitting in an occasional acting or directing gig. He played on Broadway in *Embezzled* (1944), *Crime and Punishment* (1948) and *The Cold Wind and the Warm* (1958), the latter directed by Harold Clurman. He directed the much-lauded revival of William Saroyan's *The Time of Your Life* in 1955. When **Elia Kazan** and Robert Lewis set up the **Actors Studio** in 1947, Meisner also gave classes there – prior to Lee Strasberg being drafted in to head up the teaching programme in 1951. (Meisner was allegedly furious that Strasberg later took credit for some of the students that *he* had actually trained while at the Studio.)[6]

In 1959 he moved to Hollywood to become director of the New Talent Division of 20th Century Fox. While in Los Angeles, he was able to indulge in a bit of film acting, and one can see his performances in *The Story on Page One* (1958), *Tender is the Night* (1962), *Mikey and Nicky* (1975).

In 1964 he returned to New York, to the Neighborhood Playhouse, where he continued as Head of Drama until he retired in 1990. Did I say 'retired'? Not quite. In 1985, he and his companion, actor/dancer James Carville, had established the Meisner/Carville School of Acting as a summer school, at their home on the island of Bequia in the Caribbean. Then, in 1994, Meisner's protégé, Martin Barter, persuaded him and Carville to cofound the Sanford Meisner Center for the Arts, in North Hollywood, Los Angeles.

He finally 'officially' retired from active teaching in 1994. But in 'retirement', even though confined to a wheelchair, he always managed to attend meetings and performances at his school. Sanford Meisner was the embodiment of the phrase: 'You can't keep a good man down.' When a car accident in New York made him severely lame, he bought a walker and carried on teaching. When a cataract operation resulted in a detached retina and near blindness, he obtained hyper-thick glasses and carried on teaching. When cancer of the throat (he was a chain-smoker) resulted in a laryngectomy, he learned to speak by *belching* his words, got himself fitted with a microphone and amplification system . . . and carried on teaching. 'I can't stop . . . I'm old enough to stop. I can't see. I can't talk. I can hardly walk.'[7]

To the very end he was revered by his students for his wisdom, his incisiveness, his ability to communicate, and his honesty. A list of some of his more recognizable students include many of America's best film actors of the last century.

ACTORS WHO STUDIED WITH SANFORD MEISNER
Joan Allen
Kim Basinger
Sandra Bullock
Joan Fontaine
Lee Grant
Felicity Huffman
Anne Jackson
Jennifer Jones
Diane Keaton
Grace Kelly
Suzanne Pleshette
Mary Steenburgen
Frances Sternhagen
Jo Van Fleet
Gwen Verdon
Jessica Walter

Naomi Watts
Joanne Woodward
Alec Baldwin
Jeff Bridges
James Caan
Tom Cruise
Matt Damon
James Doohan
Robert Duvall
Leonardo Di Caprio
Peter Falk
James Gandolfini
Jeff Goldblum
Joel Grey
Gene Hackman
Stephen Harvey
Philip Seymour Hoffman
Jack Lemmon
William H. Macy
John Malkovich
Dylan McDermont
Steve McQueen
Leslie Nielson
Edmond O'Brien
Gregory Peck
Tom Radcliffe
Tony Randall
Sam Rockwell
Mark Rydell
Billy Sharp
Jon Voight
Eli Wallach
Christopher Waltz

DIRECTORS AND WRITERS WHO STUDIED WITH MEISNER

Vivian Matalon (director)
Bob Fosse (director)
John Frankenheimer (director)
Elia Kazan (director)
David Mamet (writer/director)
Antony James (director)
Arthur Miller (writer)
Sydney Pollack (actor-director)
Sidney Lumet (director)

Sanford Meisner made one further appearance as an actor, at the age of ninety, as a patient in the US television series *E.R.*, for which he was personally commended by Steven Spielberg.[8]

Meisner was not *rigidly* set on his methods. Anything was acceptable that made the actor *full* and *true* in performance, including – as a last resort – affective memory. Regarding his own teaching, he said that Robert Duvall never 'got it' – but he 'had it,' so it didn't matter. He recognized that there were many ways to skin a cat, and that much of what a good actor did was instinctive.

His techniques, like those of Stanislavski, evolved over time – in Meisner's case that's a span of fifty-nine years of teaching. During the early stages his ideas were based on the Group Theatre's (i.e. Strasberg's) interpretation of Stanislavski, even if he was opposed to the increasing emphasis on both the intellectual and 'inward-looking' exercises, especially 'affective or emotional memory'[9] – which he saw as 'introverting actors who were already introverted.'[10] It was only in the 1950s and 1960s that he fully developed his famous technique of 'repetition', as a way of taking the actors out of themselves.[11]

The principles of Meisner Technique, and a programme of study and application, are fully laid out in chapters of the companion to this book, **Working with Actors**. The principles of Stanislavski's system, as they stood in 1923, and upon which Meisner Technique is based are set out in the earlier chapter of this book **'From Russia with Love'**. Meisner's 'repetition' exercises readily lend themselves to improvisations *similar to* those of Stanislavski in his 'Active Analysis'.

I have attempted to encapsulate Meisner's teaching in the chart below.

The Essence of Meisner Technique
Listening is key. When you put your attention 100 per cent on your partner actor or something else occurring in the scene, *you come to life naturally*.
Good acting is based in *the reality of doing*. When you are doing something for real, your attention is *not* on yourself. Listening is an action.
Don't do anything unless something happens to *make you do it*. Choices, inspirations, actions, must be inspired or provoked by the action of another person, or the environment.
Don't worry about your emotions. They will *surface according to need*, in reaction to what's happening in the scene. Explore them through improvisation, then leave them alone.
Work from your heart and not your head. Work to unlock the doors to your *inner self*. Follow your instincts – each and every time.
Don't *'conceptualize'* a character in advance. *Discover* the character in improvisation with other actor/characters. 'Don't do the character. Let the character do you.'
Memorize the text like a shopping list, neutrally, without emphatic punctuation. Find its *meaning* while engaged with the other actors, especially through improvisation – *don't predetermine it*.
Analyse the script, scene-by-scene, in terms of your *character's objectives* with respect to the other characters and obstacles. *Personalize* each of the character's objectives by imagining yourself in a situation which encapsulates the *essence* of that objective. The actor's 'As if'.

Avoid use of *emotional memory* to find appropriate emotions for the scene. It is *not* as effective as using *imaginary circumstances* and is potentially dangerous.
Enter the scene (or shot sequence) emotionally *'full'*. To do this use an *'emotional preparation'* based on what's happened to the character just before the scene. An 'emotional preparation' is another form of *personalization*.
The director needs to determine the *'spine'* or *SuperObjective* of the work, and of each of the characters therein. The actors, in rehearsal and improvisation, need to discover the *'spine'*, or *'throughline'* of their character, and remain faithful to their character's point-of-view.
Be specific in your choices. Particularize *everything* in the text with a *specific* and personal meaning. The greater the *specificity*, the greater the *reality*.
When presenting a monologue, conceive it as a *dialogue*, imagining the listener as another character, and have a *clear objective* as to what you want to obtain from them in the telling.
Live moment-to-moment. React spontaneously. *Don't anticipate anything*. Enjoy the journey. 'Acting can be fun.'

Further reading

Sanford Meisner and Dennis Longwell, *Sanford Meisner on Acting* (New York: Vintage Books, for Random House, 1987).

Sanford Meisner Masterclass from the Sanford Meisner Center, available on DVD or by streaming: https://www.sanfordmeisnermasterclass.co

Notes

1. Meisner Center website: https://www.themeisnercenter.com, posted 2019.
2. Meisner and Longwell, 5.
3. Matt Trueman, 'Did Daniel Day-Lewis see his father's ghost as Hamlet? That is the question . . .' *The Guardian*, 29 October 2012, https://amp.theguardian.com/stage/2012/oct/29/daniel-day-lewis-hamlet-ghost
4. *Rebel Without a Cause* [film], dir. Nicholas Ray, Warner Bros., 1955.
5. *East if Eden* [film], dir. Elia Kazan, Warner Bros., 1955.
6. https://en.wikipedia.org/wiki/Sanford_Meis
7. Meisner and Longwell, 186.
8. Peter B. Flint, 'Sanford Meisner, a Mentor Who Guided Actors and Directors Toward Truth, Dies at 91' [obit], *The New York Times*, 4 February 1997.
9. Philippa Strandberg-Long, Philippa, 'Mapping Meisner – How Stanislavski's System influenced Meisner's Process', ResearchGate, February 2018, https://www.researchgate.net/publication/323272368: 3.
10. Meisner and Longwell, 182.
11. Ibid., 184.

31 Viola Spolin
1906–1994

Everyone can act. Everyone can improvise. Anyone who wishes to, can play in the theater and learn to become 'stage-worthy'.[1]

Viola Spolin maintained that acting was a natural impulse. She discovered this while training as a settlement worker in the slums of Chicago when she began using games to bring out the expressive potential in underprivileged children. Over years this evolved into a body of exercises involving storytelling and games – at first for children, then later for adults – which she called 'Theatre of Games'. Having gone to New York and trained in 'The Method', she observed that its effect was to entangle actors in *'seriousness and thinking'*. She dedicated herself to disentangle them. With a group of Chicago-based actors, including her son, Paul Sills (1927–2008), she developed her theories and formed the USA's first *improvisational* theatre company (Compass Theatre). While her work sometimes felt nearer to psychodrama and sociodrama, it provided the basis for the renowned comedy improvisational work of Chicago's famous Second City Company.

Looking at Spolin's work one might assume a direct line to the two **Jacques – Lecoq** and **Copeau**. In fact, the only professional-level actor training Spolin received was **Stanislavskian**, with the **Group Theatre**. In 1935 she went to New York to study with The Group, leaving her children behind in Chicago. But she couldn't bear the separation and returned to them before the end of the year. From that time onwards her teaching was based on elements of Stanislavski – the 'who', 'what', and 'where', the *objective*, and *actions* supporting that objective. But she seems not to have been infected by Strasberg's notions of 'affective memory' and character analysis. Spolin proposed acting *without thinking*, and reliance on intuition rather than intellect. It may have been that she acquired some knowledge of Jacques Copeau – especially his love of games – from **Harold Clurman** who, as stated elsewhere, was enamoured of Copeau's work and would have interacted with Spolin while at the Group Theatre.

Returning to her native city she was able to combine the Stanislavskian *études* she'd experienced with The Group, with the freer style improvisation she had developed with children, creating her own improvisational *acting tools for adults*. Viola Spolin is sometimes called the 'Mother of Modern Improvisation', and her book, *Improvisation for the Theatre*, written in 1963, contains a valuable collection of games – all highly social, and always containing a problem which needs solving – which are still in use today for drama workshops for all ages. For directors interested in incorporating games in their rehearsal process, it would be worth studying *Theatre Games for Rehearsal*. Noted film director Rob Reiner (b. 1947), once a pupil of Spolin and a member of the Second City Company, uses them in film rehearsals.[2] They are widely used by directors and coaches working with children for film and theatre. Spolin wrote:

> We learn through experience and experiencing, and no one teaches anyone anything. This is as true for the infant moving from kicking and crawling to walking as it is for the scientist with his equations. If the

environment permits it, anyone can learn whatever he chooses to learn; and if the individual permits it, the environment will teach him everything it has to teach. 'Talent' or 'lack of talent' have little to do with it.[3]

Further reading

Viola Spolin, *Improvisation for the Theatre: A Handbook of Teaching and Directing Techniques* (Evanston, IL: Northwestern University Press, 1963).

Viola Spolin, *Theater Games for Rehearsal* (Evanston IL: Northwestern University Press, [1983] 2011).

Notes

1. Spolin, *Improvisation* (London: Pitman, 1973 edn.), 3.
2. Noted in a biography of Spolin, written by Aretha Sills and Carol Sills, published on the Viola Spolin Estate website: https://www.violaspolin.org/bio
3. Spolin, *Improvisation*, 3.

32 Robert Lewis
1909–1997

Truth must not be made into a static, stultifying thing. In art, truth should be the search for truth.[1]

Robert Lewis grew up in a lower middle class Jewish family in Brooklyn, took up the cello as a kid, and studied music. He had an early fascination with opera, which led him, via the backstage, as it were, to an interest in theatre. To the chagrin of his mother, he abandoned his music studies in his teens and embarked on a career in show-business. He took bit parts in stock companies, and eventually landed a full-time job as a puppeteer in Sue Hastings' Marionette Theatre touring company – 'acting out every voice from the villainous giant in Jack and the Beanstalk to Eeyore, the donkey in Winnie the Pooh'.[2]

The story of how he obtained his first acting job in actress Eva Le Gallienne's Civic Repertory Theatre illustrates the cheekiness of the man. He snuck, undetected, into the back of the theatre, into the stalls, being mistaken for the photographer's assistant. When Ms. Le Gallienne (1899–1991) shouted to the actors resting in the auditorium requesting more *figurants* (extras) in a scene, Lewis, the interloper, jumped on the stage and insinuated himself in the crowd. He ended up getting small parts in five plays that season, kick-starting his professional career.[3]

He next joined a group called The Actor's Workshop. One evening, **Harold Clurman** and **Lee Strasberg** came to see their chum, **Sanford Meisner**, in one of the Workshop plays in which Lewis had a part. Afterwards, backstage, Strasberg asked him, coldly: 'What were you trying to do?' Despite this initial frosty criticism, Bobby (as everyone called him) summoned up the courage to audition for the **Group Theatre**. He was given a place amongst the first twenty-eight actors in the first-ever Group summer camp, in rural Connecticut.

He was the youngest member of The Group. Due to his stature and girth, his self-image limited his horizons to working as a character actor, and not a leading-man type. There was an abundance of such roles in Group productions, including Strasberg's production of *Men in White,* and Clifford Odets' plays *Waiting for Lefty*, *Awake and Sing!*, *Paradise Lost* and *Golden Boy*. According to Mel Gordon, Bobby 'added comic subtlety and variety to The Group's normally tendentious productions'.[4] He revelled in his life in The Group's summer camps, making life-long friends, and bonding especially with another character actor, **Elia Kazan**.

Like Kazan, Lewis was politically active. He initiated a call to reform the actors' union, Equity, demanding that it represent its members better. He rallied other Group Theatre actors to the cause – eventually achieving the desired reforms.

Of the three Group leaders, Lewis found his greatest inspiration in Harold Clurman, whom he described as 'passionate and evangelical.' 'Harold exhorted us all to relate the theatre to life. He defined the word theatre as something that need not only be the presentation of a production for the entertainment of the public.'[5]

In 1937, with Clurman's approval, Lewis set up the Group Theatre Studio – a school with twenty-five paying pupils who supported twenty-five full or part scholarships, using Group actors as teachers. There were over a thousand applicants for the fifty places. The Studio lasted only one season. It was impossible to sustain due to the teachers' touring obligations, including those of Bobby, who was sent by Clurman to London in 1938 to direct the production of Clifford Odet's *Golden Boy*.[6]

In 1937, as a result of a revolt against the leadership on the part of disgruntled Group members (fomented by agitation on the part of its Communist cell) Lee Strasberg and Cheryl Crawford resigned as directors (this is elaborated in the **Group Theatre** chapter). A year later, Lewis and Kazan restarted Group workshops, as well as the Group Theatre Studio, which resumed with fifty actors chosen from the 400 who auditioned. Lewis, Kazan and Sanford Meisner were the principal teachers. In 1941, Clurman finally closed the Group Theatre (and with it the Studio) due to its insolvency.

In the meantime, Lewis had his Broadway directorial debut, with a critically successful production of William Saroyan's *My Heart's in the Highlands* (1939). The show's producer, Clurman, had chosen Bobby 'because he had both a talent and a taste for fantasy and the non-realistic forms generally'.[7] **Sidney Lumet** was a cast member.

After the Group Theatre wound down in 1941, Kazan and Lewis attempted to form something to replace it – the Top Dollar Theatre – new plays appealing to a mass audience, and cheap seats. It proved financially unfeasible and never saw the light of day. They 'bought a script, issued a bulletin, published a preliminary article of faith, and disappeared'.[8] As Mel Gordon points out: 'The theatre's title revealed its blatant fiscal naivety.'[9]

However, Lewis was distracted. He was beginning to be offered character parts in movies, necessitating a move to Los Angeles in 1940. In Hollywood he specialized in characters of different nationalities, such as the German officers he played in *Paris After Dark* (1943) and *Son of Lassie* (1945), or the French collaborationist in *Tonight We Raid Calais* (1943). His most famous role was that of the villainous Japanese Colonel Sato in *Dragon Seed* (1944), opposite Katharine Hepburn (1907–2003). His favourite experience of this era was playing a Frenchman opposite his friend Charles Chaplin in *Monsieur Verdoux* (1947). There were other notable performances, and Lewis also had the chance to direct or co-direct a few musicals. Nonetheless, he felt bored, underused and frustrated in Hollywood, and struggled for some years to get out of his contract at MGM so he could return to the East Coast.[10]

He finally managed. In 1947, he returned to New York to direct his first commercial success on Broadway – Alan Jay Lerner and Frederick Loewe's fantasy musical set in the Highlands of Scotland, *Brigadoon* – a box office smash and long-runner (581 performances).

There's a debate in print about who first proposed forming the **Actors Studio**. (See Kazan's account in his chapter, and the chapter on The Actors Studio.) Lewis said it was his idea. In any event, Cheryl Crawford facilitated it and became the third partner. The first intake comprised approximately fifty young actors. Lewis taught advanced classes in the afternoon, with emphasis on 'inner action' and 'intention', while Kazan, in the mornings, taught 'basic training' to the younger actors, focusing on sensory memory, imagination and improvisation. Strasberg was left out of the picture because Lewis disagreed with his ideas, and Kazan preferred Lewis's style: 'Bobby's teaching had characteristics Lee's did not have: simplicity, clarity, and a sense of humor. Bobby stressed the bolder, imaginative side of acting, rather than emphasizing the interior emotional event.'[11]

Lewis left The Studio due to what he considered to be an act of treachery on the part of Kazan. Lewis had been offered a musical to direct by Crawford. Kazan advised him to turn it down, and Bobby did so – then Kazan, later, agreed to direct it himself, leaving Crawford to break the news. Lewis was deeply hurt.[12] Again, different versions of the story have been told. Kazan brushed it off, saying, 'He quit The Studio after the first year, for reasons I thought absurd.'[13]

In any event, Broadway was calling, and Lewis went off to enjoy a most fruitful career as a Broadway director. Older readers may recognize some of his productions: *Regina* (1949); *The Happy Time* (1950); *An Enemy of the People* (1950); *The Grass Harp* (1952); *The Teahouse of the August Moon* (1953); *Witness for the Prosecution* (1954); *Mister Johnson* (1956); *Jamaica* (1957); *The Hidden River* (1957); *Handful of Fire* (1958); *Chéri* (1959); *Kwamina* (1961); *Foxy* (1964); *Traveller Without Luggage* (1964); *On a Clear Day You Can See Forever* (1965); and *Harold and Maude* (1980).

In 1952 he created another outlet for his teaching, the Robert Lewis Theatre Workshop, which lasted until his retirement in 1974. In 1957 Bobby Lewis gave a series of late-night lectures at the Playhouse Theatre in New York. It was sold out, packed to the rafters with the *curious* and *confused* – actors and directors. Lewis had promised a demystification of 'The Method' – every young actor aspired to become a 'Method' actor, but few understood what that meant. He started by showing the chart which **Stella Adler** had drawn to the instructions of **Stanislavski** during her classes with the master in Paris in 1934.

The original chart, which you can find in Lewis' book *Method or Madness?* is not available for republication.[14] It's a fascinating curiosity, representing Stanislavski's belaboured attempt to codify a diverse range of concepts into a 'system'. It's somewhat unfathomable, much like his writing. I'm not sure it helped in the demystification Lewis was after. The drawing is in the form of an organ – the actor's 'organ', if you will – played by three pedals: Feeling, Will and Mind. The set of thirteen organ pipes on the right-hand side, represent the *external* aspects of the actor's organism (e.g. vocal technique, movement, external tempo and rhythm) and, on the left-hand side, seventeen pipes representing the *internal* conduits for arriving at a performance (e.g. units and objectives, imagination, the 'magic if', emotional memory). Pushkin's dictum, often quoted by Stanislavski**,** was scribed in the upper right-hand corner: 'The truth of passion, the verisimilitude of feeling, placed in the given circumstances, that is what our reason demands of a writer, or a dramatic poet.'

Lewis reported in his lecture that Adler's discoveries in Paris revealed that Strasberg's 'Method', while valid in its particulars, was a *misrepresentation* of Stanislavski, emphasizing only some parts of Stanislavski's theories, and giving a lopsided weight to the actor's internal self or psychology, rather than to the action required of the actor by the given circumstances of the scene. Referring to Method actors playing Shakespeare, he said: 'What they do is take Richard III and bring it to themselves. I said to one of those actors once: "Did you ever think of taking yourself to Richard III?"'[15]

Lewis shared with Kazan a clear understanding of the centrality of 'action'. Like Stanislavski, he believed that actors should place their attention on *action/intention* instead of *emotion* or *character*. It was his belief that if actors concentrate on actions/intentions, then emotions and character will emerge accordingly, in a logical and artistically truthful manner. **Sanford Meisner** also held this view. When Lewis talks of *action*, he is referring to internal action, i.e. the *intention* which gives the *impulse* to action – the *internal* experience leads the actor to the *external* physical manifestation of action.

One of Lewis's lectures concerns the actor's and director's role as an endless quest for *truth*. His definition of truth embraces not only the *truthful feelings of the actor*, but also the truth of the *role*, the truth of any given *moment* of the circumstances of the scene, the truth of the *author*, and the truth of the *particular style* of the production. 'Those are all truths that make up a certain moment,' and not simply the actor's internal truth.'[16]

Lewis was a proponent of Stanislavski's *'magic if'* concept, as opposed to Meisner's *'as-if'*. The 'magic if' is about the character in given circumstances, and not about the actor in personal circumstances. '[It's] the character's situation: his life in his city in his time, and so forth; not my life in my city in my time.'[17] The actor asks themself what they would I do if they were that character, in that time and place, social class, etc. How would they truthfully react to those circumstances? Whereas, in the 'as-if' the actor imagines circumstances within the *framework* of their own life (using people, places, and things they know), which might engender a similar emotional reaction to the circumstances the character confronts, and the subsequent action/intention. Both approaches use the actor's imagination. If it's a contest, I'd vote for the 'as-if' because it reaches the truthful emotions of the actor, however, the 'magic if', in the way Lewis proposes, is useful in characterization.

As actor-turned-director Lewis had a great sympathy for his own actors. His directing style borrowed a page from Clurman's book: 'It is better to evoke than to command.'[18] He spoke of *deluding* the actors into thinking they are using themselves and not just doing what the director tells them. 'I never say to an actor. "Come in here! Then walk over there!" I always say, "Don't you remember yesterday when you came in here and then walked over there . . ." and they say, "Oh yes, of course." You have to make them feel it's theirs.'[19]

Lewis had a practical non-dogmatic approach to Stanislavski, and to 'technique' in general. 'The whole point is to know that when you get in trouble with a role you can then turn to your technical knowledge for help. Otherwise, forget it.'[20] 'My one fear in training is dogmatism – sense that there was only one way to do it, and that is your way.'[21] In 1952 Bobby Lewis returned to teaching, in the 1970s becoming head of the Yale School of Drama Acting and Directing Departments, where he taught, among others Meryl Streep (b.1949) and Sigourney Weaver (b. 1949). Students and actors alike loved working with him because Bobby always imparted joy in the work. He was fun-loving, a showman, and admired by his students with few exceptions. One of those was Barbara Kazan, Elia's wife, who found his teaching to be 'superficial,' complaining 'He shows off and camps all the time.'[22] Lewis's homosexuality did not appear to be an issue in his career. When asked why he never discussed his sexuality in his memoirs, he replied that 'he assumed everyone in theater was queer; there was no particular reason to even mention it'.[23]

Further reading

Robert Lewis, *Method – or Madness?* (New York: Samuel French Inc., 1958).
Robert Lewis, *Advice to the Players* (New York: Harpers and Row, 1980).
Robert Lewis, *Slings and Arrows: Theatre in My Life* (Briarcliff Manor, NY: Stein & Day, 1984).

Notes

1. Lewis, *Method*, 102.
2. Lewis, *Slings*, 23.
3. Ibid., 28.
4. Mel Gordon, *Stanislavsky in America* (Abingdon: Routledge, 2010), 167.
5. Lewis, *Slings*, 37.
6. Harold Clurman, *The Fervent Years* (London: Dennis Dobson, Ltd., 1946), 212.
7. Ibid., 248.
8. Ibid., 280.
9. Gordon, 171.
10. https://en.wikipedia.org/wiki/Robert_Lewis_(director), as modified 2 September 2020.
11. Elia Kazan, *Elia Kazan: A Life* (New York: Da Capo Press,1997), 302.
12. Lewis, *Slings*, 188. The musical, *Love Life*, had music by Kurt Weill and book by Alan Jay Lerner, and was reasonably successful.
13. Kazan, 302.

14. Lewis, *Method*, 34–5.
15. An interview reported by Charles Marowitz, *Prospero's Staff, Acting and Directing in Contemporary Theatre* (Bloomington: Indiana University Press, 1986), 79.
16. Lewis, *Method*, 163.
17. Robert Lewis, Foreword to Konstantin Stanislavski, *Creating a Role*, trans. Elizabeth Hapgood (New York: Theatre Arts Books, 1968), vi.
18. Harold Clurman, *On Directing* (New York: Fireside Books, 1997), 115.
19. Marowitz, 89.
20. Lewis, *Advice*, Preface, (x).
21. Lewis, *Slings*, 282.
22. Kazan, 653.
23. Gordon, 165.

33   Elia Kazan
1909–2003

The material of my profession is the lives the actors have led up to now. The basic channel of the role must flow through the actor.[1]

If the SAG or Actors' Equity were ever to establish a special *Actors' Director* award, Elia Kazan would surely be its first honorary recipient. Just as **Sanford Meisner** might be said to represent the flowering of **Stanislavski's** ideas on acting, Kazan can be considered as the embodiment of the Stanislavskian approach to directing, most especially in film. Indeed, he represents a pedigree line from the 'master', through **Boleslavsky**, via the **Group Theatre** teachings of **Strasberg** and **Clurman**, and the **Actors Studio (**refer to chapters on each**)**. The copious Oscars, BAFTAs, *Palmes d'Or*, etc. garnered by his actors and for his direction are a testament to the success of his methods.

In common with Lee Strasberg, Kazan viewed life through the prism of an immigrant outsider. He was born *Elia Kazanjoglou*, in Constantinople. His parents were Anatolian Greeks – a persecuted minority in Turkey. When Elia was four years old they emigrated to the USA, settling in a Greek ghetto in New York City. Kazan later immortalized their journey in his autobiography, *America America* (1962), from which he created a film of the same title in 1963. His parents had the good sense to enrol Elia in a Montessori school at the age of five – the first step in a solid education, taking him eventually to Williams College, and the Yale School of Drama. As a college student he struggled to support himself, taking on part-time jobs, the most demeaning of which was waiting on tables in a fraternity house. According to his biographer Michel Ciment, this experience serving macho Aryan males created in him a proletarian hostility 'to privilege, to good looks, to Americans, to Wasps'.[2]

Before finishing his last semester at Yale in 1932, 'Gadg' (from Gadget, a nickname he'd picked up at Williams because he was 'small and handy') applied for the summer camp programme of the Group Theater and was accepted as an apprentice. As he half-expected, at the end of an intense summer of learning, he was turned down for membership in The Group by Harold Clurman and Lee Strasberg. Clurman told him: 'You may have talent for the theatre, but it's certainly not for acting.'[3]

In addition to providing a conduit for his love of the stage, his summer with The Group had nurtured his political interests. In the autumn several younger members, mostly radicalized middle-class, left and joined one of the far-left political theatre companies springing up in New York City – ideologically cemented collectives aligning themselves with the masses.[4] Kazan followed suit, and joined one called the Theatre of Action, directing a play for them (*The Young Go First*), and living communally with his committed comrades. Ultimately, he found their didactic brand of theatre to be rigid and limited, discovering that most of his fellow-travellers were ideologues rather than artists. Moreover, the commune was squalid. He decided that he was, after all, an elitist and not a collectivist . . . and left.

Two-thirds of the members of the Group Theatre were 'left-wing', and several, including Kazan, were members of a Communist cell, whose ambition, he discovered, was to take over The Group from within. Kazan became a 'spy' for his cell in this endeavour, but ultimately baulked at the idea of a 'putsch'. For his defiance he was summarily tried by Party cadres in a kangaroo court. He quit the Party in anger. He still held on to his beliefs in the Revolution, but when Stalin made a pact with Hitler, he, like many leftists, gave up on the USSR.[5] His disillusionment did not, however, extend to Russian theatre, which he continued to fervently believe offered the way forward for American drama. He was especially impressed with **Yevgeny Vakhtangov's** ideas which were being promoted by Strasberg after his visit to Russia.

As compensation for his rejection as an actor from The Group by Clurman and Strasberg, Cheryl Crawford offered Kazan a stagehand job, and invited him back to the next Group summer camp. In addition to stagehand duties, he was given some small parts. Bit by bit, he cranked up a professional career as an actor. The irony is that five years after his rejection by Clurman he was 'playing leading roles in Group productions under Harold's direction and getting excellent notices.'[6]

Success at theatre directing started in 1934 with *Dimitroff*, a polemic play about the Reichstag fire, and continued gradually through 1947, when he mounted Thornton Wilder's *Skin of Our Teeth* – a runaway success, which put him on the map as a top Broadway director. Suddenly he was being offered every play on the market. That production also marked for him the moment in which, he proclaims, 'I became a director.'[7] His leading lady, Tallulah Bankhead (1902–68), a diva and 'bitch' of the first order, had resented the young director and had tried her damnedest to get him fired (Orson Welles was the originally proposed director). Tallulah had also been stirring up trouble with other actors in the cast, especially Frederick March (1895–1975) and his wife, Florence (1901–88). Kazan's initial tactics in dealing with this megastar had been to swallow his pride, to tolerate and cajole, until one day Ms. Bankhead, in front of the cast and crew, went off on a rant (an *aria furioso*) about the sets and directorial matters in general not to her satisfaction. Kazan *exploded*, surprising himself, telling her that *he* was the director, and the sets were *his* province – effectively, to get back in her box and shut the lid. She stomped off, as the cast and crew applauded Kazan's bravery. It was that moment when he knew he had 'arrived'.[8]

In parallel with his New York theatre success, Kazan's film career on the West Coast got off to a good start, with a seven-picture contract with 20th Century Fox. His first feature film, *A Tree Grows in Brooklyn*, was one of the top money-makers of 1945, and garnered quite decent reviews, some commenting on Kazan's incisive 'representation of human existence'.[9]

Gentleman's Agreement (1947), a film about anti-Semitism in America, won Kazan his first directing Oscar, as well as Best Picture, and a slew of nominations and wins for his actors. Now, in addition to his Broadway success, Kazan was considered a top director in Hollywood. While the movie was highly praised at the time of its release ('brilliant blow against racial and religious intolerance'),[10] it is now generally considered to be clichéd and restrained – not one of Kazan's best.

In 1947, in the midst of a tug-of-war between the East and West Coasts over his services – Oh lucky man! – Kazan found time, in league with Cheryl Crawford and **Bobby Lewis**, to establish the Actors Studio. By his account, the idea had come to him while visiting the Philippines during the War, advising the Army on the establishment of 'self-entertainment units' as an adjunct to the USO. In Manila, he had a sudden 'fevered' desire to create something to replace the Group Theatre – namely, a place to train and for actors to practice the techniques of *realism* and *psychological-based* performance, to breed more actors with whom he could work creatively. He was, at that moment, *literally* fevered – in bed, semi-comatose with the dengue, cursing the mosquito that bit him, and thinking he was going to die.[11] When he returned to New York he went for a long walk in Central Park with Bobby Lewis, and mapped out the plan for the Actors Studio. It would be different to The Group, in that it would function as a 'lab', and not a production entity, and was to be established as a non-profit organization. At its inception The Studio 'belonged' to Kazan, with Lewis as his henchman. 'It was his place the way the Group Theatre had been **Clurman's**'.[12]

Initially Kazan and Lewis split the teaching responsibilities, but the two fell out with each other and Lewis left. Kazan asked Lee Strasberg to step in. He refused at first, miffed that he hadn't been asked in lieu of Lewis in the first place. Kazan's eyes had been abruptly opened some years earlier regarding Lee Strasberg, when his former teacher and director humiliated him in front of cast and crew on a show (*Gold Eagle Guy*, 1934), in which he was working as a stagehand. Strasberg had ruthlessly passed the blame for his own bad decisions on to Kazan (this was said to be a Strasberg character trait). It hurt and humiliated Kazan deeply, and he never forgave him.[13] Nonetheless, with the demands of his increasing East and West Coast workload, Kazan needed someone with the qualities Strasberg possessed, so he swallowed his pride. He found that once Strasberg agreed, 'No one could have been more committed or more devoted. Or more valued by everyone there. Over the years, respect became hero worship, and hero worship idolatry.'[14]

In 1947 Kazan had another runaway success on Broadway – *A Streetcar Named Desire*, in which Marlon Brando displayed his Method wares (and other assets) for all the world to admire. More films, and more plays quickly followed. He made the movie version of *Streetcar* in 1951, followed by *Viva Zapata!* in 1952, both with Brando. Kazan was riding high in the saddle. Then, suddenly – to continue the metaphor – he was thrown from his horse.

The House of Representatives Un-American Activities Committee (HUAC) had been convened as a Standing Committee in 1947, investigating Communist influence in Hollywood, leading to the conviction of the Hollywood Ten and the infamous blacklist.[15] In 1952, Kazan was called to give testimony in a HUAC session. In that *in camera* session, he openly declared that he had been a Party member but refused to give the names of his cell members in the Group Theatre. An irate anti-Communist gossip columnist leaked news of that private session, just days before the release of *Streetcar*. The studio held its breath – but the news had no visible impact on the public reception of the film. At a second session of the HUAC, Kazan went ahead and named The Group cell members (including Lee Strasberg's wife, Paula, who had hosted Kazan's kangaroo court at her flat). This 'naming' produced an outcry and condemnation on the part of Hollywood and theatre-world liberals, and many thereafter refused to work with him. Explaining his position he said, 'I don't think there is anything in my life towards which I have more ambivalence, because, obviously, there's something disgusting about giving other people's names . . . I've had two feelings: one feeling is that what I did was repulsive, and the opposite feeling, when I see what the Soviet Union has done to its writers, and their death camps, and the Nazi pact and the Polish and Czech repression – well.' He goes on to admit, 'and I've never denied, that there was a personal element in it, which is that I was very angry, humiliated, and disturbed – furious, I guess – at the way they booted me out of the Party.'[16]

There may have been further holding-of-the-breath on the part of Hollywood screen moguls over all the bad publicity generated by the HUAC outing, but it proved to be a momentary glitch, and Kazan was soon busily making movies: *On the Waterfront*, 1953 – ironically featuring a snitch justifying himself; *East of Eden*, 1955 – Method actor James Dean's last film; and *Splendor in the Grass*, 1961. This movie featured Warren Beatty – **Stella Adler's** protégé – and Natalie Wood, who was not Method trained. Her casting is illustrative of Kazan's methods. Wood was considered, at that moment, to be 'a washed-up child star', but the studio had a contract with her, and she was cheap. Kazan wasn't keen, but when he met her, he perceived an 'unsatisfied hunger' in her. 'I talked with her more quietly then and more personally. I wanted to find out what human material was there, what her inner life was.'[17] And when she told him that she was being psychoanalysed, that clinched it. He cast her, and in the process of developing the role managed to get Wood to reach the deepest corners of her psyche and deliver a multi-layered performance matching the intensity of Beatty.

Given his abiding interest in the psychology of the character, and that of the actor, Kazan's casting methods were based not on what the actor could *show* but what Kazan could *sense* is inside. 'I don't cast by reading. I take the actor for a walk or I take him to dinner or I watch him when he doesn't notice it and I try to find what is inside him.'[18] He found the potential for the role within the life of the actor. He adds: 'I never cast by looks because looks are false.'[19]

Kazan was always prepared to go on a personal journey of exploration with his actors, continually focusing on their *internal self*. Brando, in contrast to his normal distain for directors, said: 'Gadg was the only [director] who ever really stimulated me, got into a part with me and virtually acted it with me.'[20]

He shot his movies intensively, urging his actors to stay 'in character', remain near the set, and to rehearse between scenes, with freedom to improvise. He frequently used what was produced in these last-minute impromptu rehearsals in the filming. For example, in *On the Waterfront*, rehearsing with Brando while a set was being lit, the female lead, Eva Marie Saint (b. 1924), accidentally dropped her glove. Brando picked it up, possessing it as an 'object' in the Stanislavskian sense, full of sense memory. This was used in the film – a classic 'Method' example of an object being imbued with emotional significance. Brando said that Kazan frequently told him: 'Listen, go work on it, then bring it to me and show me what you've got.' Fifty per cent of the time he liked it.[21]

He always made certain that in any given scene the actors worked with *clear objectives*, otherwise a scene had no energy: 'The key word is . . . "to want". "What do you want?"' '. . .my actors come on strong, they're all alive, they're all dynamic – no matter how quiet.'[22] Additionally, he always insisted that they worked on the pre-circumstances of the scene, in order to be emotionally prepared upon entrance.[23]

As mentioned above, Kazan loved the use of objects. Put your attention on an object and you take it off yourself. Common things are charged with personal meaning, infused with sensory and emotional memories, adding psychological layers. A scene in *East of Eden* (1953), in which James Dean's character comes to ask a favour of his mother (Jo Van Fleet), is a lesson in the use of objects. She has numerous to work with (wearing gloves – an affectation of the period – lighting/smoking a cigarette, removing a hat, fixing her hair, writing a cheque with a dip pen, closing the door of the pot-belly stove), but James Dean unfortunately has none, which perhaps contributes to his embarrassing self-consciousness in the scene.

Kazan clearly had respect for the actor, having been one, and his working methods were collaborative to a degree, but he was adamant that the creation of a stage or film work was not a 'democratic' endeavour – *the director is in charge*. The director is the repository of the *artistic vision* which is, in fact, a personal interpretation of the *author's vision,* or in Stanislavskian terms – the 'spine'. Kazan – like Clurman – believed it is essential for the director to understand and articulate the 'spine' – both the SuperObjective of the work, and the through-lines of each of his characters (see **Working with Actors**, 'A Director Prepares'). They both learned this, of course, from Boleslavsky . . . who got it from Stanislavski.

For Kazan, like Stanislavski in later years, action was everything. Describing his directing methods, he said: 'I will say nothing to an actor that cannot be translated into action.'[24]

Further reading

Michel Ciment, *Kazan on Kazan* (London: Secker & Warburg, 1973).
Foster Hirsch, *A Method to Their Madness* (New York: Da Capo Publishers, 1984).
Elia Kazan, *Elia Kazan: A Life* (New York: Da Capo Press, 1997).
Brian Neve, *Elia Kazan the Cinema of an American Outsider* (London: I. B. Tauris & Co Ltd., 2009).

Notes

1. Ciment, 42.
2. Ibid., 12.
3. Kazan, 81, also Ciment, 15.
4. Kazan, 105. Kazan sensed they were paying penance for their bourgeois backgrounds. 'Our rebellions were, as much as anything, against who we were, and I suppose the saturating color was guilt.'
5. Ciment, 22.
6. Kazan, 82.
7. Ibid., 212.
8. Ibid.
9. Neve, 12.
10. *New York Herald Tribune,* 11 July 1947.
11. Kazan, 290–1.
12. Hirsch, 122.
13. Kazan, 111.
14. Ibid., 303.
15. Neve, 59 ff. gives a thorough account of Kazan's involvement in HUAC processes and the repercussions.
16. Ciment, 83–4, gives a more elaborate justification of the 'naming', and of Kazan's hatred of Stalinism.
17. Kazan, 603.
18. Ciment, 41.
19. Ibid.
20. Marlon Brando and Robert Lindsey, *Songs My Mother Taught Me* (New York: Random House, 1994), 170.
21. Ibid., 171.
22. Ciment, 40–1.
23. Ibid., 41.
24. Hermine Rich Issacs, 'First Rehearsals: Elia Kazan Directs a Modern Legend', *Theatre Arts*, Vol. 28, March 1944: 147.

34 Joan Littlewood
1914–2002

I do not believe in the supremacy of the director, designer, actor, or even of the writer. It is through collaboration that this knockabout art of theatre survives and kicks.[1]

The mention of the name of the doyen of British political theatre elicits markedly different reactions. While Joan Littlewood was given to voicing her belief in 'collaboration', she equally had a reputation as being dictatorial, outspoken and opinionated – to the extent of being given the epithet the 'Stratford Stalin'.[2] She famously told Michael Caine, who tried his best for her, 'You can't act, so you might as well fuck off up the West End or get a job in films.'[3] Personality issues aside, in Britain she is regarded as the indisputable 'Mother of Modern Theatre'– she was the principal conduit for the European ideas of **Stanislavski**, **Appia**, **Meyerhold**, **Piscator**, **Copeau** and **Brecht**.

Joan Littlewood was born out of wedlock of humble origins in Cockney South London. She played in the streets where Charlie Chaplin grew up. She never knew her father. Her extraordinary life, framed by political action, is vividly chronicled in her autobiography, *Joan's Book*, suitably subtitled *'A Peculiar History'*. In her late teens she auditioned and was given a scholarship at the 'posh' Royal Academy of Dramatic Art (RADA), where she 'seethed at the way her classmates used it as a finishing school for squeaky debs'.[4] Barring one course, she thought RADA was a 'waste of time' – the exception being classes on the methods of **Rudolf Laban** which she claimed 'influenced [her] whole life.'[5] She left RADA and got a job in repertory theatre in Manchester. There she fell in love with folksinger and Communist Ewan MacColl (Jimmie Miller was his real name). She also became enamoured of, and engaged in, MacColl's political work in the *Theatre of Action*. Together, in 1936, the two of them formed an agitprop theatre group, the Theatre Union, performing in pubs, working men's clubs and on the street. Her productions at the time were heavily influenced by what she had learned in researching **Meyerhold**, including his fascination with *commedia dell'arte* – which she took up as a lifelong passion.

Joan supplemented theatre work with journalism for the BBC in Manchester. However, the 'red' rhetoric she used in her theatre work resulted in her being put under surveillance by the British spy agency, MI5, and in 1941 she was banned from the BBC for allegedly extremist Communist views. The ban was lifted two years later when she claimed she had dropped her membership to the Party. Nonetheless, she remained under surveillance into the 1950s.[6] The situation did nothing to tone down her politics.

In 1945 she formed the Theatre Workshop with Ewan MacColl – an ensemble group which toured the UK and Europe for eight years before settling in 1953 in a derelict theatre in the East End of London – the now famous Theatre Royal at Stratford, E15 (known colloquially as Stratford East). By that time, she and MacColl had split up amicably, and she had fallen in love with her stage manager, Gerry Raffles, who became her partner and collaborator until his death in 1974.

The Theatre Workshop was the first to bring the work of **Brecht** to Britain, mounting *Mother Courage and Her Children* in 1955. The production closed after three days. Theatre critic Martin Esslin – one of the few to have seen it – called it a 'disaster', lamenting that the company couldn't afford the music, so the songs had to be cut – the heart of the work. Littlewood played the eponymous protagonist, 'an impossible feat for the director of such so complex a play.'[7] Littlewood recovered from this defeat by putting forth a bold programme. Among other works, she championed the Irish playwright, Brendan Behan (1923–64), premiering both *The Quare Fellow* (1954), and *The Hostage* (1958), thus catapulting the famously alcoholic poet/dramatist to fame.

Littlewood's first big hit was Shelagh Delaney's *A Taste of Honey* (1958) – pure British Realism of the **'Kitchen Sink'** variety, which transferred to the West End. This was followed by an even bigger success, *Fings Ain't Wot They Used T'be,* a musical about the London underworld, which ran from 1959–62, also transferring to the West End. There was much interesting work to follow, but for all its international recognition, by the late 1950s the Theatre Workshop was becoming financially untenable – there were insufficient funds to run the huge draughty old building and support a large ensemble of actors. Fortunately, the company was able to transfer a few productions to the West End and thus generate income, but this led to the diminution of Littlewood's *ensemble* and the diversion of attention away from the Stratford East project.

The years 1961 to 1963 represented a hiatus. It was the moment when they became financially able to purchase the theatre, but she and Gerry had widely divergent points of view as to its and their future. She had a brief affair with architect Cedric Price (1934–2003), then packed her bags and went to Nigeria, intending to work there on a film project with playwright Wole Soyinka (1934–). After eighteen months waiting for him, and then a little time working with him, the film was eventually aborted.

In 1963 Littlewood returned to London and produced her *chef oeuvre*, the musical *Oh! What a Lovely War*, based on a radio play that Gerry Raffles had heard, juxtaposing jolly black-and-white minstrel renditions of First World War songs with a harrowing account of the War. Joan took the concept, and with her cast, improvised the stage musical. Its central conceit was the projection of images of devastation and statistics of the War behind the joviality of the singing and dancing on stage. The work was a corporal manifestation of the spirit of **Meyerhold** (using *commedia dell'arte*-type characters), **Piscator** (film projections counterpointing the drama), **Appia** (tightly focused lighting) and **Brecht** (Epic Theatre *par excellence*). The production moved to Wyndham's Theatre in the West End, and on to Broadway in 1964. Richard Attenborough made a film version in 1964, which Littlewood, along with many critics, did not like. The film is an object lesson in how what's magical in a theatrical setting can seem fake and banal when translated directly to celluloid.

Stylistically, Littlewood did not have a one-size-fits-all approach. She researched assiduously (she was called 'one of the leading theatre researchers of our time'[8]) and was able to draw on a range of drama theories and acting techniques in her productions. '. . . Joan worked specifically on each play to find the style of performance through which the play could communicate to its audience. No production was ever the same, but there was an underlying technique and obsessive search for perfection underlying them all.'[9] At the heart of what she learned and applied were the ideas of Stanislavski – that *action* was key, the actor finds personal *truth* and *belief* in their actions, and that actions are played based on the character's *objectives*. She refrained from writing any works of theory because her methodology was so eclectic.

The principle of 'ensemble' was fundamental to Joan Littlewood's approach. She dismissed the 'genius' director with contempt. She held that the Theatre Workshop was analogous to a *jazz combo*, as opposed to the usual model of a conductor-driven classical orchestra. She claimed that collaboration and improvisation were fundamental in the rehearsal process. She stated: 'I do not believe in the supremacy of the director, designer, actor or even the writer. It is through collaboration that this knockabout art of theatre survives and kicks.'[10] There is a self-delusional quality of that statement because by all accounts in the late stages of rehearsal she turned into a fierce dictator. As one of her actors said: 'In the end, after all the playing about, it was Joan who told the actor what to do in quite specific terms.'[11] And she often lost her temper – although actor/biographer Peter Rankin maintains that was only a directing technique: '. . . often manufactured. "Denouncing" she called it, calculated to humiliate the actor in front of the others and send out a warning. The actor's ego, only there, in her opinion, to serve the actor's interest, no one else's, was to be crushed.'[12]

Littlewood seems to have had little or no contact with the American Method. But she had read and digested Stanislavski's *An Actor* Prepares, and somehow must have picked up on the Russian's later ideas because for her, *action* preceded *emotion*. If an actor were to say, 'I don't feel it' her response was 'You're not fucking here to feel, you're here to fucking do.'[13]

Her approach to actors learning their lines followed 'late Stanislavski' and was like that used by Elia Kazan in film and theatre. In early rehearsals, action prevailed over memorizing the dialogues. Actors were not to learn their lines at home alone, in isolation, but in the studio – in collaboration. 'Action and dialogue were integrated, and one informed the other . . . the possibility of an actor "drying" [on stage] was barely conceivable and, if this happened, it was considered axiomatic that the other actors in the scene would be able to improvise from their own integrated understanding to carry the scene forward without difficulty.'[14]

One of her special rehearsal techniques was called *siffluese* ('whistling' in French), in which a prompter moves behind the actor whispering the lines in advance of their being spoken by the actor – with a speed, rhythm and intonation which, by that point, has been agreed. The idea is to free up the actor of the conscious work of remembering the lines, in order that they may experience the action and the emotions it engenders without the hindrance of memory.[15]

Laban technique was an integral part of Littlewood's programme, assuring that actors approached the character through movement in terms of habits and relationships. Littlewood employed games to explore Laban's concepts of time, weight, direction, and flow. 'We are not made of words alone, we human animals . . . our dress, movements, manners, physical reaction to the pressures in the air, reveal our nature before we open our mouths.'[16] While Laban's ideas had been widely used in dance and choreography, Littlewood's Theatre Workshop was the first theatre company to explore the use of his work in theatre.[17]

Her toolkit of rehearsal techniques included Brechtian devices such as having given lines spoken by different actors speaking the same lines, to find the irony or social *gests* (as per Brecht). 'In all cases, the social background was explored at the same time. Actors brought books and other research materials to rehearsal and the insights these gave were incorporated into the discussions.'[18]

Littlewood hated conservatoire-trained actors. She thought that most British actors, in accordance with what was taught in the acting schools, were given to what she termed 'past tense acting', which is to say everything they did depended on 'doing their homework' – preparing everything in advance, which of course leads to an 'indicated' performance. For Littlewood, nothing was to be 'preconceived'. It should be noted that prior to her work no British actors were training in Stanislavski, and many who came to her were terrified of improvisation and 'living-in-the-moment', and quickly dropped out. These days that would not be the case, but there remain many older generation British actors and directors for whom *past tense acting* is lamentably still the form.

Further reading

Joan Littlewood, *Joan's Book: Joan Littlewood's Peculiar History as She Tells It* (London: Methuen Publishing Ltd, 1994), reprinted 2003 as: *Joan's Book: The Autobiography of Joan Littlewood* (London: Methuen, 4th ed. 2012).

Peter Rankin, *Joan Littlewood: Dreams and Realities* (London: Oberon Books Ltd., 2014).

Notes

1. Letter to *Encore* theatre magazine, September 1961, cited in Philip Hedley's intro to the fourth edition of *Joan's Book* (2016), 15–16.
2. Roger Lewis, 'A Stratford Stalin: the nasty, aggressive and stupid world of Joan Littlewood', *The Spectator*, issue: 8 November 2014: 3.
3. Rankin, 111.
4. Lewis, Ibid.
5. Littlewood, 69.
6. Richard Norton-Taylor, 'MI5 surveillance of Joan Littlewood during war led to two-year BBC ban', *The Guardian*, posted online 4 March 2008.
7. Martin Esslin, 'Brecht and the English Theatre', *The Tulane Drama Review*, 11 (2) (Winter 1966): 66.
8. Clive Barker, 'Closing Joan's Book: Some Personal Footnotes', *New Theatre Quarterly*, 9 (2) (May 2003): 104.
9. Ibid., 107.
10. Joan Littlewood, 'Goodbye Note from Joan', *The Encore Reader: Chronicle of the New Drama*, eds. Marowitz, Milne and Hale (London: Methuen University Paperbacks, 1965), 133. The letter was written in September 1961 as she left the Theatre Workshop, and London. She came back two years later, reformed the Theatre Workshop, and mounted *Oh! What a Lovely War* – arguably her greatest success.
11. Barker, 'Closing Joan's Book', 106. Quoted from an unnamed actor.
12. Rankin, 125–6.
13. Clive Barker, 'Joan Littlewood,' in Alison Hodge, ed. *Twentieth Century Actor Training* (London: Routledge, 2000), 121.
14. Ibid., 119.
15. Ibid., 122.
16. Notes on rehearsing *'Oh! What a Lovely War'*, from Joan Littlewood Archive, British Library, ref: MS 89164/4/26.
17. Littlewood, 7.
18. Barker, *Littlewood*, 118.

35 Uta Hagen
1919–2004

The five senses are the avenues of our psychological as well as of our physical perceptions.¹

An actress of considerable renown on Broadway, Uta Hagen went on to become one of the great teachers in the **Stanislavski** lineage. Having had several years of stage experience from a young age – she played Ophelia in Eva Le Gallienne's production of *Hamlet* at seventeen years of age, and Nina in the Lunt's production of *The Seagull* when eighteen – by the time she reached thirty-six, youthful exuberance no longer was enough to sustain her. She felt jaded, that she had lost her way as an actress. Then, in 1947, she was directed by **Harold Clurman**, and experienced an epiphany . . .

> He opened a new world in the professional theatre for me. He took away my 'tricks'. He imposed no line readings, no gestures, no positions on the actors. At first I floundered badly because for many years I had become accustomed to using specific outer directions as the material from which to construct the mask for my character, the mask behind which I would hide throughout the performance. Mr. Clurman refused to accept a mask. He demanded ME in the role. My love of acting was slowly reawakened as I began to deal with a strange new technique of evolving in the character. I was not allowed to begin with, or concern myself at any time with a preconceived form. I was assured that a form would result from the work we were doing.²

Clurman had opened the door for Hagen, to the world of Stanislavski's 'system' and **Strasberg's** 'Method'.

In 1962 Hagen originated the role of Martha in Edward Albee's play, *Who's Afraid of Virginia Woolf*. She was at that time married to actor Jose Ferrer, with whom she had a daughter. The couple played together in *Othello*, along with Paul Robeson (1898–1976). But Ferrer divorced her when he discovered she was having an affair with Robeson. Her association with left-wing Robeson backlashed in another way, causing her to be blacklisted during the McCarthy witch-hunts, resulting in the curtailment of a potential film career. She later married actor/director Herbert Bergdorf (1909–90), founder of the school in which they both taught, and they were together for 30 years until his death.

Hagen was a wonderfully practical and down-to-earth teacher. She argued that the two essential talents required of an actor are *responsiveness to the senses*, and *an ability to observe human behaviour* – including one's own behavioural responses to stimuli, both sensorial and emotional. She insisted that actors strive to fully develop a sense of themselves in both of those areas, and that they bring those elements to the scene with confidence in their own being. To help the actor achieve this, she proposed a series of 'object' exercises. The first is to re-create two minutes of one's life while alone, pinpointing all the psychological and physical sensations inherent in the experience. One analyses this, rehearses it, then presents it to class, or to a coach, as one would a scene.³ Simply examining two minutes in one's life in minute detail churns up a plethora of questions – the same questions which require answers when an actor is portraying a character in a scene.

- Who am I?
- What are the circumstances?
- What are my relationships?
- What do I want? (long and short-term objectives)
- What's in my way? (obstacles)
- What do I do to get what I want? (action)[4]

These questions are those proposed by Stanislavski in *An Actor Prepares*. Hagen suggests that the actors' first job is to read the play in a detached manner to see how it impacts one, almost as a spectator: 'You are still on the other side of the footlights, and not yet on the stage.' She then suggests the actor follows Stanislavski's process, and determine the *throughline* of the work, and their character's *spine* (noting that the throughline is ultimately the province of the director). Once this overview has been set out, the actor can get on with 'scoring' the scene, which is essentially working out responses to all the questions above.[5]

While Hagen recognized the potency of imagination, her notion of 'substitution' (which she later redefined as 'transference') was along Strasbergian lines – i.e. based on remembered experience, or sensory experience of an 'object' associated with that experience, such as a dress one was wearing or a certain food one was eating. 'Substitution' for her had a broad meaning and should 'have its effect on every moment of the actor's life on stage.'[6] It embraces both *objects* and *situations,* for which she proposed the use of emotional memory:

> Each object or thing that I see or come in contact with must be made particular so that it will serve the new me and bring about the psychological and sensory experiences necessary to animate my actions.[7]

'Where am I?' is an additional question that the actor needs to pose – and if the real environment of the film location or theatre stage doesn't provide the real conditions, the actor should use sensory memory to *endow* them (I use the term *imbue*). Endowing is also used to give reality to actions which cannot be duplicated in the scene because they are dangerous or too complex, such as a hot iron a sharp knife, etc. (See **Working with Actors**, 'Faking It.')[8]

Hagen proposed that the actor from day one refers to the character as *'me'* as a way of identifying with that person. I have a different approach. I urge my actors to use the third person pronoun, *he/she/they*, throughout the early stages of the analysis, until the character's objectives have been determined, thus allowing the actor's identification with the character to develop organically through both the personalization of the character's objectives *and* engagement with other actors, until they have achieved what Stanislavski called the 'Third Being', where they feel as one with the character. (See **Working with Actors**, 'Final Phases Rehearsal'.)

Uta Hagen wrote two extremely useful books for actors, *Respect for Acting*, and *A Challenge for the Actor* – the second being an update and elaboration of the first, eighteen years on. Both contain useful practical exercises for actors. Additionally, the exercises as set out in the second book can be viewed on an informative DVD: *Uta Hagen's Acting Class*, which contains testimonials of former students Jack Lemmon, Whoopi Goldberg and Christine Lahti, among others. Highly recommended.

ACTORS WHO STUDIED WITH UTA HAGEN
Al Pacino
Robert De Niro
Gene Wilder
Whoopi Goldberg
Jack Lemmon
Amanda Peet
Sigourney Weaver
Matthew Broderick
Christine Lahti

Further reading

Uta Hagen, *Respect for Acting* (Hoboken, NJ: John Wiley & Sons, Inc., 1973).
Uta Hagen, *A Challenge for the Actor* (New York: Scribner, 1991).
Uta Hagen's Acting Class [DVD], (New York: Applause, New York, 2004).

Notes

1. Hagen, *Challenge*, 84.
2. Hagen, *Respect*, 8.
3. Ibid., 82 ff.
4. Ibid.
5. Hagen, *Challenge*, 235.
6. Hagen, *Respect*, 35.
7. Ibid., 39.
8. Hagen, *Challenge*, Chapter 15: 'Recreating Physical Sensations', and vividly illustrated in the *Uta Hagen's Acting Class* DVD.

36 Jacques Lecoq
1921–1999

Le geste c'est le dépôt d'une emotion.[1]

For Jacques Lecoq it all started with sport. He was a gymnast at seventeen and through gymnastics developed an appreciation for the abstraction of the movement of the body through space. He taught physical education for several years and undertook rehabilitation work with disabled people after the Second World War. Then in 1947 he taught physical expression in a new school called *'L'Education par le Jeu Dramatique'* – an experience which presaged his concept of athleticism for theatre.

In 1948 he joined the *Comédiens de Grenoble*, under actor-director Jean Dasté (1904–94), who was the son-in-law of **Jacques Copeau**. Dasté introduced him to the ideas of **Antonin Artaud** and Copeau.

In 1951 Lecoq moved to Milan, where he worked for eight years with *commedia dell'arte*, immersing himself in mime, masks and the physicality of performance. Here he met and became friend and collaborator with the actor, playwright and clown, Dario Fo (1926–2016). In 1956 he returned to Paris and founded his own school, where he taught for forty years, until his death in 1999. The Lecoq School's brochure of 1980 set out his philosophy of teaching, which never changed:

> Mime and Theatre based on movement and the human body . . . a school of dramatic creation; it relies on knowledge of the organic and emotional dynamics of man and nature . . . the school concerns itself with theatre to be created; this theatre belongs to pupils, their ideas, their quest.[2]

Lecoq had no theatre or ensemble of actors, so his legacy is not in his directing, but in his theories and training methods. His training was *actor-centric* and consisted of an investigation of approaches to performance that functioned for each individual. There was no codified set of skills, but rather a series of exercises and improvisations aimed at allowing the creativity of an individual performer to blossom. On the school's thirtieth anniversary Lecoq erected a banner over the courtyard which read: 'Don't do what I do. Do what you do.'

Lecoq's approach is predicated on the idea that *movement* provokes *emotion*, that the gesture is a representation of emotion. 'He proposed that it is the *actor's body* – rather than simply the spoken text – which is the crucial generator of meaning in theatre.'[3]

An essential part of the training is mask work. If the actor is deprived of facial gesture as a means of expression, or outlet for emotion, they will rely on their body as a tool of expression. And by exploring emotion through corporal means they will build up a sensory emotional memory bank. One starts with a 'neutral' mask. 'Since this mask aspires to being open, available and ready to respond to the world it encounters, the actor must be prepared to engage willingly with that world – a world that moves and will move him. Each encounter with the world creates a state of 'off-balance' since we experience something new and unknown.'[4] Lecoq believed in 'the pleasure of play'. The 'play' in the neutral mask lies in the actor repeatedly allowing themself to go 'off-balance' to find a new 'balance'. In further training Lecoq took the actors on to larval (archetypal) masks, and then to half-masks, culminating in the smallest mask: the clown's red nose.

Lecoq did not teach mime, per se. His was not a mime school. But he incorporated elements of mime in his developmental exercises as a tool of discovery for his students.

Disponibilité and *complicité* were two terms Lecoq employed frequently. With the first he did not mean psychological or emotional openness, as commonly taught in dramatic realism, but openness through the body and movement to find this quality. '*Complicity*' is generally thought to be a basic requisite for ensemble acting, but according to Simon Murray, Lecoq's spicier interpretation was 'a shared, gleeful pleasure: more the camaraderie of rogues and revolutionaries, than the quiet, self-satisfied handholding of saints'.[5] This 'naughty fun' ethos was integral to the work of the *Théâtre de Complicité,* formed in London in 1983 by Lecoq graduates, headed by **Simon McBurney**. Other former Lecoq students include directors Steven Berkoff, Robert LePage, Ariane Mnouchkine and Julie Taymar. If you are familiar with the work of any of these directors, the Lecoq influence will be clear.

In addition to the L'École Internationale de Théâtre Jacques Lecoq in Paris, there are numerous Lecoq centres of study in Britain, several in European cities and a few in the USA. The most esteemed one in Latin America is the La Mancha School in Santiago de Chile.[6] One former student describing his studies at the Paris school said: 'Lecoq's pedagogy was less a formal instruction of skills than a training in wonder and adaptation.'[7]

Further reading

Mark Evans and Rick Kemp, eds, *The Routledge Companion to Jacques Lecoq* (London: Taylor & Francis Group, 2016).

Simon Murray, *Jacques Lecoq*, in *Routledge Performance Practitioners* series, (London: Routledge, 2003, reissued, 2017).

Notes

1. Dick McCaw, director of the International Workshop Festival, reporting a conversation with LeCoq. He elaborates the metaphor, using 'deposit' in the sense of sediments building up in a riverbed. Murray, 54.
2. Murray, 19.
3. Ibid., 34.
4. Ibid., 132.
5. Ibid., 16.
6. Ibid., 71.
7. Ellie Nixon, 'La Mancha Theatre Company and School – Chile', Evans and Kemp, chapter 42.

37 Sidney Lumet
1924–2011

He was a true master who loved directing and working with actors like no other.[1]

Phillip Seymour Hoffman

Knowing Sidney, he will have more energy dead than most live people.[2]

Woody Allen

He had a unique gift with actors.[3]

Martin Scorsese

If you prayed to inhabit a character, Sidney was the priest who made your dreams come true.[4]

Al Pacino

The 'actor's director' *par excellence*, Sidney Lumet never won an Oscar himself, although he received Best Director nominations for *four* of his movies (*Twelve Angry Men*, *Dog Day Afternoon*, *Network* and *The Verdict*). *Fourteen* of his films received Oscar nods (totalling over *forty* nominations) and he was accorded a Lifetime Achievement Award by the Academy of Motion Pictures in 2005. Significantly, he guided his *actors* to *nineteen* Oscar nominations, varying from Rod Steiger for *The Pawnbroker*, to River Phoenix for *Running on Empty*. His Oscar winners included Ingrid Bergman for *Murder on the Orient Express*, and Peter Finch, Faye Dunaway and Beatrice Straight – all three for *Network*. Along his fifty-year-long career directing movies, his actors swept up innumerable *Palmes d'Or*, Golden Globes, BAFTAs and other international awards.

He was prolific, to say the least – forty-three films in fifty years. As Woody Allen indicated in his epigraph, Lumet was renowned until the last for his *energy*. His final film, *Before the Devil Knows You're Dead* (2007), was made when he was eighty-three. ('Thirty-three seemed more like it', commented lead actor Philip Seymour Hoffman.[5]) Co-star, Albert Finney, who had acted in Lumet's *Murder on the Orient Express* twenty years previously, observed: 'He shoots just as fast now as he did then.'[6] Lumet was respected by actors and crew alike for his preparedness. Treat Williams, his lead actor in *Prince of the City*, said: 'He was just a ball of fire. He had passion for what he did and he "came to work" with all barrels burning. He's probably the most prepared director I've ever worked with emotionally. His films always came in under schedule and under budget. And everybody got home for dinner.'[7] Actress Lee Grant commented: 'Physically, he flew, and in his mind flew. He thought at twice the intensity of anybody else. Keeping the house in order . . . and enjoying the unexpected that came from his actors.'[8]

It's commonplace, but true, to say that the best of the *actor's directors* have been actors themselves. That was the case of **Elia Kazan** and **Sydney Pollack**, and so it was with Lumet. The son of parents who both worked in the Yiddish theatre in New York, he was only four years old when he debuted on the Yiddish stage. Attending the Professional Children's School afforded him the opportunity to act in roles on Broadway, starting at the age of eleven, with a part in *Dead End* (1935), a Depression-era play about a gang of kids growing up 'tough' in the Bowery. He was 'political' from a young age, reading Karl Marx at the age of eight and joining the Young Communist League in his teens.[9]

He began his studies for a degree in literature at Colombia University, but the Second World War interrupted that plan (and his acting career) after only one semester. He served as an army radio engineer in Burma and India, before being demobbed in 1946. At that point he once again picked up his acting career, taking over from Marlon Brando on Broadway in *A Flag is Born*. He was part of the original intake of the **Actors Studio** in 1947, but he was let go after the first year by **Robert Lewis** (for 'bitchy' reasons according to Lumet's ex-wife, Rita Gam).[10] He formed an off-Broadway theatre group called the Actors Workshop, with some friends, including Rita Gam (1927–2016), and Yul Brynner (1941–85) – his soulmate from the Actors Studio. No one volunteered to direct, so the group asked Sidney to do it. And thus began a most illustrious career.

At the same time, he was studying with **Sanford Meisner** at the **Neighborhood Playhouse**. Thereafter, Meisner's action-oriented approach, and attention to specifics, heavily influenced Lumet's methods.[11]

The first professional directing job in his career occurred when Brynner, who had been directing bits for television between acting gigs, got a job for Sidney as his assistant. Lumet displayed great aptitude, and in 1950 was given a staff-director position at CBS. These were the Golden Days of television, when much of the content was drama, and much was produced live. Therefore, the most important quality for a director was to be able to think quickly on their feet, as well as (and I know this from my own experience) possessing the logistical brain to *not* cross the three camera cables on the studio floor when calling shots. Lumet directed more than 500 shows at CBS and would have employed more than 2,000 actors.[12] As a result of this baptism of fire, he became one of Hollywood's most efficient movie directors, wasting very little time or film footage.

One of the secrets of his legendary *quick shooting* was spending more time in *rehearsal.* However, his rehearsal methods were not just a way of saving the producer money but were in line with his approach as a Meisner/Method actor, namely, allowing the actors time and space to explore, and find themselves in the character. His rehearsals lasted between two and four weeks, depending on the emotional complexity of the text. They were always run in chronological order because the shooting itself could not be done so, thus allowing the actor to acquire a clear sense of their character's '*spine*', and thus be able to *drop into the narrative* at any point. Lumet said: 'Rehearsing in sequence gives the actors a sense of continuity, the 'arc' of their characters, so they know exactly where they are when shooting begins, regardless of the shooting order.'[13]

Lumet's pre-eminence as 'master' of American cinema Realism can be attributed to the confluence of his own *background* and the *conditions* attaining in the movie market at the time. His training in Method acting, his apprenticeship with the intimate camera of television drama, his background growing up as a Jew in New York's working-class Lower East Side, his wartime experience amongst men from all walks of life, his social and political engagement – all converged to fit neatly into a particular gap in the market. In the 1950s, Hollywood was desperately trying to counter the growth of television, promoting the slogan 'Movies are better than ever.' Cinema offered audiences spectacle, wide-screen, lurid colour and epic stories.[14] On the other hand, television, still in *black and white*, was offering small-scale, domestic, suburban stories. There was a lacuna to be filled. 1940s '*film noir*', with its formulaic storylines and stylized lighting, borrowed from German Expressionism, was becoming *passé*. But there was something new out there – art-house cinema audiences were lapping up imported **Italian Neo-realist** movies – stories of ordinary people caught up in the struggles of life, depicted in a flat, objective, almost newsreel format, shot in black-and-white. This opened the door for Lumet's brand of 'urban realism' – a genre already proving itself commercially viable with two movies: Kazan's On the *Waterfront* (1954), set in the docklands of Hoboken New Jersey, and *Marty* (dir. Delbert Mann, 1955), a film featuring a butcher and a schoolteacher in the Bronx. Both were box office hits.[15]

Lumet clearly understood the difference between *realism* and *naturalism* – namely, that realism involves *interpretation*, that reality is filtered by the director's vision, and that truth can be served up poetically. 'I want to find a way of telling real stories in abstract terms that make it even more real.'[16]

Given his formation in the theatre, Lumet remained fond of film adaptations of stage plays, and made movies of, among others, Eugene O'Neill's *Long Day's Journey into Night*, and Chekhov's *The Seagull*. In these films he demonstrated his mastery of theatrical realism, with its focus on performance. But it was when he broke away from the stage, and out on to the streets, that his cinematic vision took flight, and he was able to develop his own film style – or should one say styles? – movie by movie. For Lumet, each film should be accorded a different style, depending on its subject matter and themes – style should develop based on *form follows function*. Moreover, style would not be allowed to dominate the drama. 'I want [stylization] to be done with such subtlety that you can't see it happen.'[17]

Early in his film career Lumet developed a distaste for Hollywood, and repeatedly opted *not* to go to Los Angeles, even turning down important films such as *A Raisin in the Sun* because they had to be shot there.[18] He hated the artificiality of studio production, the bottom-line mentality of the studio execs, the cardboard cut-out film extras of the Screen Actors Guild. 'They have sets, but not the genuine thing. Even the lampposts are wrong – they're made of Styrofoam. I hate being separated from life. There's nothing organic about Los Angeles.' Filming in New York, on the other hand was: 'like sitting on a big lid ready to blow off. And this energy reaches the screen.'[19] The credibility of Lumet's dramas has much to do with the fact that the stories are *embedded* in the reality of their settings. *The Pawnbroker* provides an early example. Chases through the streets, people dodging *real* traffic, crowds milling around to observe a young man bleeding to death on the pavement – as a spectator . . . you are right there. 'He sets his film in the City [New York] with an unfailing sense of locale. He knows which architecture or neighborhood fits the atmosphere. Walls and lampposts work as silent bit players. His characters, like cab drivers at a red light, twitch with the edgy impatience that at any moment may explode into violence.'[20]

Lumet's brand of realism is also marked by his interest in anti-heroes. Sol Nazerman in *The Pawnbroker*, Frank Serpico in *Serpico*, Harold Beale in *Network*, Frank Galvin in *The Verdict*, Sonny Wortzik in *Dog Day Afternoon*, Daniel Ciello in *Prince of the City*, DiNorscio in *Find Me Guilty* – typical Lumet characters: imperfect, seedy, beset by their own devils; heroic only in the sense of fighting against the isolation foisted upon them by a society. Lumet was convinced that what he found compelling – namely, the complexity and self-contradictions of the anti-hero – would be interesting and engaging for the audience. They are *real* to us because, like all of us, they have conflicting desires and are sometimes quite lost. These were *familiar* people fighting their way out of the limitations and strictures of society – anti-heroes 'struggling to extend their identities and moral capacities in an ever more challenging world'.[21]

Being Method trained, Lumet knew how get the actors to dig into their own psyche and work off the *subtext* – to explore what lies beneath the surface. He achieved this through a Meisner approach to script analysis, in which the character's intentions and actions were identified early on. His extensive rehearsals sometimes included improvisation of two types. One was exploring the actor's 'substitution' – to deepen their emotions – and the other was doing dialogue improvisations – expressing the author's ideas in the actor's own words. This allows the actor to 'own' the character. Sometimes the results of these improvisations were used in the final film. On rare occasions the actors were even allowed to improvise during filming. Exceptionally, approximately 60 per cent of Al Pacino's dialogues in *Dog Day Afternoon* were improvised.

While he eschewed psychoanalysis as a technique, Lumet used a lot of common *psychology* in directing. If an actor had a block, he didn't offer his own analysis, but instead gave the actor space to discover the reason behind the block. Any conversations were carried out in a very personal, one-to-one manner, out of earshot of others. On one occasion Lumet, famously known as a 'one take wonder', allowed Marlon Brando to do *thirty-four takes* when he was emotionally blocked – giving him the time to find his personal psychological connection.[22] Afterwards, Brando hugged Sidney, by way of thanks. Lumet believes that the director must respect the *actor's process*, above all if it involves delving deeply into emotionally difficult territory. He says, 'The actor has a right to his privacy; I never violate his private sources knowingly.'[23] He was confident in talking to the actors on this level because he had done his own careful preparation, working out the 'spine', or SuperObjective of each character, so he came to rehearsal armed with clues to their psychology.

Lumet has much to teach young filmmakers, especially those who wish to get the most out of their actors. His book, *Making Movies*, spells out clearly his own *modus operandi* by giving examples of his work. Here's just one of his helpful tips: He points out that a director will be dealing with actors possessing a wide range of methods. The *unifying factor* of those methods is, in rehearsal, simply to get them all to *listen* and to *talk* to each other *directly*. He cites Sanford Meisner – whom he calls one of the best acting teachers of his time. He remembers that the first six week of Meisner's training were getting the actors to listen to each other. 'It's the great common denominator where different acting styles and techniques meet.'[24]

Preparation was key for Lumet. It was the key to 'freedom' to be in-the-moment. The reason he prepared, he frequently said, was for the *lucky accident* to happen. Focused preparation in advance allows flexibility on the day of shooting. His sometime-assistant director, Frank Leicht (1925–2015) bears this out: 'Sid was spontaneous. Some directors would map it all out at home over a week, and they wouldn't budge. That's the way they were going to do it. Sid would block well, but he was ready to make a change whenever he had to. He wasn't locked into it.'[25] Lumet himself comments, 'Does mountains of preparation kill spontaneity? Absolutely not. I've found that it's just the opposite. When you know what you're doing, you feel much freer to improvise.'[26]

Al Pacino, in talking about working with Lumet on *Dog Day Afternoon*, said: 'He frees the actors instinctively by setting up his camera and lighting, and allowing them freedom within that framework.' He said that Lumet helped him explore the depths within himself that he didn't even know were there.[27] An actor friend who observed how Lumet worked with Pacino likened it to pulling the pin out of the grenade and watching it explode.[28]

Lumet's way of working sets a benchmark for my own work as a director. The actor Van Dyke Parks (b. 1943) describes it: 'Sidney was tremendously invitational. . . . empowering, drawing on his subjects' invention and contributions. He was not disciplinary in any way.'[29] Essentially, Lumet *invited*, induced, coaxed, but rarely *told* the actor what to do, and yet managed, by and large, to get the results he wanted, earning him the well-deserved sobriquet: *'actor's director'*.

Further reading

Richard A. Blake, *Street Smart, The New York of Lumet, Allen, Scorsese, and Lee* (Lexington, KY: The University Press of Kentucky, 2005).
Sidney Lumet, *Making Movies* (New York: Vintage Books, 1996).
Aubrey Malone, *Sidney Lumet, The Actor's Director* (Jefferson, NC: McFarland & Company, Inc., 2020).

Notes

1. Hellomagazine.com, 11 April 2011, https://www.hellomagazine.com/celebrities/201104115240/sidney-lumet/tributes/woody-allen-al-pacino/
2. Ibid.
3. Ibid.
4. *The Guardian* [obit], 10 April 2011, https://www.theguardian.com/film/2011/apr/10/sidney-lumet-obituary
5. Malone, 187.
6. Ibid.
7. PBS interview cited on Wikipedia, https://en.wikipedia.org/wiki/Sidney_Lumet; edited 1 September 2021.
8. The Classic TV History Blog, 18 July 2011, https://classictvhistory.wordpress.com/tag/yul-brynner/
9. Frank R., Cunningham, *Sidney Lumet, Film and Literary Vision*, 2nd ed. (Lexington, KY: The University Press of Kentucky, 2001), 14–15.
10. Classic TV History Blog.
11. Cunningham, 18.
12. Malone, 1.
13. Lumet, 63.
14. Blake, 49.
15. Ibid. *Marty*, directed by Delbert Mann, was written by the pre-eminent writer of television Realism, Paddy Chayefsky (1923–81), and it kickstarted Ernest Borgnine's brilliant career (1917–2012), garnering several Oscars.
16. Cunningham, 10.
17. Ibid.
18. Blake, 46.
19. Malone, 65.
20. Blake, 41.
21. Cunningham, Preface to the 2nd ed., xv.
22. Malone, 32; during the filming of *The Fugitive Kind*, playing opposite Anna Magnani and Joanne Woodward.
23. Lumet, 66.
24. Ibid., 67.
25. Classic TV History Blog.
26. Lumet, 26.
27. Malone, 95.
28. Ibid., 96.
29. Classic TV History Blog.

38 Peter Brook
1925–2022

For Artaud, theatre is fire; for Brecht, theatre is clear vision; for Stanislavsky, theatre is humanity. Why must we choose among them?[1]

Any serious director *of theatre* should acquaint themself with the work of Peter Brook. Less so, a film director – as Brook's focus has been primarily with theatrical form. The epigraph is misleading, as Brook was *not* directly influenced by **Stanislavski**. He once admitted in an interview: 'Stanislavski, I never really read'.[2] His sources of inspiration were eclectic – **Grotowski**, **Meyerhold**, **Vakhtangov**, **Craig**, **Artaud**, **LeCoq**, **Brecht** and **Laban**, as well as the theatre and folklore of Africa, Asia and the Middle East.

This giant of the theatre was already a successful stage director by the age of eighteen, having mounted Christopher Marlowe's *Doctor Faustus* in a professional production. He became director of productions at the Royal Opera House (1947–50) when only twenty-four years of age. In the early 1960s he was invited by Peter Hall to join the newly organized Royal Shakespeare Company, as head of 'chief of exploration'.[3] By then he had already directed every type of play – contemporary or historical – primarily in the arena of commercial theatre.

At the RSC, Brooks began to push boundaries. Mega-critic Kenneth Tynan called his highly praised production of *King Lear* in 1962 'revolutionary' – unlike any before it, both in its setting ('flat white, combining Brecht and Oriental theatre against which ponderous abstract objects dangle'), and in its fresh approach to the protagonist ('not the booming, righteously indignant Titan of old, but an edgy, capricious old man, intensely difficult to work with').[4]

But Brook kept one eye trained on developments outside of the relatively luxurious bubble of the West End, the RSC and the Old Vic – looking towards **Joan Littlewood** at the Stratford East Theatre, on the periphery of London, who was devoted to producing *popular political theatre* using elements of circus, cabaret and the fun fair. Jaundiced by mainstream theatre, Brook was beginning to become radicalized. He counselled **Charles Marowitz**, the American director who came to England to work with him on *King Lear*, that in order to mount a play the director must start with 'the instinctive feeling that the play needs to be done "now"; that it has become pertinent or relevant to artists and public because of a coincidence between the work and certain immediate social, spiritual, or political circumstances.'[5]

At the RSC in 1964 he mounted the 'Theatre of Cruelty' season in collaboration with Marowitz, exploring the ideas of Antonin Artaud in the form of improvisations. The idea was to reinvigorate theatre using a vocabulary not tied to language. (He later said of Artaud: 'Mainly, it was his intensity that interested me. I thought his theories were absolutely useless.'[6]) That same year, drawing on some of the 'Cruelty' ideas, he mounted Peter Weiss's ground-breaking *Marat/Sade* in London, which transferred to Broadway in 1965, winning Tony Awards for Best Play and Best Director. In 1971 he returned to New York with the acclaimed

RSC *aerial* production of *A Midsummer Night's Dream* with Oberon, Titania and Puck largely working from trapezes in a set resembling a gymnasium.

Facing *westward,* Brook was stimulated by the weird and wonderful ideas in the theatre emerging in the sixties in the USA, especially in New York (the **Living Theatre**, **Joe Chaikin's** Open Theatre, La Mama Café, etc.), and facing *eastward*, Jerzy Grotowski's Laboratory Theatre in Poland. Brook's interests increasingly lay in the *theatre of provocation*. He became friends with Grotowski and wrote the Foreword to the English language publication of *Poor Theatre*. They collaborated on a production of *US* – an ensemble-devised piece about the Vietnam War – at the RSC. Eschewing the commercial and institutional theatre which had been his world, Brook moved to Paris in 1970 and co-founded (with Micheline Rozan, 1928–2019) the International Centre for Theatre Research (CIRT) based at the Bouffes du Nord Theatre, where he was Artistic Director until 2008. There he was free to experiment with ideas garnered from Grotowski, Meyerhold and Artaud, *commedia dell'arte*, masks and theatre forms from other cultures. The first compliment of students/actors joining the ensemble came from around the globe.

Soon after its foundation, and well before 'multiculturalism' came into fashion, Brook toured Africa and Asia with his group, surveying theatre practice in the places he visited, putting on plays *in situ*, and gathering insight into the universal human condition. He became fascinated by the Greek-Armenian mystic, G.I. Gurdjieff (1866–1949), to whom his wife, actor Natasha Parry, had introduced him. After immersing himself in Sufism, and extensive research in Persia, he made a biographical movie about Gurdjieff, shot in Afghanistan, *Meeting with Remarkable Men* (1979).

Brook made several films during his career, but they were mostly versions of his stage productions. The notable exception was his adaptation of William Golding's anarchistic fantasy, *Lord of the Flies* in 1963 – worth reviewing for the handling of its all-child cast in extreme situations. Brook claimed that his inspiration in matters of film was Jean-Luc Godard (1930–2022), who carried the torch for Bertolt Brecht in the realm of cinema.[7] This influence is evident in the unorthodox film grammar of the *Lord of the Flies*.[8]

In 1985 he mounted another landmark theatre production – an eight-hour version of the Indian Sanskrit epic *The Mahābhārata* – a mixture of ritual and performance. It was an attempt to make accessible the Hindu myth to a wider public, albeit with a tendency to 'orientalism', according to some critics.[9] The play was later filmed.

Brook was fascinated with Brecht, especially his *concept of alienation*. In *The Empty Space* he offers a very clear definition of the practice:

> Alienation can work through antithesis; parody, imitation, criticism, the whole range of rhetoric is open to it. It is the purely theatrical method of dialectic exchange. Alienation is the language open to us today that is as rich in potentiality as verse: it is the possible device of a dynamic theatre in a changing world, and through alienation we could reach some of those areas that Shakespeare touched by his use of dynamic devices in language . . . It aims continually at pricking the balloons of rhetorical playing.[10]

Alienation, according to Brook, can consist of simple devices. He cites Joan Littlewood dressing her First World War soldiers as Pierrots, as an example. He cites Charlie Chaplin's deliberate contrast of *sentimentality* and *calamity* as another form of alienation.[11]

The Empty Space (1968), his first publication, is a theatre classic, and a must-read for every aspiring *theatre* director. In a sense the book is his manifesto, and its minimalist essence is set out in the first lines:

> I can take any empty space and call it a bare stage. A man walks across this empty space whilst someone else is watching him, and this is all that is needed for an act of theatre.[12]

Brook classifies theatre into four types: Deadly, Holy, Rough and Immediate. *Deadly* refers to the commercial theatre, stuck in the old forms, and any practice of theatre lacking energy and invention. *Holy*, he also calls the 'Theatre of the Invisible-Made-Visible'. 'The notion that the stage is a place where the invisible can appear has a deep hold on our thoughts.'[13] In other words, theatre that induced reflection or particular mental states. For Brook, Artaud represents the apotheosis of Holy Theatre: 'A theatre working like the plague, by intoxication, by infection, by analogy, by magic. A theatre in which the play, the event itself, stands in place of the text.'[14] *Rough Theatre* is inspired, among others, by the work of Gordon Craig – who, in his designs, stripped away the superfluous. It is exemplified by Brecht in his theatre of alienation. It is theatre of minimal means, kindled by social and political imperatives. Joan Littlewood's popular theatre, with elements of circus and cabaret is a clear example. *Immediate Theatre* is the symbiosis of the Holy and the Rough. It is theatre of the moment: 'The destruction of old forms, the experimenting with new ones: new words, new relationships, new places, new buildings'.[15]

Brook's other literary works are largely reflections on his experience – elaborations and developments of the themes developed in *The Empty Space*. There is no attempt to codify his aesthetic philosophy, and very little guidance for the actor. He is essentially a practitioner, not a theorist. His second book, *The Shifting Point* (1988), traces his forty years in the theatre revisiting his productions of *King Lear* and *Romeo and Juliet*, and his discoveries about the power of ritual in theatre while producing *The Mahābhārata*. *The Open Door* (1995) consists of three lectures, amplifying earlier themes.[16]

Throughout his career Brook mounted dozens of inciteful, innovative productions of Shakespeare's plays, blazing a trail for all directors who followed. His books, *Evoking Shakespeare* (2002) and *The Quality of Mercy: Reflections on Shakespeare* (2013), are recommended reading for any director about to take on the Bard.[17]

Brook's 2019 play, *Why?* continues his unending quest for an open theatre. It is based around the death of Vsevolod Meyerhold, who, despite being a Communist and ardent supporter of the Russian Revolution, fell afoul of Stalin's decree that **Socialist Realism** was the only permitted art form, was labelled a subversive, and was brutally executed months after his wife was killed under torture – as recounted in Meyerhold's chapter. Meyerhold was one of Brook's main influences. The play, co-written and co-directed with Marie-Hélène Estienne was presented in January 2020, in New York. Brook was at the time ninety-four years of age, in his seventy-sixth year of directing theatre.

Further reading

Peter Brook, *The Empty Space* (New York: Touchstone/Scribner, 1968).
Peter Brook, *The Shifting Point* (London: Bloomsbury Publishing, 1988).
David Richard Jones, *Great Directors at Work: Stanislavsky, Brecht, Kazan, Brook* (Los Angeles: University of California Press, 1986).

Notes

1. Brook, *Shifting Point*, 43.
2. Margaret Croyden, *Conversations with Peter Brook 1970–2000* (New York: Theatre Communications Group, 2009), 392.
3. Jones, 213.
4. Kenneth Tynan, *The Guardian*, 11 November 1962, republished online 24 January 2014. https://www.theguardian.com/stage/2014/jan/24/kenneth-tynan-paul-scofield-peter-brook-king-lear
5. Charles Marowitz, *Recycling Shakespeare* (London: Palgrave Macmillan,1991), 91.
6. Croyden, 392.

7. Brook, *Empty Space*, 91.
8. *The New York Times* characterized it by 'the spirit of experimentation that marks Mr Brook's stage works'. Peter M. Nichols, 'A Less Lovely "Lord of the Flies"', 26 March 2000, https://www.nytimes.com/2000/03/26/movies/video-a-less-lovely-lord-of-the-flies.html. The cameraman, Tom Hollyman, was a stills photographer, and the anarchic action required a style of 'grab shooting' which didn't always cut together using conventional grammar.
9. Gautam Dasgupta, 'The Mahabharata: Peter Brook's Orientalism', in *Interculturalism and Performance: Writings from PAJ*, eds: B. Marranca and G. Dasgupta (New York: PAJ Publications, 1991), 81.
10. Brook, *Empty Space*, 82.
11. Ibid.
12. Ibid., 11.
13. Ibid., 47.
14. Ibid., 55.
15. Ibid., 151.
16. Peter Brook, *The Open Door* (New York: Anchor Books/Random House, 2007).
17. Peter Brook, *Evoking Shakespeare* (London: Nick Hern Books, 1999), and *The Quality of Mercy: Reflections on Shakespeare* (London: Nick Hern Books, 2013) Also see: Peter Brook, *Evoking (and Forgetting) Shakespeare* (London: Nick Hern Books, 2002) based on a lecture given in Berlin in 1998.

39 Julian Beck
1925–1985

When Julian Beck was given a pre-publication copy of the English translation of **Artaud's** *Theatre and Its Double* in 1957, he read it immediately cover to cover – then again and again and again. It represented for him a *total meshing* of visions. In the *Theatre of Cruelty*, Beck had found the theoretical justification for the anarchist spectacle he had been attempting to create with the **Living Theatre**. The Becks were the first Americans to read, understand and incorporate Artaudian principles into theatre production. Between them they succeeded in finding a means to transform the abstruse vision of Artaud into a concrete form, converting what many thought were the ravings of a madman into comprehensible principles adaptable to modern theatre. (See **Grotowski's** views on the utility of Artaud's madness.)

The story of Beck meeting his partner in work and life and the subsequent formation of the Living Theatre is covered in the following chapter on **Judith Malina**.

Julian Beck trained as an artist but gave up formal education abruptly on a whim, walking out one day in the middle of a lecture during his sophomore (second) year at Yale University, having decided that he had better things to do with his time – namely writing and painting. His art was Abstract Expressionist in style, suiting his anarchist viewpoint. He was accomplished enough as a painter to continue to exhibit well into his Living Theatre days, while indulging in what he had always dreamed of as a career – stage design. Philosophically, his primary influences beyond Artaud were Paul Goodman (1911–72), the libertarian philosopher of the New Left, psychologist, and sometime playwright (writer of the best-seller, *Growing Up Absurd*, 1960); and the psychologist Wilhelm Reich (1897–1957), the pre-eminent promoter of 'free love'. Beck picked up knowledge about stagecraft plus an enthusiasm for **Piscator's** ideas by monitoring classes at the Dramatic Workshop. His role with the Living Theatre, apart from acting and designing the sets, appears to have been as 'chief ideologue', always ready to expound his anarchist views. Critic Charles L. Mee somewhat unkindly suggested that Beck joined Malina in forming the Living Theatre 'in the search for a soapbox'.[1]

In 1972 he wrote something akin to a manifesto, *The Life of the Theatre: The Relation of the Artist to the Struggle of the People*.[2] Now, fifty-plus years on, I read it as a badly organized anarchist stream-of-consciousness rant, peppered with references to the beloveds of hippiedom – Wilhelm Reich, surrealist poet Rimbaud (1854–91) and Mao Zedong – seemingly fuelled by acid. In the book Beck chronicles the birth of Free Theatre, the precursor concept to the Living Theatre. Free Theatre was a form of *absolute improvisation* ('improvisation unchained') devised on an individual basis – 'Do nothing, Do anything. Be.'[3] – without an orchestrating concept behind it. According to Beck, when it was first attempted – in Italy – the only *action* was the action of the audience who protested vehemently about the actors *doing nothing* – so vehemently, in fact, that the police were called to break up the ensuing melee.[4]

'We insisted on experimentation. That was an image for a changing society. If one can experiment in theater one can experiment in life.'[5] True to his credo, experiment in life he did. Beck had an open marriage with Judith Malina, which produced two children. They shared a lover – a bisexual shipyard worker. Additionally, Beck had a gay relationship with Ilion Troya, a member of the company, while Malina enjoyed a heterosexual with Hanon Reznikov (1950–2008), another company member. Never one to follow society's rules, Beck was indicted a dozen times on three continents for charges such as 'disorderly conduct, indecent exposure, possession of narcotics, and for failing to participate in a civil defence drill'.[6]

In his later years Beck found some unexpected success as an actor in mainstream Hollywood movies, e.g. in Coppola's *The Cotton Club* (1984), Adrian Lyne's *9½ Weeks* (1986), and finally with his iconic portrayal of Reverend Henry Kane in Brian Gibson's *Poltergeist II*. It was filmed while he was suffering the final stages of his stomach cancer. He died in 1985, and the film was released in the following year.

Further reading

Julian Beck, *The Life of the Theatre: The Relation of the Artist to the Struggle of the People* (San Francisco: City Lights, 1972). Further editions published by Limelight Editions.

Signals Through the Flames [docu-film], dir. Sheldon Rochlin, 1983, Mystic Fire Video. Rights now owned by Yale University. Available on Internet Archive and other free access sites online.

Notes

1. Charles L. Mee, Jr. 'The Becks' Living Theatre', *Tulane Drama Review*, Vol. 7, No. 2 (Winter 1962): 195.
2. Beck.
3. Ibid., 83.
4. Ibid., 82–3.
5. Samuel G. Freedman, *Julian Beck, 60, is Dead* [obit], *The New York Times*, 17 September 1985.
6. Ibid.

40 Judith Malina
1926–2015

As Piscator had used real disabled people in *The Good Soldier Schweik* . . . so we had real addicts among the actors and musicians in *The Connection*.[1]

Judith Malina's mother was an actress, and her father a rabbi – both from Poland, although they were living in Kiel in Germany when Judith was born. In 1929, in reaction to the mounting antisemitism in Germany, her father moved the family to New York.[2] She met **Julian Beck** when only seventeen. He was eighteen – training to be an artist in the Abstract Expressionist vein. Together they went on a quest for 'culture' – not difficult to find in the Big Apple – visiting museums, seeing movies and mostly plays. They shared another interest – of an ideological nature – contemporary revolutionary movements, especially in the anarchist and pacifist veins. They exchanged and discussed pamphlets and books. Julian was aspiring to become a stage designer, Judith to become an actress.

At the age of nineteen, Malina enrolled in **Erwin Piscator's** Dramatic Workshop course at the New School for Social Research. As well as exposure to the **Stanislavskian** ideas being taught by **Adler**, **Strasberg** and **Meisner** she received a thorough indoctrination into **Brecht** and Piscator's version of 'Epic Theatre'. It took no time at all to decide that she preferred directing to acting. She revered Piscator and has fully documented her time at the Dramatic Workshop in her autobiographical book *The Piscator Notebook*. The Workshop's programme is covered in an earlier chapter on Piscator.

In 1947, she and Julian Beck founded the Living Theatre, dedicated to developing an anarchistic and non-violent version of the theatrical principles of Piscator. They took as inspiration his proclamation that he wanted theatre 'to explode outside of the theatre buildings on to the streets; to take from real life and surge back into real life.'[3] The Living Theatre started by producing avant-garde plays, such as the work of Jean Cocteau (1889–1963), but with little means. Their first production was staged in their own sitting room with an audience capacity of twenty people – a bill of one-act plays of Gertrude Stein, Bertolt Brecht, Paul Goodman and García Lorca. Subsequently, the troupe based itself in a succession of small New York locations, having to move regularly due to failure to pay rent. This peripatetic existence meant they were unwittingly pioneers in the emerging phenomenon of the 'off-Broadway' and 'off-off-Broadway' theatre scene, where innovative, avant-garde and counterculture works flourished through the 1950s, 1960s and 1970s.

The Becks' ideas for experimental theatre didn't exist in a vacuum. In the avant-garde New York art world at the beginning of the 1950s event described as 'happenings' were being mounted, initially as a kinetic development of the plastic arts, in painting, collage and sculpture. In a 'happening' (not named as such until the late 1950s) there was no narrative or plot, only *incident*, in real time. Antecedents could be found in the work of the Dadaists and Surrealists in the twenties. In the 1950s, John Cage (1912–92) began experimenting with musical 'happenings', further popularizing the concept.

In 1957 Julian Beck discovered **Artaud** and infected Malina with his enthusiasm. She called the Frenchman her 'madman muse'.[4] In the *Theatre of Cruelty*, the Living Theatre had found the justification for its anarchistic creations. *The Connection* in 1959, directed by Malina and designed by Beck, scandalized public and critics alike with its brash depiction of drug addiction and coarse language. Its *mise-en-scène* consisted of the actors mingling with the audience, panhandling them, and addressing them directly one-to-one. Its depiction of drug addiction, including a death by overdose, was harrowing. Among the cast were real addicts. It's doubtful that it ever achieved the 'free flow of feeling and thought' between spectators and actors which Beck desired – increasingly less so as it became notorious and successful, with audiences flocking to see what was deemed 'a freak show'.[5] Critic Charles L. Mee described the phenomenon as 'a kaleidoscopic vision of reality and illusion breaking apart, jarring and insulting the audience, coming back together again to evoke a feeling of agonizing verisimilitude; a mating of the tawdriest naturalism and Brechtian acting bringing forth the Becks' vision of half-drama, half-ritual.'[6] Mee also comments on the acting, uniformly forced and self-conscious, and delivered with a **Brechtian** *V-Effekt*.

In 1963 the Living Theatre moved to what they hoped would be a permanent home in Clinton Street, New York. They opened there with *The Brig*, by Kenneth H. Brown (1936–22). This visceral production depicted a typical day in *real-time* in a US Marine Corps military prison. Directing it Malina drew on four sources: the Marine Corps Brig Regulations for authenticity; **Meyerhold** for evoking the rhythmic discipline of 'biomechanics' in her actors; Artaud's *Theatre of Cruelty* for its exhortation to 'a theatre so violent that no man who experienced it would ever stomach violence again';[7] Piscator for teaching her that theatre can galvanize people to act.[8] By simply depicting in a naturalistic – or rather, veristic – manner the violence inherent in the Marine regulations for treating court martialled soldiers, the production was so physically shocking and so scandalous that it even elicited calls for a congressional investigation. The play has no plot, per se. Nothing happens. It has no characters whose personal journeys we follow. Simply by enacting a book of regulations to the letter in a hyper-intense manner it exposes extreme institutional cruelty, and the routine depersonalization and degradation which occurs in the brig. Audiences felt battered. The role of 'victim' was so gruelling that the actors had to rotate roles to survive playing it. This Artaudian device also gave the victims the chance to experience being the victimizer. In the 1964 Obies (Off-Broadway Awards), Malina and Beck received Best Production, Best Director and Best Design.

Despite such accolades, the play was shut down by the Internal Revenue Service for defaulting on a $23,000 tax debt, and the events which unfolded became theatre in themselves, starting with protestors carrying placards stating 'Art Before Taxes' and such like, outside the company's home. The spectacle continued in the ensuing trial, in which Malina, dressed as Portia in *The Merchant of Venice*, represented the defendants, protesting that their nonviolent civil disobedience was a legitimate reaction against unfair administration of the law. There was much speechifying, Malina read her poems, and there were outbursts of protest.[9] The Becks were eventually convicted, given brief sentences, but upon appeal, allowed to leave for Europe where they had some gigs lined up. They remained abroad for most of ten years, either in Europe or Brazil, touring old work and developing new.

The Brig and the exile following it marked a turning point in the Living Theatre's development, in which they took up a more improvisatory style of rehearsal and production – the Free Theatre espoused in Julian Beck's 'Life of the Theatre' essay. The result, according to Professor Judith Rodenbeck, was 'a redefinition of "acting" that retained a degree of veristic intensity while dispensing with the matrices of naturalism and character.'[10] A sort-of 'Stanislavski' turned on its head – a search for truth with its own style. The Living Theatre's next major production, *Paradise Now*, took a giant step forward in using these methods, obliterating narrative and 'subordinating individual bodies to the status of graphemes or emblemata.'[11]

How does one describe *Paradise Now*, the Living Theatre's most notorious work? A jumble of nonlinear vignettes, rituals, mantras, group embraces, theatre games, anarchic anti-capitalist slogans, exhortations to free sex, marijuana use and nudity – often resulting in both actors and audience members alike stripping naked. *Paradise Now* was *iconic* – perfectly in tune with 1960s hippy counterculture. Devised while the group were in Europe at the time of May 1968 in Paris and the Prague Spring in Czechoslovakia, it was eventually presented in the USA later that year at Yale University, where members of the cast and audience were arrested for indecent exposure. The work captured the *zeitgeist* of disaffected youth. It was revolutionary, in-your-face, notorious wherever it played, attacked by censors and reactionary forces, infiltrated by police who made arrests, mostly for indecency. Venues were closed down; performances were cancelled. A *succès d'estime*.

The critics were divided. Some like Henry Hewes in *The Saturday Review* were in awe, saying it was 'beyond theatre'.[12] Richard Gilman in *The Atlantic* said, '. . . the Living Theatre has lost almost all its never more than marginal abilities for the rudimentary processes of acting: speech, characterization, the assumption of new invented life.'[13]

The Living Theatre continued to spend most of its time abroad, principally in Europe and Brazil, but had gravitated back to New York by the time that Julian Beck died in 1985. Malina married her associate and lover, Hanon Reznikov in 1988, who wrote and performed many subsequent Living productions – all political and non-realistic. They reprised *The Brig* with great success in 2006. Reznikov died in 2008. The Living Theatre was evicted from its premises in Clinton Street, Manhattan in 2013, but the indefatigable Ms. Malina continued working, presenting her production *Nowhere to Hide* in the streets of New York and in 2014 at the Burning Man Festival. She lived out her last days in the Lillian Booth Actors Home, dying in 2015 of lung disease caused by lifelong smoking. She is buried in New Jersey in a grave contiguous to those of Julian Beck and Hanon Reznikov.

The Living Theatre is still in existence, principally giving street theatre workshops entitled 'A Day in the Life of the City'. Its Board is headed by Garrick Beck, son of Judith and Julian. Al Pacino is on the Advisory Board. Julian Beck's original mission statement for the Theatre can be found on its website, echoing Piscator in its concluding lines: '. . . to move from the theater to the street and from the street to the theater. This is what The Living Theatre does today.'[14]

Further reading

Judith Malina, *The Diaries of Judith Malina: 1947–1957* (New York: Grove Press, 1984).
Judith Malina, *The Piscator Notebook* (New York: Routledge, 2012).
Charles L. Mee, Jr. 'The Becks' Living Theatre', *Tulane Drama Review*, Vol. 7, No. 2, Winter, 1962: 194–205.
Signals Through the Flames [docu-film], director Sheldon Rochlin, 1983, Mystic Fire Video, now defunct. Rights now owned by Yale University. Available on Internet Archive and other free access sites online.

Notes

1. Malina, *Notebook*, 136.
2. Ibid., 3.
3. Ibid., Foreword by Richard Schechner, xvi.
4. Malina's director's notes to Kenneth H. Brown, *The Brig: A Concept for Theatre or Film* (New York: Hill and Wang, 1965), 86.
5. Mee, 194.

6. Mee, 199.
7. *The Brig*.
8. Ibid., 87.
9. Bruce Weber, 'Judith Malina, Founder of the Living Theatre, Dies at 88' [obit.], *The New York Times*, 10 April 2015, https://www.nytimes.com/2015/04/11/theater/judith-malina-founder-of-the-living-theater-dies-at-88.html#:~:text=Judith%20Malina%2C%20an%20actor%20and,of%20civic%20authorities%20on%20three
10. Judith Rodenbeck, 'Madness and Method: Before Theatricality', Grey Room Vol. 13 (Fall 2003): 54–79.
11. Ibid., 71.
12. Cited by Weber.
13. Ibid., Gilman was, in this case, reviewing the Living Theatre production of *Antigone*.
14. *The Living Theatre* website: https://www.livingtheatre.org

41 Augusto Boal
1931–2009

Everyone can do theatre: even actors.[1]

Augusto Boal, a Brazilian, had his formation in the 1950s as a student at Columbia University and during his subsequent time in New York City. His mentor at Columbia, the critic John Gassner (1903–67), urged him to study **Brecht**, but Boal also immersed himself in the ideas of **Stanislavski**, and 'observed' at the **Actors Studio**,[2] where he was exposed to **Lee Strasberg's** version of the 'system', with its emphasis on affective memory.

Gassner also connected Boal with a key politicizing influence in the Brazilian's own country, namely, the *Teatro Experimental do Negro* (TEN, or Black Experimental Theatre). This ground-breaking company had been formed in 1944 with the goal of subverting the pervasive stereotyping and demeaning of Black characters in the arts and developing a praxis which was uniquely Afro Brazilian – revolutionary in its day. The connection with TEN lead to Boal's acquaintance with the American black activist Langston Hughes (1901–67) who opened for him a world of dissident Black literature and theatre.

Putting aside the fact that his English was still 'in development', Boal cleverly decided that one way to meet interesting people was to interview them. 'All artists like to appear in the newspaper. It is a necessity of their profession'.[3] He managed to get a correspondent (stringer) post for the *São Paulo Courier*, and brazenly set about dropping off requests for interviews at stage doors – with phenomenal success. Amongst his interviewees were **Harold Clurman**, Ben Gazzara, **Stella Adler**, José Ferrer, Geraldine Page, **Elia Kazan**, Barbara Bel Geddes, Deborah Kerr – the exercise was an education in acting and directing.

Upon completion of his studies, he returned to Brazil, to take up the post of director of the *Arena Theatre* in São Paulo. There he was able to promote a Stanislavskian approach to acting hitherto unknown in his country. In its early years, the *Arena Theatre* became known for producing socially relevant and political Agitprop plays – in the eyes of the establishment, subversive and controversial. In 1971, with the military junta in full flow, Boal was labelled a Marxist, arrested on the street, tortured, and exiled to Argentina.

During his exile in Argentina he developed and published his ideas for the *Theatre of the Oppressed*, proposing that traditional theatre is 'oppressive' because the audience are not given a chance to express themselves, and that if you can give the audience a chance to intervene – even perform – such collaboration allows spectators to perform actions that are socially liberating. The 'spectator' becomes a '*spect-actor*'.

While Boal is structurally associated with the ideas of Brecht and the concept of 'Epic Theatre' (albeit with a Hegelian twist),[4] his approach to acting is fundamentally rooted in Stanislavski.

> I have had a fascination for actors who truly live their characters – rather than those who pretend to. To see an actor transforming himself, give life to their human potentialities, is marvellous. Seeing an actor create is the best way to understand the human being.[5]

Boal put the emphasis clearly on the character's *objective* as the driver of the narrative. Not 'Who is this?' but 'What do they want?' He rejected **Brecht's** 'alienation' concept because he felt the spectator should be emotionally involved with the plight of the characters on the stage.

During his years of exile Boal travelled to numerous Latin American countries and worked politically with local communities, out of which arose his *Forum Theatre* concept in which the actor presents a problem dramatically – a *real and actual* problem someone in that community is facing – and the spectator replaces the actor to determine the solution to the given problem. At this stage, shifting from earlier revolutionary goals, Boal's work took on a more 'therapeutic' approach to society's ills – how can people *cope* with the capitalist society, rather than *change* it – which some considered to be a lapse into bourgeois individualism.[6] He also spent two years in Paris, where he taught at the Sorbonne, and set up centres of Theatre of the Oppressed.

Boal's methods have been adapted globally by educational theatre groups, (e.g. TIE in the UK and Teatro Espontáneo in Cuba). Like **Viola Spolin**, he believed that one doesn't need to be an actor to act. In common with Spolin, he understood the utility of games. Ideas emanating from *Forum Theatre* can be found in Boal's book, *Games for Actors and Non-Actors*, in which he suggests a range of exercises and games designed to heighten the participant's ability to interact physically and emotionally with their playing partners. These exercises refer to Stanislavskian psychophysical notions – the interlinking of emotions and physical action.

> Scientists have demonstrated that one's physical and psychic apparatuses are completely inseparable. A bodily movement 'is' a thought, and a thought expresses itself in a corporeal form.[7]

Boal never stopped building and innovating. His *Legislative Theatre* concept was an imaginative development of *Forum Theatre*, created when he served as a city councillor in Rio de Janeiro from 1993 to 1997. When a law was proposed *spect-actors* would take the stage, express their opinions – even formulate their own proposals for legislation. In his time as councillor, forty such proposals were submitted (only thirteen were passed by the conservative council).

Lest we forget, Boal was also an accomplished playwright. He was studying writing under Gassner at Columbia University and only accidentally came to directing in having to stage two of his university plays in 1955, *The Horse and the Saint* and *The House Across the Street*. He went on to write numerous plays throughout his career, especially prolific during his time at the Arena Theatre. They include the musicals *Arena Conta Zumbi* (1966); *Arena Conta Tiradentes* (1967); *Arena Conta Bolivar* (1969); *Torquemada*, an allegory about torture (1971) and *Revolucão na América do Sul* ('Revolution in South America', 1970).

Boal's autobiography, *Hamlet and the Baker's Son*, is an enjoyable read, told in a personal and modest manner indicative of his personality, allegedly warm, inclusive and humble.

Further reading

Augusto Boal, *Theatre of the Oppressed* (London: Pluto Press 1979).
Augusto Boal, *Games for Actors and Non-Actors*, trans. Adrian Jackson (London: Routledge, 1992).
Augusto Boal, *Hamlet and the Baker's Son*: *My Life in Theatre and Politics*, trans. A. Jackson and C. Blaker (London: Routledge, 2001).

Notes

1. Boal, *Hamlet*, 320.
2. Ibid., 16.

3. Ibid., 128.
4. Boal, *Oppressed*, 88. Boal cites Hegel: 'The event does not appear to proceed from *external conditions*, but rather from *personal volition* and character.'
5. Boal, *Hamlet*, 129.
6. David Davis and Carmel O'Sullivan, 'Boal and the Shifting Sands: The Un-Political Master Swimmer', *New Theatre Quarterly*, Vol. XVI, Issue 63: 288–97.
7. Boal, *Games*, 49.

42 Susana Bloch
1931–
(Alba-emoting™)

Breath is the physiological element essential to life. We live between two extremes. We are born with an intake of breath, and we die exhaling it.[1]

Though she is not a drama theorist *per se,* I include some notes on Susana Bloch and her work on a technique which she has trademarked as '*Alba-emoting*'™. Ms. Bloch is a neuroscientist, based in Chile. She has specialized in the study of emotions for many years. She is not a theatre or film practitioner, but she has adapted some of her discoveries in the field of emotions as a tool for actors to effectively induce an emotion – as required – via the physiological changes that manifest themselves with each emotional state. Breath is a key factor. In addition to its physiological utility, breath can be used as a regulator of emotional states. Her methods are widely recognized in Latin America, and there is a growing awareness of them in Europe and the USA.[2]

In the early 1970s Bloch and her fellow scientists, Pedro Orthous and Guy Santibañez-H, developed methods for physiologically activating emotion, which they named the 'BOS Method'. These techniques recognized the physiological changes which occur when experiencing emotion – in breathing, heart rate and muscle tension, breath being the most measurable and elemental. They were interested in six basic emotions: joy, sadness, fear, anger, eroticism and tenderness. The study consisted of professional actors reliving emotions (via affective memory), and the measurement of the physiological changes that occurred, especially, breathing patterns. Breathing was the key distinguishing feature of different emotions, but posture, and facial patterns also featured.[3]

Bloch and Santibañez followed this study by asking participants to reproduce the respiratory-posturo-facial manoeuvres without naming the emotion and found a reverse correlation to the previous experiment – specific emotions were *generated* by a specific set of *stimulators*.[4]

Recognizing the utility of this psychophysical relationship for actors (who had been used as subjects of some of the experiments), Bloch and her colleagues began to work on a set of respiratory-posturo-facial patterns for the six emotions, which could be taught to actors as a way of *inducing* appropriate emotional states. They also described a neutral pattern, and a 'step-out' technique – presupposing that one enters an emotional 'zone' at will and has to know how to get out of it.

In her book *Surfeando la Ola Emocional* (Surfing the Emotional Wave) Bloch sets out the stimulatory models (*patrones efectores*)[5] for creating each of the six basic emotions. For example:

ANGER

- Breathing: rhythmic cycles of high frequency and great amplitude. Breathing through the nose, dilating and contracting the nostrils abruptly.

- Mouth: lips, teeth and jaw pinched.
- Eyes: squinting, with the gaze fixed on the point of attack.
- Head: inclined forward.
- Body: increased tension in all the muscles of the body.[6]

Susana Bloch has established workshops for actors, promulgating her methods, starting with introductory five-day courses. Typically, after four intensive days of learning the stimulatory models required to arrive in each emotional 'zone' (my term), on the fifth day exercises are undertaken to apply the technique. One of these exercises is for an actor to deliver a given text with one generated emotion, and then do it again in another 'zone'. It is informative for both performer and spectators to see how the same text can have different meanings when riding different emotions. However, a similar result could be achieved using *imaginary circumstances* (**Meisner** Technique). Advanced workshops vary according to the needs of the participants.[7]

Bloch proposes six *sets* of emotions: laughter-happiness, crying-sadness, fear-anguish, anger-aggression, love-erotic, love-tender – used as a basis for the auto-physical generation of emotion. Bloch recognizes two types of 'love' – the biological (erotic) one, and the *caring* type. Both, she points out, are necessary for the survival of the species.[8]

Bloch acknowledges that there are *'mixed emotions'* – these are defined as the ones which are *not* present in small children (i.e. not 'biological' in the Darwinian sense). 'When a little child feels angry, s/he doesn't mix it with fear, and when s/he laughs, s/he doesn't tense the body. But, as we grow up, almost all the emotions of our adult existence end up mixed.'[9] Additionally, she classifies 'superior emotions', such as *admiration* and *respect*. These are affected by psychological, historical and cultural factors impacting on one's life – the mix being extremely personal and individual. Work on mixed emotions is more complex, but not impossible.[10]

Alba-emoting™ training in a workshop format could usefully have therapeutic effects for the actor, in terms of unlocking an individual's emotions – especially if they are emotionally 'blocked'. I would leave it at that. Predetermining and manufacturing an emotion mechanically in this manner mitigates against spontaneity in performance, and therefore has extremely limited utility for a Meisner-trained actor.

Bloch takes us back 200 years (and to the beginning of this book) to **Diderot's** *Paradox,* with the hotly debated view that to 'appear natural or true on the stage, actors do not need to actually "feel" the emotion they are playing but must produce the correct effector-expressive output of the emotional behaviour.'[11]

In *Surfeando la Ola Emocional* she sets out 'maps' of emotions for scenes (for example the balcony scene in *Romeo and Juliet*) based on reading the text and ascribing the emotions and emotional mixes to each line.[12] This mechanical method is the diametrical opposite of the Stanislavskian approach to living truthfully in the moment.

To note, the method has significant potential as a tool incorporated into standard forms of psychotherapy, perhaps for people on the autistic end of the spectrum, in terms of reading emotions in other people, as pointed out by Chilean psychoanalyst, Juan Pablo Kalawski,

> A finer distinction among emotions may help clients better identify their associated needs and action tendencies. For example, the impulses associated with anger are not the same as those associated with fear. . . . When a client has experienced the respiratory-postural-facial patterns of the basic emotions, he or she is subsequently better able to recognize when those patterns are spontaneously aroused.[13]

Further reading

Bloch, Susana. *The Alba of Emotions: Managing Emotions through Breathing* (Santiago de Chile: Ediciones Ultramarinos PSE, 2006).

Bloch, Susana. *Surfeando La Ola Emocional: Reconozca Las Emociones Básicas Y Comprenda Sus Emociones Mixtas* (Santiago de Chile: Uqbar Editores, 2008).

Notes

1. Bloch, *Surfeando,* 37–8. My translation.
2. Jessica Marie Beck, 'Directing Emotion: A Practice-led Investigation into the Challenge of Emotion in Western Performance', PhD thesis, University of Exeter, 2011.
3. Juan Pablo Kalawski, 'Using Alba Emoting to Work with Emotions in Psychotherapy', PhD thesis, University of Louisville, 2013, 5.
4. Ibid., 6.
5. My translation. A more literal translation is 'effector patterns'.
6. Bloch, *Surfeando*, 85.
7. Kalawski, 7–8.
8. Bloch, *Surfeando*, 80.
9. Ibid., 73–83.
10. Ibid., 73. My translation.
11. Beck, 71. Citing an article by Bloch, Orthous and Santibañez: 'Effector Patterns of Basic Emotions: A Psychophysical Method for Training Actors'. *Journal of Social and Biological Structures,* 10: 1–19.
12. Bloch, *Surfeando*, 88.
13. Kalawski, 8. In his paper Kalawski offers a clearly laid out case study of the use of Alba-emoting™ to promote emotional awareness in a client.

43 Jerzy Grotowski
1933–1999

The song becomes the meaning itself through the vibratory qualities. When we begin to catch the vibratory qualities . . . the song begins to sing us . . . I don't know any more if I am finding that song or if I am that song.[1]

Theatre of Sources

Jerzy Grotowski's work astounded the theatre world, and profoundly influenced experimental theatre from the 1960s to the present day, yet the Polish director's engagement with production *per se* only lasted for the first decade of his working life. The rest of his career was devoted to teaching, whilst continually researching with his actors a path to one's *personal truth* and its connection to the collective subconscious.

He has self-described five distinct phases in the development of his work:

Theatre of Productions

Theatre of Participation (Paratheatre)

Theatre of Sources

Objective Drama

Art as Vehicle

Grotowski's initial formation in direction was at the Ludwik Solski Academy in Kraków, where he received a thorough grounding in **Stanislavskian** principles – *de rigueur* in the prevailing 'socialist realist' theatre in Poland at the time. In 1956, he went on to matriculate in the Lunacharsky Institute of Theatre Arts in Moscow (now the GITIS), where he was additionally exposed to the ideas of **Vakhtangov** and, notably, **Meyerhold**, whose teachings were undergoing 'rehabilitation' at that time. He claimed that it was from Stanislavski that he learned how to work with actors, but it was from Meyerhold that he discovered the creative possibilities of the stage director's craft.'[2] The central technique which Grotowski drew on from 'the master' were his end-of-life studies on the 'method of physical actions'. The 'truth' which Stanislavski proposed through these actions followed the natural laws of normal life. Grotowski claims that he was taking Stanislavski's 'unfinished' ideas a step further – maintaining that it is the *impulse behind the action* which is the more revealing than the action itself – the intention rather than the actual action, emanating deep within the actor's psyche.[3]

Returning to Poland, he started teaching at the theatre school in Kraków and obtained his first 'professional' job in that city, directing Ionesco's *Chairs*. In Kraków, he directed several plays, in more-or-less standard formats, while indulging his interest in what were to become life-long passions: ritualistic theatre, Chinese and Tibetan legends, and the ancient Indian play, *Shakuntala*, which he developed as a radio drama.[4]

In 1959, he moved to Opole in Poland where he had been asked to become artistic director of the subsidized Theatre of Thirteen Rows. Within that framework he founded his 'Laboratory Theatre', gathering together a group of nine fearless actors, most of whom went on to become part of his core group, and remained with him for years. His first production in Opole was Jean Cocteau's supernatural play *Orpheus* (1926). Grotowski's most notable early work of the Thirteen Rows was *Akropolis*, first presented in 1962, with four additional incarnations to follow, eventually debuting in New York in 1969. The work is *loosely* based on a text by the Romantic Polish poet, playwright, and painter, Stanislaw Wyspiański (1869–1907). For the presentation, the theatre space was made to represent a crematorium, and the actors, concentration camp prisoners. This is an early example of Grotowski locating the spectator within a specific setting – one of the devices used in what Grotowski later defined as 'poor theatre'.

Grotowski's set out his concept of the relationship of the spectator, the actor, and the subconscious in a pamphlet entitled *The Possibility of Theatre*,[5] produced in 1962, and distributed by his assistant, **Eugenio Barba**, who summarizes it here:

> The specific characteristic of theatre consists in the live and immediate contact between actor and spectator; for each production a new way of organizing space has to be found, creating a unity and a physical osmosis which mingle actors and spectators, and favour contact: the performance originates from the contact between two *ensembles*, that of the actors and that of the spectators; the director has to direct both these ensembles, consciously moulding their interaction in order to reach an archetype, and thereby the 'collective subconscious' of the two *ensembles*; these become aware of the archetype through a dialectic of apotheosis and derision which is applied to the text.[6]

In his 1963 production of *Doctor Faustus*, loosely based on Christopher Marlowe's play, he sat the audience around the table of Faust's last supper, eschewing props altogether and using the bodies of the actors to represent different objects – another 'poor theatre' technique. Presentation of this innovative production coincided happily with an international theatre congress taking place in Poland, thereby sowing the seeds for Grotowski's recognition abroad. Critics in the West immediately labelled his productions '**Artaudian**', but in fact Grotowski did not read Artaud's *The Theatre and Its Double* until 1964, by which time his style was already well set.[7] Later, commenting on the relevance of Artaud's madness to his own work, he said, 'Artaud teaches us a great lesson . . . This lesson is his sickness.'[8]

In 1965, Thirteen Rows, both theatre and company, moved to Wroclaw, and Grotowski began referring to it as the 'Laboratory Theatre Research Institute for the Study of Acting Methods'. While the form and structure of Grotowski's theatre works evolved increasingly towards a kind of *'anti-theatre'*, at the core of his concern was the actor, especially focused on their psychophysical resources. This interest he attributed to Stanislavski, whose pedagogy provided his model.

> I was brought up on Stanislavski; his persistent study, his systematic renewal of the methods of observation, and his dialectical relationship to his own earlier work make him my personal ideal. Stanislavski asked key methodological questions.[9]

In that same year he published his essay, 'Towards a Poor Theatre', later expanded into a book by that name, published in English in 1968 (foreword by **Peter Brook**, and essays by Eugenio Barba). The concept of 'poor theatre' has nothing to do with production finances or the economic status of the audience, but instead refers to the use of a minimum of *elements* and *artistic disciplines* in the play. Grotowski asserted that 'theatre can exist without any accoutrements, needing only the live communion between actor and spectator.'[10]

This minimalist definition interested director Peter Brook, at a time when he was fed up with the indulgence and profligacy of the English theatre. He invited Grotowski to London, to present a workshop at the Royal Shakespeare Company. According to Brook, Grotowski's course profoundly shocked the text-obsessed British actors on many levels, and it turned Brook into a 'fan' for life.[11] During the 1970s Grotowski's fame spread even more widely, as he and his small company toured internationally, performing works, as well as conducting workshops.

Two of Grotowski's Wroclaw productions especially caught the imagination of the international theatre community: *The Constant Prince* (1965) and *Apocalypsis Cum Figuris* (first mounted in 1968). Both attained the fullest expressions of what one could call 'ecstatic acting', as well as being exemplars of the 'poor theatre' concept. In *Apocalypsis*, for example, the actors wore their everyday clothes, and there were no seats for the spectators – some stood, and some sat. It was a 'devised' production, containing text from T. S. Eliot, Simone Veil, Dostoevsky and the Bible. It was presented in the style of a passion play around the Christ myth. The work was considered by the Catholic Church to be blasphemous and was roundly condemned.[12]

Apocalypsis also became a bridge to the next phase of Grotowski's explorations – 'Paratheatre' – in which members of the audience, on occasion, were invited to stay behind after the 'performance' and 'immerse' themselves with the actors, carrying on some of the themes of the piece. The piece was last performed in 1979 and was Grotowski's final public theatre production.

Eric Bentley (1916–2020), the doyen of the New York theatre critics, who largely dismissed Grotowski on the basis of pretence and 'guruism', nonetheless was profoundly affected by a performance of *Apocalypsis*, recounting:

> About halfway through the play I had a quite specific illumination. A message came to me – from nowhere, as they say – about my private life and self. This message must stay private, to be true to itself, but the fact that it arrived has public relevance . . . I don't recall this sort of thing happening to me in the theatre before.[13]

It seems that in Grotowski's terms, the work was having its desired effect, even on a most sceptical spectator.

As Grotowski's reputation and status as 'guru' grew, a number of directors who were engaged in what **Harold Clurman** called the 'New Theatre'[14] made a pilgrimage to Wroclaw. They included Peter Brook, French actor/director Jean-Louis Barrault, **Joseph Chaikin** and Eugenio Barba. The last stayed on for thirty months and became Grotowski's assistant.

In his publication in 1973 of an essay entitled 'Holiday: The Day That is Holy'[15] Grotowski clarified his second phase of endeavour – the *'Paratheatre'* explorations, which attempted to thoroughly break down the distinction between performer and spectator.

> Some words are dead, even though we are still using them. . . .what they mean has died. . . . Among such words are: show, performance, theatre, spectator, etc.[16]

What was to replace *theatre* was the actor's ongoing quest for an understanding of themselves through psychophysical work. The actor was challenged to draw from their psyche images of collective or primeval significance and bring them to life through movement and the sounds of the voice. The growth and transformation of the actor would hopefully *evoke* a similar development in members of the audience. It was nothing less than a search for *the meaning of life*.

Grotowski made a distinction between the *courtesan actor* – one who exploits their body for money and fame, using skills and effects they have learned – and the *holy actor* – one who sacrifices their body through an act of 'self-penetration'.[17] The state of *self-penetration* is achieved through a 'via negativa', which means following a route of *elimination*, ridding the body of its *resistance* to the psychophysical – essentially a negative process – in order to achieve what Grotowski called the *'total act'*.

However laudable Grotowski's goals for his actors to achieve complete openness and giving of themselves, there were only a handful who managed to realize the 'total act' and embody the 'holy' state. One of them was the actor Ryszard Cieślak (1937–90). In Grotowski's *The Constant Prince*, playing the role of someone being ritually tortured, he literally laid bare his soul. There is an extraordinary fragment of his 'ecstatic' performance one can watch on YouTube, which clearly illustrates the concept, as well as Cieślak's exceptional ability.[18]

These Paratheatrical 'events' involved communal rites and interactive exchanges with the 'attendees' (my term; Grotowski called them 'spectators', and *never* used the collective noun 'audience'). The sessions had similarities with the 'happenings' which were in vogue in London and New York in the late 1960s and 1970s, but unlike happenings were *not* just a random collection of events – different in the respect of having an end goal, in the form of *mutual enlightenment* on the part of actor and spectator.[19] Paratheater events sometimes ran on for extended periods (thirty-six hours in the case of one held in Grotowski's studio in Brzezinka), attempting to breakdown *negative impulses* in the unwitting participants – a difficult proposition, as many theatre-goers would baulk at being drawn into such a performance, having paid their admission expecting to *watch* actors, not to *be* one. Eventually Grotowski realized the limitations of this unstructured work, acknowledging that it frequently elicited banalities from participants, and that one could not expect actors and spectators to enter the theatre space with a common set of beliefs, or capabilities.[20] He closed this phase down in 1978.

During this period, in 1974, Grotowski presented a new research programme: 'Theatre of the Sources'. It was physically based in the new studio which he had built at Brzezinka, in the Polish countryside, but it took him and his associates to Mexico, Nigeria, India and Haiti, in search of a global common denominator – essentially, *archetypes* deriving from a *universal collective unconscious*. The programme resulted in a gathering of resources used in his later work on theatre as ritual.[21] Grotowski's ideas on archetypes were based on the theories of the Swiss psychologist, Carl Jung (1875–1961), but he disagreed with Jung on one fundamental point. Jung contended that the archetype could not be grasped consciously by an individual – that the collective unconscious was a *supra-individual psyche*.[22] Yet Grotowski's entire programme was based on the idea of the individual actor striving to reach the archetype in a deeply personal manner.

Grotowski left Poland abruptly in 1982, after the crackdown on the Solidarity Movement, and the declaration of martial law. He taught briefly at Columbia University in New York, then, in 1983 was appointed professor at University of California, Irvine. There he embarked on his next project/phase, 'Objective Drama', which consisted of seeking out common cross-cultural performative tools, leading to the creation of a universal ritualistic art. This followed on from his earlier Theatre of Source explorations, but with a focus on the psychophysiological aspects of ritual expression. His quest in this research was to discover a type of performance in which 'poetry is not separated from the song, the song is not separated from the movement, the movement is not separated from the dance, the dance is not separated from the acting, a type of performance associated with very ancient ritual traditions.'[23]

Meanwhile, in 1984, in Wroclaw his theatre company closed.

Becoming disillusioned with the misinterpretation and adaptation of his ideas in the USA and elsewhere, in 1985 he retreated to Italy – to Pontedera, near Pisa, where he established the Grotowski Work Centre, continuing his programme of Objective Drama, and processing the songs and rituals his group had collected during the Theatre of Sources period. He concentrated on 'vibratory songs' – certain traditional songs which preserved the corporeal impulses of the singer in their vibratory quality. To sing the song authentically, and touch the collective unconscious, one must discover its vibratory qualities, not just the notes: 'the melody is not the same as the vibratory qualities . . . modern man looks just for the melodic line without catching the differences of resonance.'[24]

In the early 1980s Grotowski began his battle with the leukaemia which eventually killed him. Perhaps intimations of his own mortality drove him to create a final chapter in Pontedera, and to fixate on the concept of 'transmission' – the notion that knowledge had been passed on to him by masters, and that he had the duty to do the same. The beneficiary of this *transmission* was an American actor, Thomas Richards, who he had met in a Yale University workshop, and who carries Grotowski's torch at Pontedera to this day.[25] Richards collaborated with Grotowski as he entered into the final phase of his work, 'Art as Vehicle' or 'Ritual Arts', embodying the themes of 'transmission' and 'Objectivity of Ritual', meaning creating a performative structure which functions as a tool for work on oneself.[26] Grotowski died in Pontedera in 1999.

With his investigations into physical theatre, one could say that Grotowski picked up on Stanislavski's *psychophysical techniques* where the master had left off – taking them to their ultimate form in the 'total act'. His intensive, and constantly evolving training in physical acting was inspired by Meyerhold's 'Biomechanics', but contained elements of mime, yoga, and the Tai Chi Chuan.[27] The programme consisted in marrying the most rigorous physical work with psychological-spiritual practices, 'What is most intimate and hidden in each individual, what is core or deep or secret, is the same as what is most archetypal or universal.'[28]

The physical exercises were of two types: the *Plastiques* and the *Corporeals*. The former consists of specifically learned body movements, executed with a partner (person or object), with a goal in mind. The various forms employed within this set of movements which Grotowski called *details*. The movements were individual, and spontaneous, and originated from one's psyche. Corporeal exercises were more gymnastic and derived from hatha yoga *asanas* (upside-down positions). 'Corporeals' worked based on an *impulse* generating an action. There is no better way to understand the exercises than by watching them demonstrated in a collection of videos, made by Eugenio Barba, and featuring Ryszard Cieślak – available on YouTube.[29]

While extraordinary to behold, the practical utility of the Grotowski sets of *physical exercises*, and their deployment has little objective bearing on the work of the actor in realistic drama. In contrast, the *vocal work* proposed by Grotowski is extremely useful in practical terms to *all* actors, and there are studios around the world teaching the techniques. There were two clear objectives:

1 The column of air carrying the sound must escape with force and without meeting obstacles (e.g. a closed larynx or insufficient opening of the jaw).
2 The sound must be amplified by the physiological resonators.[30]

He maintained that respiration is *individual*, so that each actor needed to work on their own method to achieve the above goals, in a manner that was uninhibited and natural. Voice wasn't just about words, but equally about sounds. He pointed out that *open vowels* freed the sound, where *consonants* closed the jaw, larynx or lips, frustrating sound. His productions de-emphasized *words* in favour of *gestures* or *sounds*.

The similarities in Artaud and Grotowski are noteworthy. Most creators of 'New' or experimental theatre acknowledge their debt to both. As noted above, Grotowski claims that he was not aware of Artaud until very late in his own development, relating his own pedagogy directly to Stanislavski.[31] However, once exposed to Artaud's visionary ideas, he became an admirer (even writing an homage when Artaud's book, *The Theatre and Its Double*, was published in Poland). But he pointed out that Artaud's ideas were not substantiated with practice. He called Artaud's writings: 'an astounding prophecy, not a program.'[32] **Artaud** was a 'poet of the possibilities of the theatre'.[33] Contrary to common belief, Artaud's concept of 'total theatre' and Grotowski's quest for the 'total act', both radical and innovative, ran on diverging tracks. It was left to **Malina** and **Beck** to synthesize and to find concrete applications of Artaud's ideas in the **Living Theatre**.

Further reading

Jerzy Grotowski, *Towards a Poor Theatre*, Preface by Peter Brook, ed. Eugenio Barba (New York: Routledge, 2002).
James Slowiak and Jairo Cuesta, *Jerzy Grotowski* (London: Routledge, 2007).
Lisa Wolford and Richard Schechner, eds, *The Grotowski Sourcebook* (London: Routledge, 1997).

Notes

1. Jerzy Grotowski, 'From Theatre Company to Art as Vehicle', postscript essay in Thomas Richards, *At Work with Grotowski on Physical Actions* (London: Routledge, 1995), 127.
2. Slowiak and Cuesta, 6.
3. Richards: the chapter 'Grotowski vs. Stanislavski: The Impulses', 93–9.
4. By the Sanskrit poet Kālidāsa, based on a story from the *Mahabharata*.
5. Materiały Warsztatowe Teatru 13 Rzędów (Workshop Materials of the Theatre of 13 Rows), Opole, February 1962, 23 pages, non-paginated.
6. Eugenio Barba, *Land of Ashes and Diamonds: My Apprenticeship in Poland*; including twenty-six letters from Jerry Grotowski to Eugenio Barba, translated from Italian, letters translated from Polish (Aberystwyth: Black Mountain Press, 1999), 27.
7. David Richard Jones, *Great Directors at Work: Stanislavsky, Brecht, Kazan, Brook* (Berkeley: University of California Press, 1986), 210.
8. Ibid.
9. Grotowski, 16.
10. Slowiak and Cuesta, 10.
11. Peter Brooks, Preface to *Towards a Poor Theatre*, 11.
12. The Primate of Poland tried to ban the play, focusing on the fact that the actor playing Christ masturbates into a loaf of bread. Source: Paul Allain, 'Grotowski', *Essential Drama*, https://essentialdrama.com/practitioners/grotowski/, 9.
13. See Bentley's highly critical open letter to Grotowski in *Sourcebook*, 156–60.
14. Harold Clurman, 'The New Theatre, Now', *Harpers Magazine*, February 1971. His article covers the range of significant experimental theatre of the time.
15. Jerzy Grotowski, 'Holiday: The Day That is Holy', trans. Bolesław Taborski, *TDR: A Journal of Performance Studies* 17, no. 2 (June 1973): 113–35.
16. Ibid., 115.
17. Slowiak and Cuesta, 15.
18. YouTube source: https://www.youtube.com/watch?v=5Poc5QvfWbw.
19. The concept of 'happenings' stems back to the Dadaists and Surrealists and originated in the plastic arts. For an overview of their proliferation in the late 1960s and early 1970s, and to further explore their relationship with Grotowski and Artaud see Gary Botting, *The Theatre of Protest in America* (New York: Harden House, 1972), 12–17.
20. Slowiak and Cuesta, 13.
21. As defined by Carl Jung *archetypes* are universal, archaic symbols and images that derive from the collective unconscious. *Collective unconscious*: structure of the unconscious mind which are shared among beings of the same species. Source: Wikipedia.
22. Wolford and Schechner, *Sourcebook*, 410.
23. Ibid., 252.
24. Grotowski essay in Richards, *At Work with Grotowski*, 138.

25. It was Richards who published *At Work with Grotowski on Physical Actions*.
26. Slowiak and Cuesta, 40.
27. He had met and greatly revered the French mime artist, Marcel Marceau (1923–2007).
28. Richard Schechner, 'Theatre of Productions', in *Sourcebook*, 43.
29. Training at Grotowski's 'Laboratorium' in Wrozlaw in 1972 Screener, https://www.youtube.com/watch?v=dRyLLTvs00c&list=PL7xLeLQHxPJFirnvncPjloHVb3BR-3Vrc&index=1
30. Grotowski, 147.
31. Ibid., 16.
32. Ibid., 24.
33. Slowiak and Cuesta, 18.

44 Sydney Pollack
1934–2008

I learned more about everything from [Sanford Meisner] – life, art, acting, directing, writing. I still fall back on what I learned, whether I'm in a script conference, working with an actor, editing a film, or anywhere else.[1]

Before his working life was cut short by cancer at the age of seventy-three the prolific Sydney Pollack had *acted* in more than thirty films, *directed* over twenty movies, ten TV shows, and *produced* forty-four movies. Inevitably a few of his films were box-office flops, and some were better than others, but none were without substantial elements of quality, especially in the realm of acting. Film critic Leonard Maltin (b. 1950) said the hallmark of Pollack's work was 'intelligence, both in his approach and his selection of subject matter . . . Good, bad, or in between, his films at the very least respected their audience.'[2]

Pollack was raised in South Bend, Indiana. His father, a pharmacist, divorced Sydney's mother, who was an alcoholic with emotional problems. She died at the age of thirty-seven when Sydney was only sixteen. In high school he developed a love of the theatre and aspired to become an actor. Upon graduating at the age of seventeen he fled South Bend for New York City. '[South Bend] was a real cultural desert. There weren't many Jews like us, and it was real anti-Semitic.'[3] He auditioned and obtained a place at the **Neighborhood Playhouse**, where he went on to become one of **Sanford Meisner's** star pupils, and devotee (see chapter epigraph). His studies were interrupted by the Draft and a stint in the army, but upon his return to civilian life, Meisner made him his assistant. (His respect for his mentor is evident in his 1984 documentary, *Sanford Meisner – The Theatre's Best Kept Secret*.)[4] After five years as assistant to Meisner, he began teaching the technique at the **Neighborhood Playhouse**.

With **Elia Kazan** and **Sidney Lumet**, he shared the **Group Theatre** ethos – with a Meisner slant – and like them he was revered by actors as an 'actor's director'. 'He talks in a language that actors can understand,' said actor Ed Harris (b. 1950). 'He won't just say "speed up" or "slow down"; he'll talk to you about the situation.'[5] Jane Fonda (b. 1937) who starred in Lumet's *They Shoot Horses, Don't They?* (1969), said that working with Pollack was a 'turning point for me, both professionally and personally . . . With his guidance I probed deeper into the character and into myself than I had before, and I gained confidence as an actor.'[6]

Pollack helped **Lee Strasberg** set up a branch of the **Actors Studio** in Los Angeles, and worked successfully with Studio actors, but of the two approaches he 'preferred Meisner, by quite a long shot.'[7] He felt that 'The Method' had been elevated to a religion, and that Strasberg somehow 'made the process the end in itself.'[8]

> There was something about Meisner's approach that was extremely simple. He kept trying to simplify and simplify until you had some sense of a technique, only so far as (a) it was necessary, and (b) that its objective was to get you a result. There was no book in which it said you had to go through all of this rigamarole [The Method] to get a result.[9]

Sadly, Sydney Pollack died in the full flow of his career. Thus, he never had the time to reflect upon his work, write an autobiography, or set out his methods in book form, as did Kazan and Lumet. From the accounts from his actors, we can assume that his approach to analysing the script and working with his actors conformed closely to those proposed by Meisner. He said he liked to talk to his actors at length about the *reality of doing*. He would say, 'Let's not make a movie. You're not doing this to be observed. You're doing it alone.'[10] He directed his actors to watch the TV show *Candid Camera,* a hidden camera reality show, then switch channels to a drama to see how phony real acting can look. In line with his mentor, he eschewed *intellectuality* in favour of *action*.

> . . . acting has nothing to do with intellectuality. An actor doesn't need to understand in a conventional way what he is doing – he just has to do it. And so you have to make a distinction between direction that produces behavior and direction that produces intellectual understanding, the latter being absolutely useless.[11]

He was careful not to over-rehearse, and sometimes dived into filming the scenes quickly so that his actors felt unprepared and were a little off-balance and nervous. His skill in directing actors is evidenced in his twelve Oscar nominations and two wins in acting categories – Best Supporting to Jessica Lange for *Tootsie*, 1982, and to Gig Young for *They Shoot Horses, Don't They?* 1969. Pollack was nominated as Best Director in both movies and finally won his Oscar for *Out of Africa* in 1985. He worked with Robert Redford (b. 1936) on seven films. He was very successful at working with stars, not intimidated by them, yet appreciating that he was not working with mere mortals. 'They are like thoroughbreds . . . You have to be careful because you can be thrown. But when they do what they do best – whatever it is that's made them a star – it's really exciting.'[12]

Pollack understood that working with actors was not all a bed of roses. The problems on the filming of *Tootsie* (1982) are legendary, born out of differences of approach between director and star. Pollack's approach was logical and measured, with a firm grip on the SuperObjective of the screenplay, and his lead actor Dustin Hoffman (b. 1937) was a self-absorbed Method actor – all spontaneity and inventiveness in the moment. It was bad chemistry to start with. 'His [Hoffman's] intent was to try to make every scene the best in the movie, something Sydney knew from long experience was impossible.'[13] Moreover, Hoffman was known to have a 'default' adversarial relationship to directors in general. As he had cowritten *Tootsie* and brought the project to the studio, he had a vetoing power – not a comfortable position for Pollack, and not one that he ever tolerated again. At one point during the filming David McGiffert, assistant director on this and several other Pollack pictures, wisely suggested an extraordinary tactic. He had noticed that Dustin Hoffman, in true Method style, was 'in character' as the female Dorothy from the moment he/she finished applying his/her makeup, until it was removed. Since the character Dorothy affected sweet gentile Southern manners, she might be much more receptive to the changes Pollack was suggesting . . . so script discussions from that point on were held 'in character' and Pollack was able to prevail.[14] With the multiple production problems of the movie (especially the hours required for Hoffman's fragile and problematic makeup as a woman), and the star actor's recalcitrance, *Tootsie* was the least pleasant filming experience of Pollack's life, and made him determined henceforth to produce his own movies. For all he suffered, the film's enormous box office success gave him the muscle to insist on that position with the studios.

As a director Pollack said that he enjoyed preparing a movie and the more solitary task of editing it, but he hated the actual shoot. 'It is like being a surgeon at a train wreck, except that I am trying to stop a haemorrhage of money.'[15]

At the time of *Tootsie*, Sydney Pollack had only acted in one movie since embarking on his directing career, but Dustin Hoffman pressured him to play George Fields, Dorothy's agent. He demurred at first but was eventually coerced into doing it. He was thoroughly convincing in the role, connected, and in the moment – he obviously hadn't forgotten his Meisner training. He went on to successfully play a number of acting roles including in Woody Allen's *Husbands and Wives* (1992), Robert Altman's *The Player* (1992), Stanley Kubrick's *Eyes Wide Shut* (1999), and in Tony Gilroy's *Michael Clayton* (2007), which he also produced.

Pollack was a Hollywood director *par excellence*. His films comprised several genres, but had, in common, high production values, a measured pace, and 'star' actors, starting with his very first movie, *The Slender Thread* (1965), which featured Anne Bancroft (1931–2005) and Sydney Poitier (1927–2022). His movies were broadly commercial and mainstream but connected through a filter of liberalism to the *zeitgeist* of the time. 'He had a very sharp political sensibility and a keen sense of what the issues of his world were, and he advanced and changed as the times advanced and changed.'[16]

His directorial methods derived fairly exclusively from the teachings of Sanford Meisner, but he counselled that the director's intuition is sometimes more important than technique, and that also applies to actors. 'The best actors that I've worked with have a tendency to stick with the circumstances of the play and find the emotion through that.'[17] 'If I can get them to trust me . . . I get more exciting performances from really gifted actors out of the rush of their own intuitive understanding of the part. Nonetheless technique had to be there as a safety net and to give the director 'a systematized approach'.[18]

Pollack's advice to younger directors, in line with his Meisner-trained contemporary, **David Mamet** was to 'keep it simple'. He said, '. . . if there are seven things wrong about the scene, just talk about one . . . Solve problems one at a time. You can't ask an actor to think about five different things at a time.'[19] 'I think the most common mistake a young director can make is to direct too much.'[20]

In terms of the process of developing a movie, Pollack put great emphasis on determining the *spine* as a first step in the process (see **Harold Clurman's** analysis of the spine). 'I try to determine as early as possible what the theme of the movie is, what central idea is being expressed through the story. Once . . . I have figured out a unifying principle, then any decision I make on the set will be influenced by that and will therefore fall into a certain logic.'[21]

> It's a process I often compare to sculpture: you start with a sort of spine, like a skeleton, and then, little by little, you cover it with clay and give it a shape . . . Without it, the sculpture would just collapse. But the spine must not be visible, or it would ruin everything.[22]

Pollack's movies generally are built on an A-B-A or circular structure, in which the characters begin in one place and eventually return to a place that is both physically and psychologically similar to where they began, having learned something during the journey. 'The circular structure Pollack employs coincides with the director's philosophy about human nature: though people have experiences that move them and affect some change, they are never really different people.'[23] In her critical filmography of Pollack, Janet Meyer gives examples of the Pollack A-B-A structure.[24] His movies typify 'Hollywood Realism', with an attention to naturalistic detail and characters operating on the basis of a largely predictable psychology, without layers of subtext. He professed to love the detailed observations of real life in European films but was ultimately wedded to the plot-driven movies he'd been raised on since a boy.

> Sometimes if you have a career like mine, which is so identified with Hollywood, with big studios and stars, you wonder if maybe you shouldn't go off and do what the world thinks of as more personal films with lesser-known people. But I think I've fooled everybody. I've made personal films all along. I just made them in another form.[25]

Further reading

Janet L. Meyer, *Sydney Pollack: A Critical Filmography* (London: McFarland & Company, Inc., 1998).
William R. Taylor, *Sydney Pollack* (Boston: Twayne Publishers, 1981).
Laurent Tirard, ed., *Moviemakers' Master Class, Private Lessons from the World's Foremost Directors*, 'Sydney Pollack' (New York: Faber & Faber), 2002.

Notes

1. Taylor, 20.a.
2. Cited in Dennis McLellan, 'Sydney Pollack, 73; Oscar-winning director and producer' [obit], *Los Angeles Times*, 27 May 2009.
3. Ibid.
4. *Sanford Meisner: The American Theatre's Best Kept Secret* [film], dir. Nick Doob, Columbia Pictures Corporation, 1990.
5. Harris, Pollack, Lumet and Kazan were all alumni of Sanford Meisner.
6. Jane Fonda, *My Life So Far* (New York: Random House, 2005), 208–11.
7. Carole Zucker, *Figures of Light: Actors and Directors Illuminate the Art of Film Acting* (New York: Plenum Press, 1995), 225.
8. Ibid.
9. Ibid.
10. McLellan [obit].
11. Laurent Tirard, *Moviemakers' Master Class* (New York: Faber and Faber, 2002), 22.
12. Stephen Farber, 'How Conflict Gave Shape to Tootsie', *The New York Times* (19 December 1982): Section 2, 1.
13. David McGiffert, 'Tootsie – While Dustin Was Dorothy', in *The Best Seat in the House: An Assistant Director Behind the Scenes of Feature Films* (Orlando: Bear Manor Media, 2022), 104.
14. Ibid., 105–6.
15. Brian Baxter, 'Sydney Pollack' [obit], *The Guardian*, 27 May 2008.
16. McLellan [obit].
17. Zucker, 226.
18. Stephen Littger, ed., *The Director's Cut, Picturing Hollywood in the 21st Century* (New York: Continuum, 2006), 84
19. Zucker, 21.
20. Ibid.
21. Tirard, 16.
22. Ibid.
23. Meyer, 4.
24. Ibid.
25. Farber.

45 Charles Marowitz
1934–2014

[The] point where, the text [is] analyzed and the sub-text uncovered, the mysterious abyss of the ur-text lies smouldering.[1]

Having given us **Strasberg**, **Adler**, **Clurman** and **Lumet** at the turn of the century one would think that the Yiddish-speaking community of the Lower East Side in New York had done its bit towards the advancement of Realism in dramatic art. But another influential talent was yet to come. In 1934 Charles Marowitz was born there, in District 3, to Polish parents who spoke only Yiddish, and worked in the rag trade. Having determinedly mastered English in school, in his adolescence he enrolled as a student in the Henry Street Playhouse directed by Blair Cutting, who was a disciple of **Michael Chekhov** (a fact unbeknownst to Marowitz at the time).[2] Something of a prodigy, at eighteen Marowitz formed his own theatre group and was taken on as a reviewer by the famous alternative arts paper *The Village Voice*, becoming their youngest and the most impertinent critic ever.[3] This was the start of a long career in outspoken criticism writing for the *The New York Times*, *The Times* (London), *The Los Angeles Herald-Examiner*, and various theatre magazines.

In 1954, he co-founded *Encore* magazine, proclaiming it to be 'the voice of vital theatre', railing against the staid drawing-room fare of the West End, and promoting the work of the likes of **Peter Brook**, **Joan Littlewood** and Arnold Wesker. It folded in 1965, having chronicled the 'new wave' of gritty British theatre, which had been kick-started by John Osbourne's *Look Back in Anger* in 1956. Following *Encore's* demise, a compendium of some of the best articles were published in book form, with an introduction by the critic Michael Billington.[4]

Conscription in the Korean War interrupted his career, saw him posted for a spell to France, and later resulted in a G.I. Bill scholarship to study in London. In 1956 he obtained a coveted place at LAMDA – England's premier school for actors and theatre directors. Having been weaned on the **Group Theatre** version of **Stanislavski** in New York, Marowitz became one of the first people 'championing' these techniques in London.[5] He enjoyed a long and varied professional directing career, starting with a London production of Gogol's *Marriage* in 1958 and spanning the years to his death in California at the age of eighty-two. (He re-emigrated to his native USA in 1980, where he formed the Malibu Stage Company.)

His outspoken criticism, his background in the 'American style', coupled with his training at LAMDA gave him an authoritative voice – even if one considered by some Brits to be brash and arrogant. Taking his cues from Wagner, **Craig** and **Appia** he espoused a theory of *unified* production and an insistence on the supremacy of the director's viewpoint. In his book *Prospero's Staff,* he cites **Copeau**, **Dullin**, **Vahktangov** and **Meyerhold** as 'men who leave their mark on the *material* as much as they do on *actors*; directors who begin to reveal an attitude to new and established plays that is more pronounced than before'.[6] This perspective characterizes his work as a director.

Marowitz was famous for tearing texts apart and reassembling them in a different form, he said to 'confront the intellectual substructure of the plays'.[7] His *deconstruction* style was exemplified in *The Marowitz Hamlet* in which he poses the question, 'Is it possible to express one's view of *Hamlet* without the crutch of narrative?' And further, 'Must we forever be *receiving* Shakespeare; why can't Shakespeare *receive* us?'[8] In this work, and the numerous other Shakespeare 'collages' which followed, he shuffled plot lines and assigned speeches to characters other than those to whom they were allocated in the original text. This was done *not* by way of **Brechtian** alienation, but to give predominance to the director's voice. For him a 'modern director' is marked by an 'intercession with the playwright's ideas'.[9]

In his book *Recycling Shakespeare* he sets out the advantages of his 'collage' approach in terms of *speed*, *discontinuity*, and *dramatic juxtaposition*:

> *Speed* enables it to deliver a maximum amount of information in a minimum amount of time. *Discontinuity* permits it to express interior meanings that in more conventional structures are revealed through the more plodding movements of unfolding psychology. *Dramatic juxtapositions* enable it to convey contrast and contradiction in such a way as to provide more dramatic information than is possible through sequential development.[10]

In 1964 Marowitz joined Peter Brook to co-direct the famous 'Theatre of Cruelty' season at the RSC, in which they experimented with the wild and seemingly impractical ideas of **Antoine Artaud** as the basis of a new theatre. (This is covered in the chapter on Brook.)

In 1968 Marowitz opened his own theatre, the Open Space, in a converted basement in the Tottenham Court Road, London. He was based there for eleven years, continuing the Shakespeare collages[11] as well as mounting plays of his own, which he termed 'potboilers'. Despite describing them as such, only one – *Sherlock's Last Case* (1974) – could be deemed 'commercial'. The play transferred to Broadway, made some money, and provided Marowitz with some recognition in his native country.

He also used the Open Space to form a company of actors, and do improvisational work, much of which had to do with *deconstructing* plays. It was there that he developed his theories of the Ur-text.

Dissatisfied with the psychological and naturalistic vogue of Stanislavski, as codified in 'The Method', he felt that drama should take us to a deeper level – as only hinted at by Stanislavski in his thoughts on the subconscious.[12] Drawing on Freud's demarcation of the Ego, the Superego, and the Id, Marowitz opined that Stanislavski had only scratched the surface of psychic experience, tending 'to stop his search at the very point where he should push it toward its greatest discoveries'.[13] Marowitz proposed to take his actors to 'the depths' – into the abyss of the 'Ur-text', into 'the swirl of the Primitive and the quagmire of the Precognitive'.[14]

How does one arrive at the *Ur-text*? Marowitz conceived of the process as peeling the layers of an onion to get to the essential emotional truth, in the sense that different layers represent layers of *subtext*. It involves a special form of improvisation. One starts with a Stanislavskian analysis of the character's *tasks* or *objectives*. Once the 'wants' of the character have been agreed by the actors, the scene is improvised using only the *action lines*. At this point the actors choose three or four key words which they believe contains the *essence* of the action. Then the scene is played out only using these key words. This done, the next step is for the actors to *extract a sound* from the vowels or consonants of the *key words*, and using these sounds, coupled with physical action, they interact, exploring the deepest most animalistic impulses of the scene – the *Ur-text*. The final step is to re-assemble the scene and play it 'straight.'[15] The result is that the actors are left with a 'steaming stew' of emotions in the gut appropriate for the scene.[16]

One of Marowitz's protégées at the time of his work on the Ur-text was the multi-Oscar-award winning actresses Glenda Jackson (1936–2023), also a protégée of Peter Brook. Her long and distinguished career was kick-started when they cast her as Christine Keeler (of the Profumo affair) in a Theatre of Cruelty production (1964) – incidentally, one of the first contemporary productions to feature brazen uninhibited nudity on stage. Jackson greatly admired her mentors in that both encouraged their actors to find the deepest emotional and meaningful truth, and the image of a 'steaming stew' of emotions characterized her intense performances on stage and screen.

The 'Ur-text' has certain similarities to Michael Chekhov's 'Psychological Gesture'. Marowitz had become aware of the personal connection of Michael Chekhov with Stanislavski. In studying 'the divergence of their views and the ideological nuances that colored and differentiated their respective acting theories',[17] he realized that some of the powerful, if esoteric ideas he had been taught by Blair Cutting in his youth at the Henry Street Playhouse derived from Chekhov. 'The more one became disenchanted with Naturalism in all its mundane varieties, the more the spectre of Chekhov returned.'[18] Marowitz later went on to write the definitive biography of the great actor and teacher.

It was one of a considerable number of books he wrote – upwards of fifty-nine. His early works, such as *The Method is Means* (1961)[19] were written with impetuous youthful energy but lacked mature understandings of the art of direction and are insufficiently questioning about 'The Method'. In later works, such as *The Other Way* (1999) he consolidates his technique (which was derived from disparate threads of Stanislavski, Artaud and Chekhov – Strasberg by then was a 'no-no'). In that book he offers useful approaches, among other things, to rehearsal. He maintains that we humans not only react with a complex set of *emotions*, but we also react with complex *objectives* – and that 'The Method' vastly oversimplifies human behaviour. In lieu of simply acting upon the *objectives* of one's character in a linear fashion, the 'other way' is to create a series of pathways and follow them wherever they lead, even if contradictory. The final product 'having more facets to choose from, will create a character more varied and less predictable.'[20]

One of his improvisational techniques was to get an actor to distribute one of their own specific character objectives to each member of the group. The ensemble then confronts that actor, acting and reacting using their assigned objectives. The result is a cacophony of dialogues which, in theory, offer the central actor a range of viscerally felt emotional choices when playing the scene.

Marowitz understood the value of *surprise*, and cautioned that in structuring rehearsal, one must not look at what he calls the 'futurity' of the scene, robbing the actor of freshness. The director should add *twists* or change the *objectives* of opposing characters to keep the actors on their toes.[21]

Regarding auditions, Marowitz suggested that the key skill the director needs to look for in the actor is whether they can 'process'. He suggests a simple method of assessing the actor's ability: once the actor has given a reading of the text, the director asks them to do it again as if the lines were in the mouth of another character.[22] Marowitz muses that the ideal situation for a director would be not to have to make a final decision on casting until rehearsal, once having seen how the actor works with the role.

While acknowledging the power of the collective endeavour, Marowitz asserts the greater power of the director. 'The director is a self-obsessed colonizer who wishes to materialize power through harnessing and shaping the powers of others. It is not a calling for shrinking violets or self-effacing nonentities.'[23] Given the authority implicit in the role of the director, Marowitz posits that the actor, in their subservience, should make one of two types of 'pacts' with their 'master': the Napoleonic – offering unquestioning effort to support the General's masterplan – or the Faustian – selling one's soul to achieve immortality. He submits that the Faustian is the braver route, fraught with risks, but the rewards can be greater.[24]

Further reading

Charles Marowitz, *Prospero's Staff: Acting and Directing in Contemporary Theatre* (Bloomington, IN: University Press, 1986).
Charles Marowitz, *The Other Way*: *An Alternative Approach to Acting and Directing* (New York: Applause Books, 1999).

Notes

1. Marowitz, *Other Way*, 6.
2. Charles Marowitz, *The Other Chekhov: A Biography of Michael Chekhov: The Legendary Actor, Director & Theorist* (New York: Applause Theatre and Cinema Books, 2004), 2.
3. Irving Wardle, 'Charles Marowitz' [obit], *The Guardian*, 9 May 2014.
4. Charles Marowitz, Tom Milne, Owen Hale, eds, *New Theatre Voices of the Fifties and Sixties: Selections from Encore Magazine 1956–1963,* Introduction by Michael Billington (London: Eyre Methuen, 1965).
5. Marowitz, *Other Chekhov,* 2.
6. Marowitz, *Prospero's Staff,* 2.
7. Wardle [obit].
8. Charles Marowitz, *The Marowitz Hamlet* (London, Allen Lane: The Penguin Press, 1968), 12.
9. Marowitz, *Prospero's Staff*, 2.
10. Charles Marowitz, *Recycling Shakespeare* (Basingstoke: MacMillan Education Ltd., 1991), 32.
11. Wardle [obit], described as 'hitching a lift on Shakespeare to tell a story of his own'.
12. Konstantin Stanislavsky, *An Actor Prepares* (London: Geoffrey Bles, 1937), Chapter 14, 'The Inner Creative State'.
13. Marowitz, *Other Way*, 6.
14. Ibid.
15. Ibid., 12–14.
16. Ibid., 14.
17. Marowitz, *Other Chekhov,* 2.
18. Ibid., 3.
19. Charles Marowitz, *The Method as Means* (London: Herbert Jenkins, 1961).
20. Marowitz, *Other Way*, 69.
21. Ibid., 26.
22. Ibid., 50.
23. Marowitz, *Prospero's Staff*, 'Introduction', xvi.
24. Marowitz, *Other Way*, 69.

46 Joseph Chaikin
1935–2003
(The Open Theater)

Because we live on a level drastically reduced from what we can imagine, acting promises to represent a dynamic expression of the intense life.[1]

Joseph Chaikin was only six years old when rheumatic fever struck, putting him in bed for a year-and-a-half, and damaging his heart – a condition which was to plague him for the rest of his life–ultimately bringing him down at the age of sixty-eight, in the full flow of his career. At the age of ten, when he suffered a deterioration in health, Joe's Russian-Jewish parents, quite poor at the time, sent him away from their home in Brooklyn to a charity cardiac hospital in Florida. He convalesced there for two years, masking his sense of parental abandonment and inherent loneliness by writing and mounting plays with the other children. For young Joe the imagination was the key to overcoming his handicap and acting the means of expressing it.

Eventually he was sent home – but home was now Des Moines, Iowa, where his father had obtained a teaching job. There he attended Drake University, studying acting and making something of a name for himself in the theatre programme. But he dropped out at the age of nineteen, deciding to move to New York. Joe Chaikin was famously not a very open person, and his biographer, Eileen Blumenthal, posits that the 'social mask' he wore in life was constructed during his time in conservative Des Moines, as a way of concealing his medical problems, his Jewishness and his sexual orientation.[2]

In New York in 1955 he co-founded a small theatre company, Harlequin Players, in which he was able to try his hand at directing, as well as acting. In its brief two years of life the amateur company put on several public productions, then for the next two years, in classic struggling-actor mode, Chaikin picked up bit theatre roles and a succession of office and waiter jobs, none lasting very long. He took numerous acting classes in New York, including some with Herbert Bergdorf (1909–90). (One assumes he would have had exposure to the version of **Stanislavski** taught by Bergdorf's wife, **Uta Hagen**.) He followed that with a stint in Chicago to do a workshop with **Viola Spolin**. These classes consisted largely of classic Method training, but Chaikin found the American version of Stanislavski's ideas as taught by his various teachers to be constricting and incomplete, commenting that if the 'master' were yet alive, he'd still be exploring.[3]

In 1959 Chaikin auditioned for the **Living Theatre** and was taken on. His break came when **Malina** and **Beck** asked him to replace the lead actor in the ground-breaking play *The Connection* on its European tour. He went on to play Galy Gay in Brecht's *A Man's a Man*. Out of this immersive **Brechtian** experience in *Verfremdungseffekt* he came to define *transformance* in the theatre, as both in the sense of what occurs within the actor while acting, and its political effect upon the audience.[4] He had a gradual political awakening during that play's run, as he put it, 'mostly from considering the lines of the play night after night after night. And saying them . . . . the responsibility of coming out to the audience and talking directly to them . . . knowing that what I said to the audience [at first] I didn't believe, and then coming to believe what I was saying.'[5]

The Brechtian experience, coupled with a deepening involvement in anti-nuclear protests and anti-Vietnam-war peace activities – which sometimes included getting arrested for the cause – enabled Chaikin finally to relate to the radical politics of Malina's and Beck's theatre, which he had had been trying his best to ignore. He became a principal actor in the troupe. But he felt unsatisfied, frustrated that, for all their experimentation with theatrical forms, there was a lack of attention to the *acting process*. 'At that time the Living Theatre was not really interested in acting at all, and hardly explored the actor's own powers or the ensemble experience.'[6] He persuaded Malina and Beck to set up a workshop for acting, but the tepid interest of the actors who agreed to participate was not sustained, and the cohort gradually dissolved. Chaikin decided to leave the Living Theatre and set up on his own.

He co-founded the Open Theatre in 1963, joined by seventeen actors and four writers, including a few defectors from the Living Theatre. Intellectual leftist luminaries such as writer Susan Sontag (1933–2004) and philosopher Paul Goodman (1911–72) were mentors. Sam Shepard (1943–2017) eventually became attached. Its goal, according one of the collaborators, Peter Feldman (1936–2022), a former Living Theatre member, was not unlike that of the Malina and Beck: 'to break down the actor's reliance on mundane social realism and watered-down Freud'.[7] The Open Theatre's *modus operandi* was that the actor would play a central role in generating and researching material for eventual performance, while the writer or dramaturg would shape and edit what was being produced in improvisations.[8] Chaikin directed the plays which emerged by this method – fourteen of them over a decade. The Open Theatre's first full-length ensemble piece was *The Serpent*, a collage of episodes, delivered in an impressionistic style, and thematically connected by the notion that the choices made by Adam, Eve and Cain represent the *perverse* human condition – as exemplified in the assassination of John F. Kennedy and Martin Luther King, Jr, with which the play opens, followed by an erotic depiction of the Garden of Eden in the form of a chain of naked actors slithering across the stage in the form of a snake; Cain's violent murder of Abel; a chorus uttering a roll call of Old Testament 'begats' over simulated acts of procreation – copulation, birth, aging. Chaikin toured the ensemble in Europe in 1968 and opened the piece in the USA at Harvard University in 1966, to highly favourable reviews.

The Open Theatre had gained renown for its innovatory style while on its European tour, and in 1966 **Peter Brook** invited Chaikin to join him at the Royal Shakespeare Company, to help mount *US*, a play about the Vietnam war. **Jerzy Grotowski** was also consulted in that work.

In 1972 Chaikin published *The Presence of the Actor,* a meandering impressionistic book which reveals a lack of a coherent body of theory. 'It is a book full of dreams, hopes, wishes, challenges and provocations towards creativity.'[9] Although Chaikin was one of the great innovators of the 60's and 70's experimental theatre, he left us no organized proposals for practice, only the effect of his work, unlike those who inspired him – **Artaud**, Malina and Beck. In the early years of the Open Theatre, he was searching for an alternative system of actor training, but later concluded that there should be no prescriptions to training, only *exploration.* 'There is no principle I have held in absolute terms. Not one.'[10]

Grotowski visited the Open Theatre in 1967 (one of two visits he made), with the actor Ryszard Cieślak (1937–90). They demonstrated exercises for using the body as a gateway to the *subconscious* and *collective unconscious*.[11] For a while following the visit Chaikin placed more emphasis on physical training – but eventually reverted to exercises of imagination. ('An actor should be alive to all that he can imagine possible.')[12] The process of *exploration* for **his group's** works involved the actors constantly in 'transformative' improvisations. Some of these were borrowed from **Chekhov**, Spolin and **Marowitz**.

After several successful years, and international acclaim, the Open Theatre began to wind down bit by bit, reducing the size of its corps of actors, sloughing off classes and workshops, and finally dissolving in December 1973. Chaikin continued to direct, mostly works written by other people. His health was mixed, and in 1975 he had his first open heart surgery, which slowed him down for a while.[13]

Indefatigable, and itching to get back to experimentation, in 1977 he founded a new group, The Winter Project, consisting of twenty actors, musicians, writers, directors and a dramaturg. Its name derived not solely from the fact that it only had sufficient resources to convene in the winter, but also because in terms of thematic material 'the ensemble was looking into cold and dark regions of experience'.[14] The Project presented few public performances. The works were mostly 'collages' assembled from new exercises and explorations mingled with fragments of older works.

One recurring theme in Chaikin's 'explorations' was the relationship of life and death. Having found himself repeatedly at death's door since the age of six, he had regularly reflected upon mortality. The production which followed the Open Theatre's *The Serpent* in 1966 was *Terminal*, an investigation of dying and death, again in collage style, which dealt with Chaikin's preoccupations in social, mythic and psychological terms. It was set in a terminal ward in a hospital and consisted of an impressionistic mix of institutional cruelty, dying people losing their physical functions, embalming and visits from the spirits of the dead. In the early days of rehearsal, Chaikin chided players who found it a 'downer'. 'If you think you have no relation to your impermanence, if you think it's antilife to work in that area, then you're involved in self-mystification.'[15]

It was natural that Chaikin, with his life/death obsessions, and a desire in later years to embrace his Jewishness, would choose to mount *The Dybbuk*. The play, by the Jewish Belarussian S. Ansky (1863–1920), features a dead woman possessed by the spirit of her lover – which is then exorcised by a rabbi. It was presented at the Public Theatre in 1977 to enthusiastic reviews. (**Vakhtangov** staged the definitive first version in the Habima Theatre in 1922.)

The principal Winter Project work for 1981/1982 was *Trespassing* – also set in the shadowlands – 'a subject which had haunted [Chaikin's] work since the beginning of the Open Theatre: coming to terms with one's own or a loved one's imminent death.[16] There was one further publicly performed Winter Project, *Lies and Secrets*, a three-hander, which played successfully at the La Mama in New York and the Riverside in London in March 1983, after which Chaikin abruptly, without explanation, closed down the Project.

The following years saw the flowering of his working relationship with Sam Shepherd, directing his scripts and devising and performing with him; they co-wrote *Tongues* and *Savage/Love*, both solo pieces with music, performed by Chaikin. They were in development on *The War in Heaven*, which features an angel who died on the day he was born, when, in 1984 Chaikin suffered a stroke during his third open heart surgery. This caused *aphasia* – a speech impediment in which one cannot find the words one is seeking. He attempted to rise above this disability and use it theatrically. As Sam Shepard's mother-in-law had suffered aphasia, he was able to pass on speech exercises to Chaikin. He then incorporated Joe's aphasic syntax into a revised *War in Heaven*, in a long monologue for the angel. In the 1980s Chaikin toured extensively as an actor in *The War in Heaven*, and another play about aphasia. He also led workshops for actors with aphasia.

Through sporadic bouts of ill health Chaikin continued to direct right up until his death. One obituary writer said, 'He seemed to be straying across the border into death but kept coming back again.'[17] He died in 2003 at home. The cause, of course, was heart failure.

Chaikin had become something of an expert on Samuel Beckett (1906–89), having acted in *Endgame* and having directed several of his plays. The last poem Beckett ever wrote, entitled 'what is the word' was dedicated to Chaikin, 'his aphasic friend'. It ends thusly:

glimpse –
seem to glimpse –
need to seem to glimpse –
afaint afar away over there what –

folly for to need to seem to glimpse afaint afar away over there what –
what –
what is the word –
what is the word[18]

Further reading

Eileen Blumenthal, *Joseph Chaikin* (Cambridge: Cambridge University Press, 1984).
Joseph Chaikin, *The Presence of the Actor* (New York: Theatre Communications Group, [1972] 1991).
Barry Daniels, ed., *Joseph Chaikin & Sam Shepard: Letters and Texts, 1972–1984* (New York: New American Library, 1989).
Dorinda Hulton, 'Joseph Chaikin and Aspects of Actor Training', Alison Hodge, ed., in *Twentieth Century Actor Training* (London: Routledge, 2000).

Notes

1. Chaikin, 2.
2. Blumenthal, 8. He confirms the Jewish part in *Presence of the Actor* in Chapter 8, 'Notes on Myself', 92.
3. Chaikin, 57, 58.
4. Hulton, 153.
5. Chaikin, 50, 51.
6. Ibid., 52.
7. *The Guardian* [obit], 26 June 2003.
8. Hulton, 154.
9. Ibid., 155.
10. Chaikin, 112.
11. Hulton, 164.
12. Chaikin, 5.
13. Blumenthal, 90.
14. Ibid., 31.
15. Chaikin, 86.
16. Blumenthal, 36.
17. *The Guardian* [obit], 26 June 2003.
18. Samuel Beckett, 'what is the word', *Grand Street*, Vol. 9, No. 2, Winter 1990: 17–18.

47 Eugenio Barba
1936–

It is a fundamental principle of the theatre: on stage, the action must be real, but it is not important that it is realistic.[1]

Eugenio Barba's distinction that the performer should not *relive* the action, but instead recreate their story is inextricably linked with that of **Grotowski**, to whom he served as assistant for three years, and whose work he illuminated in writings such as *Grotowski in Search of a Lost Theatre* in 1965, and *Land of Ashes and Diamonds: My Apprenticeship in Poland* (written 1996–8; published in English in 1999).

Barba was born and raised in Apulia, on the South-eastern peninsula known as the 'heel' of Italy. As a young man he did a stint in a military academy in Naples, then made his way to cooler climes – Norway – where he first trained and worked as a welder. Later he joined the merchant marine. Having learned Norwegian, he went on to study French, Norwegian literature, and the history of religion at the University of Oslo.

An obsession with Andrezj Wajda's iconic film, *Ashes and Diamonds* (1958)[2] drew him to Poland,[3] and he managed to obtain a scholarship from the Italian government to study Polish literature at Warsaw University. Once enrolled, he shifted to the Theatre Department. He wangled a commission from an Italian art magazine, *Sipario*, to write an article on Polish theatre, which gave him an excuse *and* a budget with which to tour Poland, surveying its theatres. On his initial visit to Grotowski's Theatre of Thirteen Rows in Opole he was not impressed. The play he saw, *Dziady* (The Forefathers), in which performers milled about with the spectators, he found to be banal, unpolished and amateurish; and Grotowski, aloof and uncommunicative.[4] But months later he had a chance meeting with the director in a bar while changing trains in Cracow. After the consumption of copious quantities of Polish vodka in the station bar and the consequential baring of their souls, Grotowski invited Barba to come work as his assistant. He accepted on impulse, becoming the first of a string of acolyte/companions to the charismatic director.[5]

Upon taking up residence in Opole, Barba was able to quickly assimilate Grotowski's theory and praxis, assisting in a production of *Kordian* by Juliusz Słowacki (1809–49) – a key work of Polish Romanticism which Grotowski treated in a manner anything but 'romantic'. It was set in a mental asylum, where the spectators were treated as patients and were seated amongst the metal beds of the actor-patients. Barba witnessed first-hand Grotowski's process – the exploration of the subconscious with his actors. Grotowski spelled it out for him in the interview he gave Barba for *Sipario*.

> Actors must know how to assail their own 'psychic humps' with conscious cruelty, and reach the inner layer from where they can attack the collective 'psychic hump': the community's images, myths, archetypes and dreams. It befalls the director to stimulate this creative process in the actor in order to confront myth and society, and by profaning them both to corroborate them both.[6]

Grotowski's interest in theatrical forms of other cultures infected Barba. After a three-year stint in Opole, he left Poland to visit India to research Kathakali, a dance/drama form from Southern India performed with acrobatic energy by male actor/dancers in spectacular multicoloured costumes. He intended returning to work with Grotowski after six months but was denied a visa to Poland in 1964 (the Communist authorities were getting suspicious of Grotowski's setup).

He returned, instead, to Norway. Finding it difficult to position himself as a theatre director in Oslo due to being a foreigner, he and a colleague, the anarchist author Jens Bjørneboe (1920–76), founded the independent Odin Teatret in 1965. The company took its name from the Norse god of war, a deity who wasn't simply bellicose, but was also known as the bearer of light and wisdom through the darkness – this exemplified Grotowski's approach for Barba.[7] The Odin Teatret's first play, *Ornitofilene* (The Bird Lovers) was written by Bjørneboe.

Holtsebro, a small town in Jutland in the north of Denmark, offered a barn and a financial grant to Barba, and he and Bjørneboe and a small band of actors (all rejected applicants of the Oslo Theatre School, and *non-Danish speakers*) decamped from Oslo, and set up shop in Holtsebro. Faced with the problem of having an ensemble of actors who could barely speak Danish, Barba quickly steered the group's works towards an emphasis on dance and movement (a 'theatre that dances' in Barba's words).[8] Still feeling green and un-formed Barba determined that more serious study was required for him to develop as a director, and he established the Nordisk Teaterlaboratorium, an umbrella organization for the Odin Teatret, with emphasis on laboratory work, exercises and training.

Odin Teatret's third production, *Ferai*, was highly successful, touring both in Europe and Latin America, but Barba halted it abruptly after 220 performances, and dissolved the company. He was concerned that success would divert the actors from the *training* required to grow their skills and obtain a deeper understanding of theatre. His idea was that actors should live for *the theatre*, and not for *performance* and this required rigorous ongoing training.[9] Some members of the company couldn't agree to this shift and left, but others stayed on and engaged in Barba's intense programme of training, which had its basis in Grotowski's exercises, but was embellished with the ideas of Dario Fo (1926–2016), **Lecoq** (1921–99), and Louis Barrault (1910–94), all of whom visited Holtsebro and offered masterclasses – alongside sundry invited Balinese and Indian practitioners.[10] The emphasis was on physical and acrobatic exercises. Barba had no experience in training other than observing Grotowski's exercises, so initially he drew on the skills of his actors in the areas of mime, dance or gymnastics and they collectively devised regimes. In the early days he was stabbing in the dark, not having a clue as to how this work related to performance, other than to inculcate in the actor ideas of self-discipline and control over one's organism.[11] Later he introduced elements of **Meyerhold's** Biomechanics into the regime. Like Grotowski before him, and **Chaikin** after him, he saw the potential for incorporating exercises in performance: 'Exercises are like bricks and can be put together to build performances.'[12]

Members of the troupe were required to read **Stanislavski**, Meyerhold, **Craig** and **Copeau**, and to study images of non-Western theatre. Apart from Grotowski, Barba's key influence was Vsevolod Meyerhold, whose approach involving constructing a performance 'score' is key to understanding how the Odin Teatret actors create and perform characters. 'The characters are not psychologically motivated in the Stanislavskian sense, but are governed by the physical, vocal and internal scores created by the actors.'[13] A 'score' is a series of repeatable movements created in improvisation by the actor as a personal response to the director's material – be it ideas or themes. It is honed down into simple components which, when assembled, form what Barba called an 'ideogram' (the name for a Chinese/Japanese written character – in which different elements create the whole picture of a word). Despite lip service to Stanislavski, Barba's concepts of physical theatre carry Meyerhold's footprint, and are centred on autogenerated performance, less connected on an emotional level with other actors – useless for realistic theatre but indispensable for the types of theatre-as-ritual typical of Grotowski and the theatre-as-spectacle of Jean-Louis Barrault (1910–94) or Ariane Mnouchkine (b. 1939).

As an adjunct to the work he was doing in the Odin Teatret, in 1979 Barba formed the International School of Theatre Anthropology (ISTA) to study the transcultural aspect of recurring principles in performance, expanding a vision he shared with Grotowski concerning the interweaving into their work (or appropriation of?) facets of acting practice from other cultures. For example, Barba had noticed while travelling in India and elsewhere that Asian actors constantly work with bent knees. From that observation he developed his concept of 'sats', 'a position in which the knees, very slightly bent, contain the . . . impulse towards an action which is yet unknown and can go in any direction . . . the basic posture found in sports . . . when you need to be ready to react.'[14] He incorporated 'sats' as a default posture for his Odin Teatret actors.

'Theatre Anthropology' is defined by Barba as the study of 'human behaviour on a biological and socio-cultural level in a performance situation'.[15] A synthesis of much of what Barba has learned in his explorations is laid down in his book, *The Paper Canoe* (1995).[16] The School was essentially run as an ongoing series of annual or biannual symposiums lasting four weeks, each engaged in a comparative study of acting techniques with an intercultural perspective. The first was held in Berlin in 1979 and featured teachers from Bali, China, Japan and India. While the Barba's impulse to create such an organization may have stemmed from practical considerations, the work produced by the ISTA is highly academic – as is much of Barba's writing – and sometimes pseudo-scientific sounding (indeed, Barba refers to his ISTA academics as his 'scientific staff').[17] It produced little of practical value for actors of realism.

The internationalism of Barba's approach, combined with the provincial setting of the Odin Teatret, suggested to him the concept of the 'Third Theatre' – i.e. not 'main-stream' (institutional), nor 'avant-garde,' but a third thing that lies between them.[18] He recognized that this type of 'group' theatre already existed globally, 'living on the fringes, often outside or on the outskirts of the centers and capitals of culture'.[19] Not 'ensembles' in the sense that Stanislavski constructed them, but more like collectives, where actors might live together, and take collective responsibility for things such as set building and writing or devising elements of the play.

Barba's *modus operandi* in developing Odin Teatret works is to first explore the central themes of the source material collectively, and then enjoin his individual actors to create their own personal improvisations solely through movement. The 'writers' would then decide which to keep and incorporate into the production. Only at that point did the actors begin to work with spoken text. Initially the speech improvisations were concerned with realistic dialogue, but, taking a leaf from Grotowski's book, Barba then focused the actors more on the musicality of the vocal sound rather than the semantics of the text.[20] The point of departure for Barba for creating the dramaturgy of a given piece is the individual actor's psychophysical relationship to the 'theme', and that's where he begins in rehearsal. This is markedly different to other 'Third Theatre' groups such as Joe Chaikin's Open Theatre who prioritize ensemble improvisation. Barba's long-time collaborator, actress Julia Varley (1954–) makes the distinction: 'A common voice comes from a composition of individualities and realities that come together to make simultaneously their difference and sense of belonging.'[21] From the photographs and clips I have seen of Barba productions I have the impression that the 'individualities' are paramount, and that the actors work very much in isolation, even when ostensibly 'interacting' perhaps not the case in a full live performance.

Further reading

Eugenio Barba, *The Paper Canoe: A Guide to Theatre Anthropology*, trans. R. Fowler (London: Routledge, 1995).
Eugenio Barba, *Land of Ashes and Diamonds: My Apprenticeship in Poland, followed by 26 Letters from Jerzy Grotowski to Eugenio Barba* (Aberystwyth: Black Mountain Press, 1999).

Jane Turner, *Eugenio Barba* (London: Routledge, 2004).
Ian Watson, *Towards a Third Theatre* (London: Routledge, 1993).

Notes

1. Barba, *Canoe*, 31–2.
2. *Ashes and Diamonds* [film], dir. Andrezj Wajda (Poland, Janus Film, 1958).
3. Land, 15.
4. Ibid., 20.
5. Ibid., 26. Others included the actor, Ryszard Cieślak, the American director André Gregory, and his final collaborator and heir, Thomas Richards.
6. Ibid., 28.
7. Turner, 6.
8. Ibid., 12.
9. Ibid.
10. Ibid.
11. Watson, 43–4.
12. Turner, 28.
13. Ibid., 28–9.
14. Barba, *Canoe* 5, 6.
15. Eugenio Barba, *Beyond the Floating Islands* (New York: PAJ Publications, 1986), 115.
16. Barba ,*Canoe*, 46. 'This book is a paper canoe. The currents are the multiplicity of theatres and their performers, experiences and memories. The canoe's route twists and turns, but according to a method.'
17. Turner, 68.
18. Watson, 20.
19. Barba, *Beyond*, 193.
20. Watson, 74.
21. Julia Varley, 'Ensembles, groups, networks,' in *Encountering Ensemble*, John Britton, ed. (London: Bloomsbury, 2013), 183.

48 Tadashi Suzuki
1939–

The art of a performance cannot be judged by how closely the actors can imitate or recreate everyday life on the stage. An actor uses his words and gestures to try to convince an audience of something profoundly true. It is this attempt that should be judged.[1]

Tadashi Suzuki's creative path was in large measure a rejection of the *'Shingeki'* style of theatre which emerged in Japan in the early twentieth century – consisting of imported (Russian) styles of Realism and **Socialist Realism**, promoted by left-wing movements aligned with the Soviet ideology which dominated Japanese academia until the late 1980s and the fall of the Berlin Wall.[2] Eschewing **Stanislavskian** naturalism, Suzuki believed that *truth* was more directly transmitted via sound and gesture universally understood in ancient forms of theatre

His career began in the 1960s, when, inspired by the *'Angura'*, or 'underground' theatre movement in Japan, Suzuki founded his own troupe, The Waseda Little Theatre. There, in rehearsal, he began to formulate the physical training methods which were to become the hallmark of his teaching. In 1976 he moved his company to the small rural Japanese community of Toga. During the ensuing years, he and his troupe travelled abroad extensively, presenting their innovative work to an interested Moscow Arts Theatre, and to Jean Louis Barrault's (1910–94) theatre festival in Paris. The community of the Suzuki Company of Toga (SCOT) flourished and grew eventually becoming an international theatre destination.

Suzuki's *postmodernist* approach to theatre has consistently involved reimagining classic Western plays – ranging from Euripides to Shakespeare to Chekhov – deconstructing them and creating new ironies and juxtapositions in the text. Suzuki has a penchant for poking fun at 'high culture', setting it in contrast to scatological or functional moments of action. For example: 'one character recites classical poetry while another slurps noodles'.[3] Typically, the action consists of highly stylized 'Suzuki movements' deriving from Noh drama, or Kabuki theatre. The lighting is minimal but dramatic, with the frequent use of spotlights. The action is quickly paced and sometimes overlapped. A Suzuki show is mesmerizing.

Suzuki's theatre work, and training methods both reference Noh drama and Greek theatre, in which *animal energy* and pure *human skill* present the ideas of the drama, as opposed to theatre *mechanics* of the sort proposed by the likes of **Piscator**. His style is clearly demonstrated in the video *Suzuki's Creative Trajectory in Toga*, cited below.

In parallel to **Peter Brook** in France, Suzuki developed an interest in 'Interculturalism' in the theatre. Because the style embraces separate voices within a given work, without demanding logical integration, or harmony, it lends itself to postmodernist models.[4] In 1992, Suzuki co-founded the Saratoga International Theatre Institute (SITI) in upstate New York, with **Anne Bogart**. Their mutual goal was to redefine and revitalize contemporary theatre in the United States through international cultural exchange and collaboration.

The 'Suzuki Method' consists of a rigorous physical discipline drawn from such diverse influences as ballet, traditional Japanese Noh and Kabuki drama, Greek theatre and martial arts. In common with Bogart, the concept of 'ensemble' is fundamental, having the effect of heightening the actor's emotional and physical power and a communal commitment to each moment on the stage.

The actor's attention is put on the lower body using a 'vocabulary' of footwork, which sharpens breath control and concentration. Suzuki maintains that an actor's physicality begins and ends *with their feet*. His most characteristic exercise is one of *rhythmic stomping*, where the ensemble of actors march in unison, pounding the floor. 'Sliding the feet' is another foot exercise, increasing the actor's intimacy with the ground. 'Statues' explores the actor's relationship to earth and sky. There is a catalogue of such training exercises.

Suzuki maintains that *creativity* cannot exist until *mastery of skills* is complete. When his exercises are well-performed in perfect ensemble, it is spellbinding. He explains, 'The main purpose of my method is to uncover and bring to the surface the physically perceptive sensibility which actors had originally, before the theatre acquired its various codified performing styles, and to heighten their innate expressive abilities.'[5]

When asked by *Backstage* magazine about his methods, Suzuki quipped that he simply trained his actors to 'move faster and make the voice louder' but added, 'Actors convey emotions and ideas through the sounds and rhythm of language as opposed to the words. No, this is not a realistic acting style.'[6]

Further reading

Paul Allain, *The Art of Stillness: The Theatre Practice of Tadashi* Suzuki (London: Methuen, 2002).
Suzuki's Creative Trajectory in Toga, https://www.youtube.com/watch?v=fwttjtZ0QSQ
Tadashi Suzuki, *The Way of Acting*, trans. Thomas Rimer (New York: Theatre Communications Group, 1986).

Notes

1. Suzuki, 5.
2. Allain, 14–15.
3. Ibid., 6.
4. Ibid., 9.
5. Tadashi Suzuki and Kazuko Matsuoka, 'Culture is the Body', *Performing Arts Journal*, Vol. 8, No. 2 (1984): 28.
6. Simi Horwitz, 'Tadashi Suzuki: Seeking a Common Grammar', *Backstage*, 14 November 2001.

49 Anne Bogart
1951–

I believe that the great tragedy of the American stage is the actor who assumes, thanks to our gross misunderstanding of Stanislavski, 'If I feel it, the audience will feel it.'[1]

The child of a naval officer, as a young girl Anne Bogart moved, year after year, from school to school. At each school she attended, she sought out the drama club or theatre group. In her transience she developed a vision of theatre at an early age as an intense coming together of people, like a 'bonding of atoms', producing something marvellous, thereafter dispersing into their banal lives – a metaphor for her later work.[2] At the age of fifteen, at her high school in Rhode Island, she was asked to be assistant director to her French teacher's school production of Ionesco's *avant-garde* play, *The Bald Soprano* – a bold choice in 1967. Halfway into rehearsals the teacher fell ill, and Anne was left to direct the show. That experience determined her career, and she never looked back.

As a budding director she was fortunate to have opportunities and the wherewithal to travel and study abroad in her youth. She spent her Bard College sophomore year studying Greek in Athens, imbibing the atmosphere of the ancient architecture and classical theatre. At college she became fascinated by **Grotowski's** work, and joined a company called *Via,* where she studied and performed, using his methods. From an early age, she had an *internationalist* perspective on theatre.

The dancer, Aileen Passloff (1931–2020), a former member of the Judson Church Theater,[3] by then defunct, taught a postmodern approach to dance at Bard. Passloff influenced Bogart greatly. From the dancer she learned the technique of *'composition'* – which later became a fundamental element of her directorial methods. A typical Passloff exercise: 'Make a piece about a dream which doesn't tell the story of the dream but expresses the expression of the dream.'[4]

Bogart is a child of the 1960s – those heady years when young people dared to protest, when the dominant bourgeois art forms were confronted head-on by the *avant-garde*, when artists claimed their freedom to experiment – her desire to challenge and innovate was a product of the *zeitgeist* of that era. From the outset, her work can be viewed as a reaction to the prevailing American style of Realism, which had ruled the stage for thirty years, and certainly the brand of realism promoted by the likes of **Lee Strasberg**.[5]

Choreography is at the centre of Bogart's theatrical style, which combines movements which are developed by the performers, in ensemble, as abstractions of the behaviour of the characters. In Bogart's theatre, physical expressions are equal to verbal expression. Her plays usually involve many characters on the stage at once, acting in *ensemble*, using a deconstructed narrative, where sometimes one character is played by different actors, even simultaneously.

Her rehearsal and training methods were not unlike that of **Jacques LeCoq**, in terms of the relationship of the performers to each other and to the space, as well as LeCoq's sense of 'play'. She professes to admire LeCoq's protegee Ariane Mnouchkine (b. 1939) – it was Mnouchkine who urged Bogart to form her own company.[6] She was also influenced by the German director, Peter Stein (b. 1937) and his Schaubühne ensemble, known for its *collective approach* to political theatre. While an internationalist at heart, Bogart ultimately decided that the recasting of theatre in the USA required an *American* approach.

Bogart was an early practitioner of site-specific work, staging productions not only in rooms of her own apartment in Brooklyn, but in lofts and on the street corners of the East Village. Famously, in Berlin, with her production of *Babel* (1987) she moved her audience around the city to four different dramatic locations.

In 1977 Bogart was awarded a master's degree from the NYU Tisch School, and in 1979 was employed there to teach in the Experimental Theatre Wing. There she met the choreographer, Mary Overlie (1946–2020), also teaching. Overlie had developed what one could call a *classification* system of movement in relationship to space and time, called *Viewpoints*. Its constituent elements are *space, shape, time, emotion, movement, and story*.

Bogart began to incorporate Viewpoints into her work. Gradually, she and collaborator Tina Landau (of the Steppenwolf Company in Chicago) more-or-less appropriated Overlie's system, constructing their own classification – an ordering of the elements of performance, in relation to physical space, which formed the basis of a system with its own language for training directors and performers. In their book, *The Viewpoints Book: A Practical Guide to Viewpoints and Composition*, Bogart and Landau identify nine primary Viewpoints. Four relate to Time: *Tempo, Duration, Kinesthetic Response, and Repetition*. Five relate to Space: *Shape, Gesture, Architecture, Spatial Relationship and Topography*. In addition, they determined Vocal Viewpoints, which include *Pitch, Dynamic, and Timbre*. (See definitions of each Viewpoint in the Appendix below.) The *Guide* is a handbook. In it the authors map out in detail Viewpoints training exercises – some with self-descriptive names such as the *Sun Salutations, The Chase, Peripheral Vision* – as well as specific instructions for applying Viewpoints to both rehearsal and production.

The value of Viewpoints for actors, as I see it, is in learning to work in *ensemble*, to *sensitize* oneself to the relationship of one's own movement to others, as well as to space (including the architecture of the space), and to *react instinctively* to what is happening around you. The exercises are largely non-verbal, even if vocal. They are useful for honing the actor's 'instrument', and, in that respect, could be used to develop base skills (perhaps in parallel with exercises proposed by **Stanislavski** for concentration, relaxation and external tempo and rhythm). While Viewpoints is in many ways the antithesis of **Sanford Meisner's** very focused approach to the *drama*, what both have in common is: *being in the moment, listening* and *action in response to the actions of others*. Like Meisner, Bogart proposes freedom to follow one's impulses, courage and spontaneity. Most of the exercises have no predetermined outcome. She exhorts teachers of her system: 'The most essential quality . . . is being open to what actually occurs in the group, rather than to what you hoped would occur.'[7]

A practical extension of Viewpoints training lies in what Bogart calls 'Composition', a director's tool which consists of the act of 'writing' collectively in time and space, using the language of the theatre. It is a collaborative method for finding solutions to problems generated by a play or for creating original work. Its basis is in movement, drawing on the Viewpoints classifications. It consists of creating sketches, non-verbal, which are 'expressive' of the situation being explored, as opposed to 'descriptive'. This method is an elaboration of what Bogart was taught by Passloff, which, in turn, emerged from of the Judson Church Theater experience, cited in footnote no.3.

In 1992 Bogart co-founded the Saratoga International Theatre Institute (SITI), with Japanese director and teacher **Tadashi Suzuki**, with a mission to create new work, train young theatre artists, and encourage international collaboration. In 1993 she became a professor at Columbia University in New York, where she heads the Graduate Directing programme.

APPENDIX

VIEWPOINTS TERMINOLOGY

SPATIAL/TEMPORAL VIEWPOINTS
TEMPO: rate at which something happens onstage
DURATION: length of a movement
KINESTHETIC RESPONSE: the reaction to the movement of other people, objects, or design elements
REPETITION: recreating something you have done or seen
SHAPE: outline of a body in space
GESTURE: behavioural or expressive shape with a beginning, middle and end
ARCHITECTURE: physical environment of the space/stage
SPATIAL RELATIONSHIP: distance between bodies or objects onstage
TOPOGRAPHY: pattern created by a collective design or movement

VOCAL VIEWPOINTS
PITCH: highness or lowness of the sound
DYNAMIC: loudness or softness of the sound
TIMBRE: texture or quality of the sound
ACCELARATION/DECELRATION: speeding up or slowing down the sound
SILENCE: the absence of sound

Further reading

Anne Bogart, *A Director Prepares: Seven Essays on Art and Theatre* (London: Routledge, 2001).
Anne Bogart, *And Then, You Act: Making Art in an Unpredictable World* (London: Routledge, 2007).
Anne Bogart and Tina Landau, *The Viewpoints Book* (New York: Theatre Communications Group, 2005).
Eelka Lampe, 'From the Battle to the Gift: The Directing of Anne Bogart', *Tulane Drama Review*, Vol. 36, No. 1 (Spring 1992): 14–47.

Notes

1. Bogart, *Prepares*, 36.
2. Lampe, 18.
3. The short-lived Judson Church Theater in New York (1962–4) was an experimental postmodernist dance/theatre group, which included artists Jasper Johns and Robert Rauschenberg and composers John Cage and Philip Corner. Their aim was to 'liberate choreography from psychology and conventional drama;' Lampe, 4.
4. Ibid., 19.
5. Bogart, *Prepares*, 37. 'The Americanization, or miniaturization, of the Stanislavsky system has become the air we breathe and, like the air we breathe, we are rarely aware of its omnipresence.'
6. Ibid., 15. Mnouchkine, of *Cirque du Soleil* fame, trained with LeCoq.
7. Bogart and Landau, *Viewpoints*, 61.

50 David Mamet
1947–

'Emotional memory,' 'sense memory,' and the tenets of the Method back to and including Stanislavsky's trilogy are a lot of hogwash.[1]

David Mamet has penned several provocative treatises, expressing his outspoken views on acting, directing and writing (some are listed below). His style is to make sweeping pronouncements, guru-like, frequently as the 'Devil's advocate'. In *True and False: Heresy and Common Sense for the Actor*, Mamet condemns the concepts of 'affective memory' and 'sense memory' and the notion that the actor can *work on* their own emotions *in isolation*, as proposed in 'The Method'. He points out, 'The addition of "emotion" to a situation which does not organically create it is a lie.'[2] In its place, he proposes a 'practical aesthetic', in which the actor's job is simply to say the lines written by the author, and to act on the character's goals in the scene – the emotions will take care of themselves. This is a stripped-down version of what **Stanislavski** proposed in his final years, and in line with what **Sanford Meisner** taught in terms of the primacy of action. Mamet states:

> The actor does not need to 'become' the character. The phrase, in fact, has no meaning. There is no character. There are only lines upon a page. They are lines of dialogue meant to be said by the actor. When he or she says them simply, in an attempt to achieve an object more of less like that suggested by the author, the audience sees an illusion of a character upon the stage.[3]

In the same book, Mamet attacks Stanislavski as an amateur and a theoretician whose ideas don't work, opining, 'Stanislavsky's trilogy is a bunch of useless gack',[4] and dismisses 100 years of acting theory from the likes of Tovstonogov (1915–89), **Nemirovich-Danchenko**, 'and the rest of the Reds', **Brecht**, **Lewis**, **Artaud**, **Grotowski** and so on.[5] In his polemic against Stanislavski, he is off-base in two important respects: (1) He conflates 'The Method' with the *totality* of Stanislavski's ideas – failing to acknowledge that **Lee Strasberg's** teaching was limited to only the earlier ideas of 'the system', based on affective memory and *not* the later 'Active Analysis'. (2) He fails to recognize that the actor's *substitution* should be done *only* by way of *preparation* and *not* be actively processed during the enactment of the scene. Moreover, he fails to acknowledge that the ideas he developed in his own 'Practical Aesthetic' system echo the 'Active Analysis' of Stanislavski.[6] Actor and teacher, Bella Merlin, has written an excellent rebuttal of Mamet's anti-Stanislavski diatribe, entitled 'What's True and False in "True and False"'.[7]

David Mamet studied under Sanford Meisner for a year, but by some accounts spent much of his energy 'begging to differ' with his teacher. The **Neighborhood Playhouse** is run on the basis that there is a larger intake in the first year, and a culling for the second year. Many perfectly capable actors get the chop after the first year and go on to great things in their careers. Mamet was one of these. And what great things, indeed. Albeit *not* as an actor. He has written thirty-nine plays, including *American* Buffalo,[8] *Glengarry Glen Ross*, *Speed the Plow*, *and Oleanna*; thirty-one films, of which he directed eleven, including *Heist* (2001), *House of Games* (1987)*, Wag the Dog* (1997), *Hoffa* (1992), *and The Untouchables* (1987); twenty-two published books (including a novel, several novellas, and four seminal textbooks on film and theatre); six children's books; several television series; and some poetry. He was, by his own admission, 'a lousy actor'.[9]

He started out in show business as a child actor doing a Sunday morning radio programme for Jewish children, encouraged by his rabbi uncle in his home town, Chicago.[10] As a teenager, Mamet became involved in theatre programmes at the Hull House Settlement Project in that city, and enrolled in the workshops of **Viola Spolin**, famous as the 'Mother of Modern Improvisation'. Her concept of acting as a reciprocal, spontaneous, outward-directed event, responsive to stimuli, would have meshed well with Meisner's action-oriented techniques at the Playhouse. (As has been noted, Spolin, had spent a brief time with the **Group Theatre**.)

Mamet has a certain distain for formal education – he claims that his own occurred *not* in school, but in the Chicago Library and at the back of a bookshop, where he voraciously read plays.[11] His scepticism regarding actors' training institutions is evident in his writings. 'One doesn't have to be constantly trained to be aware of the opportunities on stage any more than one has to be constantly trained to be aware of all the opportunities in trying to talk a cop out of a traffic ticket. We're born with this capacity.'[12] He believes that all that is required of actors by way of training is voice, diction, and movement – the rest is down to instinct.

Practical aesthetics

Using ideas he would have learned from Sanford Meisner,[13] and tossing in some Stoic philosophy and a pinch of psychology – especially William James (1842–1910) and Bruno Bettelheim (1903–1990) – Mamet, and some of his acolytes, set out the 'Practical Aesthetic' system – a useful method for creating a role in preparation, which will free the actor to *live* the actual performance in-the-moment. These concepts crystalized while working with a group of students at Goddard College in Vermont and were later refined with students at the Atlantic Theatre School (ATC), which he co-founded with Meisner-trained actor William H. Macy (b. 1950). A team of ATC students subsequently published a handbook entitled: *A Practical Handbook for the Actor* (1986). In 2021 Lee Michael Cohn, one of the original ATC students, published his own book on the methods, specifically for directors (see reading list below).

Practical Aesthetics proposes looking at the script strictly scene-by-scene, as per Stanislavski's idea of analysing 'event-by-event'. 'The correct unit of study is not the play; it's the scene.'[14] The scene itself contains everything on which the actor needs to focus to determine their appropriate *actions*. 'Choose a simple action for the scene, and play the scene . . . After you finish one scene, you will encounter another one, with its own task; the total of them is the play.'[15] To boil it down, a simple scene analysis, looked at from the point of view of each character consists of:

1 The Literal: literally what is the character *doing* in the scene?
2 The Want: what does the character want to get from the other character(s) in the scene?
3 The Essential Action: a simple definition of what the actor is doing in the scene to achieve The Want.
4 The 'As If': what's the Essential Action like in terms of the actor's own experience of life lived, or better still, imagined.

Troy Dobosiewicz adds a fifth question, 'What are my Tactics?'[16] These are what I call *strategies* or *tools* – predetermined behaviours designed to achieve one's objective.

The Practical Aesthetics approach is an extremely simple and effective way for directors *and* actors to build scenes and construct roles in collaboration with the actors. The scene analysis I propose in my book **Working with Actors** is a modification of it, embracing Meisner's and Stanislavski's ideas. In common with Meisner, Mamet used the 'as if', as well as the notion that *everything* the actor does in the scene must be *in response* to the other actor(s). The key difference is that Meisner talks about emotions, and Practical Aesthetics avoids this word.[17] The focus should never be on one's emotions. Another difference is that Meisner never codified his system – while others, including myself, have tried to do so. Actor's training for Practical Aesthetics, also uses variations of Meisner's Repetition Exercises (even though in Mamet's book, *Theatre*, he says they don't work).[18] The clearest explanation of the Exercises and the whole of Practical Aesthetics that I have found is in Robert Bella's article (see reading list below), and I would recommend it as the first step for researching the subject.

Both *True and False* and *Theatre* are full of aphorisms and pronouncements on the nature of acting, designed to be witty and provocative (providing helpful epigraphs in books such as this one). Mamet tends to elevate the writer over the actor ('Most plays are better read than performed.'[19]) He denigrates acting schools, bad teachers, and standard audition methods. He exhorts the young actor to *forget* preparation, even if one finds the prospect frightening, and to boldly address the scene unprepared – simply say the author's lines, and the illusion of character will manifest itself. He cautions against *interpretation*, most of which is irrelevant, and exhorts us to simplicity in acting, directing, and scene analysis. His famous motto was the 'KISS' rule – 'Keep it simple, stupid'.[20]

Further reading

Leslie Kane, ed., *David Mamet in Conversation* (Ann Arbor: University of Michigan Press, 2001).
David Mamet, *On Directing Film* (New York: Penguin Books, 1991).
David Mamet, *True and False* (London: Faber, 1998).
David Mamet, *Theatre* (New York: Faber and Faber, 2010).

Practical aesthetics further reading

Robert Bella, 'Practical Aesthetics, an Overview,' in *Handbook of Acting Techniques*, ed. Arthur Barlow (London: Nick Hern Books, 2008).
Melissa Bruder, Lee Michael Cohn, Madeleine Olnek, Nathaniel Pollack, Robert Previto, Scott Zigler, *A Practical Handbook for the Actor* (New York: Vintage, Random House, 1986).
Lee Michael Cohn, *Directing Actors: A Practical Aesthetics Approach* (New York: Routledge, 2021).
Troy Dobosiewicz, *Teaching Acting with Practical Aesthetics* (New York: Routledge, 2020).

Notes

1. Mamet, *True*, 12.
2. Ibid., 78.
3. Ibid., 9.
4. Ibid., 144.
5. Ibid. Tovstonogov was a noted Russian theatre director, a student of Stanislavski, and leading proponent of 'Active Analysis'.

6. With the exception of Tovstonogov, most of the analysis of Stanislavski's concept of 'Active Analysis' was published after the writing of *True and False*. See James Thomas, *A Director's Guide to Stanislavsky's Active Analysis* (London: Bloomsbury Methuen, 2016) and Maria Knebel, et al., *Active Analysis* (Abingdon: Routledge, 2021).
7. Bella Merlin, 'Mamet's Heresy and Common Sense: What's True and False in "True and False".' *New Theatre Quarterly*, Vol. XVI, Issue 63 (2000): 249–54.
8. *American Buffalo* was his 'breakout' work, playing on Broadway when he was only twenty-seven years old.
9. Kane, 60, 170.
10. Ibid., 139.
11. Ibid., 60.
12. Ibid., 204.
13. Christophe Collard, 'Living Truthfully: David Mamet's "Practical Aesthetics",' *New Theatre Quarterly* 26.4 (2010): 329–39. 'Mamet's views are little more than an almost verbatim rendition of the first part of Sanford Meisner's two-year actors' training.'
14. Mamet, *True*, 75.
15. Ibid., 76.
16. Dobosiewicz, https://doi.org/10.4324/9780429290688, 57.1 / 451
17. Ibid., 66.7 / 451
18. Mamet, *Theatre*, 34–5.
19. Mamet, *True*, 64.
20. An expression used widely by David Mamet in his teaching. It originated with the US Navy design unit's 'Project KISS' in 1960; Source: Chicago Daily Tribune, 4 December 1960: 43.

51 Simon McBurney
1957–
(Théâtre de Complicité)

A brief mention of *Théâtre de Complicité*, now known simply as *Complicité*, is included because, just as **Judith Malina's** theatre represented the practical modern-day application of **Artaud's** theoretical ideas, so the work of Simon McBurney and his company in London represents the embodiment of the principles laid down by McBurney's mentor, the Frenchman, **Jacques LeCoq**, which he had little opportunity to put into practice before the public in Paris.[1] Although its approach has little to do with theatrical realism, the company excels in imaginative staging, using the communicative power of space, and working in *ensemble* with a shared working language. Théâtre de Complicité was formed in 1983 by four graduates of Jacques LeCoq's École Internationale de Théâtre: Annabel Arden, Fiona Gordon, Marcello Magni and Simon McBurney, who became the group's artistic director. Their *raison d'etre* at the outset was to create an alternative to the conformist, text-based, realistic British theatre, and to proselytize on behalf of their own 'more European methods.'[2]

Forty years on from its inception, Complicité remains, as *The Times* put it, '. . . the most influential and consistently interesting theatre company working in Britain.'[3] From the outset the company's work has been idiosyncratic, distinctive and difficult to categorize. The name of the group derives from LeCoq's own distillation of his principles into three words: *disponibilité, le jeu* and *complicité*. LeCoq and his associate Philippe Gaulier (b. 1943) originally coined the term 'complicité' to mean the connection between the actor and the audience, however in English it connotes an element of conspiracy or shared naughtiness. LeCoq's principle of *le jeu* (the game) has been enthusiastically embraced by the group, and McBurney's 'naughty fun' has greatly enlivened their productions.

Simon McBurney's uses a musical analogy for the creation of his 'fully theatrical' theatre, pointing to three equally balanced elements: (1) 'the text as the principal melody', (2) 'the bass clef as what actors are doing', and (3) 'light and music and the objects onstage as harmonies'.[4] For him, *image* takes precedent over *the spoken word,* and *movement* is an equally essential means of expression. He claimed to be influenced by watching archives of the dancer Isadora Duncan (1877–1927), finding in her movement the embodiment of what **Stanislavski** called 'the truth of the inner creative urge'.

Complicité's customary *modus operandi* is devising the work, but the group also successfully applies its imagination and sense of fun to written plays. The widow the playwright Frederick Durrenmatt (1921–90) on seeing their stunning production of *The Visit* in 1989, said that it was the most revealing version of the work she had ever seen.[5]

Initially all productions were devised in house, in a similar form to that which **Joe Chaikin** was doing in New York, albeit with a LeCoq-ian spin. Notwithstanding their stand against text-based theatre, the group's improvising has provided much rich and witty dialogue. Today, for every work undertaken, whether completely devised or text-based, *devising* is the first step, with actors responding to the themes identified in the piece, creating improvisations with words, movement, soundscapes, video footage – or whatever. Their performances are energetic and alive, and seemingly spontaneous. McBurney puts it down to preparation: 'A moment of inspiration, whilst sounding haphazard, can only exist as the result of profound preparation.'[6] Like Chaikin, McBurney is gifted in making collaboration work. 'He rips and trashes through the mounds of material and crafts a show. He wrestles with subject, space, form, sound and actor to make something new. Most importantly, he allows himself and everyone around him to struggle.'[7]

Complicité's themes and subject matter are predominantly British – political without being didactic. McBurney cites **Joan Littlewood**, with her blend of political engagement and 'vibrant theatricality' as his heroine.[8]

In addition to excelling in non-naturalistic highly theatrical work with Complicité, Simon McBurney has distinguished himself over the years as a sought-after film actor in the realist Stanislavskian vein, usually playing character roles, such as Oliver Lacon in *Tinker Tailor Soldier Spy* (2011) or Dr Atticus Noyle in *The Manchurian Candidate* (2004).

Further reading

Michael Fry, 'Théâtre de Complicité', in *British Theatre Companies 1980–1994*, Graham Saunders, ed. (London: Bloomsbury Methuen Drama, 2015).

Notes

1. This, of course, is not the only example. Ariane Mnouchkine in France and Robert LePage in Canada are latter day practitioners of LeCoq's techniques.
2. Fry, 166.
3. Tom Overton, 'Our History', Complicité, https://www.complicite.org/about-us/our-history/
4. Ibid.
5. Ibid.
6. Simon McBurney, cited by his collaborator Catherine Alexander, 'Theatre de Complicité and Storytelling' British Library online, published 8 January 2019: https://www.bl.uk/20th-century-literature/articles/theatre-de-complicite-and storytelling#:~:text=Catherine%20Alexander%20discusses%20Theatre%20de,by%20looking%20for%20a%20story
7. Ibid.
8. Fry, 171.

52 The Neighborhood Playhouse
1915–1927, 1928–

The Neighborhood Playhouse today is a full-time conservatory for actors, located in mid-town New York City, and inextricably bound to the name of **Sanford Meisner**, who taught there for fifty-five years – the reason for its present-day renown. Meisner arrived in his post in 1935, but the institution had its origins twenty years earlier and carried its own social-political pedigree.

The Settlement Movement was a reformist social movement which began in the 1890s in the USA and Britain, based on the patronizing idea that if members of the privileged classes were to establish residence amongst the poor, that they could acculturate them, enlighten them and elevate them socially through educational and cultural programmes, while at the same time charitably aiding in their basic needs like food and medicine. The movement peaked in the 1920s. It aimed to establish "settlement houses" in poor urban areas, in which volunteer middle-class 'settlement workers' would live and work. In 1905, two philanthropist sisters, Alice and Irene Lewisohn, orphaned Jewish heiresses of a mining fortune, volunteered at the Henry Street Settlement House in Lower East Side of Manhattan. Alice (1883–1972), who had pretensions to act, began to give classes in drama and dance to the 'locals'. They discovered an abundance of talented actors and dancers in the principally Jewish immigrant neighbourhood whom they could involve in their popular dramatic productions. In 1914, they drew on their inheritance to build the handsome new Neighborhood Theatre in nearby Grand Street and donated it to the Settlement. The Lewisohns were well-educated, well-informed, and were aided in their fledgling Neighborhood Theatre endeavour by an all-female board of directors inclining towards the *progressive* theatre production of the time. As sometime visitors to Europe, the sisters were well versed in the emerging Continental artistic and dramatic movements – Constructivism, Symbolism and the like. They knew the Moscow Arts Theatre, and, in their own country, the progressive work of the Provincetown Players collective founded in the same year, 1915. They organized the Neighborhood Playhouse as an *ensemble theatre* along the same lines. By 1920, the Playhouse had replaced its amateur casts with a resident professional company. It gained wide recognition for their 1925 production of *The Dybbuk* – only two years earlier premiered by **Yevgeni Vakhtangov** at the Habima Theatre in Moscow. What they lacked in comparison to other *ensembles* that followed, such as the **Group Theatre**, was a conceptual framework, a coherent credo, a pedagogy and a training programme. In 1927, following a hugely popular production of its annual *Grand Street Follies* – the must-see show in New York that year – the company splintered, divorcing itself from the Henry Street Settlement House, and reforming as the Actors-Managers Company to remount the successful *Follies* production in an uptown venue. It was the proverbial camel's straw breaking the back of an organization by then characterized by 'mission confusion, internal rivalries, poor financial planning and an unsustainable philanthropic model for a non-commercial theatre.'[1] The Playhouse died.

Out of the ashes arose a phoenix in the form of Rita Wallach Morgenthau (1881–1964). The daughter of a highly successfully lawyer and wife of Max Morgenthau, Jr, she had been associated with the Henry Street Settlement since its early days and was a board member of the theatre. Addressing a need that the previous incarnation of the Playhouse had failed to satisfy, Morgenthau, along with Irene Lewisohn (1892–1944), established the Neighborhood Playhouse School of Theatre in 1928, dedicated to training. Morgenthau became its director, maintaining a presence in the school for thirty-five years. In addition to her work in that capacity she published many educational materials and was the first vocational counsellor in the New York City public school system.[2] Out the outset, Irene Lewisohn served as an adviser, assuring some continuity with teaching from the original Playhouse, especially in dance.

It's not known who had the foresight to bring Sanford Meisner on board. The Group Theatre, with its new 'Russian' ideas, had been making waves and the Lewisohn and Morgenthau were well aware of the revolution in theatre it represented. The first class in 1928 comprised only nine students, who had the good fortune to be taught by the likes of dancer/choreographers Martha Graham (1894–1991) and Agnes de Mille (1905–1993), composer/choreographer Louis Horst (1884–1964) and actress Louise Elliott (aka Kasey Rogers, 1925–2006), all of whom were part of the original Playhouse teaching cohort.[3] When Sanford Meisner arrived in 1935 it was largely attended by 'slum youngsters' – the legacy of the 'social assimilation' of Henry Street. Within five years he converted it into a conservatory centre of excellence for professional actors becoming Head of the Acting Department in 1940.[4]

Martha Graham is variously called the 'Mother of Modern Dance' and the 'Picasso of Dance'. By the time of the opening of the Playhouse she had established her own dance studio[5] where she was developing her revolutionary style, stripping away the decorative movements of classic ballet and creating performance arising from the rawness of the human experience. The form of the new dance was corporally grounded – energy derived from the earth, in contrast to the floating and flying of traditional ballet. Graham subscribed to **Stanislavski's** concept that truthful acting emanates from one's 'inner forces' and that each actor is unique.

> There is a vitality, a life force, an energy, a quickening that is translated through you into action, and because there is only one of you in all of time, this expression is unique. And if you block it, it will never exist through any other medium and it will be lost.[6]

Her style was the perfect form of movement to complement Meisner's challenging his students to reach into their inner emotional depths. (Meisner's teachings at the Playhouse are covered in his chapter and elaborated in **Working with Actors**.)

In 1990, Meisner retired, but then served as director emeritus of the Acting Department until his death in 1997. The school today is a full-time professional conservatory for actors, training in acting, movement, speech and voice. It is highly respected, on a par with top American university courses. The core of the acting programme is, of course, Meisner Technique. The full-time course is of two years duration. There is also a six-week summer programme, and several other specialized short courses.

Further reading

John P. Harrington, *The Life of the Neighborhood Playhouse on Grand Street*, (Syracuse: Syracuse University Press, 2007).

Notes

1. Harrington, 268.
2. Ibid., 264.

3. Neighborhood Playhouse website.
4. 'Rita Morgenthau Socialworker, 84' [obit], *The New York Times*, 9 April 1964.
5. The Martha Graham Centre of Contemporary Dance was formed in 1926 and is still in existence as the oldest dance company in the USA.
6. Agnes de Mille, *Martha: The Life and Work of Martha Graham* (New York: Random House, 1991), 264.

53 The Group Theater 1931–1941

> The unity of theatrical production . . . is a unity of background, of feeling, of thought, of need, among a group of people that has formed itself consciously or unconsciously from the undifferentiated masses.[1]
>
> **Harold Clurman**

The germ of the idea of the **Group Theatre** grew out of discussions between director **Harold Clurman** and actor/director **Lee Strasberg**, but the *visionary* of the project was Clurman. It seemed a perfect symbiosis – Strasberg's *adaptation* of **Stanislavski's** early principles provided the techniques required for Clurman's dream of building a radical new American theatre. Like the Moscow Arts Theatre it was to be an *ensemble* theatre, drawing its inspiration not only from Stanislavski but more directly from Clurman's admiration for, **Jacques Copeau** (who was copying André Antoine.) It was to be the site of shared values and artistic unity distinct from the undifferentiated commercial theatre of the day.

One of the first people to share his vision was Cheryl Crawford (1902–86), an ambitious young producer at the Theater Guild. In 1930, with Crawford doing the promotion, Clurman began to hold lectures and discussion groups in which he preached to anyone who would listen about the need for a revolution in theatre. And listen they did. The Friday evening sessions initially took place in his own hotel room, then, as more people attended, it moved to Cheryl's flat, and eventually – as interest among the theatre community swelled – to the Steinway Hall at 11:30 at night, after the theatres had let out. Inspired by the Moscow Arts Theatre (see **From Russia with Love**) and the teachings of **Richard Boleslavsky**, Clurman talked passionately of forming 'an ensemble of dedicated artists – actors, playwrights, directors, designers – collaborating through a common technique, to create unified presentations of plays that would reflect, for their audience, the life of their times.'[2] He preached the need, not just for new acting techniques, but for an ideas-based theatre which was socially relevant.

Out of these meetings, The Group was born. Cheryl was to be the business head, Harold the spokesperson, public relations chief, and literary director, and Lee, the teacher, and principal director. A corps of committed actors was assembled – by interviews and not auditions. On a rainy evening in June 1931, twenty-eight young actors, the three Group directors, sundry wives, and a few children, set off in a motley caravan of cars – symbolically departing from in front steps of the Guild Theatre – and headed to 'summer camp' at the Brookfield Centre in Connecticut.[3] The youngest actors amongst them were Sanford Meisner and **Robert Lewis**.

The troupe spent the summer rehearsing a new play by Paul Green (1894–1981), *The House of Connelly*, jointly directed by Strasberg and Crawford, which then opened in New York in September. The box office was good, and the notices were excellent – several mentioning the quality of the *ensemble playing*, which reinforced The Group's *raison d'être*. The rehearsal methods which Strasberg had used that summer were innovative, involving a new form of improvisation. 'This required the actors to do extemporaneous scenes based on situations emotionally analogous to those in the play, but not actually part of the play's text.'[4] Strasberg exhorted his actors to find meaning for their character from within their own psyche and taught them the use of 'affective memory'. Although Clurman, in retrospect, recognized that *The House of Connelly* was flawed in several respects, he points out that this production marked a turning point in American theatre. For the actor, the improvisation methods used in rehearsing the play (Stanislavski-via-Boleslavsky-via-Strasberg) represented a radically different approach to creating a role.[5]

The pattern of that first summer was repeated every year through 1939 – 'summer camps' outside of New York, to rehearse much of the work to be staged in the ensuing season.

The production output was not insignificant – twenty-two plays over the ten years. Some were flops and a few were hits. *The Men in White* (1933), directed by Strasberg, was the first real commercial success, running for three hundred and fifty-one shows, and garnering glittering reviews. In rehearsal, Strasberg emersed his actors in the detailed reality of hospital life and their individual professional roles. The naturalism thus created on the stage was framed in abstracted and beautifully lit sets by designer Mordecai Gorelik (1899–1990) – the experience was both *theatrical* and *truthful* at the same time. It won the Pulitzer Prize for Drama.

The other major success for the Group came later, in 1937, with *The Golden Boy*, written by Group member Clifford Odets (1906–63), and directed by Clurman. Its initial Broadway run numbered 250 performances, followed by two substantial New York revivals. It also toured extensively, including a London production (directed by Robert Lewis).

But financial success was a rarity, and during its ten-year life, there was a constant struggle for existence, which lead to conflicts over The Group's priorities – was it to be *commercial success* or *artistic* and *social integrity*? Additionally, Hollywood was calling. Jobs in the movies – on offer to some members, but not others – also created resentments – not to mention scheduling problems.[6] Moreover, there was a wide disparity of financial standing amongst the members. **Stella Adler**, who came from a well-off actor family and lived in a relatively luxuriously 'uptown' flat, had no intention of joining other members (including Clurman and **Elia Kazan**) when they were resigned in the lean times to living in a low-rent commune, which they dubbed The Group's 'poorhouse'.

Regarding principles of remuneration, it was determined at the outset that all actors were to be paid the same fee, irrespective of the importance of their role in any given play. However, some weighting was given for marital status or child responsibilities, as well as tenure within The Group. The three directors received a middle-level salary. Profits were to be largely ploughed back into the company, except that exceptional profits would be shared in dividends, equally distributed.[7] Members and apprentices had to pay for their own lodging at the summer camps – cheap, but nonetheless representing a hardship for some. Robert Lewis, for example, totally broke, but desperate to enrol in the first summer camp, found a stock-broker friend who 'invested' in his talent, and covered the $90 lodging fee.[8]

The *'ensemble'* idea was not easy for everyone. American individualism was engrained. 'The Group's non-star system was particularly painful for [Stella Adler], and she never did adjust to it.'[9] **Stella** had been a respected actress in the Yiddish theatre since she was a child and aspired to be a Broadway star. Even though her lover and husband-to-be, Harold Clurman had a hand in the casting for The Group's productions, she was rarely offered leading-lady roles. She allegedly made life quite difficult for Clurman over this. She said retrospectively, 'For me the Group was a miserable experience. I wasn't a part of it, ideologically, or any other way. I am not a Group member; I only joined because I believed in Harold.'[10]

The harmony and collective euphoria of that first camp didn't last long. Halfway into the summer the first of many deputations of actors showed up at the directors' doors. The founding members had imagined a transparent, progressive environment, but found it to be far from democratic. As his power as a teacher and director grew, Strasberg's personality was changing – he became increasingly autocratic. Even **Clurman** could see it.[11] Strasberg's petty jealousy, inflexibility, and inability to admit that he was wrong – combined with Crawford's and Clurman's closed style of management (not to mention a perceived favouritism by Clurman for his lover/wife, Stella Adler), fostered discontent.

A few years into The Group experiment, as might seem natural in an organization devoted to creating 'workers theatre', a Communist cell sprang up. As Kazan recounts in his chapter, the cell fomented resistance, and secretly plotted to take over *artistic control* of The Group, at which point he dropped out of it.

It's not surprising, given the *zeitgeist* of the times – the Depression, rampant unemployment, strikes, Roosevelt's social New Deal and the perceived successes of the Russian Revolution – that The Group was politically committed. However, it wasn't until Clifford Odets, then an actor in the Group, wrote *Awake and Sing!* (1935) that The Group's politics began to be channelled into its artistic output. Odets' plays, which were expressed in the language and circumstances of their working-class characters, fulfilled The Group's hopes of creating a theatre which spoke both *to* and *for* its audience. Odet's *Waiting for Lefty*, and *Paradise Lost* were among the most memorable productions of the decade.

The beginning of the end, so to speak, came in August of 1936, when Stella Adler returned from her trip to Paris, full of excitement about what she had learned at the feet of the 'master', Stanislavski. By way of reporting, she gave two lectures to The Group (see **From Russia with Love**). In these lectures she explained that Stanislavski had shifted away from the use of 'affective memory', having determined that appropriate emotions arise naturally from reactions to the given circumstances of the play – and that emotions should not be *self-generated* in *advance* of the action, via an actor's psychological introspection. As noted in other chapters, this rejection of 'affective memory' resonated widely with the members. There was a growing resentment towards Strasberg's ruthless method of putting his actors through emotional wringers.

Lee Strasberg was a deliberate *non-attender* to Stella's first lecture. The very next day he convened a meeting of his own, in which he disputed Stanislavski's approach, insisting that true emotion had to be found before an action could be played. Jaws dropped as he declared 'I don't teach Stanislavski's method, I teach Strasberg's Method.'[12] From that day forth, Strasberg dropped all mention of Stanislavski, at least until after the Russian's death. Many of the members were shocked and appalled at Strasberg's arrogance and intransigence. On the other hand, they lapped up every word Stella had to say. Strasberg was stripped of his position as 'unblemished arbitrator of Stanislavski in America. . . . The Group's despotic schoolmaster and his lessons were now disputed.'[13]

Robert Lewis was one of those most relieved. The new accent on *action*, and the use of the *actor's imagination* completed his own concept of what makes effective acting. Sanford Meisner, as well, felt liberated – he readily grabbed on to the concept of 'imaginary circumstances.' He said, 'The net effect of Stella's report to the Group . . . was to drive a chink into what was, up to then, Lee's impenetrable armour, and also to let some fresh air into the fetid atmosphere in America surrounding the theories of Stanislavski.'[14]

The growing lack of faith in Strasberg was compounded by growing discontent amongst the ranks towards the management – financial, administrative, and artistic. An Actors' Committee had been formed in 1933 to undertake a post-mortem on the management's incompetence attending the closing (after only nine days) of one of The Group's biggest flops, *Big Night*. This Actors' Committee, of which Elia Kazan was a member, was reconstituted in the spring of 1936 over some other management issues. Following Adler's lectures, and the subsequent diminution of respect for Strasberg, the Committee doubled its attack on the directors, in December delivering in a letter an ultimatum to the leadership, demanding that they change and restructure, or step down. Crawford and Strasberg resigned, but Clurman clung on, going on to direct *Golden Boy* and *Rocket to the Moon* for The Group. Even the success of these late plays couldn't stop the inevitable. The Group's financial model was no longer sustainable. It collapsed definitively in 1941. As Clurman said in *The New York Times*, 'our means and our ends were in fundamental contradiction.'[15]

Despite its relatively short life span, the Group Theatre has been called the bravest and single-most significant experiment in the history of American theatre. It set the bar for realistic acting and produced numerous brilliant actors and directors. However, its legacy lies in its teachers. A number of its members became teachers, carrying forward the spirit of The Group (and its Moscow predecessor), and perpetrating the realistic 'American style' of acting which has come to dominate theatre and cinema globally . . . the three most prominent were Lee Strasberg, Stella Adler, and Sanford Meisner.

Further reading

Harold Clurman, *The Fervent Years* (London: Dennis Dobson Ltd., 1946).
Robert Lewis, *Slings and Arrows: Theatre in My Life* (Briarcliff Manor, NY: Stein and Day, 1984).
Wendy Smith, *Real Life Drama: The Group Theatre and America, 1931–1940* (New York: Alfred A. Knopf, 1990).

Notes

1. Clurman, 33.
2. Lewis, 37.
3. Smith, 32.
4. Clurman, 43.
5. Ibid., 60.
6. Amongst The Group members most sought-after by Hollywood were directors Kazan, Lewis and Clurman, and actors Franchot Tone, John Garfield, Stella Adler and Francis Farmer.
7. Ibid., 57.
8. Smith, 32.
9. Robert Lewis, *Method – or Madness?* (New York: Samuel French Inc., 1958), 73.
10. Ibid., 106.
11. Clurman, 52.
12. 'Method' teacher Robert Ellermann in an interview, in Ruthel Honey-Ellen Darvas, 'A Comparative Study of Robert Lewis, Lee Strasberg, Stella Adler and Sanford Meisner in the Context of Current Research About the Stanislavsky System' (2010), Wayne State University Dissertations,15.
13. Mel Gordon, *Stanislavsky in America* (New York/Abingdon: Routledge, 2010), Kindle edition, 168.
14. Lewis, 71.
15. Smith, 411.

54 The Actors Studio 1947–

The demise of the **Group Theatre** in 1941 created a vacuum. There was no opportunity for the 'converted' to continue the momentum that had been generated by the **Stanislavskian** 'Russian invasion' which had occurred some fifteen years previously (see **From Russia with Love**). The Actors Studio, formed in 1947 to fill that vacuum, was the brainchild of **Elia Kazan**, **Robert Lewis** and Cheryl Crawford, who were lamenting that there was no place 'where a working or professional actor could go to work on his craft'.[1] The partial exception had been **Erwin Piscator's** Dramatic Workshop at the New School, 1941–7– a broad church of acting methodologies which Piscator had attempted to house under the umbrella of 'Epic Theatre'. **Strasberg**, **Meisner** and **Adler** had all been invited by him to teach there, even though he had basic disagreements with their ideas.[2]

The original concept of the Actors Studio was as a 'workout' space, where professionals could meet, practice their craft and try out new methods. Crawford claimed it was set up 'as a philanthropic gesture'.[3] And, until Strasberg arrived, there was only *one* salary paid – for the secretary. The Studio is generally thought of as the 'domain' of Lee Strasberg, whereas Elia Kazan and Bobby Lewis were the original teachers. Lewis taught 'Scene Study and Advance Acting', and Kazan, 'Beginning Acting'. Kazan basically focused on *action* and subtext. In the early days Sanford Meisner moonlighted from the **Neighborhood Playhouse** and gave supplementary classes.

In 1949, Kazan and Lewis fell out, the partnership broke up and Kazan then invited Lee Strasberg to join him. He was recalcitrant, thinking he should have been asked in the first place, but eventually accepted, taking over Kazan's teaching duties.[4] In 1950, he became The Studio's Artistic Director – salaried. Strasberg's arrival inhibited many former Group Theatre members from joining the venture – much bitterness towards him lingered from the time of his autocratic, and some thought, misguided direction.

Once ensconced, Strasberg took over, branding The Studio teaching 'Stanislavski as reformulated by Vakhtangov'.[5] Kazan's course, with its Stanislavskian emphasis on *action* was replaced with pure Strasberg Method, focusing on *affective memory*. The heart of The Studio became Strasberg's Tuesday and Friday morning sessions, eleven to one, where he discoursed about acting, and remained so until his death in 1982.[6] Strasberg made it clear that The Studio was not a school but was designed for actors who already had voice and body training and were ready to do the 'inner work' on themselves. With Strasberg in charge, the tone changed: 'an atmosphere of challenge had replaced the familial cordiality of the first 1947–1948 season with Kazan'.[7] The more dogmatic Strasberg 'brooked no contradictions and invited no opinions on acting theory.'[8]

The modality for accepting students for classes established by Kazan in the early days has become the standard procedure for membership to The Studio even to this day.[9] Applicants with professional experience are the main target, but neophytes (over eighteen) are also allowed to audition. It consists of two stages: the first, a five-minute scene (contemporary preferred) with a partner (no monologues). For the second, a drastically reduced shortlist is invited back to present another contemporary scene with the same partner. It was originally adjudicated by Kazan, Strasberg and Crawford, and now by a group of senior members.

The teaching part of the Actors Studio has migrated to Pace University in New York, qualifying as a master's degree.[10] The membership part remains much the same – regular sessions consisting of group discussions moderated by senior Studio members such as actor Ellen Burstyn (b. 1932), where member actors present scene-work or characterization in development, for critique.

Many members of The Studio have become well-known screen actors: Al Pacino, Julie Harris, Paul Newman, Geraldine Page, Maureen Stapleton, Anne Bancroft, Rod Steiger, Eva Marie Saint, Eli Wallach, Anne Jackson, Sidney Poitier, Shelley Winters, Dennis Hopper, Sally Field, Gene Wilder, James Dean, Karl Malden, Ben Gazzara, Jane Fonda, Steve McQueen and Marlon Brando. Jack Nicholson auditioned five times before he was accepted, Dustin Hoffman, six, Harvey Keitel, eleven. Marilyn Monroe had a 'special' relationship with The Studio, which can be viewed as more of a Svengali-effect relationship with Strasberg (covered in his chapter). Many of these actors studied with other teachers – for example, Dean and Brando with **Stella Adler**. Jackson, Wallace and McQueen studied separately with Meisner, who had been teaching the 'basics' to many of the early members before the arrival of Strasberg. Strasberg's later insistence that he had trained them allegedly distressed Meisner, creating animosity with his ex-mentor which lasted until Strasberg's death.[11]

Further reading

David Garfield, *A Player's Place: The Story of the Actors Studio* (New York: Macmillan, 1980).
Foster Hirsch, *A Method to Their Madness: The History of the Actors Studio* (New York: Norton, 1984).

Notes

1. Hirsch, 117.
2. Ibid., 118.
3. Ibid., 117.
4. Garfield, 44.
5. Ibid., 45.
6. Hirsch, 124.
7. Garfield, 82.
8. Ibid.
9. The current application process is set out in: https://theactorsstudio.org/membership/audition-process/#:~:text=All%20members%20of%20The%20Actors,of%20a%20five%2Dminute%20scene
10. https://theactorsstudio.org/who-we-are/the-actors-studio-drama-school-at-pace-university-mfa/
11. https://en.wikipedia.org/wiki/Sanford_Meisner, last edited 19 March 2023.

55 Dramatic Realism in Cinema

There is not one but several realisms. Each era looks for its own, that is to say the technique and the aesthetic which can best capture it.[1]

André Bazin

The French critic André Bazin (1918–58) described cinema as 'the art of reality',[2] arguing that cinema, by its photographic nature, lends itself to Realism as an art form. From its inception film has attempted to create verisimilitude and depict life as we know it in a naturalistic manner. The first films of the Lumière brothers (Auguste, 1862–1954 and Louis, 1864–1948) were called *'actualités'*, moving snapshots of actual events, precursors to the documentary film. Simple events reproduced on celluloid were awesome in their day. In 1896 – two years before Stanislavski's *Seagull* enthralled Moscow theatregoers – the Lumière brothers' film *L'arrivée d'un train en gare de la Ciotat* famously caused spectators to flee the cinema as the train approached the camera and seemed to leap out of the screen.[3]

In Britain, the Calvinist Scotsman John Grierson (1898–1972) – sometimes called the 'Father of Documentary' – was inspired by the high ideal that the camera could 'view reality with a new intimacy',[4] and made that his life's work, inspiring generations of documentalists to follow. With Presbyterian rigour he railed against the fakery and artifice of the work of Georges Méliès and others in creating fictitious and fantastic narratives such as Méliès' *Journey to the Moon* (1902), proclaiming that cinema's 'natural destiny' was 'discovering mankind.'[5]

While a simple photographic representation of a subject can be considered as a form of *naturalism*, the subjective choices the filmmaker makes in terms of where to put the camera, which lens to use, when to start and stop filming, and how the shots are assembled – i.e. the mediation of the image in the service of storytelling – take us into the realm of *realism*, in other words, a *representation* of reality vs. an actual reality. Documentary films, which purport to depict reality, are mediated in the filmmaking process, and thus become subjective works of art – and in that sense qualify as *realism*. Even in the filming of the fifty-seconds of *L'arrivée d'un train* decisions were made by the Lumière brothers as to when to start and stop filming and where to put the camera to maximum effect, elevating the mere 'mechanical' to a work of art.

Perceptual psychologist Rudolph Arnheim (1904–2007) refuted thoroughly and systematically 'the charge that photography and film are only mechanical reproductions and that they therefore have no connection with art'.[6] His case for cinema as an 'art form' is based on the numerous ways that filmmakers manipulate the image and, fundamentally, the essential difference in the time-spatial relationship between film sequences and real life. 'In real life every experience or chain of experiences is enacted for every observer in an uninterrupted spatial and temporal sequence . . . Not so in film.'[7]

Cinema author Richard Armstrong proposes a useful paradigm for film realism as a blend of both the *actuality* proposed by Grierson and the *trickery* possible in the manipulation of images.[8] (With modern CGI there is no limit.) Armstrong proposes that between Lumière and Méliès the values within a given work can be measured on a sliding scale, delineating the degree to which a film reveals *real experience* versus *filmic techniques*. As examples he situates *The Blair Witch Project*[9] on one end of the scale, and *Lara Croft Tomb Raider*[10] on the other.

Hollywood Realism

While the publishing of literature has always been a 'business' – sometimes blatantly commercial (from Dickens to potboiler novels) – the *entertainment value* of cinema has been usurped since Day One for commercial purposes to a far greater extent than any other 'art form'. The pressure to get bums on seats has given rise to a form of Realism developed in Hollywood, which subsequently became the dominant model of Realism with its own rules of 'verisimilitude' within strict parameters. Those rules dictate a classic three-act narrative structure, with emphasis on plot, plausibility, rationality and continuity. The characters are given heavy arcs and are basically used as tools to further the plot. The audience must know what's going on within the first thirty seconds. Spectators relate to each character primarily by relating to their *predicament*. The films are slickly edited to drive the plot, and music is applied to manipulate the audience emotionally. There is always *catharsis* so that audiences can leave the theatre satisfied. Directors such as **Elia Kazan**, **Sidney Lumet** and **Sydney Pollack** brought progressive sensibilities and **Stanislavski** to Hollywood, but their work remained largely within the parameters dictated by the 'business' ethic, i.e. in the format of Hollywood Realism, leaving it to other American filmmakers to break the mould – directors such as **John Cassavetes**, **John Sayles** and **Sean Baker**, all of whom acknowledge their debt to an influential foreign subset of Cinema Realism – **Italian Neo-Realism** – covered in a chapter below.

Further reading

Rudolf Arnheim, *Film as Art* (Berkeley: University of California Press, 1957).

Notes

1. Quoted in R. Southwell, 'Media and Its Cultural Implications', *Managing the Media*, P. Block, ed. (London: Focal Press, 2001), 140.
2. Hugh Gray introduction to André Bazin, 'The Ontology of the Photographic Image', *Film Quarterly,* Vol. 13, No. 4 (Summer, 1960): 4.
3. This was not their first film. In 1985 *La sortie des ouvriers de l'usine Lumière* (1895), in the same style, was screened at the Grand Café in Paris and is considered to be the first public screening of a movie.
4. Quoted in Geoff Brown, 'Paradise Lost and Found: The Course of British Realism', *The British Cinema* Book, Robert Murphy, ed. (London: BFI Publishing, 1997), 28.
5. Ibid.
6. Arnheim, 8.
7. Ibid., 20.
8. Richard Armstrong, *Understanding Realism* (London: British Film Institute, 2005), 7.
9. *The Blair Witch Project* [film], dir. Eduardo Sánchez and Daniel Myrick, Lionsgate, 1999.
10. *Lara Croft Tomb Raider* [film], dir. Simon West, Paramount, 2001.

56 Arrival of the Talkies
1927

While other forms of dramatic expression challenged Realism in the theatre (e.g. Symbolism and Constructivism in the 1920s, Epic Theatre in the 1940s, Experimental Theatre in the 1960s) the style found a natural home with the arrival of sound in the cinema. In 1927, the first 'talkie', *The Jazz Singer,* hit the screens in the USA – essentially a musical drama. Shortly thereafter, in 1929 in England, Alfred Hitchcock (1899–1980) presented the first European sound film, *Blackmail*, a dark drama containing elements later to become his trademark – notably 'the woman in peril'.

Overnight, there was a different requirement for the film actor. In lieu of '*showing*' with broad gesture and exaggerated expressions, sound film demanded of the actor reasoned statement and applied psychology. Theatrical gesture gave way to subtle facial expression – it was all in the eyes. *Ad lib* dialogue was replaced with precise scripted lines. A new style of acting was required, making it difficult for actors such as Douglas Fairbanks (1883–1939), whose active athletic body was his main mode of expression, to adapt. A new type of 'swashbuckling' was required for sound – the *psychological* type. Other actors couldn't adapt for reasons of voice quality, or foreign accents. John Gilbert (1897–1936), a hugely popular MGM silent screen actor dubbed 'The Great Lover', is alleged to have possessed a stilted manner of speaking, and the talkies precipitated his career nose-dive and an eventual alcohol-related death.[1] Lillian Gish (1896–1993) gave up her career in movies for the theatre because she couldn't adapt to the subtleties of the closeup. Silent film actors collectively called this period the 'Talking Terror'. Mary Pickford's biographer, Scott Eyman describes the change:

> 'Talkies' were less romantic than 'silents', more real; less utopian, more democratic; less behavioural, more psychological. Because silent films were such an anomalous hybrid, and closer to ballet than to anything else in the arts, actors who had an aptitude for them often seemed comparatively ordinary, if not inadequate, in the more plebian talkies.[2]

A Hollywood recruitment drive for Broadway theatre actors began in 1928. It was assumed that good voices and proper enunciation would be required for the speaking films – especially as the technical quality of the sound was rather rudimentary. There was a Westward stampede. But the studios miscalculated. Celebrity appeal and fan-base were already firmly rooted in the commercial studio market, and audiences preferred the bad acting of the silent stars to the more polished performances of the Broadway 'newbies' – at least for a time. By September 1930, the *émigrés* to Los Angeles were folding their tents and slipping away back East.[3]

But the novelty of sound soon wore off, and its quality improved incrementally with technical advancements. It didn't take long for people to demand something more sophisticated in the writing as well as a more multi-layered type of acting to match.

Enter **Stanislavski**. As described in previous chapters, in the mid-1920s two of his disciples, **Maria Ouspenskaya** and **Richard Boleslavksy**, brought the teachings of the Moscow Arts Theatre to New

York, and captured the interest of several writers, actors, and directors who would later form the **Group Theatre** to study and apply the Russian Realism. These ideas were readily adapted for the theatre in New York, but eventually found favour with the Hollywood studio machine, hungry for realistic acting required for the *closeup*. Actors trained by The Group's 'troika' – **Stella Adler, Sanford Meisner,** and **Lee Strasberg** – set the benchmarks for the new film acting style being demonstrated by the likes of Gregory Peck, Marlon Brando and Marilyn Monroe. **Elia Kazan** and **Sydney Lumet**, both associated with the Group Theatre, came to be considered two of the most important movie directors. The realistic acting of the Stanislavski brand became irreversibly embedded in the movies.

In the early days of sound there was great confusion as to what was required of the actor, and the Fox studio employed two directors for each film, one from the silent movies and one from the stage who would be more sensitive to the thespians talents and working methods – a method endorsed by Actors Equity.[4] For example, for the film *Air Circus* (1928) the prolific Hollywood director Howard Hawks (1896–1977)[5] directed the non-talking action scenes while another director handled the speaking sequences.[6]

It was Russia that had provided America with the acting techniques which were to become the backbone of Hollywood Realism (see **From Russia With Love**), so it's ironic that the Soviet Union was not able to develop a fully-fledged, stylistically catholic narrative realistic cinema of its own until after the death of Stalin. The advent of sound in the USSR, four years after it was launched in the West, had coincided with Stalin's ascendancy and his authoritarian imposition of **Socialist Realism** (1934–91) on the arts. Socialist Realism was a *cul-de-sac* in the history of Realism – an arts movement which impacted heavily on cinema, but which had a negligible effect on artists outside the Soviet Union, and a stultifying effect on those within. Eventually, with Stalin gone, directors such as Grigori Churkray (1921–2001) began to emerge. His *Ballad of a Soldier* (1959) brought a refreshing whiff of **Poetic Realism** to Soviet cinema.

Further reading

Donald Crafton, 'The Talkies: American Cinema's Transition to Sound, 1926–1931', in *History of the American Cinema,* C. Harpole, ed. (Berkeley: University of California Press, 1999).

Notes

1. There is conspiratorial theory which says that studio head Louis B. Mayer (1884–1957) as part of a vendetta, ordered the bass level turned down on Gilbert's recordings to effeminize his voice. Crafton, 504.
2. Scott Eyman, *Mary Pickford: America's Sweetheart* (New York: Donald I. Fine, 1990), 226.
3. Crafton, 497.
4. Ibid., 221.
5. Hawks had previously made seven silent films and *Air Circus* was his first sound film. He went on to direct thirty-two more films, in a number of genres, including classics such as *The Big Sleep* (Warner Bros.,1946), *Gentlemen Prefer* Blondes (Fox, 1953) and *Rio Bravo* (Armada Prods., 1959).
6. Crafton, 280.

57 Socialist Realism
USSR
1934–1991

Codified in the proclamations of the First Congress of Soviet Writers in 1934, the seeds of Socialist Realism dogma can be found as early as 1905 in a pamphlet by Vladimir Lenin (1870–1924) in which he urged, 'Down with literary supermen! Literature must become part of the common cause of the proletariat, a "cog and screw" of the single great Social-Democratic mechanism set in motion by the politically conscious vanguard of the entire working class.'[1] For Lenin it was a given that art and literature must at the service of the Revolution. At the outset he had an enlightened view of the diverse forms in which that service could occur, embracing the vibrant the Russian *avant-garde* of the time. But by 1921 he had become more dogmatic and un-enamoured of Dadaism and Constructivism on ideological grounds. A number of leading artists including Wassily Kandinsky (1866–1944) decided it was time to emigrate; as did the writer Maxim Gorky (1868–1936), who had criticized Lenin's approach.[2]

Josef Stalin (1878–1953), having become General Secretary of the USSR following the death of Lenin in 1924, dictated that art should be strictly used for 'agitation' – serving the cause of Soviet construction – in other words, *propaganda*. In this endeavour he solicited the help of Maxim Gorky, who, as we have pointed out, wrote in a naturalistic style in his earlier work (e.g. *The Lower Depths*, 1902). Stalin invited Gorky to return to Russia, and he did so. In an address to the First Congress of Soviet Writers the writer proclaimed a new Soviet style born out of Classic Realism, depicting reality, but strictly within the context of 'its revolutionary development,' exhorting writers to take up their role as 'engineers of the soul.'[3] In his speech to the Soviet Writers' Congress Gorky set out four defining conditions for Soviet Realism.[4]

- It must be relevant and coherent to the workers.
- It must represent the everyday lives of the Russian people.
- It must be stylistically realistic.
- It must be partisan, i.e. support the aims of the State and the Party.

Gorky's 1906 book, *Mother* was retrospectively deemed to have been the first novel written in the new style.

Stanislavski's brand of Realism was readily appropriated for the new genre, for both theatre and film. During the early 1920s three master filmmakers – Lev Kuleshov (1899–1970), Dziga Vertov (1896–1954) and **Sergei Eisenstein** (1898–1948) – held sway. Between them they had developed the art of film montage and had little interest in Stanislavskian Realism. They struggled to try to adapt to the requisite banal, formulaic, non-poetic 'Socialist Realism', and their work was ultimately supressed or defamed by the Party bureaucracy.

An inevitable result of Gorky's first point was that Socialist Realism tended to 'talk down' to the masses. In the plastic arts, styles such as Impressionism and Cubism were banned because it was deemed that they could not be understood by the proletariat, and as such could not be used as propaganda.[5] In literature a straight-forward narrative style was required. Abstraction, formalism, surrealism, expressionism, religion and eroticism – all were forbidden. Psychology and subtext were taboo, and formal experiments such as internal dialogue, stream of consciousness, magic-realism and free-form association were off the menu as being unintelligible to the proletariat.

The net effect was sugar-coated anodyne art, literature and theatre, accessible to the masses, embodying little depth or contradictions, always looking on the bright side, accentuating heroism, eschewing individualism and psychology – formulaic, predictable and banal. Ultimately, this form of realism had little in common with Classic Realism.[6]

Socialist Realism has had no effect on art, literature or drama outside of the Soviet sphere of influence. However, within the Soviet Union the story was different. As discussed in earlier chapters, the Classic Realism of the Moscow Arts Theatre continued to be respected for providing the base techniques for the new Socialist Realism, but **Nemirovich-Danchenko** and Stanislavski had to steer the ship through dangerous waters, being mindful to minimize the psychological, spiritual and individualistic aspects of 'the system' and strip any traces of Symbolism or Constructivism from their theatrical presentation. It has been pointed out that Stanislavski's later development of Active Analysis, with its physical, spiritual and psychological elements, were squelched by the powers-that-be on ideological grounds, but were quietly kept alive by his disciple, Maria Knebel, even if they were not openly taught until the 1960s.[7] The impact of the Stalinist codes on Eisenstein's filmmaking and **Meyerhold's** tragic downfall and eventual assassination have been previously discussed.

Stalin died in 1953. In 1956, Nikita Khrushchev (1894–1971) delivered his famous 'Secret Speech' condemning the former dictator's artistic policies. Socialist Realism lost its 'official' status in the early 1960s, but because Leonid Brezhnev (1906–82) reinstated many Stalinist policies when he succeeded Khrushchev, the doctrine only finally disappeared (one can hear the collective sigh of relief) in 1991 with the breakup of the Soviet Union. In the brief window of Khrushchev's liberalization, a couple of notable movies were made in the Socialist Realist style, but with a poetry and complexity not seen in earlier iterations of the style. Both films promote anti-war sentiments. *The Cranes are Flying* (dir. Mikhail Kalatozov, 1957) tells a story of two star-crossed lovers amongst the victims of war. It was the first Soviet 'art' movie to be distributed broadly in the West and won the *Palme d'Or* at Cannes in 1958. *Ballad of a Soldier* (dir. Grigory Chukhray) was released in 1959 and was not only popular in the USSR, but had a successful international distribution, winning a BAFTA Best Film Award and an Oscar nomination for its screenplay. The film follows a young Red Army soldier on his journey home on a brief leave from the front lines of the War with Germany, and realistically portrays the damage of the War in physical and humanitarian terms. The movie is stylistically redolent of French **Poetic Realism** of the 1930s.

Further reading

Brandon Taylor, 'Socialist Realism', in *Adventures in Realism*, M. Beaumont ed. (Oxford: Blackwell Publishing, 2007) 142–157.

Notes

1. Taylor, 143.
2. Werner Haftmann, *Painting in the Twentieth Century* (London; Lund Humphries, 1965), 196.

3. A concept coined by Stalin. Maxim Gorky et al., *Soviet Writer's Congress 1934: The Debate on Socialist Realism and Modernism in the Soviet Union* (London: Lawrence and Wishart, 1977), 21.
4. Ibid., 'Soviet Literature', 27–69.
5. Haftmann.
6. Ibid., 303.
7. Sharon Marie Carnicke, *Stanislavsky in Focus: An Acting Master for the Twenty-first Century,* 2nd ed. (London: Routledge, 2009), 100.

58 Poetic Realism
France
1930–1939

This was a glorious era in French cinema that emerged from a particularly inglorious phase of French history.¹

The reconstruction period in France after the First World War was, at first, a time of optimism. The Great Depression hit late (1931), due largely to France's gold reserves. And hit it did. The economy tanked, inflation and unemployment resulted in strikes and the formation of a left-wing Popular Front. The darkening cloud of Fascism was approaching, with Mussolini's invasion of Ethiopia (1935) and Hitler's military occupation of the Rhineland (1936). Following the invasion, first of Austria, then of Czechoslovakia and Poland in 1939, France and Britain declared war on Germany. In 1940, Germany invaded Belgium and the Netherlands. The defeatist government of Marshal Philippe Pétain (1856–1951) agreed to a division of France into the Occupied and Unoccupied Zones. The clandestine French Resistance was born. It was a dark and desperate decade.

The short-lived subgenre of cinema Realism that arose in France in these years, distinctive and memorable, wasn't a movement as such, but more of a serendipitous coalescence of individual talents, inspired by the adventures in Surrealism of the 1920s, but responding to the grim realities of France of the decade. It involved a collection of directors from diverse backgrounds, of whom Jean Renoir (1894–1979), son of the painter, is the best known. Others are Jean Grémillon (1901–59), a documentary filmmaker; Jean Vigo (1905–34), son of a famous anarchist; Jacques Fevder (1885–1948), Belgian/French, (1885–1948), a silent film director and screenwriter; Julien Duvivier (1896–1967), formerly an actor with André Antoine (see **Jacques Copeau**); and Marcel Carné (1906–96), formerly a film critic who found his way to directing by working as assistant director for both Rene Clair (1898–1981) and Feyder.

Film historian Roy Armes termed this non-movement 'an affair of individuals'.² The rest of the talent pool comprised composers such as Maurice Jaubert (1900–40), cinematographers like Boris Kaufman, Russian (1906–80), screenwriters such as the sometime Surrealist poet Jacques Prévert (1900–77), the prolific author Charles Spaak, Belgian (1903–75), and designers such as Lazare Meerson (1900–38) and Alexandre Trauner, Hungarian (1906–93).

There are clear literary antecedents. The themes and settings for these films were already gaining popularity in the late 1920s with novels such as *Quai des brumes* (1927) by Pierre Mac Orlan (1882–1970), *Hotel du Nord* (1928) by Eugène Dabit (1898–1936) and *Pépé le Moko* (1931) by Henri la Barthe (1887–1963) – all of which were made into Poetic Realist films. Jean Renoir's poetic crime film, *La Bête Humaine* (1938) – precursor to the *film noir* genre of the 1940s – was, of course, based on Émile Zola's naturalistic novel of 1890.

Poetic Realism wasn't defined as a genre until much later, by French film theorist Jean Mitry (1907–88), who qualified it as 'a sort of neo-romanticism often mixed with psychoanalysis or pseudo-Marxism'.[3] Another film theorist describes it as an amalgamation of 'urban romantic realism' and 'melodrama'.[4] Despite its international recognition it comprised a relatively small production of films which stood outside of, and had very little connection with, the prevailing commercial production in France, essentially 'military adaptations and family melodramas produced for the Saturday-night audience'.[5]

The subgenre is distinguished from Classic Realism in that it is *stylized* – naturalism or documentary filming are sublimated into the overall *aesthetic design* of the work. Films are mostly studio-bound, and all craft elements of moviemaking – set design, cinematography, sound and music – are brought to bear to create a poetic resonance for otherwise bleak settings. Its characters are generally working class, frequently unemployed or criminal, living 'on the margins'. As anti-heroes they are flawed, frequently by jealousy or obsession, and have a fatalistic view of life. Sometimes, after a life of disappointment they are given a final chance of love or redemption – but are ultimately disillusioned.[6]

The actors of these films were not cast for movie-star looks, but for a down-to-earth quality befitting the gritty lower-class characters they were playing. The men tended to be intense and brooding. Jean Gabin (1904–76), rugged and charismatic, was first cast by Julien Duvivier in the 1934 production of *Maria Chapdelaine* and went on to play the lead in a number of films in the subgenre, gaining international fame in Duvivier's *Pépé le Moko* in 1937, opposite Simone Signoret (1921–85). Jean Dasté (1904–94) was another 'regular' in the subgenre, beginning with *L'Atalante* in which he played Jean, the impulsive jealous bargeman who abandons his wife, then regrets it. Juliette, his wife, was played by Dita Parlo (1908–71), a German (deported to Germany as an enemy alien during the war). Parlo had a natural naivety which made her perfect for the role. She also played as Elsa in Renoir's *La Grande Illusion* (1937). Michèle Morgan (1920–2016) was another actor in the pool capable of playing strong women. She was cast in Marcel Carné's *Quai de Brumes* (1938) opposite Gabin, and in Jean Grémillon's *Remorques* (1941). Michel Simon (1895–1975), Swiss, was a popular comedic theatre actor, whose eccentric down-to-earth looks won him a number of film roles in the Poetic Realism style. He features in *Quai de Brumes*, Renoir's *Boudu sauvé des eaux* (Boudu Saved from Drowning,1932), and others. His performance as the bumbling first mate of *L'Atalante* is unforgettable.

Not all of the films by these directors in this period fall within these parameters, and thus do not qualify as Poetic Realism. Regarding Renoir for example, Roy Armes points out, 'The terms 'poetry' and 'realism' can be variously applied to all the nine works which stretch in an unbroken line from *Toni* (1935) to *La Règle du jeu* (1939), but there is no single stylistic paradigm towards which Renoir's work aspires.'[7]

While the subgenre largely died out in France as the Second World War rolled in, its influences were felt elsewhere, starting with **Italian Neo-Realism**. Luchino Visconti (1906–76) and Michelangelo Antonioni (1912–2007) both had worked as assistants to Renoir and Carné in France and carried the torch to Italy. **Satyajit Ray** (1921–92) had assisted Renoir while he was filming in India, and the poetic filmic style of Ray's early movies such as *Pather Panchali* (1955), set in the grim reality of poverty, is clearly influenced by Poetic Realism. Less directly, we can imagine that the amorality depicted in Duvivier's *Pépé le Moko* (1937) influenced Graham Greene's *The Third Man* (1949), and that its mixture of grit and lyricism influenced Terence Davies (1945– 2003) and Aki Kaurismäki (b.1957).[8]

The collection of Poetic Realism films makes for rich and rewarding viewing, as much for the films' style as the content. Filmmakers all have their favourites. If I had to choose five amongst the twenty-five or so one can identify with the subgenre, my choice would be:

- *L'Atalante*, Jean Vigo, (1934).
- *Pépé le Moko*, Julien Duvivier (1937).

- *La Grande Illusion*, Jean Renoir (1937).
- *La Bête Humaine*, Jean Renoir (1938).
- *Le Jour Se Lève*, Marcel Carné (1939).

Further reading

Roy Armes, *French Cinema* (New York: Oxford University Press, 1985).

Notes

1. P. De Semlyen, I. Freer and A. Wibrew, 'Poetic Realism', *Empire*, 8 August 2016, https://www.empireonline.com/movies/features/poetic-realism-movie-era/
2. Armes, 91.
3. Jean Mitry, *Histoire de cinéma: Art et industrie: Vol. 4, Les Années Trente* (Paris: Jean-Pierre Delarge, 1980), 339. 'Realism is not univocal. Its only duties are to respect concrete logic . . . and to be conscious of social reality (in other words, any milieu seen in its social context). Nothing more.'
4. Peter G. Christensen, in 'Feyder's *Le Grand Jeu* and the Idea of Poetic Realism', *Film Criticism*, Vol. 12, No. 2 (Winter, 1987–88): 3–17, https://www.jstor.org/stable/44077588
5. Armes, 89.
6. Wikipedia, 'Poetic Realism', last edited 24 November 2023, https://en.wikipedia.org/wiki/Poetic_realism
7. Armes, 103.
8. De Semlyen, Freer and Wibrew.

59 Italian Neo-Realism
Italy
1943–1952

The most precious moment in film history.[1]

Martin Scorsese, *My Voyage to Italy*

Other than being indisputably *Italian*, the term 'Italian Neo-Realism' is a bit of a misnomer. The roots of this post-Second World War genre lie in the late nineteenth century, in the 'Verismo' literary movement of Italian novelists and playwrights,[2] which was itself inspired by the *French naturalism* of writers such as Émile Zola (1840–1902) and Guy de Maupassant (1850–1893) – authors who depicted the humblest social class in its naked impoverishment and sordidness. Accepting the distinctions between naturalism and realism set out elsewhere in this book,[3] *Italian Neo-naturalism* or *Italian Neo-verismo* would be more appropriate designations for the cinematic movement which arose in the waning months of Mussolini's Fascist Italy.

Ossessione (1943), directed by Luchino Visconti (1906–76) – arguably the first Neo-realist film – illustrates the point, being thematically related to Zola's defining work of naturalism, *Thérèse Raquin* (1868/73) – both stories are set in a working-class milieu and concern adultery and matricide.

The emergence of what's known as Neo-Realism in Italian cinema corresponded to a resurgence in the late 1940s and early 1950s of Realism in Italian literature, with the novels of Alberto Moravia (1907–90), Cesare Pavese (1908–50) and Elio Vittorini (1908–66), but the cinematic movement's direct roots lie the *Verismo* of seventy-five years earlier, notably in the works of Giovanni Verga (1840–1922), who wrote about the life of the common man in his native Sicily. His novel *I malavoglia* (The House by the Medlar Tree, 1881), about a poor family of Sicilian fishermen, was brought to the screen by Luchino Visconti in 1948 with *La Terra Trema* (The Earth Trembles). An additional touchstone for the movement was a short-lived vein of *Verismo* in the Italian silent cinema in the years 1913–16, with films such as *Sperduti nel Buio* (Lost in the Dark, 1914) directed by Nino Martoglio (1870–1921) depicting life in the slums of Naples.[4]

Although the nascent Neo-realist movement had literary antecedents and cinematic precedents – hence some sort of framework in place – it was the fall of Fascism which brought it into being (as well as providing the subject matter for its initial productions). In July 1943, Mussolini, who had been arrested by his own Council and the king, was freed by the occupying Germans, enabling him to re-establish his Republican Fascist government at Salò on Lake Garda. The Cinecittà Studio in Rome was closed, and all film equipment and existing films were removed to the north of Italy. Thus Cinecittà, the temple of Fascist cinema, was abandoned, and filmmaking was forced to take to the streets, establishing – by necessity – a modality for Neo-Realism.[5] A conceptual proposal for this new cinematic form was formulated a month before the fall of the regime by the progressive film critic Umberto Barbaro (1902–59) in the magazine *Il Film*, June 1943. Barbaro's article was written in reaction to what were called the 'white telephone' movies of the Fascist studios – trivial romantic comedies set in blatantly artificial studio surroundings and symbolized by an ever-present white telephone – dominating film production at the time.[6] Barbaro decreed, 'If we in Italy wish to abandon once and for all our trashy histories, our rehashes of the 19th century, and our trifling comedies, we must try the cinema of realism.'[7] His Neo-realist dogma demanded the following: (1) get rid of the 'naïve and mannered cliches which have formed the larger part of Italian films'; (2) abandon 'those fantastic and grotesque fabrications which exclude human problems and the human point of view'; (3) dispense with 'historical set-pieces and fictional adaptations'; (4) exclude the rhetoric which pretends that all Italians are 'inflamed by the same noble sentiments'.[8] In the same article Barbaro references the silent *Verismo* film *Sperduti nel Buio* mentioned above.

Visconti's *Ossessione* was made in 1943 prior to Barbaro's pronouncements. Its director, Luchino Visconti, was an Italian left-wing aristocrat who had once been assistant to Jean Renoir (1894–1979) and schooled in Renoir's style of **Poetic Realism**. The film is, in effect, an uncredited adaptation of the American James M. Cain's 1934 novel, *The Postman Only Knocks Twice*.[9] It concerns a drifter who shows up in a café, falls for the café-owner's wife, and conspires with her to murder her husband. Though it relies heavily on plot, and some elements of the film don't conform strictly to the Neo-realist dogma soon to develop, it is starkly realist, authentic in its settings of rural poverty – its characters confronting at every turn the realities of life. Completed during the Fascist regime, it outraged the Church with its unqualified depiction of adultery, and its distribution was halted. Mussolini viewed the movie, urged to do so by his son who was editor of the principal film magazine, *Il Film*. Having been persuaded that it was harmless, Il Duce approved its release with a few cuts. However, it was later banned. *Ossessione* represented something utterly new – 'the sudden intrusion of social and psychological authenticity into a cinema that had previously thriven on the novelettish and the two-dimensional. It was the revelation of an Italy completely different from that of the romantics and the tourists, an Italy of poverty and suffering, yet still mindful of its past grandeur.'[10]

The movie which definitively set the parameters of Italian Neo-Realism, and brought the movement to international attention, was Roberto Rossellini's *Roma città aperta* (Rome Open City), shot in 1945, shortly after the Germans abandoned Rome and the Americans moved in. The story occurs amongst a diverse group of ordinary Romans coping on a day-to-day basis with the German occupation, and centres on a Resistance fighter who is trying to escape the city, helped by a Catholic priest. Film historian Peter Bondanella contends that the tone of the work is 'far more indebted to Rossellini's message of Christian humanism than it is to any programmatic attempt at cinematic realism'.[11] Nonetheless, the film encapsulates the hallmarks of the Neo-Realism genre.

HALLMARKS OF NEO-REALISM

- Everyday subject matter. The *naturalism* of poverty, struggle, and survival for the lower and working classes.
- Use of non-actors mixed with professionals and local people rather than professional extras.
- A high degree of reality in day-to-day activities.
- Child characters in featured roles.
- Location shooting.
- Avoidance of over-dramatic or intrusive editing.

In Italy, *Rome Open City* was slow to take off at the box office, with Italian audiences reluctant to relive the deprivations of the recent occupation and to face up to what their country had become, 'no longer the Rome of the *palazzi*, but the Rome of the suburbs, the Rome of misery, of children playing amidst tragedy, of simple-mindedness, or strife, and of death'.[12] Once the movie had been awarded the *Palme d'Or* at the

Cannes Festival and an American Academy Award nomination for the script, it caught on at home, achieving first place in the box office in 1945–6.

The film most commonly associated with Neo-Realism is Vittorio De Sica's *Ladri di biciclette* (Bicycle Thieves, 1948), written by Cesare Zavatinni (1902–89). The movie has the simplest of plots: a workman spends a whole day searching for his bicycle which has been stolen. The bike is the tool of his trade and if he doesn't get it back, he will be unemployed. In desperation he too steals a bike. Unfortunately, he is apprehended, then released, left as poor as ever, but now branded a thief. As French film critic André Bazin put it, 'the whole story would not deserve two lines in a stray-dog column'.[13] The *plot* is not the point in this film. Bazan remarks, 'In itself the event contains no proper dramatic valence. It takes on meaning only because of the social (and not psychological or aesthetic) position of the victim'[14] – the *victimizer* in this case being *unemployment*. Zavattini defended his approach, 'When you scrutinize a social fact you come to realise that it is, in reality, a complex and multiple phenomenon, and far from banal.'[15]

It is easy to see how this concept directly informed the social realism of British director **Ken Loach** in his desire to make political films without them appearing didactic. Bazan notes, 'Its social message is not detached; it remains immanent in the event, but it is so clear that nobody can overlook it still less take exception to it, since it is never made explicitly a message. The thesis implied is wondrously and outrageously simple: in the world where this workman lives, the poor must steal from each other to survive.'[16] In 1945, the occupation and liberation had created social conditions for which the workers took the brunt of the suffering. By 1948 unemployment was the peril affecting the lower classes, many of whom were one step away from starvation.

Bicycle Thieves won a Best Foreign film *Oscar*, as did an earlier collaboration with Cesare Zavattini, *Sciuscià* (Shoeshine, 1946), a story of two shoeshine boys who are saving up to buy horse but get involved in criminal activity to achieve their goal. Zavattini is a key figure in Neo-Realism (and in Italian cinema generally – he wrote over one hundred screenplays). He collaborated regularly (but not exclusively) with Vittorio De Sica (1901–74), both in the strictly Neo-realist vein and in later in more mainstream fare, such as *Miracolo a Milano* (Miracle in Milan, 1951), *Umberto D* (1955), *Ieri, oggi, domani* (Yesterday, Today and Tomorrow, 1963), *La ciociara* (Two Women, 1960), *Il giardino dei Finzi-Contini* (The Garden of the Finzi-Continis, 1970), never abandoning elements of Neo-Realism, which he considered to be 'an unfinished project'.[17] Zavattini's style was more suited to De Sica's interest in human stories, than, say Rossellini's focus on ordinary people being caught up in the epic sweep of events. According to critic Pierre Leprohon, 'His warm sympathy for his fellow men was largely responsible for steering neo-realism towards the humanitarian outlook that can frequently be detected even in its most sordid and violent works.'[18]

To devise stories, Zavattini proposed an 'ethnographic' approach associated with documentary technique, which included 'shadowing' (*pedinamento*) – literally following a person, or persons, going about their daily business and investigating the reality of *events* in their life within a social, cultural, and political context.

Zavattini was a journalist, cinema critic, novelist and painter. He was a Communist, but never a card-carrying member of the Party. Another aspect of his writing worth noting is his use of 'magic realism' as manifested, for example, in his novella, *Totò il Buono* (Toto the Good, 1943), later made by De Sica into the film *Miracle in Milan* (1951). The leading proponent of the style, Colombian writer Gabriel García Marquez, met Zavattini while a student at the Italian film school and was greatly influenced by his work. He later said, 'I'm a son of Zavattini.'[19] García Marquez credits De Sica's film 'as the most probable source of "magic realism" in the Latin American novel.'[20] Thus it could be said that Zavattini, leading advocate of Neo-Realism, was instrumental in creating its sub-genre, **Magic Realism**.

The Neo-realist phenomenon had faded by 1950, the causes of its demise being both financial and political. Firstly, 'social' films didn't make money. The battered post-War Italian public had little appetite to see their problems and suffering displayed on the screen, preferring the escapist comedies akin to those which the Fascists had made. In fact, of the 882 films produced in Italy between 1945 and 1953 only ninety (roughly 10 per cent) could carry a Neo-realist label.[21] Moreover, a flood of American movies entered the country hard on the heels of the 'liberators' and quickly dominated the market.

The second factor was the coming to power of the Christian Democratic Party in 1948, which brought in a rigorous censorship of the arts, spearheaded by Giulio Andreotti (1919–2013), then a vice-minister, later to become prime minister. This was especially directed at films with dark subjects and controversial aspects. Andreotti attacked the Neo-realists, and especially De Sica's *Umberto D,* released in 1952, saying the film represented 'dirty laundry that shouldn't be washed and hung to dry in the open'.[22]

Alberto Lattuada (1914–2005), a writer/director and sometimes collaborator of Federico Fellini (1920–93) replied to this sort of criticism – offering a credo for Neo-Realism:

> So we are in rags?' Then let us show our rags to the world. So we are defeated? Then let us contemplate our disasters. So we owe them to the Mafia? To hypocrisy? To conformism? To Irresponsibility? To faulty education? Then let us pay our debts with a fierce love of honesty. . . . We will meet at last with comprehension and esteem. The cinema is unequalled for revealing all the basic truths about a nation.[23]

While Neo-Realism's full bloom had withered by 1952, it continued to be championed by some – principally Zavattini, who set out its principles clearly in a 1953 article entitled 'Some Ideas on the Cinema'.[24] Zavattini's proposal was hotly contested in a Conference on Neo-Realism held in Parma in that year, largely by Umberto Barbaro, whose Marxist leanings now inclined him to the new form of **Socialist Realism** being promoted in Russia.[25] The debate was academic because Neo-Realism continued to be practised, even if not in its full particulars, in various iterations, such as the *activist* movies of Francesco Rosi (1922–2015), *Salvatore Giuliano* (1961) and Gillo Pontecorvo (1919–2006), *La battaglia di Algeri* (The Battle of Algiers, 1966). They shared the same screenwriter, Franco Solinas, and imitated Rossellini's style of ordinary people caught up in epic events. Federico Fellini's, *La Strada* (1954), though poetic and mystical, was grounded in realism. The sensibilities of De Sica and Zavattini are clearly evidenced in the smaller more humanistic stories of Ermanno Olmi, *Il Posto* (The Job, 1961), Taviani Brothers', Vittorio and Paolo, *Padre Padrone* (My Father, My Master, 1977), Giuseppe Tornatore, *Cinema Paradiso* (1988).

Just as the Moscow Arts Theatre had been a watershed in theatrical realism fifty years earlier, Neo-Realism was a defining moment in world cinema. Its effects reverberated to all corners of the globe and impacted other film genres. It was the inspiration for **Satyajit Ray** (1921–92) and the Parallel Cinema movement in India; Ousmane Sembène, Souleymane Cissé and the new African cinema; the Iranian New Wave with Abbas Kiarostami (1940–2016); and Andrzej Wajda (1926–2016), *Pokolenie* (A Generation, 1955) and Jan Rybkowski, *Godziny nadziei* (The Hours of Hope, 1955) and members of the Polish Film School – a group of young filmmakers dedicated to adapting the principles of Neo-Realism to a Polish context.

The British 'New Wave', called **'Kitchen Sink Drama'**, was not directly based on Neo-realist principles, but had its own impetus. Although **Ken Loach,** developing his own naturalist vein at the time, professed to be dazzled by the Neo-realist films.

In the USA Neo-Realism did little to break the mould of the dominant slick form of Hollywood Realism, other than in its influence on the *film noir* genre, opening the door for crime dramas to be darker, raunchier and more in touch with the common man. There have been notable American exceptions along the way, such as **John Cassavetes**, whose film *Shadows* (1959) has been described as pure Neo-Realism. Many filmmakers we identify with the American Independent Film Movement, exemplified by **Sean Baker**, director of *The Florida Project* (2017), have been inspired by Neo-Realism. Low budgets have forced young filmmakers out of the studios and into the streets. (Sean Baker famously shot *Tangerine* (2015) on an iPhone.) We shall consider some of them in the chapter **Neo Neo-Realism**.

Further reading

Peter Bondanella, *Italian Cinema, From Neorealism to the Present*, expanded edition (New York: Continuum, 1990).
David Brancaleone, *Cesare Zavattini's Neo-realism and the Afterlife of an Idea* (New York: Bloomsbury, 2021).
Bert Cardullo, ed., *André Bazin and Italian Neorealism* (New York: Continuum Books, 2011).
Pierre Leprohon, *The Italian Cinema*, trans. R. Greaves and O. Stallybrass (London: Secker & Warburg, 1966).

Notes

1. *My Voyage to Italy* [film], dir. Martin Scorsese, Miramax, 2001. Scorsese's two-part documentary survey of Italian cinema.
2. From the Italian word 'vero' meaning 'true'.
3. Realism as a political tool is discussed in 'The Case for Realism' in **Working with Actors**.
4. Cardullo, 20.
5. Leprohon, 91.
6. Cardullo, 24.
7. Leprohon, 86.
8. Ben Lawton, 'Italian Neorealism', *Film Criticism*, Vol. 3, No. 2 (Winter, 1979): 8.
9. Bondanella, 24. Visconti had been given a French translation of the book by Jean Renoir.
10. Leprohon, 88.
11. Bondanella, 38.
12. Leprohon, 93.
13. André Bazan, 'Bicycle Thieves', Cardullo, 64. It was the French critic, André Bazin (1918–58) who brought Neo-Realism to the attention of the international film community and elaborated its elements.
14. Ibid.
15. Brancaleone, 131.
16. Bazan, 65.
17. Brancaleone, 131.
18. Leprohon, 114.
19. Brancaleone, 43.
20. Ibid.
21. Bondanella, 35.
22. Cited in Wikipedia article on Italian neorealism https://en.wikipedia.org/wiki/Italian_neorealism edited 23 September 2023.
23. Leprohon, 98.
24. Published in English in *Sight and Sound*, October 1953, 64–9.
25. Brancaleone, 137.

60 Satyajit Ray
1921–1992

In the previous chapter I mentioned some of the global movements and directors influenced directly by **Italian Neo-Realism**, amongst them the revered Indian director, Satyajit Ray, whose first feature film, *Pather Panchali* (Song of the Little Road, 1955) is universally acknowledged as a masterwork. It tells the story of a family living in penury in a village in Bengal, largely seen through the eyes of two children. It could just as easily be set in a slum on the outskirts of Rome.

Ray was an authentic twentieth-century Renaissance man, well-educated, from an intellectual Calcutta (now Kolkata) middle class family – a proficient painter, graphic artist, specialist in Eastern classical music, novelist, writer of children's books and, above all, a cineaste with a passion for world cinema. In his early twenties he formed the Calcutta Film Society (1947) and wrote critical articles for Indian film magazines.[1] One of his first paying jobs was creating covers and typography for the publishing house Signet, which specialized in Bengali literature. It was there that he discovered the novel *Pather Panchali,* which he resolved to adapt for film. In 1949 Jean Renoir (1894–1979) was scouting in Calcutta for his Hollywood-produced movie *The River*. Young Satyajit, with his impeccable English, wangled an assistant's job, and was assigned to accompany the French director on his location hunts. While on the road Renoir opened up to Ray, lamenting the artistic downturn in his career in American movies and expressing his hope to use *The River* as a return to his roots in realism – all the while taking in both the 'enchantment and novelty of the [Indian] landscape on the one hand, and the picture of filth and misery and poverty on the other.'[2] Ray reported that the Frenchman would 'go into ecstasies over a simple hut, and pass into gloomy despondency at the sight of a beggar'.[3] His time with Jean Renoir strengthened Ray's resolve to become a filmmaker. And Renoir's **Poetic Realism** manner of using observational detail is clearly evident in Ray's filming style for *Pather Panchali,* in which landscapes are beautifully framed for effect, and the crumbling family abode is made intriguing in its decrepitude through use of mysterious lighting and interesting camera angles, while the poverty of the people living within it is simply heart-breaking.

Ray's day job just after the time of Renoir's visit – doing illustrations for D. J. Keymer, a British publisher with a Calcutta office – took him to London. During the long ocean journey, he started drafting a script for *Pather*. In London, as was his wont, he greedily consumed as much cinema as his free time would allow, discovering and being dazzled by the **Italian Neo-Realist** movies he saw there, most particularly by De Sica's *Bicycle Thieves*, which solidified a resolve to create a realist Bengali cinema. During the homeward voyage to India, he completed a first draft of *Pather Panchali*.

Financing the movie was not as easy as writing it. Being an accomplished illustrator, he produced a meticulous storyboard (held today by the Cinémathèque Française). Beautiful as it was, it failed to attract finance in the commercial world of Indian cinema. Like many independents to follow, Ray turned to self-funding the movie with loans and contributions from friends – his wife even sold her jewellery for the cause. Shooting occurred bit-by-bit over two years due to the piecemeal 'drip' financing.

In this movie, as in the ones to follow, Ray used a mixture of non-actors and professionals, the most notable of whom was the remarkable Chunibala Devi (1872–1955), an eighty-year-old professional actress coaxed out of retirement to give an unforgettable and totally naturalistic scene-stealing performance as the grandmother, endowed with a reality that **Eleanora Duse** would have envied.

By coincidence, as the film was being edited, another great director was visiting Calcutta, preparing to shoot his movie. It was the American, John Huston (1906–87), and the film was *The Man Who Would be King* (1975). Ray got a rough cut of *Pather* to Huston, who in turn recommended it to the MoMA (Museum of Modern Art) in New York, where it was accepted for an American premiere. Ravi Shankar (1920–2012) already composing for film but not yet a musical superstar, set to work on the exquisite score. The film subsequently had an eight-month run in New York, was lauded in Cannes, and garnered eleven international awards. Only after its international success did it find a proper distribution in India.

Satyajit Ray possessed no-dyed-in-the-wool political (or religious) affiliation, unlike a number of the directors in the Italian Neo-Realist movement, and he has been criticized for not being committed to the cause of the downtrodden people he was depicting. His films were more concerned with the psychology of relationships and the authenticity of human behaviour. As *The New Yorker* critic, Pauline Kael put it, 'No other artist has done more than Ray to make us re-evaluate the commonplace.'[4] Ray was unconvinced about the idea of film as a political agent. 'Show me a film that changed society or brought about any change.'[5] In his film *Pratidwandi* (The Adversary, 1970), two brothers take differing positions regarding the Bengali Naxalite rebellion. The elder vacillates and is conflicted in his loyalties, and given these contradictions his character is interesting on a psychological level. The younger brother gives himself totally to the Naxalite movement and has no contradictions. To Ray, 'He, as a person, becomes insignificant.'[6]

Pather was to become the first film in what came to be known as *The Apu Trilogy*. The second, *Aparajito*, garnered even more praise for Satyajit Ray, and lead to a long career in which he made thirty-six movies and won multitudinous awards. Over time he gradually drifted away from his particular form of poetic observational realism into other styles and genres, eventually finding himself developing a project for a big budget Hollywood movie entitled *Alien*, brokered with Columbia Pictures by Ray's friend, the sci-fi writer Arthur C. Clarke (1917–2008). Ray wrote the script, and Peter Sellers and Marlon Brando were slated to star. But Brando dropped out and the project was canned. It has been alleged, but not proven, that Stephen Spielberg's *E.T.* (1982) plagiarized Ray's script. Certainly, the friendly alien in *E.T.* conformed precisely to the one depicted by Ray.

Satyajit Ray was not the only Indian director influenced by Italian Neo-Realism. In the 1950s and 1960s, the *Parallel Cinema* movement emerged in West Bengal, out of a frustration with the prevalent song-and-dance drama dominating cinema screens at the time. In addition to Ray, the movement included Mrinal Sen (1923–2018), Ritwik Ghatak (1925–76), Bimal Roy (1909–66), among other directors. Frequently supported by state funding and influenced by the wave of socially conscious Italian films, these filmmakers depicted social themes using realism and naturalism, drawing on Indian social literature and earlier social-realist films.[7]

Ray and his films won innumerable awards during his lifetime, including with the American Academy Honorary Award in 1992. His unique poetic style of realism was admired by and influenced many great directors. Akira Kurosawa (1910–98) proclaimed, 'Not to have seen the cinema of Ray means existing in the world without seeing the sun or the moon.'[8]

Further reading

Andrew Robinson, *Satyajit Ray: The Inner Eye: The Biography of a Master Film-maker* (London: Bloomsbury Academic, 3rd ed. 2021).

Notes

1. A selection of his criticism was collected and published in the volume *Our Films, Their Films* (Bombay: Disha Books, 1992).
2. Ibid., 119.
3. Ibid.
4. Pauline Kael, 'Lost and Found', *The New* Yorker, 17 March 1973.
5. Udayan Gupta, 'Satyajit Ray: In retrospect', in *The Cineaste Interviews*, eds. D. Georgakas and L. Rubenstein (Chicago: Lake View Press, 1983), 385.
6. Ibid., 387.
7. Notable earlier social-realist films include *Dharti Ke Lal* (Children of the Earth, 1946) depicting a family caught up in the Bengal famine of 1943, directed by K. A. Abbas (1914–87), later considered a member of the *Parallel Cinema* movement.
8. *The Guardian,* editorial, 6 July 2022.

61 Kitchen Sink Drama (British Social Realism) 1956–1970

Kitchen Sink Drama – once humorously dubbed 'The View from the Fridge'[1] – did not derive from **Italian Neo-Realism**. Its roots lie in the new theatrical Naturalism which burst upon the English stage in 1956 with John Osbourne's play *Look Back in Anger*. The protagonist of that play, Jimmy Porter, is a young working-class man living a life of hard graft despite having achieved a university degree. He harbours deep resentment for the upper classes who have ruled England, and projects his bitterness towards his unfortunate wife, Alison, progeny of that class. Jimmy behaves badly throughout. He is not a likeable character – angry, conflicted, misogynistic and, contradictorily, deeply in love with his wife. In effect, Osbourne (1929–94) had created the modern *anti-hero*. The working-class protagonist and the gritty setting of these people trapped in poverty in the grimy, smoke-choked Midlands of England, presented a radical departure from the cosy drawing room plays of Noël Coward (1899–1973) and Terrence Rattigan (1911–77) which dominated post-war British theatre – set in high society and dealing with the trials and tribulations of the upper classes.

Osbourne's example inspired a mixed bag of novelists and playwrights, political, sometimes anarchistic, who were lumped together because of their critical voices and their treatment of the alienated, disenfranchised and misused sectors of society. They were called the 'Angry Young Men' after the label applied to Jimmy Porter, and by default, to John Osbourne. They included playwrights like Shelagh Delaney (1938–2011), whose play *A Taste of Honey* (dir. **Joan Littlewood**, 1958) is about a seventeen-year-old white woman who sleeps with a black sailor, gets pregnant, then moves in with a gay friend who becomes her protector. Shocking at the time, the play treated unwanted pregnancy, racial intermixing, and homosexuality as ordinary facts of life. Other 'angry' dramatists included Harold Pinter (1930–2008), Arnold Wesker (1932–2016), Alan Sillitoe (1928–2010), David Storey (1933–2017), and Edward Bond (1934–2024).

Contemporaneous with the emergence of the Angry Young Men was the Free Cinema Movement – a loose association of filmmakers making 16mm documentaries primarily focused on the working lives of working-class characters. The 'movement' established a forum for showing such work in regular screenings at the National Film Theatre and issued its own 'manifesto', the first line of which stated: 'No Film Can Be Too Personal.'[2] Free Cinema's mission was to have 'freedom' from commercial constraints, and 'freedom' to choose the subjects that interested them as artists. Their aim was to make low-budget movies outside of the commercial financing and distribution system. Aesthetically they wanted to advance the realist project in cinema begun some thirty years earlier by John Grierson (1898–1972).[3] Three of its members, Karel Reisz (1926–2002), Lindsay Anderson (1923–94) and Tony Richardson (1928–91) went on to become leading lights in the British New Wave. Early Free Cinema films included Anderson's sordid portrayal of life in an amusement park, *O Dreamland* (1953), and Tony Richardson's *Momma Don't Allow* (1956), set in a North London jazz club. There is a direct connection between the documentaries of the Free Cinema, and the fiction films which followed, in personnel, style and subject matter – the fascination with traditional working-class culture, 'and the ambition to represent what is contemporary about contemporary Britain'.[4]

In 1959, Tony Richardson directed the film version of *Look Back in Anger*, the first of the British New Wave of movies which dealt with factory workers, prostitutes, office underlings, homosexuals, small shop keepers and others of the under-class. These films were set in regional settings, filmed in real places giving an authenticity of location, and featured a new generation of British actors like Alan Bates (1934–2003), Tom Courtenay (b. 1937) and Albert Finney (1936–2019) – who were allowed to speak in their own regional accent, freed from the 'received pronunciation' which they had been force-fed in drama schools.

Look Back in Anger was the first in a chain of New Wave films which examined economic and social pressures impact on sexuality and relationships, especially as seen through the eyes of their (angry) male protagonists. *Room at the Top* (dir. Jack Clayton,1959) features an ambitious young accountant, Joe Lampton, who decides to seduce the factory owner's daughter as a step up the social ladder, but simultaneously falls for a married older woman. *Saturday Night and Sunday Morning* (dir. Karel Reisz, 1960) features another angry young man, Arthur, who finds himself entrapped in tangled relationships. In John Schlesinger's film, *A Kind of Loving* (1962), the protagonist, Vic, is yet another working-class male victim of a surprise pregnancy. *This Sporting Life* (dir. Lindsay Anderson, 1963) is a relationship drama with no birth control issues – a more psychological story of a maladjusted young rugby player/coal miner, Frank, who falls for his older landlady. The unifying thread for British New Wave films was that they dealt with everyday situations of ordinary people confronting problems, social and economic, imposed by a class-bound society. They comprised a genre soon to be developed further in British television, and later reworked by the likes of **Ken Loach**, **Sean Meadows** and the emerging directors of the British **Neo Neo-Realism** school, all to be considered in later chapters.

More or less contemporaneous with *Look Back in Anger* was the naming of a new movement in British art which portrayed the grimmer social realities of the time. It was called 'kitchen sink realism', and was inspired by the work of John Bratby, RA (1928–92), whose paintings consisted of ordinary kitchens and bathrooms peopled by grim, desperate people, in everyday scenes illustrating the banality of life.

The term 'Kitchen Sink Drama' was subsequently applied to the British New Wave of Social Realism, a genre which continued into the 1970s and beyond. It more specifically attaches to the outpouring of naturalism in television drama emerging in the 1960s exemplified by made-for-telly films such as *Cathy Come Home* (BBC, *The Wednesday Play*, 1966), directed by Ken Loach, which depicted the downward spiral of a young mother into homelessness due to inequities of the system. Subsequent Kitchen Sink plays spawned a bevy of socially committed writers such as Alan Plater (1935–2010) and Jim Allen (1926–99), feeding a popular appetite for real life drama easily accessed at home watching 'the box'.

That appetite was fed by another popular realist format – the soap opera – the first of which was *Coronation Street* (Granada Television/ITV 1960–) set in a fictitious working-class terrace near Manchester – still broadcasting today. It was followed by *Brookside* (Channel Four, 1982–2003) set in a lower middle-class estate near Liverpool, and *EastEnders* (BBC from 1985) set in a fictitious working-class borough of East London. These serials endlessly portray everyday human dramas – one could say melodramas – of ordinary people played out within a specific cultural context and the framework of current social issues, albeit more superficially and sensationally. To note, the dramatic serial format is not a new concept for Brits – it has existed on *radio*, since 1 January 1951 when the BBC initiated a daily drama called *The Archers* – now the longest running serial in the world. It is set in rural England and was conceived with a hidden agenda – to bring British audiences up to date on the latest farming methods.[5]

The film version of Bill Naughton's 1967 play, *Spring and Port Wine* in 1970[6] is considered by film theorists to be the end of the Kitchen Sink cycle, but the form didn't die in the cinema, so much as gradually morph into other forms of social realism. The distinguished director Mike Leigh (b. 1943) created a unique version of the genre, sometimes labelled 'Neo-Kitchen Sink'.[7] Leigh started out as an actor, graduating from RADA (where he said Pinter was dismissed as 'rubbish', and that he had learned little more than elocution).[8] He went on to study set design at the Central School of Arts and Crafts,[9] and filmmaking at the London Film School. He claims he had a single moment of enlightenment at RADA – an *improvisation* class conducted by the actor Peter Barkworth (1929–2006). That, and a movie he saw around that time – **John Cassavetes**' *Shadows* (1959) – an improvised film with themes of racism set in the Beat generation in New York – planted the seeds of the methodology for which Leigh is so well known.

Leigh usually starts his projects with a blank canvass – merely some themes and an idea of how things might develop. He then works individually with each actor to invent their character – creating backstory, describing their tastes and ways of looking at life. The actors tend to reference people they know. Intimate moments are explored for the character – which won't necessarily be revealed in the improvisations or final script – in order to give them a more complete life. A distinction is always made between the 'actor' and the 'character'. Sometimes the actors are asked to go out into the real world and carry out a simple task such as shopping 'in character'.[10] The actors are eventually introduced to each other, always in the order in which their characters would have met in their fictitious lives. They will then improvise scenes jointly, based on situations Leigh proposes. When stopping an improvisation Leigh always tells the actor to 'come out of character' before discussing what has happened. Rehearsing and scriptwriting are one, and the process lasts for many weeks, even months, until the script is whittled down and polished. Actors are obliged to work on Leigh's films as an act of faith, being told little in advance about their character or what happens to them.

Apart from a few deliberately bleak movies (e.g. *All or Nothing*, 2002), Leigh's films tend to have a wry comedic vein, sometimes expressed in tragicomedy (e.g. *Life is Sweet*, 1990). His biographer Tony Whitehead notes that Leigh's characters often say with irony 'You gotta laugh.' when there is nothing to laugh about. 'Laughter and a sense of humour are seen as valid indeed vital, responses to life.'[11] Leigh is essentially a humourist working in an ostensibly realist mode who, it's been noted, 'often treats ordinary life as the subject for cruel satire'.[12] His films have an affectionate, if somewhat patronizing, view of their working-class characters, who sometimes border on caricature. The result is something quite different to the social realism of Ken Loach, who has a more straightforwardly compassionate view of his characters and whose films are driven by their message and could be said to be 'realism with a cause'.[13] Leigh is particularly fond of poking fun at the pretensions of the upwardly aspiring lower middle class (never more so that in his 1977 play *Abigail's Party*).[14] As evidenced especially in his design, he has an interest in the influence of social class on aesthetic taste, redolent of the work of British artist Grayson Perry (b. 1960) in his tapestries, *The Vanity of Small Differences* and other works.[15] Two filmmakers deeply admired by Mike Leigh were Jean Renoir and **Satyajit Ray**, and one can see the influence of their heightened, 'hyper-realist' styles in his work,[16] as well as their perspectives as filmmakers, that of outsiders looking in affectionately on the life styles and foibles of their subjects.

By the 1990s, some felt the Kitchen Sink Dramas had outlived their purpose and were labelled as 'miserabilist' – a 'political and aesthetic dead-end'.[17] During that decade, as if in rebuttal to the charge, there emerged in Britain a strand of social realism in comedic form; feel-good movies such as Mike Leigh's *Life is Sweet* (1990), *Brassed Off* (dir. Mark Herman, 1996), *The Full Monty* (dir. Peter Cattaneo, 1997) and *Billy Elliot* (dir. Stephen Daldry, 2000). In fact, there had been even earlier examples, such as *My Beautiful Laundrette* (dir. Stephen Frears, 1985) – and my own work with social comedy in the mid-eighties with writer Ruth Carter, exemplified by our Welsh-language films such as *Y Gwaith* (The Works, dir. Stephen Bayly, 1984) and *Coming up Roses* (dir. Stephen Bayly, 1986).

The social comedies of the 1990s have been criticized by dyed-in-the-wool social realists as being 'Ealing in the North' – 'conservative, backward-looking elegies, steeped in masculinist ideologies of the past'.[18] Notwithstanding how politically 'right-on' they may or may not have been, it's true that these films were inevitably influenced by the Ealing comedies (mine quite consciously so), and their accessible storylines have fed the public's appetite for real-life narratives of people's struggles against the political and social constrictions of the system, complementing the more acute work of others such as Ken Loach.

Further reading

Michael Coveney, *The World According to Mike Leigh* (London: Harper Collins, 1996).
Samantha Lay, *British Social Realism* (London: Wallflower, 2002).
Tony Whitehead, *Mike Leigh* (Manchester: Manchester University Press, 2007).

Notes

1. Expression coined by cultural commentator Paul Allen, first heard on BBC4, 27 August 1979.
2. Free Cinema's spokesperson Lindsay Anderson disavowed the term 'manifesto' even though he was its co-author.
3. Lay, 57. John Grierson is featured in a previous chapter: 'Dramatic Realism in Cinema'.
4. Lay, 61.
5. A market for socially relevant episodic popular fare featuring the trials and tribulations of working people had existed, albeit in a different medium, since the days of Charles Dickens's nineteenth-century serialized novels set in the East End of London. They were sold in cheap monthly instalments, called 'books in part'.
6. Dir. Peter Hammond, distributed by Anglo-Amalgamated Distributors.
7. Molly O'Hagan Hardy, 'Gendered trauma in Mike Leigh's Vera Drake', in *Studies in European Cinema,* Vol. 3 (2004): 211–21.
8. Whitehead, 12.
9. Merged with Saint Martin's School of Art in 1986, becoming the Central Saint Martin's College of Arts and Design.
10. Whitehead, 15.
11. Ibid., 4.
12. Geoff Brown, 'Paradise Lost and Found: The Course of British Realism', in Robert Murphy (ed), *The British Cinema* Book (London, BFI Publishing, 1997), 35.
13. Ibid.
14. A play improvised by Leigh, and first presented at the Hampstead Theatre in 1997, then televised later that year by the BBC.
15. A series of large tapestries created by Perry in 2013 ironically portraying the foibles and tastes of the British socio-economic classes, based on the series *The Rake's Progress* by eighteenth-century painter William Hogarth.
16. Coveney, 12.
17. David Thompson, former head of BBC Films, touting the British comedies in Cannes in 2005, as reported by Vanessa Thorpe in *The Guardian* https://www.theguardian.com/uk/2005/may/15/cannes2005.film
18. Paul Marris, cited by Paul Dave in 'Tragedy, Ethics and History in Contemporary British Social Realist Film', in *British Social Realism in the Arts Since 1940*, ed. David Tucker (London: Palgrave Macmillan, 2008), 17, referring to the 'Ealing Comedies', a series of films produced at the Ealing Studios in London between 1947 and 1957 reflecting the spirit of Britain during its post-War recovery.

62 John Cassavetes
1929–2008

Improvisation is at the centre of Cassavetes' work – the primary instrument in his search for truth. Performance, for him, was based on *character creation,* and was not to be restrained by the strictures of *narrative*. He was not interested in plot*,* '*I hate* plot points! I don't like focusing on plot because I think the audiences don't consist of only thirteen-year-old kids and also that each person that you see in life has more to them than would meet the eye.'[1] *Personality* replaced *plot*. The characters Cassavetes and his actors constructed in his movies were rich in complexity and full of unexpected reactions. Regarding his style of improvisation, he said, 'If the film is created out of the actors, then the work has as many facets as there are actors; the action is seen in the round – the communal creation of several imaginations.'[2]

While he studied acting at the rather 'establishment' American Academy of Dramatic Art,[3] his formation was really 'in the field'. He readily found work in tv series soon after graduation – not held back in the least by his marriage to the actor Gena Rowlands (1930–2024) four months after he met her at the Academy. Their marriage later produced three children, additionally benefitting Cassavetes with a fruitful working relationship with an actress of exceptional talent. She acted in most of his movies and they shared a complementary approach to their work in that they had both studied with **Sanford Meisner**.

Cassavetes hated 'The Method', considering it to be 'more a form of psychotherapy than of acting'.[4] He set up his own acting workshop in NYC with actor Burton Lane (1912–97). Their approach can be seen as a reaction *against* two prevailing conditions: the banal nature of characterization in the commercial movies of Hollywood, and the dominant approaches to training actors to act in those movies, namely, **Lee Strasberg's** 'Method' and other bastardizations of **Stanislavski**.[5]

The Cassavetes-Lane Theatre Workshop specialized in improvisation. This was not the improvisation of Strasberg, delving into the actor's psychology, nor that of Meisner, based on action/reaction and eschewing language and intellectuality. It was based simply on the actors' natural reactions, as expressed in every-day speech, to what was happening to them in the context of a given situation. One major Theatre Workshop improvisation project, entitled *Shadows*, developed into a movie (1957), directed by Cassavetes. He tried out a cut of the film in Paris and then at a late-night screening in New York in 1958. Afterwards he reshot and re-edited much of it, releasing the new version for public consumption in 1959. The single existing 16mm print of the first version – he could only afford one print – was found by his biographer Ray Carney after much detective work; was restored and released and is generally considered to be better than the second version.[6]

After *Shadows,* Cassavetes directed two studio pictures, *Two Late Blues* (1961, for Paramount) and *A Child is Waiting* (1963, for United Artists) – demoralizing experiences, especially the former, where the studio edited a version with which he could never agree. It wasn't until 1968 that he was able to make another film independently – *Faces*, starring Gena Rowlands. In the intervening years he (and Rowlands) did a considerable amount of lucrative paid acting work, including *The Dirty Dozen* (1967), for which he was nominated for a Best Supporting Actor Oscar. (See IMDb for his *prodigious* acting credits.)

Faces, and the films which followed, were characterized by two things: the *impression* that we are watching improvisation (even though the actors were assiduously following the script), and an 'antifilmic' use of the technical elements, which do not *construct* the performance, but rather *allow* it to take place. This approach was a *cinema verité* style of filming – frequently making the audience feel like the proverbial *fly on the wall*. He used camera angles, lighting and camera movement sparingly – performance was always given top priority.[7] Film technique was something 'to keep out of the way of the performance'.[8] His style was rough and not classically cinematic, the editing quite 'open' with non-Hollywood rhythms to allow performances to play out. The dialogues, originally improvised in rehearsal, but religiously adhered to in the filming, *felt like* improvisation, because they consisted of the rambling, disconnected speech of daily life, didn't exist simply to drive forward a narrative, but to create a living breathing character.

It was a style not loved by many mainstream critics. Pauline Kael (1919–2001), the doyenne of US critics, writing for the *The New Yorker*, called *Faces* 'dumb, crudely perceived, and badly performed'. *Variety*'s review said *Minnie and Moskowitz* was 'an oppressive and irritating film . . . in which a shrill and numbing hysteria of acting and direction soon kills any empathy for the . . . characters.'[9] John Simon (1925–2019), the characteristically vitriolic critic of *New York Magazine* called *A Woman Under the Influence* 'dreadful, muddle-headed, pretentious, and interminable'.[10]

A stylistic relationship of Cassavetes movies to the French New Wave has been noted – filming in black and white, natural lighting, improvising during filming, hand-held cameras and long takes. But Cassavetes differs in that his *mise-en-scène* is less subjective, lacking the quick cuts and fancy editing of the French films. He experimented with 16mm in two films (*Shadows* and *Faces*– anathema to New Wave auteurs, in love with the full luminous 35mm celluloid frame – but gave up, wanting more latitude in the film stock to give more freedom to his actors to work within the frame.

Cassavetes' movies offered up a smorgasbord of characters: housewives, hippies, gangsters, children, businessmen, actors and strippers. They are the people we encounter in the real world. Even his actor characters seem like ordinary people. 'They live in specific social environments and their actions are a consequence of their personal histories and environmental forces.'[11] In comparison to characters in New Wave films – frequently quirky, edgy types – those of Cassavetes lack self-reflexion and are less consciously existential. They are too busy being intensely engaged with other characters. Frequently they 'cannot express or even understand the situation in which they find themselves. Like real people . . . they improvise as they go along.'[12]

In rehearsal, Cassavetes spent little time at the table on analysis, other than to study the general theme of the work as laid down by the director. It was important that all in the ensemble 'share the same overall conceptions but each actor must come at his own interpretation of his role, without the sort of group study and mutual criticism which one associates with Method work'.[13] He and Burton Lane once famously played a prank on Lee Strasberg. They auditioned for the **Actors Studio** having been instructed to present a scene from a recent stage production. However, in the audition they simply improvised something on the spot. Strasberg loved it an offered Cassavetes a full scholarship to The Studio. Cassavetes turned down the offer on the basis that this man – so easily *duped* – had nothing to offer him. Cassavetes was not only 'anti' 'The Method', he was 'anti' *any* method, pointing out that Stanislavski himself 'acknowledged that every artist must in the end discover his own, personal method'.[14]

In filming he dived into the shooting quickly before the actors could come up with any fixed line reading. He would use devices to elicit surprise, including tactics similar to those of Ken Loach, sometimes changing the lines of one actor without telling another. Discussing the filming of *A Woman Under the Influence*,

Cassavetes explains. 'We lit up the entire room and set up the camera to be open to the actors who would use the entire space. . . . What I try to do is anticipate the movement of the scene, to leave the actors as free as possible in the space. I can't demand that the actors fit their motion to a pre-planned camera movement. They could only make it work by repetition, but that's boring and tiring, and the crew starts to become their audience.'[15]

He rejected Stanislavski's counsel in *An Actor Prepares* that the actor works off the character's 'SuperObjective'. Instead, he and the actors would establish several disparate objectives, scene-by-scene. This led to the characters having complexity and the self-contradictory quality of real life. He used *subtext* as a tool but was also known in rehearsal to create double or even triple subtexts for the characters, so that if one action or intention didn't work another could be called into play as an *indirect* action.[16] This was in deliberate contrast to 'Hollywood Realism' which required an actor to play one specific subtext at a time.[17]

Although born in New York, Cassavetes lived in Greece until the age of seven, when he returned to the USA, speaking no English. Profoundly influenced by his father, a rags-to-riches Harvard-educated businessman who made *and lost* millions, he attributed his instinct of gambling on films (money, property, whatever) to his father.[18]

Between 1954 and 1960 he acted in more than ninety live TV dramas, and several movies, including a starring role with Sidney Poitier in *Edge of the City* (1957). He specialized in gangsters and detectives and was especially well-known for his performance in the long-running TV series *Johnny Staccato*, as the eponymous detective/jazz musician (1959–60 ABC/NBC).

Cassavetes vies with **John Sayles** for the title of 'progenitor of American independent film'. Like Sayles he used his acting earnings to finance his own movies and maintain total control over them. Starting with *Shadows* he made eight films that were solely under his control, but unlike Sayles, he brought to his films a style utterly distinctive from mainstream Hollywood. Film critic Joe Leydon called him the 'the gray eminence of American independent moviemakers . . . creator of such rough-edged, defiantly unpolished . . . pictures in which life is served up like steak tartare: Raw and not appealing to every taste.'[19]

I close this chapter with a helpful note for young directors: Cassavetes had great faith in his actors delivering to him what he needed: 'as long as they are given praise. That's what an actor needs. Praise is his prime nourishment.'[20]

Further reading

Ray Carney, ed., *Cassavetes on Cassavetes* (London: Faber & Faber, 2001).
Gabriella Oldham, ed. *John Cassavetes Interviews* (Jackson: University Press of Mississippi), 2016.
Maria Viera, 'Playing with Performance, Directorial and Acting Style in John Cassavetes's *Opening Night*', '*More Than a Method*', eds. C. Baron, D. Carson and F. Tomasulo (Detroit: Wayne State University, 2004).

Notes

1. Carney, 419.
2. 'Mr. John Cassavetes on the Actor and Improvisation', *The Times*, 11 August 1960, in Oldham, 12.
3. The Academy was the first acting school in the USA, established in 1884 in NYC. It's acting programme currently *includes* elements of Strasberg, Meisner and Hagen. One assumes that given Cassavetes' distain for Strasberg's The Method that it was being taught in some manner when he attended, and one assumes that Meisner's mitigating modifications of Stanislavski's teachings were not being taught.

4. Carney, 52–3.
5. Ibid.
6. According to experimental filmmaker and critic Jonas Mekas, 'the tones and rhythms of a new America' were perfectly caught in the first version, and the second version should be taken out of circulation. Jonas Mekas, *Village Voice*, 27 January 1960.
7. Viera, 153.
8. Ibid.
9. *Variety*, 13 December 1970.
10. John Simon, *Reverse Angle: A Decade of American Films* (New York: Crown Publishers Inc.,1982), 169.
11. Viera, 154.
12. Ibid.
13. Oldham, 12.
14. Ibid.
15. Michel Ciment and Michael Henry, *Positif*, April 1976, in Oldham, 107.
16. Viera, 162.
17. Viera, 163.
18. Joe Leydon, 'The Lost Interview: John Cassavetes', *MovieMaker, The Art and Business of Making Movies* (online), 29 January 2009, in Oldham, 151.
19. Leydon, in Oldham, 148.
20. Oldham, 12.

63 Ken Loach
1936–

It grows ever more apparent that there are two classes in society, that their interests are irreconcilable, and that one survives at the expense of the other.[1]

British director Ken Loach's politics are clear. They are inherent in his films, yet in watching a Loach movie one is caught up in the storyline and the life of the characters, and one understands the message viscerally, not intellectually. In **Working with Actors**, in the chapter 'The Case for Realism', I examine the *power of realism* to stimulate political thought and galvanize the spectator to action via an emotional attachment to the personal real-life predicaments and reactions of the characters in the drama. There is no one who more fully understands this principle than Ken Loach, whose films exemplify the art of marrying the personal and the political – of making didactic films without them seeming to be didactic.

> The politics are embedded into the characters and the narrative . . . a more sophisticated way of doing it. It's a balance, because on one hand you don't want it embedded so that only film professors can read it but, equally, you don't want to be that crude that every film ends with a fist in the air.[2]

Loach's distinctive approach to filmmaking is clearly a product of his formation – reading law at Oxford, trying his hand at acting, directing television **(see Kitchen Sink Drama)**, studying Marxism, and making documentaries – all coalesce in his mature cinema art from the 1990s to the present day. While studying for a law degree at Oxford, young Loach moonlighted as President of the Oxford University Dramatic Society as well as Secretary of the Experimental Theatre Club through which he had his first experience in acting and directing. Upon graduation he found jobs in repertory theatre, mostly as an assistant director. In 1963 he was taken on as a trainee television director at the BBC, which was gearing up for the opening of its second channel. At the BBC he cut his teeth directing *live* television productions of a police drama, *Z Cars*, followed by episodes of a half hour studio drama, *Diary of a Young Man,* about the adventures of two northern working-class lads seeking their fortune in London. In 1964 – the year of Britain's return to a socialist government led by Harold Wilson – the BBC, catching the *zeitgeist*, launched its long-running series *The Wednesday Play*, devised and edited by the Canadian Sydney Newman (1917–97) consisting of weekly dramas, many concerned with social issues, and written by a talented group of Britain's emerging socialist writers, including Jim Allen (1926–99), David Mercer (1928–80), Alan Plater (1935–2010) and Johnny Speight (1920–98). By Loach's own telling, it took some time for him to gain confidence as a director,[3] but in 1965 he was deemed accomplished enough by Newman to direct a Wednesday Play. The first of the ten plays he mounted for the series was *Up the Junction* – a drama portraying the new sexual freedom of young working women and its consequences, based on a book by Nell Dunn (b. 1936). Its candidness, especially in its depiction of an abortion, raised the ire of conservative Britain, including the outspoken arch-conservative moralist Mary Whitehouse (1910–2001). Benefitting from the notoriety she generated, the show achieved a wide viewership, and much praise.

Loach's next play, *Cathy Come Home* (1966), concerned a working-class couple's descent into poverty and homelessness. Its producer Tony Garnett (1936–2020) convinced Sydney Newman to allow shooting of the entire play for the first time 'on location' (he had shot some sequences of *Up the Junction* on a lightweight 16mm camera). This gave the drama a level of reality impossible to achieve in the studio. Loach, who at that time was drawn to some of the ideas of **Bertolt Brecht** and **Joan Littlewood**, broke the realistic thread by editing-in snippets of vox pop as well as housing statistics by way of contextualizing the drama, creating Brechtian V-Effekts to complement the naturalism. These two plays are the best of Loach's *Wednesday Play* output, and arguably among the best of the six-year series, and considered to be a turning point in British TV drama. *Cathy Come Home* was named by *Broadcast* magazine as the most influential UK television programme of all time.[4] It caused debates in Parliament, and spurred on the formation of the housing charity, Shelter. The plays were the start of a working relationship with producer Tony Garnett that lasted for years. By Loach's account, Garnett was the more politically progressive of the two and opened him up to a Marxist point of view of class betrayal which distinguished the products of their collaboration throughout.[5] With characteristic modesty Loach understates his contribution to *The Wednesday Play*, 'I know I personally made several howlers, but I think it was a time when a group of us collectively made a few pushes forward.'[6]

Loach's first feature films were an extension of his television work in naturalism centring around the lives of ordinary people. *Poor Cow* (1967) was based on another novel by Nell Dunn and features a young mother in an abusive relationship with a petty criminal, and her descent into prostitution. *Kes* (1969), based on the novel *A Kestrel for a Knave* by Barry Hines (1939–2016), is about a troubled adolescent finding solace with his kestrel. It was the first of several Hines-Loach collaborations, produced by Tony Garnett, and was distributed to acclaim worldwide. (In English-speaking territories it was subtitled in English due to its thick Yorkshire accents.) In both of those early films, Loach demonstrated an attitude towards casting which he would carry through for years to come, namely, recruiting non-professionals (or actors with local or vocational backgrounds) who could bring 'authenticity' to a part – which he considered to be more important than acting experience. In *Poor Cow* he cast John Bindon (1943–93), an actor, bodyguard and a bit of a thug, as Tom, the husband, because he had been 'inside' on an assault charge. In *Kes* he cast Colin Welland (1934–2015), because he had been a teacher. Loach never used a complete cast of non-professionals but tended to mix pros and non-pros on the basis that they help each other – the actors help the non-pros technically, and they in turn cause the actors to be more 'authentic'.[7]

In 1971 Loach's world collapsed. An accident while he was at the wheel of his car killed his five-year-old son and his grandmother-in-law. Overwhelmed with grief, it was over a year before he could work again. He eased back in with a television adaptation of two Chekhov plays entitled *A Misfortune*. His next project was substantially meatier – Jim Allen's four-part epic *Days of Hope* (1975) which followed a working-class family left in turmoil from the First World War until the time of the General Strike of 1929. Again, it was produced by Tony Garnett. This was followed by yet another Hines-Loach-Garnett collaboration, *The Price of Coal*, a two-part BBC *Play for Today* (1977) with comic overtones and serious undertones set in a northern mining village expecting a royal visit (Prince Charles).

In the 1980s, Loach's career floundered. *Looks and Smiles* (1981), set in the era of Margaret Thatcher, concerns two kids whose high hopes graduated from school are dashed. Based on Barry Hines's novel of the same name, it was not well received, even though the acting of its young (untrained) principal actors and the black and white photography of Chris Menges (b. 1940) were generally praised. Some of its lack of success might be attributable to the heavy Sheffield accents, which were incomprehensible to Americans and many Brits. *Fatherland*, the other film he made in the 1980s was, by his own admission, a failure – a mismatch of his freewheeling naturalism with writer Trevor Griffiths' (1935–2024) more literary style.[8] Loach's feature film career languished. He says of this period, 'I couldn't direct traffic.'[9] However, Margaret Thatcher's rise to power, with her attacks on the trade unions and social services galvanized him and provided an impetus to make more documentaries. Unfortunately, his socialist critique became the victim of repeated censorship, and much of what Loach made in those years has never been seen or was tucked away in late night regional programming. His four-part Channel 4 documentary *A Question of Leadership* (1981) was blocked by the Independent Broadcasting Authority (or perhaps by someone higher-up). A film about miner's art and music during the 1984–5 strike was pulled from the *South Bank Show*. The Jim Allen play he directed at the Royal Court Theatre caused another type of political backlash, and closed before it opened. That play, *Perdition* (1987), was based on the true story of the betrayal of certain Zionist leaders in Hungary who made a deal with the Nazis to free 'key' people, while leading the mass of Jews to the trains bound for the concentration camps. It was viciously attacked by British Zionists as being anti-Semitic when it was not anything of the sort (presaging the problems of one of Loach's biggest fans, former Labour leader, Jeremy Corbyn, whose anti-Zionist stance got him branded as anti-Semitic and led to his loss of the leadership of the Labour party).

The 1990s saw the full flowering of Ken Loach's talent as a filmmaker. By then in his fifties, he had a wealth of experience under his belt, a distinctive and confident approach to making movies, and newfound writers and political soulmates, especially in Jim Allen and Paul Laverty (b. 1957). He also connected at that time with producers Rebecca O'Brien (b. 1957) and Sally Hibbin (b. 1953) of Parallax Pictures, who offered him a base and continuity for the first time since leaving television drama, as well as their unstinting support. The critically acclaimed *Hidden Agenda* (1990), a political thriller set in Northern Ireland, written by Allen, coproduced by O'Brien, and featuring the formidable talents of Brian Cox (b. 1946) and Frances McDormand (b. 1957), put him back on the map, and set the stage for a long chain of movies in the Loach vein of realism which has not stopped at the time of this writing (despite his declaration of retirement in 2014).[10] Below is his impressive filmography from 1990 on, listing the writers. Since the death of Jim Allen in 1999, Loach has enjoyed a fruitful, trusting and exclusive relationship with Paul Laverty.

Hidden Agenda (1990) Jim Allen

Riff-Raff (1991) Bill Jesse

Raining Stones (1993) Jim Allen

Ladybird, Ladybird (1994) Rona Munro

Land and Freedom (1995) Jim Allen

Carla's Song (1996) Paul Laverty

My Name is Joe (1998) Paul Laverty

Bread and Roses (2000) Paul Laverty

The Navigators (2001) Paul Laverty

Sweet Sixteen (2002) Paul Laverty

11'09"01 September 11 (2002)

Ae Fond Kiss (2004) Paul Laverty

Tickets (2005) with Ermanno Olmi and Abbas Kiarostami

The Wind That Shakes the Barley (2006) Paul Laverty

It's a Free World (2007) Paul Laverty

Looking for Eric (2008) Paul Laverty

Route Irish (2010) Paul Laverty

The Angel's Share (2012) Paul Laverty

Jimmy's Hall (2014) Paul Laverty

I, Daniel Blake (2016) Paul Laverty

Sorry We Missed You (2019) Paul Laverty

The Old Oak (2023) Paul Laverty

Loach at eighty-seven years of age, ten years on from his first declaration of retirement, has claimed that *The Old Oak* was to be his final film. Time will tell.[11]

There is ample material in print and online by way of biography and analysis of Loach's work. Our narrow focus here is his handling of actors and performance in the context of realism. I start with casting, which could be said to be Loach's greatest strength as a director. He rehearses minimally, believing that the more a cast is rehearsed the less convincing the performances. Hence, he needs to have great faith in his casting decisions. As mentioned above, Loach believed that those who had lived an experience could represent it more faithfully. Sometimes that approach backfired, as in the case of former thug John Bindon in *Poor Cow* whose performance was flat and unnatural. But usually it resulted in credible, even moving, performances, such as those he achieved in his 2019 film *Sorry We Missed You*, which was cast by Kahleen Crawford (b. 1979), who has worked on all of Loach's films since *Ae Fond Kiss* in 2004. On that movie, following his usual pattern, Loach and Crawford started with the characters' socio-economic profiles, then travelled to the local area where the story takes place.

The Loach casting concept is, in general, to use professional actors who fit the character's profile for meaty roles requiring subtle emotions, and local actors, both *pro* and *non-pro*, as foils. The 'pro' in the case of *Sorry We Missed You* was Kris Hitchen (b. 1974), a trained actor who came from Salford but had been a plumber for most of his working life. Debbi Honeywood (b. 1972), a local educational worker, was the 'non-pro' – with astonishing results. Debbi was cast after a hunt on social media, local gyms, and a background actors' agency.[12] Her truthful and moving performance won her the Best Actor Award at the Chicago Film Festival and she has now 'gone pro'.

Loach's MO in casting, according to Rebecca O'Brien is to meet 'thousands' of people for main roles, sometimes casting them in parts they didn't come in for, shortlisting those he thinks have energy, wit and can think on their feet. He looks for someone he believes will *be* that person. 'Not a performer, just someone who is.'[13] According to Kahleen Crawford, to cast for Ken Loach 'you've got to be open-minded about the whole script – about all the possibilities for that person'.[14] He prefers to cast lesser known and inexperienced actors, both for their greater availability for long shoots, but also because they tend to have less 'actorly' pretention. The following comment by Loach is telling: 'I've always preferred to watch documentaries rather than television dramas because of the way they grind down the spontaneity of the actors' performances.'[15] Loach is very clear about what makes a good or bad actor.

> A good actor lives off the people he's acting with; a bad actor acts in a vacuum. A good actor gives support to other people in the scene; a bad actor gives nothing. That generosity is vital. That's why you should never audition in isolation and say, 'Read this,' because it denies the very first principle of acting, which is response. I wouldn't dream of having an actor try out for something by having them act or read on their own.[16]

Listening was a base-line skill for **Sanford Meisner** and a case for casting using a 'connected reading' is made in ***Working with Actors***, in the chapter 'Cast the Actor not the Character'.

Loach's shooting practice is legendary. To achieve the realism that he is after he wants the actor to *live* in the story 'as if they were participating in a documentary', and this means not knowing what fate is going to befall their character. To this end he shoots the script chronologically (an expensive approach), and only issues the scenes to the cast a day at a time. He wants the actors to come to the scene fresh – to *react* rather than act. This method creates an emotional energy in the filming of every scene that carries over into the next. During the shooting he allows his actors to vary the dialogues and openly react to other actors or occurrences. He is a great believer that 'surprise' is an indication of truth in performance, and will go to great lengths to achieve it, setting up situations in scenes introducing unscripted elements and events not revealed to his actor-victims. He can be quite manipulative in these tactics, and occasionally his tricks have reached the limit of acceptability. One classic early example is the heart-wrenching final scene in *Cathy Come Home* where the actor Carol White is sitting on a bench in a railway station with her two *real-life* children in the midst of real-life passers-by when social workers suddenly appear from the crowd and snatch her children from her. It was filmed with a hidden camera. Unsuspecting Carol was genuinely horrified, and the children terrified. Another oft-mentioned example occurred in *Kes* in the scene in which the headteacher canes a group of smokers. The youngest boy, who was innocent, was not told in advance he would be caned. He is stoic and steadfast, and the camera homes in to a closeup as his real tears escape. There are many more examples. In *The Wind That Shakes the Barley* (2006) in the scene where the Black and Tans ambush everyone at Sinead's house, the actors playing the Brits were kept out of sight from the others, hence the victims had genuinely shocked reactions when attacked. The actors also were not told that the soldier would emerge from the barn with blood all over his hands. The actor playing Dan didn't know his character was going to die until the actual event. Loach's devices have become industry legend and now when actors are tricked into surprise situations, such as when the alien suddenly explodes from John Hurt's chest in Ridley Scott's *Alien* (1979), it's termed 'getting Loached'.

As noted, Loach, like Sanford Meisner, places great value in listening. When an actor is not listening, he instructs the partner actor to say: 'Sorry, what did you say?' forcing the actor to repeat the line in a *connected* manner and listen.[17]

People who have worked with Ken Loach have commented to me on his personal qualities, namely that he is extremely considerate and maintains a respectful attitude to all who work with him – none more so than to his actors. On the set, like the best of the 'actors' directors' he respects the actor's preparatory process, and doesn't shout 'action'. He says quietly in quaint English, 'Off you go' – similar to another well-known 'actor's director', Clint Eastwood (b. 1930), who famously intones: 'Alright, go ahead.'

Loach's belief in collaboration was illustrated recently when he was praised for *his* ground-breaking film, *Kes*. He countered:

It was Barry Hines' book . . . and I met Barry through Tony Garnett the producer . . . So I'm always embarrassed when they say that's your film. It's *our* film. And Barry's book is a real classic. I think the problem with our business is that it does create egotists if you're not careful. A film 'by' the director is embarrassing. A film is by Kodak if it's by anyone.[18]

In his early television days Loach, as noted, was heavily influenced by **Joan Littlewood**.

I admired and enjoyed her work enormously and tried to emulate it – the way you often emulate someone when you're start out. I was trying to get the same sense of randomness that she got in live theatre. It was a way of telling a story where the images appeared arbitrary but none the less a story emerged . . .

It still seems to me that a lot of films and television dramas just show you the main actors, as though they live in a vacuum.[19]

The Littlewood effect can be seen clearly in *Up the Junction* which consists of a series of vignettes of multiple characters. As for cinema, excepting a brief technical interest in early Godard, Loach professed *not* to be influenced by the French New Wave. 'Their fascination with Jean Paul Belmondo didn't interest me one bit.'[20] Loach's greatest inspiration was **Italian Neo-Realism** – Luchino Visconti (1906–76), Roberto Rossellini (1906–77), Vittorio De Sica (1901–74), who took their cameras on to the streets and made stories about the working-class. 'The Neo-Realist films were about comradeship, about solidarity, about a sense of mutual support . . .'.[21] His greatest debt is to Vittorio De Sica who made him realize that 'cinema could be about ordinary people and their dilemmas'.[22] He greatly admired the affinity De Sica had with his writer, Cesare Zavattini (1902–89), and aspired to and achieved a similar relationship with his own. 'Without the writer the director has nothing to direct'[23] He was also drawn to the Czech New Wave – the films of Miloš Forman (1932–2018) and Jiri Menzel (1938–2020) in particular: 'they were the kinds of films we wanted to make . . . humanist, compassionate films. They weren't soft in any way, but had a very sharp, wry wit.'[24]

Ken Loach's films have only had sporadic and moderate box office success in the USA. In Europe they are highly valued. Sixteen of his movies have been officially invited to the Cannes Festival, and he shares the record for winning two *Palmes d'Or* (*Wind that Shakes the Barley*, 2006 and *I, Daniel Blake*, 2016). Additionally at Cannes, he has garnered three jury prizes, three FRIPESCI awards and two Ecumenical Jury honours. In Europe his films have won multiple Césars, Goyas, Golden Lions, etc. The American Academy has not once acknowledged him.

Ken Loach's work has a significance beyond itself. His legacy is as deep as its spread is wide. He has inspired an entire generation of British Neo neo-realist filmmakers (see below) and influenced innumerable filmmakers globally, such as the American **Sean Baker** (see his chapter).

Further reading

Nick Grant, 'Keeping it real: the brutal art of Ken Loach,' *International Socialism*, Issue 160, 18 October 2018, http://isj.org.uk/keeping-it-real/

Anthony Hayward, *Which Side on You On?: Ken Loach and his Films* (London: Bloomsbury, 2004).

Ken Loach, *Loach on Loach*, ed. Graham Fuller (London: Faber & Faber, 1998).

Notes

1. Loach, 113.
2. 'Ken Loach. Meet one of Britain's most controversial filmmakers', *Slate Magazine*, posted 27 August 2011, an article republished from the *Financial Times*. https://slate.com/human-interest/2011/08/ken-loach-meet-one-of-britain-s-most-controversial-filmmakers.html
3. Loach, 8. At the time of making *Diary of a Young Man* in 1963 Loach said in directing he was 'still rigid with fear'.
4. 'Cathy tops TV shows that changed our world', *The Evening Standard*, London, 22 July 2005. https://www.standard.co.uk/showbiz/cathy-tops-tv-shows-that-changed-the-world-7271892.html
5. Loach, 9, 13.
6. Ibid., 31.
7. John Hill, *The Politics of Film and Television* (London: BFI and Palgrave Macmillan, 2011), 121.
8. Loach, 60.
9. Ibid., 61.

10. Alex Ritman, 'Legend of the Croisette: How Ken Loach Conquered Cannes', *Variety*, 15 May 2023, https://www.hollywoodreporter.com/movies/movie-features/ken-loach-interview-cannes-film-festival-history-1235483548/
11. Loach's second declaration of retirement, having completed *The Old Oak* in 2023 at the age of eighty-seven. With his age and the loss of sight in one eye he said, 'I can't see getting around the course again.' Then as an afterthought he added, but 'you only need one eye to look through the camera'. Diane Taylor, 'Braverman knows what she's unleashing' *The Guardian*, 2 October 2023, https://www.theguardian.com/film/2023/oct/02/suella-braverman-knows-what-unleashing-ken-loach-film-old-oak
12. Valentina I. Valentini, 'Casting Director Breaks Down How She Assembles Unique Casts for Ken Loach Films', *Variety*, 12 March 2020, https://variety.com/2020/artisans/production/casting-ken-loach-sorry-we-missed-you-1203530527/
13. Grant.
14. Valentini.
15. Loach, 20.
16. Ibid., 6.
17. Alex Ritman, 'Ken Loach on Retiring After 60 Years of Filmmaking and his Respect for Jonathan Glazer's "Hugely Valuable" Oscars Speech', *Variety*, 2 April 2024, https://variety.com/2024/film/global/ken-loach-retirement-the-old-oak-jonathan-glazer-oscars-speech-
18. Hayward, 252.
19. Ibid., 19.
20. *Slate Magazine*.
21. Grant.
22. Tom Lamont, 'Films that changed my life: Ken Loach', *The Observer*, 16 May 2010, https://www.theguardian.com/film/2010/may/16/bicycle-thieves-ken-loach
23. Grant.
24. Loach, 38.

64 John Sayles
1950–

John Sayles was a pioneer in the field of American independent filmmaking. His debut film, *The Secaucus Seven* was made in 1979, and returned $2 million on a self-funded $60K budget, setting a model for the independent movies a full ten years before *Sex, Lies, and Videotapes* (1989) so vividly demonstrated the potential rewards for low-budget films.[1] Sayles went on to make eighteen more feature-length films to date, only one of which was for a studio. (Five don't count as drama, as they were essentially long videos about Bruce Springsteen.) His films are well structured, morally complex, full of complicated characters, and well-acted. His stories contain a deterministic point of view, redolent of the great American social novels of Stephen Crane (1871–1900), Theodore Dreiser (1878–1945), Upton Sinclair (1878–1968), John Dos Passos (1896–1970), in which characters are in large measure a product of or victim to the society in which they live. Film critic Roger Ebert (1942–2013) referred to John Sayles as 'the conscience of American independent filmmaking'.[2]

Sayles's film style is sometimes labelled 'neorealist' to distinguish it from the dominant commercial 'realism' (or *faux realism*) of Hollywood. He mixes experienced and inexperienced actors in his casts, which tend to be larger ensembles than those of **John Cassavetes**, but similar in terms of the *naturalistic* performance style. Sayles's *auteur* movies are markedly different to those of Cassavetes in that they deal with broader political themes, being perhaps nearer to the 'social realism' of **Ken Loach**. *Matewan* (1987) is about union organizing; *City of Hope* (1991) looks at corruption and urban conflict in New Jersey; in *Eight Men Out* (1988) underpaid baseball players fall prey to bribery. He has treated a wide variety of themes, from a ground-breaking lesbian coming-out story (*Lianna*, 1983), to mythical Irish sea creatures called 'Selkies' in contemporary Ireland (*The Secret of Roan Inish*, 1994). His writing style tends to flesh-out numerous minor characters in an attempt, 'rare in contemporary cinema, let alone Hollywood – to depict a social totality.'[3] The overall effect is to 'de-centralize' the protagonist.[4]

Sayles came to directing via writing. He had no formal training in directing or acting. 'I'd seen a lot of movies. That was my film school.'[5] He entered the Hollywood arena via his fiction writing, persuading his literary agent to represent him as a screenwriter. He has written three novels, two short story collections, and one work of non-fiction.[6] He attended Williams College as a psychology student, allegedly not applying himself much to his subject, instead spending much of his time reading books and starting to write. At Williams he met his life partner, who later became his producer, Maggy Renzi. With her he joined the college theatre group. After graduation, following a few years of living in poverty and working tough jobs – day labourer, medical orderly, meat packer and a stint in a summer rep company in New Hampshire – he published his first novel, *Pride of the Bimbos* (1975) about a baseball team who play in drag in scraggly small towns in the southern USA. His second novel, *Union Dues* was published in 1977. Presaging his film work, it was a piece of social realism centring around a dysfunctional mining family, reading as a metaphor for the disintegrating social and political climate Sayles witnessed in the USA in the late 1960s.

The success of his novels got him a writing gig with Roger Corman's notorious B-movie factory for whom he wrote three scripts, starting with a *Jaws* pastiche called *Piranha* (1978) directed by Joe Dante. He is credited in IMDb for writing forty films (not including rewrites on uncredited movies). His Hollywood rewrites include *Apollo 13* (1995), *The Fugitive* (1993) and *The Howling* (1981). Sayles made a pile of money writing for Hollywood and, just as **Cassavetes** had done with his acting earnings, he pumped it back into his own movies. Like Cassavetes, the movies he made with Maggie Renzi are labours of love. He said: 'The things I write and direct are things I'm not going to see unless I do them.'[7] Two of his films, *Passion Fish* (1992) and *Lone Star* (1996), garnered Oscar nominations for Best Screenplay.

And then there is his acting . . . Sayles has thirty-one IMDb acting credits, essentially small character roles, several of which are in his own movies. Among the performances I have seen I found no 'stand outs'. There are some quirky ones, such as the garage owner in *City of Hope* (1991) or the drug dealer in *Hard Choices* (1986) but none which struck me as revealing the deep inner truth of the character. Perhaps it's understandable, because by his own admission most of the characters he has played 'are guys who don't change. They are able to stay outside of the action emotionally.'[8] Sayles never attended an acting class and professes to have no acting technique. Regarding his impulse to act, he says it's similar to the impulse to write, 'which is getting into somebody else's head'.[9] The point of view of the character – 'How does this person think?' – is what interested him in playing any given role.[10] As a director Sayles had only a limited appreciation for his actors' formation. 'In working with actors, it's been about 60/40: 60 percent of the time I think that recently being in an acting class has gotten in their way, and 40 percent of the time, I feel it's been helpful.'[11] There was one exception: 'For my particular style of moviemaking, which is a kind of naturalism, the people who consistently seem to be on the same wave-length and have gone to classes tend to be people who are connected with Sanford Meisner. He works on inhabiting a character and really listening.'[12] In contrast he said that conservatory training, such as the Juilliard School, which is more related to the British style of acting, was not 'especially useful for what I do.'[13]

By Sayles's own account, he is a 'hands-off' director.[14] In his direction he continues to exercise the writer's perspective. Regarding casting he has said, 'I look for actors who can inhabit the character so if I change the lines, they can do those lines exactly as the character would.'[15] He writes short biographies for the characters and hands them to the actors before shooting – giving them just the backstory they need and nothing more, so they can't wander off on tangents when filming or offer up weird backstory justifications for their character's actions. On his tight budgets Sayles does not rehearse, so his potted biographies inform the actor where the character is coming from, and they can adjust to script changes more easily.[16] The limits of his budgets imposed a technical approach to filming which mean that scenes tend to use a master shot only for the opening, then devolve to closeups or two-shots – easier on the actor in terms of line memory and not getting tired but compromising the possible energy and connection of the performances. When he had the budgets, as was the case in his only studio film, *Baby, It's You*, he would play the entire scene in a master shot to allow maximum freedom to his actors to interact. On that movie he did have rehearsal time, and he relished working with Michael Ballhaus (1935–2017), Rainer Werner Fassbinder's cameraman doing his first USA job, who was used to the German director's theatrical style. Sayles points out, Ballhaus actually 'listened to what the actors are saying' and adjusted the frame accordingly. 'Most operators don't'.[17]

Sayles's brand of realism is sometimes said to be didactic, and perhaps that is true in terms of some of his narrative. But he is to be credited with opening up an original vein of naturalism in which we can encounter ordinary people living out the challenges of society – an antidote to the slick anodyne characters of Hollywood movies. He is above all a humanist. 'Sayles cares about people. Even his repellent characters have reasons for being who they are.'[18]

Further reading

Jack Ryan, *John Sayles Filmmaker: A Critical Study and Filmography* (Jefferson, NC: McFarland & Co., Inc., 2010).
John Sayles and Gavin Smith, *Sayles on Sayles* (London: Faber & Faber Ltd., 1998).

Notes

1. The film earned $36,741,667 in global box office against a $1.2 million budget.
2. https://www.rogerebert.com/reviews/casa-de-los-babys-2003
3. Mark Bould, *The Cinema of John Sayles: Lone Star* (London: Wallflower Press, 2009), 3.
4. Ibid.
5. Tom Schlesinger, John Sayles, 'Putting People Together: An Interview with John Sayles', *Film Quarterly*, Vol. 34, No. 4 (Summer, 1981): 2.
6. John Sayles, *Thinking in Pictures* (New York: Houghton, Mifflin, Harcourt, 1987), the story of the making of *Matewan*.
7. Quote from 1983 interview: https://www.imdb.com/name/nm0000626/bio/?ref_=nm_ov_bio_sm
8. Sayles and Smith, 156.
9. Carole Zucker, *Figures of Light: Actors and Directors Illuminate the Art of Film Acting* (New York: Plenum Press, 1995), 329.
10. Ibid.
11. Ibid.
12. Ibid.
13. Ibid., 330.
14. Diane Carson, 'Plain and Simple, Masculinity through John Sayles's Eyes', in *More Than a Method,* C. Baron, D. Carson and F. Tomasulo, eds (Detroit: Wayne State University, 2004), 182.
15. Ibid., 175.
16. Ryan, 194.
17. Sayles and Smith, 85.
18. Ryan, 3. An illustration of Ryan's point is how we understand the vile behaviour of the garage-owner Carl in *City of Hope* as a product of his circumstances, without delving into tedious psychology.

65 Sean Baker
1971–

American cinema in general finds it necessary to follow the three-act form . . . and the audience needs to know what's going on in the first 30 seconds . . . I find this so closed-minded and not progressive.[1]

Sean Baker's films are sometimes criticized for being deficient in plot structure. Critic Amy Taubin disparages his film *The Florida Project* (2017) for its lack of narrative.[2] But his approach is deliberate. Ian Dartley, reviewing Baker's film *Anora* (2024) puts his finger on it, 'Sean Baker wants his audience to be locked into the present. There's no need for a backstory, no requirement for extensive exposition and a refusal to "tell" — it's all show.'[3]

The most striking thing about Sean Baker's films is the casting. Taking a leaf from **Ken Loach's** book, Baker uses – in all his movies – a scrambled mix of actors and non-actors – one inspiring the other. The *non-pros* bringing an energy and veracity to the *pros* who, in return, provide technique for the *non-pros*. As he puts it: 'An experienced actor might have a method that influences the non-professionals; the rawness of non-professionals rubs off on a seasoned actor.'[4] The strategy works. In *The Florida* Project, the highly accomplished actor Willem Dafoe, plays the manager of a seedy motel, coming across as a natural 'Joe' playing opposite a six-year-old girl, Brooklynn Prince.[5] Both actors garnered American Academy, BAFTA and Golden Globe nominations for their performances.

Baker does what he calls 'street casting' – the term is precise.[6] In *Red Rocket* (2021) – shot in secret in Texas during the Pandemic – the lead actor, Simon Rex (b. 1974) is a comic rapper and an MTV video-jockey by profession, whom Baker spotted in a club in Los Angeles. He plays Mickey, a failed porn star returning to his home town in Texas. Mikey's wife is played by Brooklyn-based Bree Elrod (b. 1978), an off-Broadway theatre actress with little exposure and zero film experience. Baker literally picked up other actors *on the street*: a former bar owner he met in New Orleans, a refinery worker who lost her job during the Pandemic, and a woman to whom he offered a jump-start when her car broke down. He met Brittney Rodriquez (b. 1993), the refinery worker, while she was out walking her dog. He cast her as the enforcer in a petty drug-pushing setup, later expanding her part as well as using her as a consultant on local Texas language and customs. The role of Strawberry, the donut-shop sales assistant who Mickey grooms to do porn work, was played by Suzanna Son (b. 1995), spotted by Baker and his wife/collaborator, Samantha Quan (b. 1975) in the lobby of a cinema in Los Angeles. Suzanna was twenty-two at the time and had studied music and theatre in college (she sings in the film). It's impossible to image anyone more perfect for the role than Son.

Before gaining a place at the Tisch School of the Arts at NYU to do a Bachelor's degree, Baker studied non-linear editing at the New School in New York. His training as an editor enabled him to find work cutting wedding and corporate videos, which helped to pay the bills for his education and sustained him financially in his early years of directing. More importantly it provided the skills he needed to edit his own films and have total artistic control. Baker emphasizes that he is both director *and* editor of his movies, and that editing is 50 per cent of directing.[7]

Sean Baker is a political creature and openly acknowledges his debt to Ken Loach. 'British social realism has had an incredible impact on my career.'[8] Baker, like Loach, sets out in his films to expose the injustices of the prevailing system, and their effect on ordinary people and marginals in society. His political objective with *Florida Project* (2017) was to shine a light on hidden homelessness in the United States. He explains, '. . . we have families, individuals, and children using budget hotels as their last refuge before having to resort to the streets.'[9] Like Loach, Baker takes us into the lives of ordinary working and unglamourous people. The protagonist of his earlier second film, *Take Out* (2004), is a Chinese immigrant unable to pay a smuggling debt. His next film, *The Prince of Broadway* (2008) features an undocumented Ghanian immigrant selling knock-off goods. Both films illustrate the hopeless trap in which immigrants in the USA find themselves. (Both won the Independent Spirit John Cassavetes Award). Baker was more widely recognized for his next film, *Tangerine* (2015), technically ground-breaking for being shot entirely on an iPhone. The movie follows a Los Angeles trans sex worker on the street, depicting the daily events, transactions and abuses of her world. It does so without judgement, inviting us to share her experience as a multi-dimensional person with a life full of joys, failures, hopes, and regrets. The iPhone filming facilitated Baker's free-flowing quasi-documentary style, where the camera follows the action – reminiscent of **Cassavetes'** work.

One device used by Baker is the 'dialogue-free take', in which, having filmed the scene with enough coverage to assure the eventual editing, he runs the entire scene without dialogue.[10] The actors connect with each other and move through the blocking, acting out the scene without dialogue. This gives the director/editor marvellous *listening* material. (A bonus of the process is a *live synchronized* effects sound track clear of dialogue.)

Ken Loach, as was pointed out in his chapter, found kindred souls in a succession of writers with whom he worked over many years (Jim Allen, Paul Laverty). They shared his political beliefs and his sensibilities with respect to film realism. Similarly, Baker has similarly benefitted by a close collaboration with screenplay writer and fellow graduate of NYU, Chris Bergoch (active 2012–) who wrote or co-wrote *Starlet* (2012)*, Tangerine, The Florida Project* and *Red Rocket.* At least until his most recent film, *Anora*, where Baker is credited as sole writer.

Keenly aware of his audience, Baker is dedicated to the proposition of creating entertaining, engaging movies for *thinking* people as an antidote to the slick so-called realism of Hollywood. He points out that he is not alone in this regard, citing Spike Leigh's films, Barry Jenkins's *Moonlight* (2016) and Jordan Peele's *Get Out* (2017) as contemporary American examples of *political* cinema operating within genres other than social realism.[11]

Sean Baker's approach can be viewed in the context of a movement of independent filmmakers, first curated in the Sundance Film Festival, established in 1978, and formalized in the establishment of the Independent Film Project/West (now Film Independent) founded in 1981. Robert Rosen (1940–2024), former Dean of the UCLA School of Theatre, Film, and Television, and founder board member of IFP/West, defined an 'independent' movie as one which (1) takes risks in content and style, (2) embodies a personal vision, (3) is funded by non-Hollywood sources, and (4) embodies the 'valuation of art over money'.[12] Baker's movies tick all those boxes. Film Independent established the Independent Spirit Awards in 1985 and the Los Angeles Film Festival in 2000. Baker's films have garnered five Spirit Awards.

Notes

1. Rebutting Amy Taubin's criticism of *Florida* Project as being devoid of narrative: Amy Taubin, 'Interview: Sean Baker', *Film Comment*, 4 September 2017, https://www.filmcomment.com/blog/interview-sean-baker-florida-project/
2. Ibid.
3. Ian Dartley, 'The Chaotic Calamity Sean Baker and Mickey Madison bring to Anora', *The Huntington News*, 5 November 2024, https://huntnewsnu.com/81371/uncategorized/review-the-chaotic-calamity-sean-baker-and-mikey-madison-bring-to-anora/
4. Ben Kenigsberg, 'In His Films, Big Roles Go to Passers-by and Professionals Alike', *The New York Times*, 16 December 2021, https://www.nytimes.com/2021/12/16/movies/red-rocket-sean-baker.html
5. In a BAFTA Screenwriting Masterclass (22 November 2027) Baker calls Dafoe a 'transformative' actor and said that work with him consisted largely of discussing the character during preproduction. Dafoe did his own research consisting largely of 'hanging out' with local motel managers, and then brought the character intact to the filming, https://www.bafta.org/media-centre/transcripts/bafta-screenwriters-lecture-series-sean-baker
6. Taupin.
7. Writing in *MovieMaker Magazine*, 3 October 2017, https://www.moviemaker.com/sean-baker-11-rules-for-editing-your-own-films/
8. Daniel Dylan Wray, 'An Interview with Sean Baker, Film's Brightest Activist', *Huck*, 16 March 2018. https://www.huckmag.com/article/the-florida-project-sean-baker-interview
9. Ibid.
10. *MovieMaker Magazine*.
11. *Huck*.
12. Sherry B. Ortner, 'Against Hollywood, American independent film as a critical cultural movement,' *HAU: Journal of Ethnographic Theory* 2 (2), 2012: 6.

Neo Neo-Realism

... how extraordinary so-called ordinary lives are.[1]

Clio Barnard

In the chapter on **Italian Neo-Realism**, I pointed out that the movement had had little immediate effect on American filmmaking, other than in *film noir* (which saw a shift to an emphasis on working class characters and settings in sordid *milieux*). *New Yorker* film critic Richard Brody puts the lack of interest down to the increasing dominance of *method acting* in Hollywood – certainly **Lee Strasberg's** version – which brought on a degree and an intensity of psychological reality '. . . opening up characters' sex lives, hidden desires, deep emotional wounds – nothing less than the acknowledgement of the dignity of the individual over the limits of the social category.'[2] While **Cassavetes**, **John Sayles** and a few others readily embraced elements of Italian Neo-Realism, it was not until the 1980s and 1990s that elements of the post-war Italian style re-emerged in the USA, in the burgeoning independent film movement, united in rejecting mainstream Hollywood, and embracing a range of *genres* – including low budget horror films such as *The Blair Witch Project* (1999) and the short-lived *subgenre* of 'Slacker' movies (1990–2000), sometimes called the Gen X films. Those films heralded a new iteration of Realism, enabled by new technologies which allowed its proponents to make films outside of the system – Neo Neo-Realism.

The name 'Slacker' came from the eponymous film written and directed by Richard Linklater in 1990, in which the camera follows a succession of misfits and marginals around the director's adopted hometown, Austin, Texas, during a single day. While comic in tone, *Slacker* can be thematically classed as Neo neo-realist in that its characters are ordinary people it treats issues of social exclusion, joblessness, political marginalization and government control of the media. Moreover, it lacks plot, and is filmed in a simple style. It was made for $23,000 and went on to gross $1.25 million.

What Linklater is to Austin, Texas, director Kevin Smith is to New Jersey. His 1994 comedy, *Clerks*, again taking place over one day, observes two young convenience-shop clerks as they annoy customers, discuss movies and play hockey on the shop's roof. The two clerks, Dante and Randal, exemplify the lost generation of the 1980s, nihilistic and ironic – their philosophy being that there is no point in working, trying or caring – a viewpoint which defines Slacker movies. Note that not all films in the Slacker category can be classed as Neo Neo-Realism – for example, the zany comedy *Wayne's World* (1992), directed by Penelope Spheeris, or Michael Lehmann's crime comedy *Airheads* (1994). On the other hand, *Singles* (1992), by director Cameron Crowe, with its social-anthropological look at the *grunge* music phenomenon in Seattle, and it's ambling naturalistic style, could qualify as Neo Neo-Realism.

Sean Baker a prime example but not the only American Neo neo-realist of his generation worth noting. Kelly Reichardt, in her film *Wendy and Lucy* (2008) depicts a young woman (Michelle Williams) in the hopeless trap of poverty. Wendy is travelling with her dog *en route* to Alaska to find work in a cannery when her car breaks down in Oregon. Shoplifting a tin of dog food lands her in police custody, whereupon her dog is impounded. She hasn't the money to repair her car, nor extricate her dog from the pound – a scenario worthy of **Ken Loach** (perhaps with a nod to Vittorio De Sica's lost dog in *Umberto D*, 1955).

Director Chloé Zhao's work has consistently focused on situations of economic hardship in the 'land of plenty'. In *Songs My Brothers Taught Me* (2015) she explores how alcoholism devastated a Lakota Sioux reservation. In *Nomadland* (2020) Zhao cast Frances McDormand – a quintessential realist actor – as a widow, made redundant, broke, with few options in life, who packs up and drives West in her van with no fixed destination. Along the way she is persuaded to join a community of desert nomads, from whom she learns road survival skills. Taking a leaf from Loach's and Baker's books, Zhao interweaves the performances of McDormand and the highly accomplished realist actor David Strathairn (a John Sayles regular) with those of the people living in the reality of the difficult conditions of the story. Zhao's social critique is weakened, however, because, while McDormand's character is depicted as a victim of social circumstances the movie also plays on the idea of nomadism as a *life-style* choice, prompting one reviewer to quip, 'Zhao has made *The Grapes of Wrath* without the wrath.'[3] This Neo neo-realist movie won The Golden Lion at Venice, the People's Choice Award at Toronto, the Best Film BAFTA, and scooped Best Picture, Best Director and Best Actress Oscars in 2021, among innumerable other awards.

In Britain, independent films more widely align with Sean Baker's type of social realism – naturalistic and existential – sometimes called Brit Grit. They represent a continuation of traditions of the British New Wave, and share one predominant influence: namely, Ken Loach. Plots evolve from or are organized around observations of the day-to-day struggles of ordinary people, ending not with Hollywood style *catharsis*, but by offering instead an *existential* view of their characters' lives – frequently bitter and gritty. While the USA has produced notable examples of the genre, it is in Britain where we currently find Neo Neo-Realism in full flow, treating issues of immigration, racism, homophobia, poverty and exclusion full-on.

British television has had a considerable influence in the development of the new realism. As a natural consequence of the predominance of **Kitchen Sink Drama** the film units established by the BBC[4] and Channel Four Television[5] have produced an outpouring of British independent films, largely in the Neo neo-realist vein, and provided opportunities for the constant emergence of young new talent working in the genre. Recent notable examples are first-time writer/directors Aleem Khan (b. 1985) with *After Love* (2020, BBC Film), Charlotte Wells (b. 1987) with *Aftersun* (2022, BBC Film) and Molly Manning Walker (b. 1993) with *How to Have Sex* (2023, Film4), all exceptional work grounded in reality, which has led to innumerable nominations and awards.

CHARACTERISTICS OF NEO NEO-REALISM

- Rejection of mainstream Hollywood narratives with their emphasis on plot and cathartic endings – *character driven* rather than *plot driven* with no third-act redemption.
- Focus on the problems confronting ordinary people in their everyday lives, the product of institutional failures or political agendas. Dealing front-on with issues of poverty, race, immigration, sexual prejudice.
- A social anthropological documentarist approach to the material.
- Casting a mixture of actors and non-actors, using people actually living in the situations depicted.
- Use of techniques to foster natural acting and surprise, such as chronological shooting, text being fed to the actors scene-by-scene, etc.
- Stories centring on the problems faced by children and youth – using children and young people as actors.

- Use of language of the time and place, i.e. regional accents and the language of subcultures.
- Filming primarily on location.
- A straightforward shooting style, frequently with a documentary feeling.

The influence of the pedagogy of Colin Young (1927–2021), founder-director of Britain's National Film School (the National Film and Television School from 1982, NFTS), was a second significant force in the development of British Neo-Neo Realism. In 1970, the prospect of establishing a new national film school seduced Young, a Scotsman, away from his chairmanship of the Theatre Department at UCLA where he had established an Ethnographic Film programme, advised by the French filmmaker and anthropologist Jean Rouch (1917–2004). Young was enamoured of the work of Frederick Wiseman (b. 1930) and brought the filmmaker's fly-on-wall style of documentary with him to Britain.[6] From its inception, *observational documentary* took pride of place at the NFTS, breeding some of Britain's leading documentarists, including Nick Broomfield (b. 1948) and Molly Dineen (b. 1959). Young was fond of saying, 'Observational film is cinema in the present tense.' The quest for a *present tense reality* rubbed off on the fiction directors at the school, inspired by the teachings of Wiseman and the parade of ethnographic filmmakers who visited the NFTS studios at Beaconsfield. Discussions frequently centred around the *blurring of lines* between documentary and fiction – an aesthetic evolved. Among the NFTS students who embraced it were several filmmakers who are now leading exemplars of the Neo Neo-Realism style: Carine Adler (b. 1948), Joanna Hogg (b. 1960), Clio Barnard (b. 1965), Lynne Ramsay (b. 1969) and Sarah Gavron (b. 1970). May it not go unnoticed – they are all women.

Another key influence at the NFTS was Scottish director, Bill Douglas (1934–91) whose austere naturalistic autobiographical *Trilogy* (*My Childhood, My Ain Folk, My Way Home*) about a young boy growing up in material and emotional poverty in Scotland is redolent of the early naturalism of Maxim Gorky or Émile Zola. Douglas taught at the School from 1978. One student contemporaneous with his tenure at the NFTS was Terence Davies (1945–23). The second instalment in Davies' autobiographical *Trilogy,* entitled *Madonna and Child* (1980) was completed while a student there. Davies' early films were autobiographical, based on his difficult upbringing in Liverpool, and while they are too formal and poetic to be categorized as Neo Neo-Realism, they were graphic in their representation of working-class poverty and its attendant intolerance and brutality, particularly when viewed from a gay perspective. His *Guardian* obituary describes Davies' work as 'overwhelmingly evocative . . . Moments of transcendent beauty nestled alongside instances of lacerating pain.'[7]

Joanna Hogg's films portray privileged upper middle-class characters 'harbouring seething resentment under a patina of easy charm.'[8] She knows the milieu well – she is a product of it. *Souvenir* (2021) and *Souvenir, Part II* (2022) are a fictionalized version of her younger self, which include recreations of some of her experiences as a student at the NFTS. While the subject matter of her movies may not conform to a Neo neo-realist model, her playbook of techniques certainly does, and are noteworthy. Hogg doesn't work from a script, but from a 'story document', which outlines the '*spine*' of the work, the psychology of the characters, and her visual ideas. It includes photographs, paintings, and poems. It contains fragments of dialogue, but not a classic text and is peppered with footnotes on technical elements required to deliver the film's *tone*. She doesn't rehearse, and the dialogue is improvised by the actors during the shooting (where possible caught using two cameras). The method requires intensive work with the actors prior to shooting to achieve a mutually agreed understanding of their characters. She shoots in chronological order and only the principal actors (sometimes) and crew (always) get to see her 'story document'. Her regular collaborating production designer, Stéphane Collonge (also an NFTS graduate) describes her approach to working with actors. '[She is] very good at blurring the line between fiction and reality. She invites performers to explore parts of themselves with the character, as opposed to other filmmakers who construct the character. It comes from inside out, not from outside in.'[9]

Sarah Gavron categorizes her own work as 'impact' filmmaking. Coming from a political family – her mother was deputy to a colourful and outspoken Mayor of London, 'Red Ken' Livingstone – she understood at any early age the potential for film to effect change. Her first professional work was at the BBC in the political documentaries department. The shorts she made at the NFTS obtained her an agent who got her a TV drama, which in turn led to her being asked to direct the film version of Monica Ali's best-seller *Brick Lane* (2007), set in a Bangladeshi immigrant community in East London. The seven years following *Brick Lane*, apart from shooting a documentary in Greenland, were devoted to developing her passion project, *Suffragette*, eventually put into production in 2014. Gavron is committed to telling women's stories, especially about lives which are either ignored or misrepresented on film, and there had never been a film about the suffragettes from a women's perspective. This particular story was epic in scope and required an A-list writer (Abi Morgan –*The Iron Lady, Shame*), high-end casting (Carey Mulligan, Helena Bonham Carter, Meryl Streep), and a studio budget ($14 million). While aspects of the movie can be classed as *naturalistic* (especially scenes involving Mulligan's character, Maud, both in the laundry where she works, and home life) this polished period costume drama with lavish sets and hundreds of daily artists falls well outside the scope of Neo Neo-Realism. It's all the more surprising, therefore, how Gavron's next film, *Rocks* (2019), subverts the Hollywood format and places itself squarely in the 'Neo' genre in a totally unique way.

Set in multicultural working-class Hackney in London, the plot of *Rocks* is triggered by the disappearance of the mother of the eponymous teenager, leaving the girl to look after herself and her little brother. Avoiding the social services in fear of losing her brother, Rocks is supported by her schoolgirl friends. Gavron describes the making of the film as the 'total reverse of the normal process'.[10] She started with casting – without a script. The first step was for Lucy Pardee, the casting director, to visit London schools. Pardee met approximately 1,300 girls, maintaining a very wide brief. Sarah, Lucy and the production team then worked with screenwriters Theresa Ikoko (b. 2013) and Claire Wilson running workshops with the selected actors, encouraging them to reveal themes to which they related. 'Friendship' became the keynote. Then Theresa proposed a unifying arc pulling together some of the youngsters' ideas. It was a story she had in her head for some time about how a teenage girl copes when abandoned by her mother, left to look after her brother. The girls were enthusiastic about the idea and workshops continued around the plotline, resulting in a full shooting script. The scenes were shot chronologically and in real locations. Gavron says in that respect she was 'standing on the shoulders of a number of directors – Shane Meadows, Ken Loach, Andrea Arnold and Lynne Ramsay – who've worked in this way'[11] The youngsters made the dialogue their own and spoke in MLE (Multicultural London English), their distinctive London youth dialect.[12] *Rocks* was awarded five prizes at the 2020 British Independent Film Awards (BIFA) and was nominated for eight BAFTAs, including casting.

One can't exit the field without mentioning two other British filmmakers of this generation working in Neo Neo-Realism. Andrea Arnold (b. 1961) was born of teenage parents in a working-class suburb of London, and like Joanna Hogg at the other end of the socio-economic scale, claims to write from 'what she knows'.[13] She eschewed film courses in Britain, opting instead for the AFI Conservatory in Los Angeles, feeling that her 'lack of education and working-class accent held her back in the eyes of the gatekeepers' in England.[14] Arnold's best-known work, *Fish Tank* (2009), is the story of Mia, a fifteen-year-old, troubled, volatile and socially isolated, who lives with her mother and younger sister on a council estate. The arrival of her mother's new boyfriend, Connor (Michael Fassbender) opens up avenues in life, including those of a sexual nature. But it all ultimately leads to disappointment. Put so simply it sounds like a 'downer', however the performances are captivating, and the movie is ultimately emotionally satisfying, evidenced in its garnering the Jury Prize at Cannes in 2009 and the BAFTA for Best Film in 2010, among other awards.

Arnold's fiction films are characterized by the themes of deprivation and impoverishment – from her early short film *Dog* (2001), through to her recent film, *Bird* (2024) they feature teenagers living in poverty-stricken English 'edge-lands'. Her films are political but not polemic, starting with an emotional connection to the material. 'I do make my films with a social eye. It's not a huge thing, and I don't want to ram it down people's throats, but it's there all the time in the way I feel and think. It's just how I see the world.' Like other new-realists, Arnold has also tried her hand at documentary filmmaking. *Cow* (2021) is an observational documentary in the style of Jean Rouch, shot over several years, about the life of a cow. Not in the least polemic, it has the effect of attaching one's humanity to the cow's life and has caused more than one carnivore to become a vegan.

Arnold is known for giving her actors almost total control in creating their characters. Her directing style is to provide support and reassurance to her actors, to enable them to create reflections of themselves. Typically, she works with untrained or unknown actors, mixing them with professionals, as in the case of Michael Fassbender in *Fish Tank*, matched with Katie Jarvis who played Mia, who had no prior acting experience. The film was shot chronologically, and actors were only given their script one section at a time, *à la* Ken Loach. In *American Honey* (2016) the actor Shia LaBeouf (b. 1986) was matched with a band of untrained teenagers who Arnold and her scouting assistant had picked up 'in shopping malls, skate parks, and urban beaches across America.'[15] That film's casting, concept, and shooting style are not dissimilar to that of Sean Baker.

Sarah Gavron also references Shane Meadows (b. 1972), a prolific British filmmaker sitting squarely in the genre of Neo Neo-Realism. Meadows did *not* attend the National Film and Television School, nor any other school for that matter. He was self-taught, starting out by making ten-minute VHS videos of friends and situations he knew, including himself as the subject. In this endeavour he was aided by a local independent filmmaker, Graham Forde, who loaned him cameras and encouraged him to shoot a lot and learn by his own mistakes. The self-styled filmmaker made six short films in as many months. His themes were grounded in the day-to-day realities of unemployment in Staffordshire under Thatcherism, as well as Meadows's self-confessed youth of petty crime.[16]

One of the shorts, *Where's the Money, Ronnie?* earned him a commission to shoot a documentary for Film4's 'Battered Britain' series, entitled *King of the Gypsies* (1995) – a ten-minute film portrait of Bartley Gorman, a bare-knuckle fighter and leader of a clan of Travellers based in Meadows's hometown of Uttoxeter in the Midlands.[17] *Ronnie?* also caught the attention of producer Stephen Woolley (b. 1956), who raised a £1.4 million budget for Meadows's first feature film, *Twenty Four Seven* (1997), featuring Bob Hoskins (1942–2014) as a man dedicated to changing the dead-end lives of the local working-class kids by opening a boxing club to engage them in something meaningful. Meadows talks about arriving on the set for his first day ever of professional shooting. 'Suddenly I was on what appeared to be a miniature city. There were trucks and people sawing wood and lights . . . there were four people who just wanted to make me a cup of tea! It was insane and I was petrified. I was absolutely shitting myself. For the first half of the day I completely busked it.'[18] Bob Hoskins, seeing how terrified Meadows was facing an extensive film crew and a movie star, gently helped build up his confidence, and welded the film together in more ways than one, integrating himself generously with the cast of non-actors.[19] The resulting movie garnered extremely favourable reviews, BAFTA and BIFA nominations, as well as the FIPRESCI Prize at the Venice Festival. Meadows was now on the map.

His next movie, *A Room for Romeo Brass* (1999) centres on two twelve-year-olds befriended by an unpredictable young man with psychopathic tendencies – the debut film role of Paddy Considine, a boyhood friend of Meadows. The two boy characters were based on the childhood of Meadows and Paul Fraser, who co-wrote the script. The film was shot on location in Meadows's local city of Nottingham. It garnered three BIFA nominations, for film, director and screenplay.

His father having named him after a Western movie,[20] it seems inevitable that 'Shane' Meadows would ultimately come round to making one – if only a pseudo-Western. In retrospect, the director has expressed his disappointment with *Once Upon a Time in the Midlands* (UK/Germany, 2002). The film is about an outlaw who rides back into town to claim his lover – not in the Wild West of yore, but in present-day Nottinghamshire. 'By the second draft I knew it was going wrong.'[21] That was the moment when the insurance company told him to lose twenty-five pages. 'I should have closed it down.'[22] With its cast of stars (Rhys Ifans, Robert Carlyle, Kathy Burke, Ricky Tomlinson) none of whom come from the Midlands, and the strong plot and happy ending, it feels like an abandonment of Meadows's Neo neo-realist principles in pursuit of the mainstream. He was not ultimately happy with the cut nor the music, perhaps regretting that he had drifted away from his roots. His next film, *This is England* (2006) allowed him to get back there.

Again, the film was shot in Meadows's stamping ground, in locations in and around the inland city of Nottingham, with some scenes shot in Grimsby on the coast, to create a fictious port city. It is set in 1983. Its protagonist is Shaun, a twelve-year-old who lives with his widowed mother and is bullied at school. He takes refuge in a skinhead gang who at first harass him, but then take him in. The lead was played by Thomas Turgoose, a non-actor who was picked up in an open call casting in the streets of Grimsby. The boy happened to pass on his bike and was curious about the crowd waiting to be called in to be interviewed. Once given his turn he cheekily said he'd only do the audition if he was paid a 'fiver' – Meadows recognized that type of impudent behaviour in himself and cast the boy.

In common with Loach and Baker, Meadows repeatedly works with a writer-collaborator, in this case Paul Fraser (b. 1973) his childhood friend from Uttoxeter, and literally his next-door neighbour, who understands the territory. Fraser has written for most of Meadows's movies from *Twenty Four Seven* to *Somers Town* (2008).

After The 2006 production of *This is England* Meadows considered making a movie following the Dogma 95 rules.[23] But he decided the Danish parameters were too restrictive. He contrived, instead, another model: 'The Five-Day Feature'. In 2007 he made *Le Donk & Scor-zay-zee*, a mock musical documentary, shot in five days for a budget of £48,000 – an attempt to make a film independent of any outside finance and control. In the movie Paddy Considine, in his fourth collaboration with Meadows, plays the eponymous lead character, an aging failed musician ineptly trying to promote his protégé, a young rapper, for a spot at an Arctic Monkey's gig. As was standard Meadows process at this point in his career, the script was simply a framework and the dialogues were improvised – brilliantly so by Paddy Considine, whose work *The Times* critic called 'an enthralling piece of improvisation that carries the whole movie.'[24] Of his method Meadows says, 'A financier's worst fear is not having a script. And my worst fear is having one.'[25] Like Sean Baker, Meadows feels the real creative work is in the editing. For *Le Donk* it was decided to shoot for only four days, then edit, then do a fifth day of shooting at a later date to round out the story and fill in the gaps.

Meadows's idea is to give the actors maximum freedom, in the style of Cassavetes. 'We light the whole room so anyone can go anywhere. . . . For me it's letting the actors know where they're going and where the scene's going, but not forcing them to speak in someone else's voice.'[26] In a manner similar to that of Andrea Arnold, he writes his script as a 'document of intent' running no more than thirty pages. He calls it 'Scriptment' – a halfway house necessary to give the actors and crew a sense of what he is trying to capture, but not tying things down.[27]

Apart from the feature documentary *The Stone Roses: Made of Stone* (2019), made to celebrate the reuniting of that band in 2012, Meadows has made no more films, turning his attention to television. He has directed three 'continuations' of the *This is England* feature film in the form of episodic TV series, *This is England '86, '88 and '90,* which were made over four years, very much in the tradition of earlier British Kitchen Sink Drama, with a new writer, Jack Thorne (1978), with whom Meadows has maintained a continuing relationship in further television work.

Meadows continued making short films while moving on to longer forms, starting with his original six in 1994 until at least until 2007, and has a catalogue of some fifty-six-plus shorts to his name.

Further reading

Martin Fradley, Sarah Godfrey and Melanie Williams, *Shane Meadows Critical Essays* (Edinburgh: Edinburgh University Press, 2013).

Notes

1. Promo interview for *Ali and Eva*, Picture House distributors, https://www.youtube.com/watch?v=Rs4LrfqBt6c
2. Richard Brody, 'About "Neo-Neo Realism",' *The New Yorker*, 19 March 2009.
3. Sean Burns for Boston University public radio station WBUR, referring to John Steinbeck's 1939 realist novel, *The Grapes of Wrath,* depicting the hardship endured by tenant farmers in Western USA.
4. BBC Films (now BBC Film) was an independent but wholly owned production company established by the BBC in 1990.
5. Channel 4 Films was established in 1982 at the inception of the new channel itself. In 1998 it was rebranded as Film4.
6. 'Fred' Wiseman (b. 1930) is a prolific American documentary filmmaker whose style was called 'observational' or 'fly-on-the-wall', although he rejected the terms, noting that while the camera may be detached from the subject, the editing is an expression of the totally subjective viewpoint of the filmmaker. His films are predominantly studies of social institutions such as hospitals, police departments, schools. In his nineties at the time of this writing, he has made fifty films to date and continues to work. He is also a theatre director.
7. Ryan Gilbey, 'Terence Davies', [obit], *The Guardian*, 8 October 2023, https://www.theguardian.com/film/2023/oct/08/terence-davies-obituary
8. Forrest, David, 'The films of Joanna Hogg: new British realism and class', *Studies in European* Cinema, Vol. 11, Issue 1 (March 2014): 64–5.
9. *Joanna Hogg,* Seventh Row, https://seventh-row.com/directors-we-love/joanna-hogg/
10. YouTube interview with David Neville, Edinburgh Jewish Cultural Centre, 23 March 2023, https://www.youtube.com/watch?v=ocvC7-dREhU
11. Ibid.
12. Known as MLE, or Multicultural London English, a variant of English which emerged in the late nineteen-nineties and is a badge of authenticity for London-based Neo neo-realist movies.
13. Sean O'Hagan, *The Observer*, 9 October 2016, https://www.theguardian.com/film/2016/oct/09/andrea-arnold-interview-american-honey-shia-labeouf-sasha-lane
14. 'Andrea Arnold', Wikipedia, updated 26 December 2023, https://en.wikipedia.org/wiki/Andrea_Arnold
15. O'Hagan.
16. Fradley, et al., 3.
17. Viewable on YouTube: https://www.youtube.com/watch?v=IB0_QEh-KVs
18. Phil de Semlyen, 'Shane Meadows on Shane Meadows', *Empire Online*, 1 September 2010, https://www.empireonline.com/movies/features/shane-meadows-shane-meadows/

19. The David Lean Lecture: Shane Meadows, 6 December 2023, https://www.bafta.org/media-centre/transcripts/bafta-david-lean-lecture-shane-meadows
20. *Shane* [film], dir. George Stevens, Paramount, 1953.
21. De Semlyen.
22. Ibid.
23. Dogma 95 (Dogme in Danish) was a manifesto co-written by Danish filmmakers Lars von Trier and Thomas Vinterberg based on the idea of simple storytelling and simple natural acting, with a minimum of camera movement and no special effects. Shooting was to totally on location, and there was to be no post-dubbed music, among other restrictions. It attracted Sean Meadows and others because it was designed to wrest control of the movie back from the financiers and into the hands of director.
24. Kevin Mahler, *The Times*, 10 October 2009 https://www.thetimes.co.uk/article/le-donk-scor-zay-zee-8j7hx9q2k65
25. David Lean Lecture.
26. Ibid.
27. Ibid.

67 Magic Realism

'Magic Realism' is sometimes classified as a genre, but the term is more broadly descriptive and not critically rigorous, embracing elements of Surrealism, the 'fantastic' and 'post-modernism'. I include it as a footnote to other forms of Realism. In its simplest form it consists of an insertion of fantastical elements into realistic situations. When seamlessly and subtly executed, spectators (or readers) can find themselves believing situations which, if given the time to apply a bit of logic, they could never objectively accept as real. The degree to which Magic Realism is effective in creating 'truth' depends on the degree of the suspension of disbelief achieved.

The style was first identified in the plastic arts in Germany in 1925 by art critic Franz Roh (1890–1965) describing a new style of painting which emerged there, called 'New Objectivity'.[1] In literature there were some early antecedents in European Romanticism, especially in the writing of Nikolai Gogol (180–52)[2] and E. T. A. Hoffmann (1776-1822).[3]

But Magic Realism as a literary form found its feet in Latin America, and was universally popularized by the Colombian, Gabriel Garcia Márquez (1927–2014) with his novel *One Hundred Years of Solitude* (1967), in which the supernatural world blends seamlessly with the natural world. The writer claims to have taken his grandmother's storytelling as a model. 'She told me things that sounded supernatural and fantastic, but she told them with complete naturalness. She did not change her expression . . .'.[4] Franz Kafka's *Metamorphosis* (1914) and the Mexican novel, *Pedro Páramo* (1955) by Juan Rulfo (1917–86) are said to have influenced Garcia Márquez's style,[5] as had the novel *The Kingdom of this World* (1949) by the Cuban, Alejo Carpentier (1904–80) whose precursor style to Magic Realism is described as *'marvellous realism'* (recreating marvellous events occurring in the real world).[6] Another Latin, Argentinian Jorge Luis Borges (1899–1986), had earlier written *Historia universal de la infamia* (1936) in a style which he termed *'magical realism'* (creating a wholly magical world).

A later iteration of Magic Realism can be found in Postmodernism, with writers such as Günter Grass (1927–2015), Peter Handke (b. 1942), John Fowles (1926–2005), Angela Carter (1940–1992), Italo Calvino (1923–85), etc. The 'postmodernist' first novel of Chilean author, Isabelle Allende (b. 1942) *The House of the Spirits* (1982) is sometimes characterized as magic realism.

Magic Realism has never really caught on in theatre, unless one includes stage musicals. When we read a novel, our imagination creates its own reality. Belief is personal and one's mind fine tunes one's imagination to create a personal truth. In the medium of theatre, however, there is a disjuncture between the physical reality of living breathing human beings on the stage and magical elements created via stagecraft – which are rarely seamless – hence it is sometimes difficult to suspend disbelief. There have been notable exceptions, such as Tennessee Williams's (1911–83) *The Glass Menagerie* (1944) in which – if well-executed – the audience travels with the protagonist, Tom, via dreamlike sequences and music, as he comes to terms with his family's past and his own identity. Tony Kushner's (b. 1968) *Angels in America* (1993) is another example, but even in that masterwork the realistic and fantastical (staged) elements at times don't sit well together.

Not so with cinema. As André Bazin pointed out (see chapter **Dramatic Realism in Cinema**) the photographic nature of film – its verisimilitude – creates an inbuilt belief on the part of spectators. Film goers are *disposed* to believe. As long as the facticity of the narrative is credible and the performances half-way truthful, it is relatively easy to insert unrealistic elements into the film which the spectator will accept; and if they are caught up in the movement of the narrative, they will suspend disbelief. Advances in film effects, animation, the manipulation of sound and picture, and computer-generated imagery are seamlessly integrated, making the fantasy elements *real* to the audience.

In cinema Magic Realism has come into its own as a popular form, with Hollywood movies such as *Big* (1988), *The Green Mile* (1999) and *The Curious Case of Benjamin Button* (2006); and European films such as Yorgos Lanthimos' (b. 1973) *Lobster* (2017) and Jean-Pierre Jeunet's (b. 1973) *Amelie* (2001). But once again the Latin American filmmakers seem to have cornered the market, especially the Mexicans. Director Alfonso Arau (b. 1932) adopted Mexican author Laura Esquivel's (b. 1950) novel *Like Water for Chocolate* (1992) for the cinema. Another Mexican, Guillermo del Toro (b. 1964) directed *Pan's Labyrinth* (2006) set during the Spanish Civil War, in which a young girl escapes the horrors of a brutal domestic life and enters a magic world where a fantastic faun creature helps guide her through coming-of-age. Del Toro also created an exquisite fantasy creature in *The Shape of Water* (2017) in which a lovelorn cleaning lady (Sally Hawkins) falls for a sea monster in a secret government laboratory. Still another Mexican, Alejandro G. Iñárritu (b. 1963) gave us *Birdman* (2014) in which a washed-up actor, former superhero star (Michael Keaton) tries to mount a serious play to revitalize his career and interacts with his own superhero character. The Mexican collective consciousness seems well-disposed to the genre.

Magic Realism also lends itself to combining with other genres, especially horror. Yorgos Lanthimos *The Killing of the Sacred Deer* (2017) is an example, where horror invades reality when a surgeon introduces his family to a teenager whose father he has killed in an operation. *Donnie Darko* (dir. Richard Kelly, 2001) is another example – a science fiction time travel film featuring a large rabbit, in which the line between fiction and reality is constantly blurred.

Notes

1. 'New Objectivity' included painter Georg Grosz (1893–1959) and influenced Bertolt Brecht – see his chapter.
2. Gogol is profiled in the chapter The Realm of Realism.
3. Hoffman is best known for his fairy tales, such as *The Nutcracker and the Mouse King*, on which Tchaikovsky's ballet is based.
4. Peter Stone, 'Interview with Gabriel Garcia Marquez, The Art of Fiction No 69', *The Paris Review*, Issue 82 (Winter, 1981), https://www.theparisreview.org/interviews/3196/the-art-of-fiction-no-69-gabriel-garcia-marquez (accessed 23 April 2024).
5. *Pedro Páramo* isn't technically categorized as 'magic realism' in that the principal narrator admits that his mind is given over to illusion.
6. In Spanish, '*lo real maravilloso*'; it proposes a unified world of fantasy, like a fairy tale and is distinct from Magical Realism in which fantastic things happen quite naturally in the real world as we know it.

68 Errors and Omissions

Given the encyclopaedic format of this book it is inevitable that some readers will find it lopsided – too much emphasis on certain theorists and practitioners, and not enough on others. There are numerous omissions, by design or accident. First and foremost, there is the question of time and space, and the limits of reader tolerance for such a fact-packed book taken as a chronological history. Secondly, the coverage is, by admission, a factor of personal interest. For example, there is a more extensive treatment of **Bertolt Brecht** because his life story and his behaviour were fascinating to me, whereas in fact he offers no contribution to the advancement of the Realist form. I found it difficult to curtail my writing on **Ken Loach**, because his contribution is so critical – there is a *before* and an *after* Loach– and there are so many practical lessons for emerging filmmakers to learn from him.

As stated in the introduction chapter **Skinning the Cat**, I am also interested in marking out the influence of key movers and shakers on the practitioners who followed them, who would then influence others in turn. In some cases, a contribution was significant in its time, but its influence on other practitioners in years to follow less so, therefore I decided they didn't merit a chapter. Theatre directors such as André Antoine, Ariane Mnouchkine, Peter Stein and Robert LePage come to mind. In film the same would apply to Mike Leigh in Britain; the Dogme 95 movement in Denmark; Finland's director of idiosyncratic realism Aki Kaurismäki; in Iran, Abbas Kiarostami, with his use of non-actor child protagonists. It would have been interesting to explore how Italian Neo-Realism influenced Ousmane Sembène, Souleymane Cissé and the African Francophone new cinema, as well as the realist cinema of Andrzej Wajda, Jan Rybkowski and the Polish Film School, not to mention, Milos Forman, Jiri Menzel and the Czech New Wave of the 1960s. There are endless veins of Dramatic Realism to mine. If readers appreciate this book, perhaps a new edition could be more inclusive.

Stanislavski, of course, merits many 'column inches' because understanding the evolution of his ideas is critical – the bedrock of all that followed. There is a constellation of teachers following Stanislavski who merit more consideration – such as his disciple Maria Knebel who kept the flame of Active Analysis alive – as does Stanislavski's collaborator over years, Leopold Sulerjitsky, who was certainly the person who introduced yoga to actor's training.

And then there are the actors. I have covered early realist actors such **Eleanora Duse** (there were so many references to her over the years) and Mikhail Shchepkin — but not Stefano Grassi. Actors, including Duse, are notoriously not given to writing about their 'process'. There are 'tips' to be picked up from the likes of Michael Caine (*Acting in Film: An Actor's Take on Filmmaking*, London: Applause Books, 1997) or in actors' autobiographies (e.g. Marlon Brando, *Songs My Mother Taught Me*, New York: Random House, 1994, or Viola Davis's *Finding Me: A Memoir*, New York: Collins, 2022) but none seems to want to lay bare their 'process' in a systematic manner, perhaps in the interest of not destroying the illusion they conjure up in their performance. Fascinating territory for further research.

Havana, Cuba, January 2025